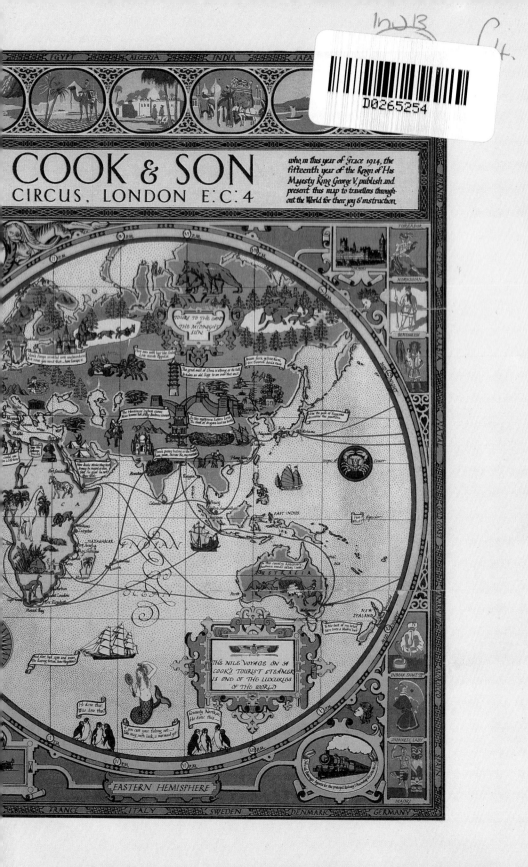

• *Thomas Cook* •

· Thomas Cook ·

150 Years of
Popular Tourism

PIERS BRENDON

Secker & Warburg
London

First published in Great Britain 1991
by Martin Secker & Warburg Limited
Michelin House, 81 Fulham Road, London SW3 6RB

Copyright © Piers Brendon 1991

A CIP catalogue record for this book
is available from the British Library
ISBN 0 436 19993 9

Set in Linotron Baskerville
Printed in England
by Clays Ltd, St Ives plc

To
Barley Alison
IN MEMORIAM

• *Contents* •

• *Illustrations* •

IN BLACK AND WHITE

IN COLOUR

Between pages 148 – 149

Cook's Scottish Tourist handbook
Cook's Continental Timetables
Cook's tours celebrated in song
A poster for the Vesuvius railway
Cook's Nile Flotilla
Cook's Excursionist

Between pages 212 – 213

Two Edwardian brochures
Four brochures for exotic holidays
A variety of Cook's posters
Trains and boats and planes

Acknowledgements: 9, 14, 22, *Illustrated London News*; 11, 46, *Punch*; 23, City of Birmingham Library; 28, Hulton Picture Company; 40, 43, 44, John Price. All other illustrations are from the Thomas Cook archives.

Acknowledgements

Before agreeing to write about Thomas Cook I made two stipula-
tions: that I should have access to all relevant information about
the company's history and complete freedom of expression. These
conditions have been met in full. This is a wholly independent work
and my only self-denying ordinance has been to respect commercial
confidentiality in the last two chapters.

Everyone I have encountered on the staff of the 10,000-strong
Cook organization has treated me with extraordinary frankness and
courtesy, and I must express my appreciation to them in general
terms as they are too many to name individually. Some names,
however, I must mention. John Brooks, current Chairman, talked
to me at length about the company and he was kind enough, in
the midst of a busy schedule, to make valuable comments on my
manuscript. Peter Middleton, the Managing Director, told me
much about the present company and something of his future
plans, as did top members of his team, Christopher Rodrigues, John
Donaldson, Colin Lamoureaux and John McEwan. I benefited too
from conversations with Mark McCafferty, Michael Braybrooke,
Paul Lovell, Lester Porter, Jim Kane, David Holden and Brian
Railton. Richard Grummitt and Desmond Harding afforded me
aid and encouragement. Lis Steele expertly fielded some last-minute
questions. Simon Laxton has given me warm friendship as well as
generous help.

I owe a special debt of gratitude to Erich Reich, who introduced
me to Thomas Cook. David Andersen, so long responsible for the
company's excellent public relations, inspired me with enthusiasm
for the firm's history. Andrew Barratt was a strong support. I have
drawn heavily on the encyclopaedic knowledge of three notable
figures now retired, Bill Cormack, John Mason and John Price,
all of whom put their personal papers and memorabilia at my
disposal. The last of these spent so much time on my manuscript
and made so many helpful suggestions, now incorporated, that I

feel guilty as well as grateful. E.H. Gerrard added useful material. I have learned an enormous amount from Sir Reginald Wilson, Sir John Cuckney, Tom Fisher and Alan Kennedy, former chairmen or chief executives of Thomas Cook, who were kind enough to submit to my inquisition. The present Thomas Cook talked to me about his forebears. Richard Lees-Milne shared his memories of Ernest Cook with me. My uncle, Colonel Oswald Cary-Elwes, did some useful investigation on my behalf. Richard and Rosemary Webster allowed me to read some fascinating diaries in their possession. Edwin Green patiently showed me round Midland Bank's archives and commented most eruditely on my manuscript. And Edmund Swinglehurst, Thomas Cook's archivist and historian, who knows more about the firm's past than anyone, was immensely generous with both time and information. It is scarcely an exaggeration to say that without his assistance I could not have written this book.

I must also thank the staff of the libraries and archives I used: the Leicester City Library, the British Tourist Authority Library, the London University Library, the Public Record Office, the India Office Library, the British Library at Bloomsbury and its newspaper department at Colindale, and the Cambridge University Library where most of my work was done.

Andrew Best, my literary agent, and Steve Cox subjected my manuscript to their usual rigorous and expert scrutiny, saving me from innumerable semantic and stylistic *faux pas*.

As always, I must express my love and gratitude to my wife Vyvyen, with her eagle eye for literary and historical errors, and to my children, George and Oliver, who stoically endure the toll taken on family life by that basilisk-eyed interloper, the word-processor.

Finally, I must pay tribute to my late editor and publisher, Barley Alison. She was enthusiastic about this book and made her usual astute comments on it in draft. But, alas, she did not live to see it published. Barley was to me, as to many, an inspiration – though during her lifetime she was too modest to let me acknowledge it in print. I mourn her passing and I dedicate this book to her memory.

Introduction

This book breaks fresh ground. Drawing on much original material, it gives a new account of the founders of modern tourism, Thomas Cook and his son John, and of the firm they created, which is now 150 years old.

Thomas Cook & Son have certainly received a fair degree of attention. Writing with an enviably light touch, John Pudney produced an entertaining portrait of them and their travel agency in 1953. Considering that Pudney was an alcoholic at the time and confessed that he found Thomas Cook's teetotal effusions 'thirsty reading', it was a remarkably sympathetic treatment. But it is marred by serious errors and omissions as well as by a generally superficial approach. Edmund Swinglehurst has filled many of Pudney's gaps with his attractive volumes about the firm, but they do not pretend to be comprehensive. Nor do learned articles by scholars like Professor Jack Simmons, valuable though these are. Until now nobody has made full use of the firm's archives and trawled widely among other sources, published and unpublished, in an attempt to tell the whole story.

It is a dramatic one, an eminently Victorian epic of achievement which began in 1841 with Thomas Cook's construction of a new industry out of nothing more than a brilliant idea. At a time when popular tourism was regarded first as a social menace and then as a bad joke, Thomas Cook engaged in a heroic struggle to make it acceptable. John Cook, who came into the business in 1865, made it respectable, turning the family firm into an institution. Under his energetic leadership it ministered to royalty, transported a British army up the Nile, arranged the travel of maharajas and pilgrims, invaded the New World, established a unique position in Egypt, and became an international adjunct of the British empire. By the time of John's death in 1899 (which was probably hastened by the effort of 'personally conducting' the Kaiser to Jerusalem) the 'Cook's Tour' was a byword from New York to New South Wales, from China to Peru. In the war-torn twentieth century Cook's 'business of peace' suffered a number of setbacks and sea-changes. But the modern company, with its sophisticated financial and other services, its computerized booking systems and data banks, its imaginative programme of tours, its global network of offices and its multi-billion-pound turnover, is the largest travel organization in the world.

That, at least, is the public account. In the following pages this outline is filled out with private details and modified by new revelations, so much so that an essentially different picture emerges – a picture of challenge and response, of controversy and conflict. It was conflict in the first instance between different temperaments and generations, between an altruistic father whose vision amounted to genius and a ruthless son with an infinite capacity for taking pains. It was also a conflict of ideas and ideals. Thomas Cook saw tourism as his mission to humanity; it was a means of emancipation for large numbers of people whose work was drudgery and whose recreation was drink. The iron-willed John was determined to forge a successful business, which could only be done, he believed, by attracting a 'select', prosperous clientele. The dissension culminated in a bitter family quarrel in 1878, after which John became the firm's 'sole managing partner'. Yet in some respects their dispute was never really resolved. It rumbled on into the present century, affecting the company's attitude to the unprecedented crises it faced. Even today a creative tension exists inside Thomas Cook between the public service and the profit-making body, between the tour operator appealing to a mass market and the travel agency catering for an elite.

The name Thomas Cook is almost synonymous with the rise of popular tourism, on which this book also sheds new light. For surprisingly little has been written about the subject. Grand tourism, its aristocratic ancestor, has been thoroughly covered, of course – Christopher Hibbert has even produced two different books about it with the same title. Travel writing, ancient and modern, also abounds, voluminously recording the independent journeys of the affluent – John Pemble surveyed such Victorian and Edwardian outpourings in his magisterial *The Mediterranean Passion* (1988). And a whole literature is devoted to exploration. Similarly, in recent years a historical industry has grown up on the subject of leisure, and there have been useful studies in the wake of J.A.R. Pimlott's fine book about *The Englishman's Holiday* (1953). But apart from a few dusty or jejune monographs the history of organized travel has been neglected. Tourism today has become the academic preserve of economists and sociologists, with predictably dire results.

This book is not a business history so much as a tale of human endeavour. It chronicles the first tentative steps of a new class of 'gregarious travellers' – exciting working-class excursions, longer middle-class tours in Britain, virgin ventures abroad. It illuminates that momentous but still obscure revolution which transformed a static society into a mobile one. It examines the furious arguments which have always buzzed about the heads of tourists. It explores the snobberies bedevilling tourism, the motives behind it (ranging from self-improvement to sexual indulgence), and its social consequences, not least the impetus it gave to freeing women from the stifling conventions of the Victorian age. Finally, using a wealth of novel information, the book traces the growth of a mass movement of human beings which dwarfs the great migrations of the past and sustains the largest industry in the world.

Novelty does not imply adequacy, quite the reverse. The evidence on the subject of popular tourism is so copious and so scattered that no pioneer could take the measure of it. Although it ploughs a new furrow this book only scratches the surface. For every source note referred to there are many thousands that might have been cited. For every unpublished letter or diary read there are hundreds mouldering unseen in attics. For every tome and article perused, every obscure journal and provincial newspaper scanned, there are libraries that remain to be opened, especially abroad. While the book quotes some foreign testimony and tries to give an impression of Cook's global ramifications, its outlook remains predominantly British. It is, moreover, deliberately lacking in balance. It concentrates on the period when the firm was moving from commercial philanthropy to imperial entrepreneurship. Cook's later metamorphoses – from family concern to international agency to nationalized industry to financial and services conglomerate – are sketched in more lightly, as are the recent, more familiar developments of tourism. The initial stage of Thomas Cook's 150-year-long odyssey was the most interesting and perhaps the most important. This book does its best to evoke that stirring time of tourist innovation and adventure.

• I •

The Birth of Tourism

On 9 June 1841 a slim, dark man set out to walk the fourteen miles from his home at Market Harborough to the provincial town of Leicester. His name was Thomas Cook and he was thirty-three years old. Cook's business was printing but his passion was temperance and it was to a temperance meeting that he was going. Drink, he believed, was the root of nearly all the evils afflicting early Victorian England and Cook, who had once been a Baptist preacher, was eager to spread the teetotal gospel. As he later wrote, about halfway along his road – 'my mind's eye has often reverted to the spot – a thought flashed through my brain – what a glorious thing it would be if the newly developed powers of railways and locomotion could be made subservient to the cause of temperance'.[1] His idea was to rally support for the temperance movement by organizing a railway excursion, which would not only gain publicity but would provide a more attractive and wholesome form of recreation than the alehouse. Cook's revelation en route for Leicester was not, despite what he seemed to imply, quite such an earth-shaking event as St Paul's conversion on the road to Damascus. Yet it was, in more senses than one, an event that moved the world. It marked an epoch in the history of travel and a revolutionary change in Cook's own life. Or, as he put it a few years later, 'That moment . . . was the starting point of a career of labour and pleasure which has expanded into . . . a mission of good-will and benevolence on a large scale.'[2]

Cook put his excursion proposal to the Leicester temperance meeting, held in the large, tawdry Amphitheatre at Humberstone Gate, and the excited audience roared its approval. He then negotiated with John Fox Bell, the former grocer who had become secretary to the Midland Counties Railway Company. Though no temperance man, Bell was much in sympathy with the idea. In 1840 the Midland had opened its line from Leicester to Derby, had provided a train for an outing arranged by the Nottingham

Mechanics' Institute[3] and had become the first railway to put on excursions of its own – its earliest special train, sixty-seven carriages hauled by four engines, had 'appeared like a moving street, the houses of which were filled with human beings'.[4] So Bell agreed to convey the temperance supporters from Leicester to Loughborough and back at the very cheap rate of a shilling each,* and he even helped Cook to find the preliminary expenses. Cook himself advertised the event, sold the tickets and dispatched invitations as far afield as Derby and Nottingham. Hoping to make the day 'one of pure and exalted delight, and great usefulness', he worked out his arrangements with particular care. He was determined to produce a 'grand demonstration' such 'as has no parallel in the history of Leicestershire'.[5]

The excursion took place on 5 July 1841; this was a Monday, perhaps a variety of 'St Monday', the unofficial holy day, or holiday, which workers often awarded themselves. Anyway, in the morning a large body of excursionists, variously numbered at 570 and 485, gathered at Leicester station. They were accompanied by temperance officers and a uniformed brass band, and watched by a crowd some two or three thousand strong. Marshalled by Cook, they climbed on board one second-class carriage and nine 'tubs', the open, seatless carriages in which third-class passengers travelled during the early days of rail, and set off on the eleven-mile journey. Every bridge along the line was thronged with spectators and when the train arrived in Loughborough it was greeted by a crush of temperance supporters and onlookers. Among them, the *Leicestershire Mercury* reported, was a company of dragoons, some of whom climbed onto the roof of their Nottingham Road barracks and,

> being stripped to their shirts and wide white trousers, their
> fine proportions appeared swelled to those of Patagonians. The
> windows were also crowded with fierce mustachiod faces, one
> of which, in particular attracted our attention. This soldier, like
> those on the roof, was stripped, his head was clothed with a
> queer red woollen nightcap, his mustachios were black and large,

*At the time of writing (1990) a day return by British Rail for the same journey costs £2.20. During the Victorian age the value of sterling was relatively static, but it has fallen sharply this century. What you could buy for 2 (new) pence in 1900 would cost about £1 in 1991.

and he regarded the moving, joyful crowd beneath him with the imperturbable gravity of a Turk.

The teetotal procession made its way through the town to South Fields, in the park of a certain William Paget Esq. He graciously received them while the band played the National Anthem. After lunch (bread and ham provided by quartermaster Cook) they set off for the station again to meet the delegations from Derby, Nottingham and Harborough. All then 'perambulated the town in goodly array – the whole population lining the streets, and filling the windows as they passed along'. In the Market Square they halted, formed a circle and sang the Teetotal National Anthem.

Next they marched back to Mr Paget's park, a colourful crowd, men and women, old reformed drunkards and young teetotallers from birth, sporting temperance medals, ribbons and rosettes, white wands and bright banners. The purple Derby flag which featured the Prodigal Son being forgiven was much admired, as was the white satin Loughborough standard which was trimmed with lace and bore the motto, 'Do not drink wine nor strong drink'.[6] After grace and tea, the band played lively tunes and the teetotallers played energetic games: cricket, 'kiss in the ring', 'running under the handkerchief' and 'tag'. There was also dancing and general jollification even among the 'Anti's', who had swollen the crowd to about three thousand. One gentleman of the press, not himself a teetotaller, felt bound to 'acknowledge that the "steam" generated by tea takes quite as long to condense as that generated by the "Fiend Alcohol" – (as our friends the Total Abstainers somewhat unpoetically designate the whole class of fermented liquors) – if not longer'.[7]

Between six and seven o'clock Thomas Cook announced that the speeches would begin, and various dignitaries, mostly local ministers, made earnest, good-humoured and predictable addresses in support of the cause. (One speaker, incidentally, condemned the use of drink to treat or demoralize electors, a piquant instance of which occurred during the 1841 general election when a number of voters were kept drunk and cooped up in the grounds of Melbourne Hall, where Cook had worked as a boy.)[8] Finally, at about nine, the meeting broke up and all returned home 'highly delighted with the day's proceedings'.[9] Encouraged by some parting words from Cook, they looked forward to further outings along the same lines.

Cook himself was already conjuring with the notion of bigger and better excursions. Thrilled by the success of his idea, and inspired by millenarian hopes of redeeming an entire people, he saw that it was capable of almost infinite extension. 'One cheer more,' he cried, 'for Teetotalism and Railwayism!!!'[10]

From this acorn grew the mighty oak of modern tourism. Yet although it is right to trace the development of today's mass movement back to Thomas Cook's first temperance excursion, and fair to claim that in carrying his work to fruition Cook 'made the largest single contribution of any man to the growth of a new industry',[11] his achievement must be set in a broad historical context if it is to be properly appreciated. Only thus can his originality be gauged and his 'genius'[12] assessed. So before examining Cook's own antecedents, let us look back at the evolution of tourism over the ages.

The first point to stress is that, despite Cook's claim that his was the 'first public excursion train ever known in England',[13] he by no means originated railway excursions. Such outings began virtually with railways themselves, though the earliest special train at reduced fares apparently dates from 14 June 1836, when it took a party of 800 from Wadebridge to Wenford Bridge.[14] Cook was anticipated by all sorts of other excursionists, from groups of spectators going to boxing matches, horse races and public executions to members of educational bodies, churches and, indeed, temperance organizations. Whether any of these expeditions was 'personally conducted' in the manner Cook made his own is unclear. Without question, though, there were tourist agents before Cook – long before.

In 1818 a Mr Emery of Charing Cross began to organize fourteen-day coach tours of Switzerland at a cost of twenty guineas.[15] In the eighteenth century entrepreneurs like John Anthony Galignani arranged group travel and sightseeing on the Continent as well as supplying passports and guide-books. In 1650 there was an embryo travel agency, the Bureau d'Adresses et de Rencontres, in Paris.[16] In the late fifteenth century the Venetian Agostino Contarini provided pilgrims with a complete package tour of the Holy Land. It included transport there and back, guides and two hot meals a day. The cost was sixty gold ducats (the equivalent of £1,650 in the money of 1980) and there were no 'extras' in the shape of fees, tolls or bribes.[17] Earlier still Crusaders entrusted their travel arrangements to a 'patronus' or personal conductor.[18]

As all this suggests, Cook did not invent tourism or the conducted tour. Indeed, the habit of travelling for pleasure is as old as recorded history. Among the graffiti on Djoser's pyramid at Gizeh is a note, written in 1244 BC, of how 'Hadnakhte, scribe of the treasury . . . came to make an excursion and amuse himself on the west of Memphis.' The ancient Greeks also visited Egypt, already with its quota of guides to explain that the pyramids extended into the earth the same distance as into the air or that they were 'Joseph's silos'.[19] Greece in turn became a holiday goal of wealthy Romans, who often travelled in parties using Pausanias as their guide-book. In fact classical civilization could boast most of the features of later tourism, from road-maps to signposts, from flea-ridden inns to decadent spas and seaside resorts like Baiae, from tatty souvenirs to critics like Seneca who mocked the travel mania. During the Middle Ages that mania took the form of pilgrimages, whose often profane character is well illustrated by Chaucer's Wife of Bath. The Church condemned this 'epidemic' of medieval tourism[20] just as moralists would later denounce the aristocratic Grand Tour. Tobias Smollett, for example, declared that Britain apparently sent her raw youths abroad solely 'on purpose to bring her national character into contempt'.[21] The Grand Tourists were not the Golden Hordes but, according to Lady Mary Wortley Montagu, they were such boobies that Italians called them the 'Golden Asses'.[22]

To some extent, of course, travel is a state of mind, and the Grand Tour was knowledge to the wise man as well as folly to the fool. But it is interesting to notice that these blue-blooded endeavours were subject to many of the strictures which were later visited on Cook's tours. Particular criticism was directed at the ignorance of the tutors, or 'bear-leaders' as they were called, and the philistinism of their charges. There were, indeed, remarkable instances of both. Lord Baltimore managed to get through the Villa Borghese in ten minutes. Discovering that there were no fine pictures at a Roman house he was about to visit, Lord Webb exclaimed: 'God be thanked. Nobody will plague me to look about me.'[23] On the other hand, many young men clearly derived enormous benefit from the experience. Among them was Edward Gibbon.

> I do not pretend to say that there are no disagreeable things in it: bad roads, and indifferent inns, taking very often a good deal of trouble to see things which do not deserve it, and especially the

continued converse one is obliged to have with the vilest part of mankind, Innkeepers, post masters, and custom house officers, who impose upon you without any possibility of preventing it, all these are far from being pleasing. But how amply is a traveller repaid for those little mortifications, by the pleasure and knowledge he finds in almost every place.[24]

Samuel Johnson (though never so supercilious) would have agreed, maintaining as he did that: 'A man who has not been to Italy, is always conscious of an inferiority, from his not having seen what it is expected a man should see.'[25] Nevertheless, there was something in Johnson's definition of the Grand Tourist as one 'who enters a town at night and surveys it in the morning and hastens away to another place', acquiring in the process 'a confused remembrance of palaces and churches'.[26]

The superficiality increased as the Grand Tour changed its nature. It had begun, during Queen Elizabeth's reign, as a refined form of education, a school to 'finish' patricians by giving them first-hand experience of classical lands. But by about 1750 it was turning into a refined form of pleasure, a Continental jaunt for those who wanted to keep up with the milords. As the eighteenth century progressed, more and more people could afford to indulge in the Grand Tour. As early as 1738 one newspaper observed that the British 'fondness for gadding beyond seas' was 'epidemical'.[27] During the two years after the signing of the Peace of Paris in 1763 forty thousand English travellers, Horace Walpole estimated, passed through the port of Calais alone. It was then that the word 'hotel' first appeared in the English language, Smollett introducing it in a suitable sentence: 'The expense of living in an hotel is enormous.'[28] Towards the end of the century there were said to be more than forty thousand English people on the Continent at any one time – Gibbon blamed the 'incursion' into his Swiss refuge on the new 'fashion of viewing the mountains and glaciers'.[29] In August 1786 the new *Daily Universal Register* (which soon changed its name to *The Times*) thundered: 'To such a pitch of folly is the rage of travelling come, that in less than six weeks, the list of Londoners arrived in Paris has amounted to three thousand seven hundred and sixty, as appears by the register of that city.'[30]

In about 1811 the term 'tourism' was coined to describe this essentially modern movement. Conveying the idea of a circular journey, 'tourism' has gentler connotations than the word 'travel', which stems from travail. This was appropriate, for after the Napoleonic Wars steamships began to make the process of going abroad far easier and more reliable – the first cross-Channel service began in 1820. In the following decade there was more talk of 'travelling mania'. But whereas 'the travellers in Sterne's day were "but as one man among ten thousand"', wrote a periodical journalist, now

'all sorts and conditions' of his Britannic Majesty's subjects seem engaged . . . in steam-boats, omnibuses, and accélérés, on one common pursuit of perpetual motion; so that I verily believe that there are not in the entire parish of Cripplegate ten respectable housekeepers wholly disqualified for the traveller's club.

Never, he concluded, 'was there such a deportation of an entire people'.[31] It is difficult to estimate how many were actually involved in this annual exodus. One modern writer suggests a figure of 150,000,[32] but this seems far too high. By 1840 perhaps as many as a hundred thousand Britons (out of a population of nearly 27 million) travelled to Europe each year.

Domestic travel expanded even more rapidly. During the eighteenth century 'taking the waters' at the spa or the seaside had become increasingly fashionable (though when Smollett swam in the Mediterranean doctors at Nice 'prognosticated immediate death').[33] George III, who hoped to find sanity in salt water and breasted the waves at Weymouth to the tune of 'God Save the King' played by a band of fiddlers in a bathing machine, encouraged the vogue. (Similarly the Romantic poets later inspired journeys to the Lake District, though as early as the 1790s William Wilberforce, sent there on doctor's orders, found Windermere 'as populous as Piccadilly'.)[34] Like the spas, which they outstripped, seaside resorts gradually changed from health centres to havens of pleasure. And as more people sought to escape from city or factory these resorts developed apace. Lacking cheap or easy means of transport, many 'trippers' (the word dates from 1813) simply walked to the coast. But improved roads and the arrival of river steamers caused a dramatic upsurge in seaside traffic after the Napoleonic Wars. By the mid-1830s Margate and Ramsgate attracted over a hundred thousand visitors each year, while more than fifty thousand went to Brighton. In 1841 the eminent medical authority, Dr A.B. Granville, who recommended sea water as 'a *mineral water*', forecast that with the advent of the railway 'the whole nation, at length, will be on the move'.[35]

There were, indeed, further auguries of an imminent travel revolution in the year of Cook's first excursion. Granville himself noted that in the Midland counties the stagecoach 'is becoming more and more of a *rarity* every day, and will end up by being "a wonder"'.[36] Bradshaw, the national railway timetable, made its first regular appearance, sporting its famous yellow wrapper though not yet christened by *Punch* (born too, incidentally, in 1841) England's 'Greatest Work of Fiction'.[37] The first European hotel to be built as an integral part of a railway station was opened in York.[38] Cunard, then the British & North American Royal Mail Steam Packet Company, started operating in 1841 with a service across the Atlantic. According to its chronicler, the story of American Express, offspring of the Wells, Fargo Company, also began in that year. In short, the first act of Thomas Cook's travel drama was performed on a crowded stage.

All the same, Cook's excursion was a startling novelty – it would not otherwise have attracted such attention or provoked such excitement. And Cook himself, having brought about a significant change in the travelling habits of his contemporaries, could rightly claim the proud title of 'pioneer'.[39] For despite popular outings, despite the beginnings of modern tourism, despite considerable local migration[40] (typified by Cook's own experiences), society before the railway age was, by present standards, almost inconceivably static. Compared to the mass movements of today very few people travelled. The poor, in particular, rarely strayed far from home. As a Cornish vicar wrote, 'A visit to a distant market town is an achievement to render a man an authority or an oracle among his brethren, and one who has accomplished that journey twice or thrice is ever regarded as a daring traveller.'[41]

Yet the rich were scarcely more venturesome. In 1829 Dr Arnold, headmaster of Rugby School, said that 'more than half my boys never saw the sea, and never were in London' and he marvelled at the ignorance which stemmed from their having 'lived all their days in inland county parishes, or small country towns'.[42] Without doubt limitation of movement did often result in narrowness of ideas. In France, as Elie de Beaumont wrote, before the Victorian communications revolution 'the people born and living on the granite soil of Limousin could not think like those of the Ile de France'.[43] The historian W.G. Hoskins gives a vivid illustration of the restricted scope of Devon life, imaginative as well as geographical, which might have applied to any county in England:

> The village of Bridford lay only nine miles south-west of Exeter
> by road, yet the rector tells us that when Napoleon's invasion of
> England was considered to be imminent the well-to-do families of
> Exeter made plans for flight to Bridford as though it were another
> continent. The same parson noted that in 1818 he buried three
> very old men who had been born in the parish, never lived out of
> it, and died in it. This is a more authentic picture of the nature of
> communications in Devon than any statistics about turnpike trusts
> and stage coach timing.[44]

Stagecoach times were, of course, one factor among many in discouraging travel. Before the introduction of mail coaches in 1874 a journey from London to Edinburgh could take twelve to fourteen days; afterwards the 400 miles were covered in sixty, then in forty, hours. Such speed took its toll and 'it was whispered that passengers had died of apoplexy from the rapidity of the motion'.[45] But even at a less frenetic pace coaching was no rest cure. On a trip from Leicester to London in 1782, Pastor Carl Moritz reckoned that he had stared 'certain death' in the face and he emerged from his mobile torture chamber looking 'like a crazy creature'.[46] After a nine-hour journey from Taunton to Bath, Sydney Smith complained that he had suffered 'between ten thousand and twelve thousand severe contusions'.[47] The deplorable state of the highways – John Wesley had almost drowned in a puddle on the Great North Road – was gradually improved by turnpikes and macadamized surfaces, though not to the satisfaction of William Cobbett. In characteristic vein he laid down the law about the whole business of coaching:

> To travel in stage coaches is to be hurried along by force, in a
> box, with an air-hole in it, and constantly exposed to broken
> limbs, the danger being much greater than that on ship-board,
> and the noise much more disagreeable, while the company is
> frequently not a great deal to one's liking.[48]

Nevertheless, there were many who exulted in the new mobility afforded by the English coach, which was at least preferable to the monstrous, lumbering Continental diligence, a cross between a Wild West stage and a broad-wheeled wagon. In 1878 Thomas Cook's firm cited figures to show that before 1835 diligences had killed one in every three hundred thousand of their passengers and injured one in every thirty thousand, whereas railways killed one in 45 million and injured one in a million.[49]

No less striking were the other hazards and difficulties of travel before the establishment of the permanent way. On the road voyagers risked attack by highwaymen and extortion by postilions, whose victims must often have wished that they would be struck by lightning. They faced problems with luggage which, in the opinion of Murray's *Handbook*, had rightly been called 'impedimenta' by the Romans and was the 'source of much anxiety, trouble and expense'.[50] Abroad travellers complained of harassment by venal customs officers and bureaucratic passport officials. They protested about guides whose avarice was matched only by their ignorance and money-changers whose exactions could be limited only by long 'numismatic research'.[51] Accommodation was a further trial. Hotel touts were clamorous to the point of violence. Hotel-keepers everywhere resembled those in France who calculated their 'reckoning as if Crécy and Agincourt were items in the account'.[52] Whether eating or being eaten, guests were made miserable. Horace Walpole grumbled about dinners of 'stinking mutton cutlets, addled eggs, and ditch water'[53] and declared that vermin were the 'legal inhabitants' of every inn he visited. He particularly shuddered at a hostelry in Amiens where, behind his bedroom tapestry, he could hear 'the old fleas talking of Louis XIV'.[54]

However, more inhibiting than any of this were the time and expense of pre-Victorian travel. Speed was governed, as it always had been, by horse-power and wind-power. When Sir Robert Peel was summoned home from Italy to form a government in 1834 he travelled no faster than Roman officials nearly 2,000 years before. Slow motion meant high prices. In 1800 a journey from Scotland to London cost £14, more than half Thomas Cook's annual income as a Baptist village missionary a few years later. A thirty-seven-day tour of north-west England and Wales undertaken in the 1820s cost a total of £118, roughly half the sum for travel and half for food and accommodation.[55] This sort of expenditure put travel beyond the reach of most people, a fact reflected by poor transport capacity.

For example Portsmouth, which had a population of 30,000 in 1831, had only enough coaches to take 200 passengers a day to London. That there was a widespread demand for travel became plain when railways reduced its cost from about threepence halfpenny a mile to a penny.[56] But amid the enthusiasm which greeted this railway revolution conservative voices were raised deploring the popular new movement. For it involved the destruction of the static society of the past, in which the higher orders had a vested interest.

After all, the word 'mob' stemmed from 'mobile', and British rulers had always regarded lower-class mobility as a threat, sometimes with good reason. The feudal system had bound men to the land. Vagrancy had been punished by law. The Settlement Acts had tried to stop labourers migrating to other parishes where they might become eligible for poor relief. Some feared that the Chartists might use the iron road to make their way into the seats of power (actually it enabled the government to control the nation better).[57] The Duke of Wellington said that railways might act 'as a premium to the lower orders to go uselessly wandering about the country'.[58] And in Disraeli's novel *Sybil* Lord de Mowbray was afraid that the 'great revolution' accomplished by the railways encouraged a 'dangerous tendency to equality' and fostered 'the levelling spirit of the age'.[59] The railway companies themselves seemed to agree. Not only did they reflect, and perhaps reinforce, social divisions by separating passengers into three classes, but they treated them as suspicious persons. In the early days of the Manchester to Liverpool Railway, for example, anyone wanting to buy tickets had to apply twenty-four hours in advance giving name, address, place of birth, age, occupation and reason for the journey. Only thus could the Station Agent satisfy himself that 'the applicant desires to travel for a just and lawful cause'.[60]

This inquisition did not last long. Railway companies, which had expected to haul freight, were overwhelmed by the flood of passengers. As one Victorian put it, 'the giant Railway has . . . swallowed up and annihilated all other modes of conveyance'.[61] Prophets like Ruskin might lament 'the ferruginous temper' of the time[62] and dismiss railways as a means whereby 'every fool in Buxton can be at Bakewell in half an hour, and every fool in Bakewell at Buxton'.[63] Gregory XVI might even forbid the construction of railways in the Papal States on the grounds that they could 'work harm to religion'.[64] But liberals everywhere exulted over the power of steam to produce social change as well as physical mobility. Dr Arnold rejoiced when the Birmingham railway advanced to Rugby and thought that 'feudality is gone for ever'.[65] Thomas Cook would have agreed. In fact, on the slightest pretext he was liable to extol the railway as a democratic and progressive force, all the more so because train timetables achieved a temporal revolution – by making Greenwich time standard throughout the country.

> Railway travelling is travelling for the Million; the humble may travel, the rich may travel. Taste and Genius may look out of third-class windows, meekly rebuking Vice and Ignorance, directly opposite them . . . Railway time is London time, and London time is the sun's time, and the sun's time is common time; and Railway time all must keep . . . To travel by train is to enjoy republican liberty and monarchical security. Railway travelling is cheap, common, safe, and easy.[66]

Yet, as Cook realized, the immediate appeal of the railway lay not in its social consequences, or even in its economic ones, profound though these were. It lay in the sheer novelty and excitement of the sensation, the sheer delight in the conquest of space and time. 'Man is become a bird,' cried Sydney Smith.[67] On an early train journey the actress Fanny Kemble became entranced by 'the magical machine, with its flying white breath and rhythmical, unvarying pace . . . I felt no fairy tale was ever half so wonderful.'[68] Extending the metaphor, Victor Hugo captured the romance of the steam engine for his own age and for posterity:

> It is difficult not to think of the iron horse as a real animal. It pants when still, wails when it starts, howls as it goes; it sweats, trembles, whistles, neighs, slows down, dashes off at great speed; it leaves as its trail a spoor of burning coals and urine of boiling water; great bursts of sparks fly out of its wheels – or, if you prefer, its feet – and its breath floats over your head in beautiful clouds of white steam which tear themselves to shreds in tree branches. Only this marvellous animal could pull along a thousand or fifteen hundred passengers – the entire population of a town – at a speed of 12 leagues an hour.[69]

No wonder that, in the 1830s and '40s, railways and their promotion became 'a fashion and a frenzy'.[70]

Thomas Cook's achievement was to associate himself with the spirit of the age and to foster its most thrilling development. He not only appreciated the new opportunities for rational recreation that the railway offered but he learnt how to make use of them. For the fact was that in its early days most people found train travel neither cheap nor easy. Regular fares, even third-class ones, were too high for the Victorian working class to regard travel by train as anything more than a treat or an emergency. And although the Railway Clearing House was established in 1842 to bring some order to the chaos caused by competing companies, a specialist travel agent was still needed to organize complex journeys over several lines and to issue tickets for them at favourable rates. This is what Thomas Cook eventually became, thus making his unique contribution to simplifying, popularizing and cheapening travel. His temperance trip from Leicester to Loughborough was the first hesitant step on an immensely long and arduous journey. It was to earn him such characteristic Victorian sobriquets as 'the eponymous hero . . . of travel', 'the Peerless Excursionist' and the 'Emperor of Tourists'.[71]

• 2 •

A Mission in Life

Thomas Cook was born on 22 November 1808 at five o'clock in the morning, the event being carefully recorded in an old family Bible. This was a more than usually appropriate place to register his birth; for though Cook earned fame as a conductor of tours, the Scriptures always remained his guide-book to life. Indeed, his whole career was a 'mission'[1] and even his temperance campaign was merely part of a more sacred crusade. This is not to say that Cook was indifferent to the romance and adventure of the travel revolution which he pioneered. Even in old age he delighted in 'a work which seems to enchain our thoughts and energies the more strongly, the more intensely it is pursued. Nothing but the stagnation of mental powers seems capable of weaning us from the claims and charms of such fascinating toil.'[2] However, his essential motives were religious. By helping to bring mobility to the masses Cook accomplished much; but his most important achievement, he believed, was that 'man has been brought nearer to man and nearer to his Creator'.[3] Victorians, who could be cynical as well as sanctimonious, sometimes observed that bad men were bad, did bad, and went to the bad; but that it was surprising how much harm a really good man could do. However, it was with piety rather than irony that Cook's contemporaries hailed him as the 'patron saint' of travel.[4]

Curiously enough, the religious revival to which Cook owed his faith began in 1741, exactly a century before his first excursion, as the result of another kind of journey. This was the itinerant mission of John Wesley, who in that year visited Cook's birthplace, the village of Melbourne in Derbyshire. Here Wesley (and others – the devout Selina, Countess of Huntingdon, lived nearby at Donington Park) initiated one of the many local 'awakenings' which together made up the great Evangelical movement of the eighteenth century. A symptom of the vitality of this movement was its tendency to split into sects, each one convinced that it had found the true path to salvation. In 1770 Melbourne became a centre of the New

Connexion of General Baptists, formed to protest against the moral and doctrinal laxity of its parent body. Its main tenet (apart from insistence on the scriptural necessity for adult baptism) was that only those whose faith produced good works could be saved.

One of the founders of the New Connexion was Thomas Perkins, Cook's maternal grandfather, who acted as co-pastor of the Melbourne flock for many years. He was a '"hell-fire" preacher' who came 'with boiling enthusiasm, and in tones of thunder, to hurl verses and paragraphs of the sacred writings like huge boulders to crush down all opponents'.[5] Thanks in part to his 'highly successful' ministry, Melbourne was soon 'noted both for its evangelistic efforts and its denominational spirit'.[6] By 1785 the New Connexion could boast 305 members (Melbourne's population being about 1,750) and 'in those early days every member considered himself a missionary'.[7] Late in life Thomas Cook proudly remarked that one nearby village, Barton, had sent more Christian missionaries to Orissa than London itself. Recalling how many Melbourne Baptists, his mother included, went on 'long tours' throughout England in search of conversions, he yearned for the revival of 'some system of itineracy'.[8]

Yet religious trips were the exception, and if Cook always thought that 'travel is a form of missionary enterprise'[9] he must have felt sadly constrained by the narrow circumstances of his Melbourne childhood. For like most poor families before the railway age, his own was distinguished by what one Victorian called 'vegetative life and stationary habits and local prejudices'.[10] Admittedly, not much is known about his early life or antecedents. But for at least four generations (each one producing a single son) his family had lived in Melbourne, where it was 'not unusual to find labourers who have worked on the same farm through the greater part of their lives'.[11] Here in 1748 his great-grandfather, another Thomas Cook, married Catherine Dodge. In 1783 their child, William Cook, married Mary Mickerson, who gave birth to John Cook two years later. In February 1808 he married Elizabeth Perkins, who though a pastor's daughter could not write her name in the church register. She duly produced Thomas in November of the same year.

He could scarcely have entered the world in humbler circumstances – a labourer's cottage, 9 Quick Close, in the ailing heart of rural England. Not for nothing, nearly half a century later, did Cook extol the 'Change! Change! Change!!!' that had occurred since his boyhood. Then water had been taken from pumps and wells, now it was piped; then houses were lit by dim tallow tapers, now by gas; then thread came by the skein, now it was unbroken; then sending a letter was so expensive that one was 'afraid to write', now the penny post prevailed; then 'difficulties of transit made all fear the risk, many the time and more the cost' of going on a journey and most people heard of faraway places only by report, now steam had triumphed and 'railway travelling is travelling for the million'.[12]

Signs of that last change were already apparent in the year of Cook's birth. In the summer of 1808, for example, the inventor Richard Trevithick publicized his improved locomotive, the 'Catch-me-who-can', by taking people for shilling rides at a 'steam circus' erected near the site of what is now Euston Station.[13] At much the same time William Blake was writing of dark satanic mills blighting England's green and pleasant land, whose face was otherwise being transformed by the enclosure movement which deprived the poor of common lands. Factories were already destroying the livelihood of framework knitters, whose protests shortly took the form of Luddite riots and machine-breaking – Ned Ludd's home was in the Midlands. But although contemporaries asserted that the condition of English villagers was worse than that of black slaves in the West Indies,[14] country life, especially around Melbourne, retained much of its pastoral character and its comfortable, ancient flavour.

Labouring wages, though pitifully low at between nine and twelve shillings a week, were marginally higher than in neighbouring districts and each man had '120 square yards of ground free of expense to grow potatoes'.[15] The landscape, with its 'richly wooded scenery'[16] was both beautiful and fertile. It was well suited to market gardening and Melbourne, straddling the main road between Leicester and Derby, helped to feed these towns. Thomas Cook must have grown familiar with the carts and trains of pack-horses (whose drivers refreshed themselves at the Old Pack-Horse Inn) which threaded their way over the narrow, 'miry and almost impassable' highway.[17] Actually in the matter of thoroughfares Melbourne compared quite well with other parts of the country – as late as 1808 travellers had to be guided across Lincoln Heath by a land lighthouse seventy feet high. In that year a parliamentary commission reported on the vital need to improve England's atrocious 'interior communications'.[18] This enterprise was so huge that even the likes of Thomas Telford, 'the Colossus of Roads'[19] could not accomplish it before being overtaken by the railway.

Thus Thomas Cook entered two worlds, one ceasing to exist, the other struggling to be born. Melbourne was the past, the Domesday village with its mellow Norman church and ruined castle, its gnarled oaks which were older still, its gorse-covered, rabbit-infested commons, its lush valleys where the grass was as 'soft as velvet and as green as an emerald',[20] its tenant farmsteads held with feudal loyalty from generation to generation, all washed by the silver Trent in which young Thomas so delighted to fish that he created a little leisure by rising well before dawn on summer mornings. Melbourne was a far cry from the booming new life of the cities, from what Cook later called 'the Great Roar of London', where a countryman would 'stand appalled' at streets in which 'men and women, cabs, busses, carts, waggons, carriages, horsemen, drays, and Hansoms, sweep by like a tide'.[21] Melbourne represented peace, continuity, seclusion. It was, indeed, so remote that French prisoners were held there, one of the few reminders that the Napoleonic Wars were raging in Europe. Understandably, Thomas Cook came to feel 'an intense admiration for the village of his birth'.[22] When the local boy had made good on a global scale it was plausibly rumoured that he intended to return and establish himself in Melbourne Hall, a potential upset to the social order which prompted this spiteful newspaper comment:

> If the rumour be correct will Mr Cook, who has 'personal'
> experience of trippers, close his portals against the fraternity, or
> will he nobly disregard the broken bottles and sandwich papers
> and empty fusee-boxes [i.e. match-boxes] and create a rival Alton
> Towers with his special trains to Melbourne?[23]

As it happened, Cook did not retire to Melbourne but to Leicester, busy scene of his 'much-loved labours in the cause of human progress'.[24] Rustication was all very well but the countryside, poverty-stricken and lacking in opportunity, was the essence of backwardness. Throughout his life Cook was drawn to the brave new world being created by the industrial revolution. It seemed to offer boundless scope for improving not just the physical but the spiritual lot of humankind, a theme on which he would wax lyrical:

> The mighty and glorious achievements of science are opening up
> facilities such as people never were favoured with at any former
> period of the world's history and men seem to be inspired with
> new feelings and animated with new hopes; and amongst the
> varied agencies now at work on the minds and morals of men,
> there are few more powerful than Railways and Locomotion.
> The opening of a railway in an ignorant and barbarous district
> is an omen of moral renovation and intellectual exaltation. The
> prejudices which ignorance has engendered are broken by the
> roar of a train of carriages, and the whistle of the engine awakens
> thousands from the slumber of ages.[25]

Cook might have been reflecting on Melbourne before the railway age.

His own formal education was 'rudimentary',[26] though it was
an improvement on what 'many boys of that time were able to
secure'.[27] He was taught by three masters of 'stern integrity and
religious character', but he left school at the age of ten. His father
had died in 1812 and his mother's second marriage, to James
Smithard in September of the same year, evidently left the family
no better off. Thomas was set to work as a gardener's boy on Lord
Melbourne's estate. This was a model of its kind. In the early
eighteenth century the owner of the Hall, coincidentally named
Thomas Coke, had employed Henry Wise and George London
(who had earlier embellished Hampton Court for William III) to
lay out the gardens in the manner of Versailles. But young Cook
had little time to admire pools, parterres, statuary and intersecting
allées. He worked hard for six days a week, earning a penny a day.
One of his jobs was to hawk vegetables round the neighbourhood.
As far afield as Derby market, eight miles distant, he cried: 'Peas!
Beans! Seeds! Plants for sale!'[28]

Released from drudgery only on the Sabbath, Thomas owed his
salvation in every sense to the Baptists. Actually, showing a characteristic independence of spirit, he attended a Methodist Sunday
school until the age of thirteen or fourteen. Then 'having found
as he thought the more excellent way' (and doubtless prompted
by his strong-willed mother), he joined that of the Baptists. It
was a flourishing organization, 150 strong. Cook, described as an
'earnest, active, devoted, young Christian',[29] became first scholar,
next teacher, and finally superintendent in this Sunday school. The
learning it disseminated was not, indeed, profound. There were

few books save Holy Writ and a typical exercise was to hunt for interminable texts on the Fall of Man. Nevertheless, a number of Baptists, the 'principal men' of Melbourne as Cook called them, were surprisingly cultivated. He himself knew one who could read the Bible in Greek, translating aloud as he went. Cook later said that he was under 'obligation' to this Nonconformist elite.[30] He was particularly indebted to his uncle John Pegg, who had married another of Pastor Perkins's daughters and in 1822 took Thomas on as an apprentice 'wood-turner' or cabinet-maker, a craft in which he acquired 'considerable proficiency'.[31] During the last winter of Pegg's life Cook 'slept in his bedroom, ready to render him any little service that lay in my power'.[32] However, the man through whom Thomas Cook's 'soul was won for Christ' was Melbourne's new pastor, Joseph Foulks Winks. On 26 February 1826, thanks largely to his 'earnest and evangelical ministry', Cook was baptized.[33]

Winks, formerly a draper's assistant from Retford, influenced Cook in other ways. A fiery speaker and a 'fearless advocate of religious and civil liberty',[34] he helped to imbue the younger man with advanced ideas. Cook 'often listened with pleasure to his biting satire on the slaves' to the 'filthy practice' of smoking.[35] He also set Cook an example. Having started the *Baptist Children's Magazine* in 1825, Winks soon decided that he 'could best serve his Lord by printing and publishing'.[36] When he moved to Loughborough in 1826 Cook seems to have gone with him and assisted in the endeavour.[37] He must have found the occupation congenial, for in due course he returned to it.

Meanwhile, however, Cook was quickly drawn back to his native village. Perhaps the move was prompted by the need to complete his apprenticeship, though in fact he never did so. Or it could have been made on account of his mother's straitened circumstances – he had earlier helped her to open a shop selling books and earthenware, as curious a combination then as now. Or maybe he wished to preach the gospel more directly. At any rate, in October 1828 the Melbourne Baptists recommended 'Brother Cook . . . so far as regards his piety . . . as a suitable person for the important work of an Evangelist'.[38] So, about the time of his twentieth birthday, Thomas Cook became a 'village missionary'. His job was to spread the Word: he and another evangelist, John Earp, taught themselves to preach by climbing through a window of Melbourne chapel in the early mornings and taking it in turns to act as minister in the pulpit and congregation in the pews. Cook also had to distribute tracts and to establish Sunday schools throughout several Midland counties. In 1829 he covered 2,692 miles, 2,106 of them on foot – or as he liked to say, by Shanks's Naggie. No doubt he carried a carpet-bag, as he later recommended tourists to do, travelling light 'with the jaunty swagger of unencumbered bachelorhood'.[39] His salary was £36 a year, later reduced to £26 because he received so much free food and accommodation from the faithful. But though the financial rewards of his mission were meagre, it was a valuable introduction to the business of travel.

The mature Cook was likened to an Old Testament prophet and at this early stage of his career he resembled, so to speak, a young Old Testament prophet. Though only of medium height, he had a commanding presence, with ascetic features and penetrating eyes. They were, a grand-daughter recorded, 'the black piercing eyes of a fanatic'.[40] Cook was formidably energetic and intimidatingly serious. In fact few men of his time attached more importance to being earnest. In his flat regional accent Cook was also sternly outspoken. He had a powerful, racy style and at times, when exposing error or rebuking vice, he sounded like some soapbox Cobbett. Yet his 'kind, benevolent face was usually either placid or smiling'.[41] He had a sense of humour and was not above teasing his mentor J.F. Winks. Like many Evangelicals, from John Newton to William Wilberforce, Cook was surprisingly tolerant despite the strictness of his creed. He regarded the Church of Rome as a shrine to 'idolatry'[42] but he deplored 'sectarian animosity'.[43] He was not a rigid sabbatarian, at least not in the eyes of those Victorians who, according to vulgar wits, forbade even Epsom Salts to work on Sunday. Cook's political views were more liberal than radical. He loathed war, slavery, capital punishment and corruption. He favoured the use of moral not physical force to eradicate evil. Above all, he felt compassion for the poor, the deprived, the downtrodden. Like other members of the New Connexion, he believed that philanthropy was the outward and visible sign of inward and spiritual grace. Cook was, in short, a practical idealist, though he sometimes let his ideals run away with him.

Luckily Thomas Cook met a young woman in 1829 who would help to temper his visionary enthusiasms with 'plenty of good common-sense'. She was Marianne Mason, a farmer's daughter who taught at the Baptist Sunday School at Barrowden in the small county of Rutland. Marianne acted as housekeeper for her father and five brothers and she had an excellent head for business. Born on 11 February 1807, she was a little older than Cook. But, 'smallish and very dapper',[44] she was as attractive as he was impressive. So, when the Baptists could no longer afford to pay him, Cook went to Barrowden where he set up in trade as a wood-turner. The courtship flourished but otherwise he clearly did not prosper there. In the year of the great Reform Act he moved again, this time to the larger town of Market Harborough, a few miles south-east of Leicester. On 2 March 1833 he married Marianne Mason (at Barrowden) and they settled down in Harborough, which was to be their home for the next eight and a half years. Almost at once they conceived a child, who was born on 13 January 1834. He was given the Christian names John Mason and was to be the 'son' in the famous Cook partnership. In some ways he proved to be an even more remarkable man than his father.

The Cook family lifed in Quaker's Yard, off Adam and Eve Street, while Thomas's workshop was in Buzzard Place. The picturesque names suggest the antiquity of Harborough, where a market had been held ever since the Middle Ages – Adam and Eve Street had probably been the scene of mystery plays.[45] Cattle were still sold in the streets and twenty coaches a day rattled through Harborough, which possessed a considerable number of old inns. Admittedly the town, whose population stood at 2,272 in 1831, was modernizing itself; a Corn Exchange was built in 1837 and gas light was introduced while Cook lived there. But many of the traditional feasts and fairs continued, often accompanied by rioting and always by drunkenness.

Of course inebriation was as old as Noah and, as Sydney Smith observed, beer had always been inseparable from Britannia. But in the 1830s many people came to see strong drink as the most serious of all social ills, and it was to this that Thomas Cook now turned his attention. Influenced by Harborough's Baptist minister, a pioneer temperance crusader called Francis Beardsall, he had taken the pledge to abstain from all spirituous liquors (though not yet from ale) shortly before his marriage, on 1 January 1833. Soon afterwards he 'induced' his 'very reluctant' wife – she had rather a nervous disposition – 'to open her house for the accommodation of temperance travellers'.[46] Henceforth, as he later wrote, temperance was 'the guiding star of my public as well as private life'. Such a preoccupation may seem impossibly remote from the travel business. In fact, early tourism was the handmaid of teetotalism. Cook was quite right in saying that 'no two movements are more closely affiliated', for 'the attractions of cheap Excursions have in many thousands of instances been employed to counteract the demoralizing influences of the bottle'.[47]

It would be easy to dismiss Cook's efforts to promote the temperance cause as the work of a crank. The campaign did, indeed, become something of an obsession with him. He was quite liable to harangue complete strangers not only about the demon drink but about its fiendish ally, the 'smoky idol' tobacco.[48] Sometimes, by his own account, he even achieved unlikely conversions. However, Cook repudiated the suggestion that he was a puritanical busybody and in the context of the time his crusade was understandable.

Alcohol, cheap, relatively unadulterated, the focus of so many activities, from striking a bargain to setting out on a journey, had long been a way of life in England (and elsewhere). But thanks to the reduction of duties on spirits and the spread of gin palaces, consumption of hard liquor was apparently rising so fast by the 1830s that it seemed in danger of poisoning the nation. George Cruikshank, whose Hogarthian depictions of the drunkard's ruin signally advanced the case for total abstinence and who later supported Cook's work in person, wrote in 1833: 'Gin is become the great demi-god, a mighty spirit dwelling in gaudy, gold-beplastered temples.'[49] Its acolytes, to extend the metaphor, were barmaids, its devotees imbibed standing up (by dispensing with seats the gin palace could accommodate more drinkers) and its gas-lit interiors cast a lurid glow on mean streets. Contemporaries expressed a growing horror at the degrading effects of drink, which were graphically reported in the press. William IV's coronation, for instance, provided the occasion for a monstrous debauch. In Manchester a *Guardian* correspondent saw

> whole pitchers thrown indiscriminately among the crowd –
> men holding up their hats to receive drink; people quarrelling
> and fighting for the possession of a jug; the strong taking
> liquor from the weak; boys and girls, men and women, in a
> condition of beastly drunkenness, staggering before the depository
> of ale, or lying prostrate on the ground, under every variety
> of circumstances, and in every degree of exposure, swearing,

groaning, vomiting, but calling for more liquor when they could not stand, or even sit, to drink it.[50]

No wonder drink became known as 'the shortest way out of Manchester'.[51] No wonder Thomas Cook insisted that intemperance was 'Death's Prime Minister'.[52] No wonder the temperance movement, born in 1828, seemed the only rational response to what Carlyle called the 'liquid madness' of gin.

In fact there were alternative responses. A man like William Cobbett, with bees in his bonnet about the harmful effects of tea and coffee, could denounce temperance reformers as 'despicable drivelling quacks'. Many others were impressed by the sterling worth of beer, which seemed to be not only John Bull's natural beverage but also a homoeopathic remedy for addiction to spirits. It was partly for this reason that in 1830 the Beer Act was passed, which permitted any householder who paid a fee of two guineas to set up a beershop. The result was that some 30,000 new beershops sprang up, introducing, as one contemporary said, 'the means of intoxication and wasteful expenditure into every village and wayside hamlet in the kingdom'.[53] Sydney Smith memorably pronounced: 'Everybody is drunk. Those who are not singing are sprawling. The sovereign people are in a beastly state.'[54]

This was a comic exaggeration, for the consumption of beer rose only slightly and temporarily. As a matter of fact, the increase in spirit drinking was also something of an illusion – the figures merely showed that more liquor was being drunk legally. However, myths are often more potent than realities and many in the temperance movement, Thomas Cook among them, concluded that abstaining from spirits alone was not enough. Actually Marianne, under the influence of the Rev. Beardsall, who was now publishing the *Temperance Star* in Manchester, preceded her husband into the teetotal fold. Cook followed in December 1836, his conscience smitten by 'the sledge-hammer of John Hockings, the Birmingham blacksmith', whose combination of vigour and humour made him a formidable preacher of the teetotal gospel. The day after he signed the pledge Cook automatically brewed a 'sack of malt' for his workmen but, Marianne agreeing with him 'heart and soul', he soon concluded that they too should renounce alcohol in all its forms.

Sixty years later, celebrating the diamond jubilee of the South Midland Temperance Association, of which he had been the

Harborough branch secretary, Cook gave an amusing account of how he had had one barrel of ale carried back to his brother-in-law in Barrowden, where it arrived much lighter than it started, and had emptied another down the drain in Quaker's Yard. His cellar was now bare except for a few bottles of his wife's grape wine, which mysteriously began to disappear. Cook kept midnight vigil and discovered that the secret drinker was an apprentice, so he got rid of the remaining wine and never permitted strong drink of any kind to darken his doors again. Another apprentice, Cook's half-brother Simeon Smithard, then rebelled against the dry regime. Having 'formed drinking habits and made pot associates',[55] Simeon ran away and broke his indentures. However, within three years he was converted, became a 'teetotal singer' able to 'render a plaintive song in a peculiarly pathetic manner',[56] and later served Cook in various useful capacities.

For the next few years Cook devoted nearly all his energies to the temperance movement, so much so that he neglected both his family and his business. John Mason Cook, an only son as a result of the death of his infant brother Henry in September 1835, had what one admirer described as a 'pathetic' childhood, largely because his father 'gave to the propagation of principles much time which he might more profitably have applied to his handicraft' and to his home.[57] Thomas worked incessantly for what he called 'a cause of unbounded joy and hopefulness'. With a few friends he formed a local abstinence society. He organized meetings, conferences, bazaars, galas, and processions (accompanied by brass bands). He held temperance picnics where the revellers, sustained with 'biscuits, buns and ginger beer' supplemented by 'tea and plum-cake', played games like 'Lost my Slipper' before listening to speeches.[58] Cook himself often addressed these gatherings, apparently in a 'lively and affecting' manner.[59]

This was a form of preaching and, like many other elements of the temperance movement, it was a secular expression of the Nonconformist religious experience. Taking the pledge, for example, was a kind of conversion. Backsliding was damnation. Cook invariably employed the language of evangelism. He rejoiced that thousands who had once been 'enveloped in "gross darkness"' were 'now walking in the paths of Temperance light'.[60] He lamented that a few of Market Harborough's 'reformed drunkards' had 'imitated "the sow that was washed"', returning to wallow in their mire. Naturally enough, many in Harborough resented the crusade and some, as Cook wrote, 'indulged in the bitterest feelings towards us'. Riotous mobs tried to break up their meetings and parades. Temperance workers suffered 'molestations' to the point where their lives were endangered.[61] Cook's own house was attacked with brickbats and he was once struck by the leg-bone of a horse. Characteristically he chased, caught and secured the prosecution of his assailant.

It was easy enough for the liquor interest to mobilize rowdies, but such violence reflected deeper antagonisms than the perennial opposition between drink and sobriety. It was part of a social conflict, a conflict between the emergent working class whose hedonistic culture revolved round the pub and the largely Dissenting lower-middle class who were wedded to respectability. True, the class lines were never hard and fast; nothing indicates that better than Cook's own situation, poised between humble origins and artisan accomplishments. Nevertheless the temperance movement was part of an effort by the few to impose social discipline on the many. The many had sound reasons for resisting it. Taverns were the sole community centres for the poor. They provided most of what limited pleasure about half the population could afford – not just alcohol (deemed a tonic at best and at worst an anodyne) but sport and entertainment, warmth and conviviality. Public houses offered everything from public lavatories to public meetings, sometimes even those of embarrassed temperance reformers with nowhere else to go (itself not more of an irony than the opening of a Leicester pub in 1973 named after . . . Thomas Cook).

Nothing daunted, temperance workers persisted with their puritan assault on popular manners and modes. They seemed determined to turn the Nonconformist conscience into a moral policeman. At its most ruthless 'teetotalitarianism' was designed to quell threatening movements like Chartism and to fit workers for the new industrial yoke. At its most altruistic the temperance movement aimed to civilize the leisure pursuits of the masses. Cook was one of the altruists. During these early years it was his constant endeavour to provide humane and improving recreations in place of the brutal pastimes associated with the drinking fraternity – bull-baiting, stag-hunting, prize-fighting and the like. He harped on the 'dissipation and excess' of tavern saturnalia, in contrast to the 'exquisite enjoyment' of temperance functions. There was the teetotal soirée, for example, with its 'variety of rational and pleasing entertainments, such as singing, recitations, and speeches' celebrating the 'triumphs of sobriety'.[62]

Sobriety did have its triumphs. By 1840 Cook's branch of the Temperance Association could hold a tea party for 160 people in the Town Hall ('handsomely decorated for the occasion') without a 'whisper of opposition'. Cook saw this as 'proof of the happy change of feeling at Harborough'.[63] Admittedly, there was also at least one 'discouraging relapse' in the movement, which he attributed to the local branch's 'heavy debt' and to its lack of 'union, concord and amity'.[64] But the signs of general improvement were unmistakable. Much of the credit must go to Cook, who had by now extended his efforts into the fields of printing and publishing. He issued a number of short-lived journals, including *The Children's Temperance Magazine* (the first such periodical in England), *The Temperance Messenger* and later *The Anti-Smoker* and *The National Temperance Magazine*. Cook also helped to set up the South Midland Temperance Association's Tract Depository in Harborough, taking over full responsibility for it in 1841. In that year he printed some hundred thousand tracts, many of which were distributed by a 'tract missionary' specially employed for the purpose. Cook acknowledged that the sales of his publications were 'paltry' – each edition of the *Messenger* sold roughly 1,500 copies. He therefore made frequent, sometimes urgent, appeals for financial support, insisting that he was subsidizing the work '*without any capital*'[65] and had 'already suffered great pecuniary losses'.[66]

Cook's temperance propaganda owed what influence it had to the fact that he condemned drink not just as the most serious social evil of the day but as a symptom of more fundamental ills. It was less a cause than a consequence of the miserable condition of England. 'Temperance men are *physical* as well as moral reformers,' he declared.[67] 'We look with grief on error, poverty, crime, strife, and wretchedness.'[68] Cook thus associated teetotalism with every kind of social and political progress, from improving drainage to improving housing, from banning quack medicines to banning the opium trade, from abolishing lotteries to abolishing war. At the same time, there was no mistaking his inveterate puritanism. He not only vilified the drunkard as a 'vice-ridden slave to a beastly appetite',[69] he also included tobacco, snuff and 'other poisons' in his demonology. He even denounced 'coffee house loitering' as a preliminary to 'alehouse revelry'.[70] Needless to say, tracts on drunkenness appeal mainly to the sober and it must have been clear to Cook that for the most part he was preaching to the converted.

It must also have been clear to him that as a cure for drink exhortations were less effective than counter-attractions. He was not alone in coming to this conclusion. During the 1830s and '40s the temperance movement was the 'most important agency for recreational improvement'. It was in the vanguard of a broad-based campaign to woo workers away from the pub by providing them with wholesome and enjoyable alternatives. These ranged from Mechanics' Institutes, public libraries, museums, parks and allotments to choral societies, brass bands and dancing round the maypole. The temperance movement even had its own music hall, about which a Victorian wag commented: 'Abandon hops, all ye who enter here.' There were also temperance walks and outings. The aim of teetotallers was to compete with the tavern, whose incidental allurements were legion. In 1841, for example, a Birmingham publican called James Day organized railway excursions for his customers.[71]

It may have been this or one of the other popular excursions of the time which inspired Thomas Cook with his seminal idea of rendering 'the newly developed power and facilities of railways and locomotion . . . subservient to the advancement of the high interests of social brotherhood and morality'.[72] Or perhaps the notion did occur to him spontaneously, as he suggested in his various accounts of his Pauline experience on the road to Leicester. At any rate his first temperance excursion was the result. Successful though this was, it did not immediately or automatically turn him into a professional conductor of tourists or travel agent. On the contrary, for several years after July 1841 he continued to arrange short, inexpensive, teetotal excursions as a form of rational recreation.

For a 'mechanic' (i.e. workman), he asserted, such an 'outing' was no more costly than a visit to a public house, which might 'render him unfit for work, and perhaps finish up with a small doctor's bill'. Furthermore, said Cook, harping on his theme of the train as the great vehicle of social progress, an excursion

provides food for the mind; it contributes to the strength and enjoyment of the intellect; it helps to pull men out of the mire and pollution of old corrupt customs; it promotes a feeling of universal brotherhood; it accellerates [sic] the march of peace, and virtue, and love; – it also contributes to the health of the body, by a relaxation from the toil and the invigoration of the physical powers. And are not all these valuable objects? A few years ago a 'visit to a watering place' was a luxury beyond the reach of the toiling artizan or mechanic; his lot was to waste the midnight oil and his own vital energies in pandering to the vitiated tastes of the sons of fashion, who after their debaucheries or voluptuousness, had to avail themselves of a change of air and scenery to recruit their enervated powers . . . [Now ordinary people] revel in the delights of nature . . . [and art] and thus the broad distinctions of classes are removed without violence or any objectionable means.[73]

Though he inveighed against quack remedies, Cook in full flood could make travel seem rather like the charlatan's pill that cured all sufferers of all diseases. Nevertheless, it was by no means absurd to perceive it as a revolutionary panacea in a society being subjected to unprecedented strains as it entered the hungry Forties.

Perhaps this vision accounted for Cook's move from Market Harborough to Leicester two months after conducting his first excursion, in September 1841.[74] Once the ancient capital of Mercia, seat of the legendary kingdom of Lear, Leicester became Cook's adopted home – and he, in due course, became its most famous citizen. It was now a sprawling provincial town with about 50,000 inhabitants and it must have attracted Cook for a number of reasons. Leicester was an important communications centre. In 1840 the railway line to Rugby opened, bringing London a matter of only five hours distant, and within a couple of years five passenger trains daily travelled each way between Leicester, Nottingham and Derby. Thus Leicester was an ideal place from which to run temperance excursions. Leicester was also 'the metropolis of Dissent'.[75] Nonconformity flourished there in all its forms, from the hot-gospelling Fire Brigade of Jesus to the large Baptist community. There were no fewer than seven Baptist chapels, and two-fifths of those who attended any place of worship belonged to them, among them Cook's old mentor, now a friendly rival, J.F. Winks.

Partly as a consequence of this religious tendency, Leicester was famed for its radicalism: when the corrupt old Tory corporation was driven from power in 1835 the new champions of civic virtue sold off all the baubles of municipal office-maces, regalia and plate.[76] Cook sympathized with such puritanism and he also regarded Leicester

as a rich field for teetotal enterprise. It contained, he said, 700 spirit-
and beershops and public houses, as well as 'great numbers of
dying drunkards', not to mention 'perhaps a greater proportion of
prostitutes than any town beyond the precincts of the metropolis'.[77]
Moreover, despite efforts made in the late 1830s, there was hardly
anything in the way of rational recreation for the great mass of
the people. Cook himself complained that the new town library,
'kept in a portion of the heterogeneous mass of crazy buildings
constituting and adjoining the Town Hall', contained little but the
'learned lumber' of ancient divinity, which should be supplemented
by modern works of history, general science, 'practical utility and
amusement'.[78] So Leicester offered Thomas Cook scope for setting
up as a bookseller as well as for carrying out his philanthropic
mission.

Cook was quite specific about his priorities in Leicester. His first
aim was 'to procure the means of subsistence by diligent and persevering exertion'. His second was 'to assist in the promotion of those
objects of public interest which require the aid of every right-minded
citizen'.[79] However, as invariably happened in Cook's life, the two
aims were in conflict. His commercial incentive proved less powerful
than his moral imperative and he sacrificed private gain to public
spirit. He established himself as a bookseller and printer at 1 King
Street, where he also ran a number of side-lines. He bound books.
He sold stationery, pens and commemorative medals. He began a
registry office for servants, another for lodging- and boarding-houses,
as well as an *Almanack* for all temperance hotels in the kingdom. He
also planned to open a temperance hotel of his own. He compiled
and printed a number of useful and innovative publications, notably
a *Leicestershire Almanack* (1842) and a *Guide to Leicester* (1843), in
the face of stiff competition. Furthermore he diligently promoted
himself and his enterprises, asserting candidly that 'Advertising is
to trade what steam is to machinery.'[80]

Nevertheless Cook was clearly more interested in his philanthropic work, spending too much time and money on it for the good
of his business. In particular his subsidies to temperance tracts and
propagandist journals proved a severe drain on his purse. In July
1843, for example, he complained of having 'suffered great pecuniary losses and disappointments in his endeavours to serve the cause
of true temperance' and he issued this half-comical, half-desperate
appeal:

for several months we have been struggling between life and death [financially] . . . It is now in the power of our friends to effect an infallible cure; and if they will supply the *mineral* [i.e. coin], we pledge ourselves to persevere in exposing the absurdity and evil of converting a *vegetable* production into *smoke, dust* or 'pigtail' [a plait of tobacco] for medicinal or fashionable follies.[81]

Eventually Cook's improving efforts led to a major crisis in his affairs.

Meanwhile, however, he seemed to have energy enough to rise above financial and all other troubles, and the range of his activities during the early 1840s was extraordinary. Cook issued some half a million temperance tracts as well as printing temperance hymn-books, Baptist devotional works and many other publications. He edited *The Teetotaller's Pocket Library, The Children's Temperance Magazine* and (briefly) *Youth's Biblical Cabinet*. He opened two temperance hotels, one in Derby run by his mother, (who had become Mrs Tivey on her third marriage) and the other managed by his wife at his new premises in Leicester, 26 Granby Street – a street consisting of 'fifty houses, but few of decent architecture and comfort'.[82] Indeed, Cook became the national champion of temperance hotels when a rival journal, *The Temperance Chronicle* claimed that they were not 'suitable for the entertainment of persons of the middle rank'. On the contrary, Cook asserted, 'commercial gentlemen, tradesmen, the representatives of respectable associations and individuals of equal standing in society' (embryo Cook's tourists, in fact) were much better off in temperance hotels than in inns, which were 'little better than brothels'.[83]

Cook worked incessantly as Secretary of the South Midland Temperance Association. This was not all plain sailing, because the Association suffered from internal discord as a result of 'reported irregularities in the Coffee Houses' and did not recover until 1845, when the celebrated Dr Grindrod gave his temperance lectures illustrated by diagrams of the human system.[84] Cook arranged excursions, addressed meetings, attended conferences. He communicated with other temperance leaders, like Father Mathew, for whom he also raised money. Sometimes he travelled – by 'iron and water'[85] – quite far afield, to Birmingham, York, London and Glasgow. Always, like the itinerant evangelist he remained, Cook fostered local revivals, here praising a reformed drinker and professional hawker known as

'Drunken Ginger Jack' for refusing to sell snuffboxes, there holding a friendly chat with a temperance committee followed by a 'general break-up of pipes' and the flinging of 'several stocks of tobacco . . . into the fire'.[86] Often he was opposed, but Cook had a forthright way with hecklers. At a teetotal meeting in 1843, for example, he condemned hissing – 'Gooseism and Snakeism' – and advised the offender to 'return to Jericho until his beard is grown. Let us have no more of his puppyism and cowardly sidewinds.'[87]

Cook was also politically active. He was appalled by the poverty in Leicester, caused by the disastrous decline in the staple trade of framework knitting as a result of mass production. But Cook was even more horrified by the kind of revolutionary physical force then advocated by the local Chartist leader Thomas Cooper. He often heard Cooper 'harangue the Leicester populace',[88] those 'lounging groups of ragged men' who filled the streets, muttering 'words of misery and discontent'.[89] Like many Dissenters Cook held aloof from the Chartists, though he sympathized with some of their aims. Instead he supported the Anti-Corn Law League, looking forward to the triumph of free trade and the consequent reduction in the price of bread, not to mention the beginning of an era of international peace. As distress and disturbance increased in Leicester, so did hostility between the two movements. In January 1844, for example, the liberal *Leicester Chronicle* reported that Cooper attempted to destroy the local Anti-Corn Law League by means of a 'juvenile gang – the very *purée* of the stews – men and boys with whom the working class would be ashamed to be identified', who 'poured forth an incessant shower of the most disgusting abuse, the most awful oaths, and the foulest obscenities'.[90]

With characteristic courage Cook resisted this kind of intimidation. He issued a small paper called *The Cheap Bread Herald*. From his window in Granby Street he addressed large crowds, arguing for free trade in corn and against the 'great evil' of using 'bread-stuff' in the manufacture of 'intoxicating drinks'.[91] Fearing that the Irish famine would spread to England, he even organized an exhibition of loaves purchased from different local bakers, those who adulterated their bread or gave light weight being prosecuted. Cook thus showed that he was concerned not only with the moral but also with the physical health of his fellow citizens, something always at risk in Leicester, low-lying, insanitary, usually afflicted by an 'intolerable stench' and 'never free from the presence of epidemics of some kind'.[92] Thus free trade was not just an ideal for Cook but a practical way of improving the lot of the masses. 'We want fewer abstractions,' he maintained, 'and more general sympathy with the stirring movements of the people out of doors.'[93]

From all this it is apparent that the excursion was just one item on Cook's agenda for social improvement. Nevertheless, it began to loom increasingly large. Following his first triumph, Cook organized a series of excursion trains to temperance functions, where teetotallers experienced 'rational and exquisite enjoyment'. They also made a 'powerful impression' on the various places they visited – some towns, of course, were inaccessible and Cook once exclaimed: 'O for a railway to Leamington!'[94] In 1843 he led a huge gaggle of Sunday School children to Derby to keep them away from the temptations of horse-racing. He took teetotallers to local beauty spots. He also conducted 'the never-to-be-forgotten "Special Train to York"', which apparently annoyed passengers by stopping too often at points of interest along the line.[95]

However, it is clear that in the management of these excursions Cook soon acquired more expertise than the Midland Railway, which was widely criticized for failing to 'understand the philosophy of special trains'.[96] Being intermittent and requiring much individual attention, these did pose problems for railway companies. But by 1844 Cook had established a reputation as a travel entrepreneur with an ability to obtain cheap rates – one hundred miles for a shilling – and to fill trains with massive parties. By then railway excursions were 'becoming our chief national amusement'[97] and it was not long before Cook hit on the idea of organizing excursions for profit as well as pleasure. Of course, such a rational form of recreation would indirectly serve the temperance cause, and philanthropy was never far from Cook's mind. But, like Cecil Rhodes after him, he was not averse to 'philanthropy plus five per cent'.[98]

Cook's first professional project was a trip to Liverpool, with an enticing extension to Caernarvon and Snowdon, which took place in the summer of 1845. In the arrangements he made Cook anticipated his future working methods with remarkable fidelity. He proposed his plan to the four railway companies over whose lines he would travel, negotiating a basic return fare of fourteen shillings for first-class and ten shillings for second-class passengers – no third-class tickets were issued. On this he received a commission, probably 5 per cent. He himself explored the route and published a handbook of the journey. This was a precursor of the modern tour operator's brochure, containing a detailed itinerary, a description of places of interest and topical tips. For example, Cook warned his excursionists about the 'mancatchers' of Liverpool, a

> knot of blackguards who are in the habit of blocking up the
> gateway at the Station [Lime Street] where they are continually
> on the lookout for strangers, whom, as soon as they set foot
> upon the ground, they importune and nearly drag out of their
> habiliments, under the pretence of finding them comfortable
> lodgings.[99]

As Cook later explained, his handbooks 'possess threefold advantage – they excite interest in anticipation; they are highly useful on the spot; and they help to refresh the memory in after days'.[100]

The handbook of the trip to Liverpool was certainly a most effective advertisement and the whole enterprise 'excited an interest in these parts which has scarcely a parallel in the annals of Special Pleasure Trains'.[101] All the tickets were sold within a few days, soon there was a flourishing black market, and Cook had to put on a similar excursion two weeks later. The initial trip proved a triumph. Without alluding to Cook, the *Leicester Chronicle* declared that 'a more agreeable, rational, and delightful amusement it is difficult to conceive'.[102] Cook himself modestly reckoned that the vital element in the trip's success was his own '*personal* superintendence'.

Not satisfied with 'merely announcing arrangements for travelling',[103] Cook conducted his party, 350 strong, by train to Liverpool (where they made their own arrangements about food and accommodation) and on board the yacht *Eclipse*. He toured Caernarvon with them (where only one man could be found who spoke enough English to act as guide) and he accompanied them to the peak of Snowdon. Probably he used the climb, as he did later ones, to show excursionists disposed to fortify their strength with whisky that 'whatever labour may be performed under the stimulus of alcohol, may be done without it'.[104] But on this occasion Cook himself was intoxicated – by the success of his first commercial tourist venture. As he stood on the summit of Snowdon he conjured up new worlds to conquer: 'my thoughts took flight to Ben Lomond, and I determined to try to get to Scotland'.[105]

• 3 •

Tartan Tours

Scotland, once scorned for its backwardness by the likes of Samuel Johnson (who proposed to take a brace of pistols on his journey to the Highlands in 1773), had now become a marvellously romantic destination. This was largely due to the poems and novels of Sir Walter Scott, the 'universal reading' of the age.[1] As Cook said, Scott 'gave a *sentiment* to Scotland as a tourist country' and Cook himself tried 'to foster and develop that sentiment'.[2] In the purple prose of his trade he extolled

> the lovely attractions of the verdant landscape, the majestic grandeur of the towering mountain, the music of the rill and the chorus of the rolling flood, the spicy fragrance of Flora's bower and the reviving inhalations of nature's universal garden.[3]

In promoting Scotland Cook had an unlikely ally – Queen Victoria. She first visited the Highlands in 1842, developed a passion for the tartan and within a few years acquired Balmoral as a holiday home. In his puffs Cook unblushingly declared that 'our good Queen . . . leads the way in Excursion Trips and countenances them by her Royal example'.[4] Thanks to such sovereign allurements, thanks to the natural attractions of loch and glen, to improved communications and to his own laborious efforts, Cook made Scotland the chief tourist goal for mid-Victorians, himself taking many thousands of people there over the next sixteen years. Scotland, as he later wrote, 'almost imperceptibly, transformed me from a cheap Excursion conductor to a Tourist Organiser and Manager'.[5]

Scotland thus proved to be the making of Thomas Cook, but it was also nearly his breaking. Cook's first conducted tour north of the border, which took place in the summer of 1846, coincided with, and contributed to, the first great crisis in his life. During this stormy tour and the disastrous weeks that followed, little of Cook's bright future was visible. The hazards, too, were unforeseen, though they provide a graphic illustration of the troubled infancy of mass travel.

As usual Cook had prepared the trip with meticulous care. He later explained:

> my constant aim has been to render excursion and tourist travelling as cheap, as easy, as safe, and as pleasant, as circumstances would allow. In all my great expeditions, it has been an invariable rule first to know the field of operations, and then to secure such facilities as were best calculated to encourage the most timid travellers to avail themselves of my arrangements and personal services.[6]

Cook made two preliminary visits to Scotland, which was not yet linked to England by rail. He negotiated with the various transport companies involved and found that the best route for his large party was the western one – from Leicester to Fleetwood by train, thence to Ardrossan by steamer, and by rail once more to Glasgow and Edinburgh. Accordingly he issued his *Handbook of a Trip to Scotland*, offering the remarkable bargain of 800 miles for a guinea. Some five hundred people bought tickets and, according to the sour account in the *Leicester Chronicle*, almost at once things started to go wrong.

At that time, of course, there were no restaurant cars or lavatories on trains and Cook had apparently told his tourists that they could disembark briefly at Manchester and other stops en route. In the event they were 'rigidly compelled to keep their seats as if they had been prisoners about to leave their country for their "country's good" instead of a body of respectable citizens who had paid their fares for a pleasure trip'. There was additional cause for complaint at Preston, where the tea which Cook had promised did not materialize. Nor did matters improve at Fleetwood, where the provision of food was inadequate and Cook again failed to feed the five hundred. Worse still, once on board the steamer, famished passengers discovered that there were too few first-class cabins to go round. Cook said that the captain was at fault but they blamed the excursion agent for over-booking. One wrote sarcastically: 'I had the *pleasure* of passing the night with a wet plank for my bed and a carpet bag for my pillow!' The sea was calm when they left Fleetwood but a gale blew up during the night so, the critic added, 'we were all completely drenched, and many were very ill'.[7]

There was some compensation for all this in the warmth of their reception at Glasgow, where guns were fired and a band escorted the tourists to City Hall. Here a soirée was held accompanied by speeches, some harping on the temperance theme. This irritated drinking tourists, but Cook's missionary zeal was irrepressible in Scotland where, he noted, 'the masses . . . were very much stupefied with whisky'[8] – even Queen Victoria strengthened her claret with the national spirit. Cook's party was greeted with equal enthusiasm in Edinburgh. William Chambers, writer, publisher, and later Lord Provost of the city, welcomed its members to a musical evening and expressed his warm approval of its leader's work. Chambers reckoned that finding innocent amusement for the masses was the most important task of the day.[9] Tourism admirably accomplished this, strengthening the health and expanding the ideas of the tourists and bringing a vital infusion of 'English pleasure-money . . . to the heart of the Highlands'.[10] Cook's tour continued with sightseeing (the term dates from 1847) in Stirling and Ayrshire, and sailing on Loch Lomond. But no subsequent enjoyment could make up for the initial setbacks, at least in the opinion of the *Leicester Chronicle*'s correspondent. He swore that in future he would travel on his own,

> rather than again subject myself to such rough and unceremonious treatment! Mr Cook is a *Temperance man*, an advocate for the principle of Total *Abstinence*, and it would seem as if he wished those whom he has so shamefully duped to practise *total abstinence* too . . . a toss overboard into the projector's *favourite element* would have been almost his due. Let us beware how he again attempts to gull the public in the matter of an Excursion Train.[11]

Such criticism adversely affected Cook's fortunes, which fell to their lowest point at the end of July 1846. Ironically, though, he suffered less from these mishaps and grumbles than from the activities of a rival temperance publisher. He was John Cassell, once known in teetotal circles as 'the Manchester Carpenter' from his habit of wearing an apron on the speaker's platform.[12] Years earlier this rough, gaunt figure had actually called on Cook in his workshop at Market Harborough and offered to make him some tables, an offer Cook refused. Cassell had then proceeded to London, where he sold tea, coffee and chocolate in small, cheap quantities and became a successful publisher, founder of an imprint that exists to this day. In 1846 Cassell began the *Teetotal Times*, which Cook '*feelingly*' described as 'a shamefully cheap pennyworth' because it undercut his own *Temperance Magazine*, which sold for fourpence. Through his involvement in business Cassell could print more advertisements than Cook. And the Leicester man was additionally hampered by the fact that since January 1845 his journal had been officially stamped as a newspaper, which meant that it could print news and be sent post-free but that he had to enter heavy securities against libel. Cook actually approved of Cassell's periodical. But after 'toiling' for seven years he felt understandably resentful that now 'an amateur steps into the field' offering 'a species of competition calculated to ruin the fortunes and frustrate the designs of the trader who wishes to act on legitimate principles'.[13]

The details of Cook's business collapse remain obscure, but it is possible to discern the outlines of the story. In the final issue of the *Magazine* he explained:

> painful and sudden reverses render it impossible for the proprietor to sustain his position. After ten years of ceaseless toil in the Temperance cause, he is compelled to yield to those influences which have driven several Temperance publishers from the field. Borne down by heavy responsibilities and legal oppressions, he has no alternative but to bid, at least temporarily, farewell to his esteemed friends and supporters.[14]

On 31 July an indenture was issued whereby Cook 'assigned and transferred all his personal estate and effects whatsoever and wheresoever' to the representatives of his creditors.[15] And during the first week of August a sale was held at his premises in Granby Street 'for the benefit of his creditors'. It included all his stock of books and 'household furniture consisting of beds, bedsteads, and hangings, chairs, sofas, and tables, earthenware and kitchen requisites'.[16] Cook had announced unhappily that his desires were 'as strong as ever to "spend and be spent" in a cause to which he has mainly devoted the best ten years of his existence'.[17] But a bankrupt stood no chance of doing either. The elements at least seemed sympathetic, for in the midst of Cook's financial crash Leicester was shaken to its foundations by the worst thunderstorm in living memory.

If the causes of Cook's fall are somewhat unclear, the circumstances of his recovery are a complete blank. In his various autobiographical writings Cook never alluded to his bankruptcy and other relevant sources are equally silent about its aftermath. Perhaps Cook was helped by the Midland Railway Company, to which he always referred in terms of respect and obligation. Possibly Baptist friends like J. F. Winks came to the rescue. Maybe the temperance community rallied round its defeated champion. Or Cook could have been put on his feet by a combination of all three, eager to show their confidence in his transcendent energy, ability and integrity. What is certain is that Cook somehow managed to avoid being evicted from his premises in Granby Street and being forced to join that 30 per cent of Leicester's citizenry who were, during those years of destitution, 'on the parish'.

Furthermore, he was quickly back in business. By 1848 his temperance hotel was prospering and he had established a bookselling and news agency at 1 Campbell Street, near the station. His tourist efforts proved so successful that he was soon being publicly honoured. In 1850, for example, the citizens of Cambridge presented Cook with a gold watch and chain 'in testimony of his great exertions to afford opportunities of enjoyment to the middle classes by means of excursion trains'. As it happened, the occasion was not a complete success, for the Town Hall audience proved impatient when Cook wanted to talk statistics in his speech of thanks. They shouted witticisms such as 'Cook and his goose' and he was eventually shuffled off the stage by the musicians. But another testimonial, this time accompanied by a gift of over £12, was even more effusive. It declared:

> all his schemes and arrangements have been characterized by a
> spirit of enlarged conception, vigorous enterprize, assiduous and
> devoted efforts to economize the time and resources of his patrons,
> and unwearied attention to their comfort and pleasures.[18]

The fact that Cook so speedily climbed to this peak from the trough of 1846 is ample tribute to what one admirer called his 'wonderful strength of will'.[19]

Certainly his labours during these years were unceasing and he overcame obstacles that could and did ruin his competitors ('imitators' he called them), who were beginning to exploit the craze for excursions. In 1847 Cook conducted two parties to Scotland, the first by the western route, the second by the newly opened

Newcastle–Berwick railway to Edinburgh. He also arranged excursions to the Lake District, to Fleetwood, Blackpool, Liverpool, the Isle of Man and Belfast, taking a total of 1,200 tourists, 500 of whom went to Scotland. The following year, he recorded, was 'a blank in my Railway Excursions, owing to the unwillingness of the Companies to negotiate'.[20] This was because, during a time of commercial crisis, they were making one of their sporadic attempts to run their own excursions and cut out the middleman. Cook proved during the hiatus that his novel profession could adapt itself to antique modes of transport.

Denied cheap rail tickets, he ran coach trips to local places of interest, beauty spots and stately homes, among them Melbourne Hall gardens and Belvoir Castle. Cook made a virtue of necessity and capitalized on a Dickensian nostalgia for the old coaching days before they were well gone. In his *Handbook of Belvoir Castle* he wrote:

> The 'rail', the 'locomotive', 'first', 'second', and 'third class carriages'; 'tubs', 'stations', 'tickets', 'the bell' and the 'electric telegraph' are the general associations of modern travelling; while 'coachee', 'all right', 'boots', and the bugle are classed with the bygones of a past age.[21]

Nevertheless, coaches were fine for special occasions and at a pinch Cook was prepared to call into service 'omnibuses, flys, phaetons, stage coaches, furniture vans and carrier's wagons'.[22] Horse-drawn vehicles had the advantage of offering facilities for 'social intercourse and pleasant observation' and Cook enlivened the procession by engaging musicians to perform in the towns and villages en route. However, cautious about his future relations with the railway companies, Cook acknowledged that it was 'almost presumptuous to start a train of coaches' on a road running parallel to a railway line. He did not want 'in the slightest degree to detract one iota' from the superiority of the steam engine.

Cook was equally deferential towards that most extravagant of grandees, the fifth Duke of Rutland (a turf-loving Tory and 'the Duke' in Disraeli's *Coningsby*), whom he praised for helping the 'poor and down-trodden laborer'. He was grateful to Rutland for allowing excursionists 'free access' to Belvoir Castle 'providing they behave with propriety and decorum'. Cook even went out of his way, apparently, to assure the Duke that, although a radical, he was no revolutionary. He looked forward to the day when 'sons of toil shall live happily in the enjoyment of the just rewards of their labor, and the rich shall live at ease in the undisturbed possession of the wealth and greatness to which they have a legitimate claim'.[23] The Duke responded in kind: 'I fully concur with you in the desire which you express to see the different classes of our great community bound together by ties of increasing strength.'[24] At that dangerous time many aristocrats threw open their doors in the name of social solidarity.

At Chatsworth Cook had an interesting encounter with the Duke of Devonshire's agent, another one-time gardener's boy. This was Joseph Paxton, subsequently designer of the Crystal Palace, who was to have a considerable influence on his life. Evidently Paxton shared Cook's view that opening great houses 'did an immense amount of social good'[25] and encouraged his excursions (though his wife Sarah had a horror of trippers who invaded Chatsworth, bringing dust and dirt in their wake). Certainly the two men agreed over 'the public-house nuisance' and Paxton later testified to a parliamentary select committee that drunken revelry was much abated by visits to stately homes like Chatsworth.[26] Still, if self-made men like Cook and Paxton naturally saw eye to eye there was something equivocal about the former's rapprochement with purse-proud patricians, of whom he usually disapproved. And there was something downright hypocritical in Cook's recommending the Belvoir Inn to his excursionists. It was, he said, suitable for the first rank of people but would supply refreshments for the 'humbler classes' on 'economical terms, thus superseding the necessity for the numerous basket accompaniments and annoyances of pic-nic parties'.[27] The teetotal Cook damned inns as little better than brothels; the tour operator came to terms with them.

During the year of revolutions abroad and civil strife at home, however, commercial compromise was overtaken by philanthropic principle. Early in 1848 distress in Leicester was so acute that bands of desperate men roamed the streets on mass begging expeditions backed by the threat of force. Moderate radicals like Cook and Winks found themselves in uneasy alliance with 'moral force' Chartists, though Cook himself had no particular faith in universal suffrage, disliking any tyrant 'whether kingly, priestly or democratic'.[28] What did unite them, though, was their support for more outdoor relief and their opposition to plans for a new workhouse. In March resentment about existing conditions in the Leicester workhouse, and about the New Poor Law generally, exploded into 'the Bastille Riots'.[29] Cook was horrified and rushed into print with a denunciation of the Board of Guardians for having increased the work-load of destitute men without increasing their reward.[30] He was forced to withdraw this charge, not having taken into account seasonal variations in the hours of labour. But he stressed the 'great and long-continued patience of the poor people' over the high price of bread and put in an 'extenuating plea for those who are now accused of riot and turbulence'. He would never sanction violence – 'God forbid' – not least because it would 'assuredly throw back the cause of liberty and right'. Indeed, as a believer in 'moral force', Cook was critical of the conduct of the police who, he thought, had behaved brutally towards innocent citizens during the riot. He even spoke at a protest meeting and joined a committee to collect evidence for legal proceedings against them – with little result. Not altogether consistently, he asserted that where the rioters were concerned these were not the 'times for a vigorous infliction of the punishment of the law'. Instead he called for 'a spirit of conciliation'.[31]

That spirit did begin to spead after 1848 as Leicester's hard times became less hard and Chartism, always 'a knife and fork question',[32] collapsed. The city was not transformed overnight. There were still scenes of squalor and violence like those often witnessed by a local minister: 'a horde of drunken savages burst forth from their drinking to wind up the night with a fight – men shouting, women screaming, half-starved children crying'. But improving work went on apace and Cook was in the van. He was the leading light in reviving the old plan to build a Temperance Hall. He supported the removal of cesspools and pig-sties from the busier streets and the regular closing of pubs. He fostered the movement for allotments, issuing a periodical called *The Cottage Gardener*. He complained that 'few towns present less variety of recreative attractions than Leicester'[33] and continued to provide attractions of his own, arranging excursions for people who had seldom if ever previously strayed beyond their native fields.

Having reached an agreement with the railway companies, he took two parties (about a thousand people in all) to Scotland in 1849. He also ran tours to north Wales, the Isle of Man and

Ireland,[34] though nothing is known about the last – the previous year Cook had scouted the ground but he seems to have been mainly interested in his meeting at Cork with Father Mathew, who 'received me with extraordinary warmth and fervour'.[35] Cook was equally effusive about Mathew's having 'destroyed by the almost magical wand of his mighty temperance influence the ancient *prestige* of Donnybrook Fair; and the old riotous scenes of Greenwich Fair, and other demoralizing though chartered "Institutions" of like character'. Yet, despite the 'great changes' which both he and Cook had wrought in 'the recreations of the masses . . . faint memorials of old and debasing May-day customs' remained,[36] along with an apparently incurable addiction to horse-racing. To provide the youth of Leicester with a wholesome alternative to the races, Cook organized another of his monster excursions in 1849. He conveyed about 3,000 boys and girls to Birmingham and arranged for them to have tea at the Town Hall. Unfortunately, as he later wrote, it was 'never served, the whole party being goaded on to excitement, and a scramble being made for a good cart load of plum cake'.

This sort of experience gave Cook an understandable aversion to all forms of catering – 'as to providing for the palates and stomachs of Tourists, woe to the unlucky wight who attempts it'.[37] Indeed, it is surprising how little the father of the package tour did for his early charges. His chief service was to provide special tickets and to map out circular routes. He supplied handbooks and created a unity for tourists out of the diversity of transport companies and conveyances – trains, steamers and coaches. Cook also accompanied several large parties each year, usually to Scotland, marshalling them with that combination of amiability and authority which has been the hallmark of the tour escort ever since. He always displayed what one customer called good-humoured 'social spirit . . . and yet not at all approaching further than the most respectful familiarity'.[38] But his peremptoriness earned him a number of military nicknames, among them 'the General'. He once ordered a group of tourists (who had risen early and had no breakfast): 'Shoulder shawls – pick up carpet bags – quick march!'[39] Cook could not personally superintend all his parties, which were made up of individuals and groups from different parts of the country who converged on the Midlands and then travelled northwards together. Sometimes he left one lot to fend for themselves while he went off to look after another. And invariably his tourists found themselves in a scrum for food at railway stations and a hunt for rooms in the towns and cities where they stayed.

Still, for the most part Cook's tourists were a hardy, self-reliant breed. The accounts of their early experiences north of the border reflected zest for exploring another dimension, excitement at making new friendships, English and Scottish, and delight in an unprecedented spree. Edward Chadfield of Derby, for example, recorded how in July 1849:

> We now commenced our peregrinations in Edinburgh by going to meet Mr Cook and the excursionists. We sauntered about here very comfortably in a drizzling rain for about half an hour before Mr Cook arrived, and after a little speechifying we divided into parties of fifty, appointing a captain to each party. We paid a shilling each to our Captain, who hired a guide, and then we went sightseeing.
>
> After returning to Edinburgh, we went to a meeting at the Calton Convening Rooms where the excursionists were to fraternize with the 'cannie Scotch'. However, we found no sawnies to fraternize with, so after a good deal of bad speaking and tolerable singing, and heaps of fun and laughing, we dispersed.

Chadfield was exalted by the 'ruined towers' of Linlithgow, thrilled by the 'glorious country' around Stirling, moved by Burns's birthplace at Ayr, amused by the antics of rival coachmen at Callander and touched by a musical farewell – the 'Scotch were all singing like so many larks, full merry enough too'. He was also happy to return safe to Derby 'having travelled a thousand miles in two hundred and seven hours for an expense of five pounds ten shillings'.[40]

Not all tourists were as cheerful as Chadfield. When his train was brought to a grinding halt after colliding with a horse he regarded the incident as more of a curiosity than a danger. Cook insisted that none in his charge ever suffered a fatal accident and that he avoided 'experimental adventures in untried regions', but there were enough mishaps of all sorts to provoke quite a few 'complainers'.[41] Once Cook was 'a little disturbed by a sort of miniature mutiny on taking a steamer at Banavie, but we prefer looking at the "sunny side", and gladly draw a veil over the little unpleasantness which occurred there'.[42] Generally Cook's benign and pacific spirit prevailed. Of one huge tour – 2,000 people in 100 railway carriages – he recorded: 'Our whole "progress" was an ovation at the shrine of mutual concord and amity.'[43] In any case, as a tourist from Cambridge wrote in his local paper, it was better not to grumble because 'You can't travel without coming to a rough place now and then.' As it happened he had experienced 'three weeks of thorough enjoyment' in Scotland. He recommended 'Mr Cook, of Leicester' as a guide and concluded: 'Hurrah for the Excursion Trains, say I! – They are a fine invention for men like myself of small means and not much leisure.'[44]

'The public journals are now teeming with details of excursion projects,' Cook wrote in the mid-1850s, many of them over 'the very routes we have rendered so easy of access'.[45] But a typical programme of Cook's Scottish tours was still enough of a novelty in 1853 to merit publication in *Chambers's Edinburgh Journal*. Chambers found 'much that is commercially and socially remarkable' in the whole business, from the clearing-house system, whereby carriages were interchanged so that the tourist was not 'tumbled out of one train into another half-a-dozen times during the course of his journey towards Scotland', to the character of Cook himself, whom he christened the 'Field-marshal . . . for we can scarcely refuse military honour to one who manoeuvres large bodies of men in such a way'. The tourists spent their first night – say a Wednesday – in Edinburgh. On Thursday morning they divided into parties and visited the Castle, Holyrood and other sights. At one o'clock, Chambers continued,

they start off by the North British Railway to Melrose, have a peep at the Abbey, then go by the next train to St Boswell's, then walk to Dryburgh, and back to Edinburgh the same evening. Friday next arrives, and with it a busy day's work, for which long daylight and fine weather are needed. A special train starts betimes from Edinburgh to Glasgow, and an hour is then left to enable the Britons to get snugly on board a steamer at the Broomielaw; they start down the Clyde to Bowling, then take the little railway to Balloch, then steam up Loch Lomond to Tarbert, next walk over to Arrochar, at the head of Loch Long, and then steam down Loch Long to the Clyde and Glasgow: '100 miles' sailing, railing, and walking through the most enchanting scenery in Scotland, all for 4s.' – so says the programme. Saturday is devoted to the Oban trip, down the Firth, through the Kyles of Bute, and over Loch Fyne, to Ardishaig; thence by the Crinan Canal, and past the whirlpool of Corrievrekin to Oban. 'This,' says the programme, 'is a lovely spot for repose, amid most beautiful scenery, and a charming place for weary tourists. It will be our home for two or three days, and lodgings are plentiful and cheap; provisions also remarkably cheap.'

On Sunday, the Britons remain quiet at Oban. On Monday, they make the trip to the Isle of Skye; and each tourist is requested to read, before he starts, the *Lord of the Isles*, to prepare him for what he is about to see. Tuesday is appropriated for the Staffa trip: 'we hope that the day may be favourable for rowing into the cave; but if this is impracticable, we shall still land at Staffa, and again at Iona, there to ruminate amidst the ruins of that ancient seat of learning, and tombs of kings, warriors, chieftains, and ecclesiastics. Tourists! go with us to Staffa and Iona, the strongest sensibilities of your natures shall be awakened!' On Wednesday, the field-marshal returns to Glasgow, and thence to England; but leaves his brother Britons to make out a full fortnight as best they choose. He gives them this parting word respecting the Clyde steamers: 'Every excursionist will acknowledge that the vessels are of the first character; their commanders, gentlemen in the fullest sense of the word; their stewards, admirable caterers; their crews, a set of worthy fellows, from whose lips an oath or vulgarity never escapes!'[46]

Whatever the truth of that, Cook's system of tours was not quite as Chambers represented it, 'a rigid, stiff and formal thing that is so repulsive to free spirits'. Instead, Cook asserted, it was so 'flexible that it imposes no unreasonable restraints upon choice of routes or changes by the way, if found desirable'.[47] Still, Cook was undoubtedly gratified by such an advertisement from such a worthy. He later wrote that among the most pleasant of his Scottish reminiscences was the fact that 'the friendly eyes of the first of social reformers have been watching our progress'.[48]

Cook's progress, he invariably suggested, was synonymous with the progress of the age. It reflected not just the triumph of machinery but the triumph of morality. 'Dwelling in one nook, viewing the same class of objects through the same narrow mediums', he said, fixed old-fashioned habits and mean prejudices, whereas his trips brought 'enlargement to mind and deepening of charity'.[49] In one of his characteristic paeans of praise to the tourist movement Cook declared:

Great moral and social lessons have been inculcated; history and geography have been practically pursued with astonishing

devotion; sectarian and political bigotry have been mortally
wounded; names and parties have been lost amid the greatness
of nature's magnificence; acquaintances have been formed
and friendly intercourse engendered betwixt those who but for
these arrangements had remained strangers to each other; the
battlefield has been transformed into an arena of pleasurable and
brotherly recognition.[50]

In other words, Cook's tours encouraged people to love God by loving
their neighbours. He acknowledged that English visitors found the
Scots 'as strange to them as the inhabitants of foreign climes'.[51] Yet
his attempts to foster 'the best feelings amongst the visitors and the
visited' at soirées and other 'fraternal gatherings'[52] helped to 'obliviate'
the 'feuds and jealousies of . . . rude and barbarous times'.[53] The
Scots had lessons of their own to teach. Unlike Continentals, who
thronged bars, 'theatres, casinos, music saloons, and other houses
of entertainment' on Sundays, they kept the Sabbath in a suitably
austere fashion. Cook added that 'Amongst their ministers there are
bigots no doubt, but there are also giants of moral heroism.'[54]

As a good Victorian Cook well appreciated the value of affirming
that his 'Excursion arrangements have become invested with a high
moral[ity]'.[55] But his claims were by no means specious. Indeed,
when visiting the poorer parts of Scotland he clearly demonstrated
that 'Tours of Pleasure [were] made subservient to Objects of
Philanthropy'.[56] At Iona, for example, Cook was not only struck
by 'the soul-penetrating realities of History bursting upon us as it
were through the vista of ages',[57] he was moved to action by the
utter destitution of the several hundred islanders. Many of them
were forced to quit their pathetic hovels in the 1840s and '50s, and
Cook issued fervent appeals to provide those who remained with
the means of earning a living. When conducting tours to Iona he
must often have mounted the 'large monumental stone', as he did
in 1856, and made a 'pleasing speech' (punctuated by 'cheers')
extolling the island (particularly because it contained no alehouse
or beershop) and inviting donations.[58] The tourists gave generously
and by 1861 they had paid for the construction of a fishing fleet of
some twenty-four vessels (one called the *Thomas Cook*) plus nets and
tackle, not to mention other gifts such as books. As the *Glasgow
Daily Bulletin* declared, 'To these poor islanders, Mr Cook and his
friends may be more useful than many Dukes.'[59] Cook himself was

entitled to ask: 'May we not claim for our labours the character of a mission?' And he had reason to say that his motives for arranging tours were not primarily commercial: 'There is a pleasure in these pursuits which selfishness can never appreciate.'[60]

Pleasure was naturally the theme that Cook most stressed in promoting his tours to Scotland. He contributed to 'the pleasure of strangers by performing the functions of a guide'. They were animated by 'new beauties and fresh impulses to pleasure'.[61] Yet amid the obvious appeal of Scotland – its scenery, monuments, people – Cook made much of other, more recherché pleasures. His tours were not just journeys in space but in time, and once again Cook tapped the vein of nostalgia for the old coaching days. What had happened to the coachman, with his rolling gait, glorious paunch, acre of scarlet face and low-crowned, broad-rimmed hat, that Pickwickian figure who was so much more romantic than the railway guard, with his fine red coat and gilt buttons? 'Come to Scotland,' Cook replied, 'coachmen are still to be found there.'[62]

Royalties were also to be found in Scotland and their presence was an undoubted 'draw'. Indeed, the earliest known photograph taken by a Cook's tourist – William Brookes, squire of Croft near Leicester – captures the construction of Balmoral in 1854. It did not matter that royal personages were largely hidden from the public gaze. Mystery enhanced regal glamour and there was always the chance that in the Highlands Cook's tourists, who seem to have been more royalist than the Queen, might catch a glimpse of Victoria and her family. In 1858 the *Illustrated London News* reported just such an occasion. A 'monster train of excursionists, under the guidance of Mr Cook, of Leicester' encountered the royal party, en route for Balmoral, at Dunbar Station. 'All ranks joined in hearty cheer after cheer'; the carriage windows were let down; Queen Victoria and Prince Albert 'turned with smiling faces to the multitude' who continued their 'impromptu outburst of genuine loyalty' for five minutes and then tactfully withdrew.[63] The following year a more problematic sighting occurred, comically chronicled by Cook:

we pulled up opposite the Royal Castle at Balmoral, when the National Anthem was sung at about half past seven in the morning, a strong breeze wafting the sound direct to the Castle. One of our party, applying his opera glass, declared that he saw the Royal Prince Consort in his night-cap(!)

at a window; but for the accuracy of this vision we cannot vouch.[64]

Cook, who was openly contemptuous of 'the customary train of fashionable court-followers',[65] probably felt less awe for royalty than most of his countrymen – all the more reason, no doubt, for systematically exploiting it as a tourist attraction.

The attraction between the sexes was also something on which Cook capitalized in the discreet fashion of his day. He insisted that it was entirely proper for 'unprotected females' to go on his tours, describing them as 'heroines who required no protection, beyond what the arrangements and companionships of the tour afforded'.[66] He referred to himself as a 'travelling chaperon',[67] mentioned that his wife often accompanied him to Scotland and insisted that women could easily cope with the physical strains of long journeys. Indeed, they 'frequently put to shame the "masculine" effeminates'. It was true that

the trappings of prevailing fashion may sometimes perplex them on clambering over precipices, and amongst rude blocks of granite or basalt; but there is a large class, who, defiant of fashion and customs . . . push their way through all difficulties and acquire the perfection of the tourist character.[68]

Perhaps as a result of this special pleading, more ladies than gentlemen went on Cook's tours. Thomas Cook thus made a significant contribution to female emancipation. He assisted the angel to move away from the hearth, though she was very far from moving into a state of equality with 'the lords of humankind'. Cook himself observed that 'wife and family are generally represented in the plural adoption of the masculine gender'[69] and seemed to deplore the fact that, terminologically speaking, 'man embraced woman'. But on Cook's party passports to the Continent men had to be named while women only had to be numbered. Still, the very presence of enterprising spinsters, in an exciting new environment where the usual domestic constraints were relaxed, added a frisson of romance to Cook's tours. Needless to say, the atmosphere in no way resembled that of today's 'Club Med'. But, Cook once recorded, 'the young of both sexes appeared to drink in the rich libations of sociality and kindness'.[70] 'Even those who start out alone,' he suggested, 'will often find an agreeable companion.'[71] And he boasted that there were 'constant cases of love-matches [being] made' on his tours.[72]

As the terms 'ladies' and 'gentlemen' suggest, Cook was taking members of the middle class to Scotland. His clientele were clergymen, doctors, schoolmasters, governesses, representatives of 'the better style of London [and provincial] mercantile community'.[73] Cook himself regretted this, having 'a special regard to the humbler class of travellers'.[74] But they simply could not afford long holidays. For them, as will emerge, Cook arranged shorter excursions which (to his fury) were often 'superciliously deride[d as] "cheap trips"'. Victorian snobbery being what it was, Cook's more respectable patrons, the tourists to Scotland, were sneered at in their turn. Once more Cook leapt to their defence, berating '"stuck up people" who affect to look down on . . . an inferior grade of tourists'. He had seen 'a little of this *hauteur* occasionally on board steamers' and he attributed it to the 'independent' tourist's resentment of his costly isolation: he 'pays a sovereign a day for the privilege of sitting solitary in a crowd of free elastic spirits'.[75] Cook was moved to further wrath by meeting a 'contemptuous old lady' in the Highlands who thought 'that places of interest should be excluded from the gaze of the common people, and . . . kept only for the interest of the "select" of society'.

> But it is too late in this day of progress to talk such exclusive
> nonsense; God's earth, with all its fulness and beauty is for
> the people; and railroads and steamboats are the result of the
> common light of science, and are for the people also. Those
> who wish to live for themselves only, and to have the exclusive
> enjoyment of the earth's provisions, had better make a tour to
> Timbuctoo.[76]

This sort of tourist controversy was to become much more heated over the next few years. But during the 1850s, thanks to the success of his Scottish tours, Cook could content himself with the approval of 'the numerous and increasing "clan" known by the name of COOK'S PEOPLE'.[77] At the beginning of the decade he had overheard a stranger remark that the fame of the wèst coast of Scotland was due largely to 'one Cook, of Leicester, an excursion manager, whose Handbooks have circulated through a large part of the country'.[78] By 1860 Cook had conveyed some 50,000 tourists to Scotland and had, as a modern historian writes, 'completed the work of Scott'.[79] He had received countless marks of esteem, like the soirée held for him in Edinburgh in 1859 as a tribute to his 'personal excellencies' and the 'benefit and enjoyment he has been instrumental in conveying to thousands'.[80] He had stimulated the development of an 'array of transportation services'.[81] He had made Cook's cheap rail tickets available to all tourists and given them a new flexibility, whereby changes of route could be arranged without loss – 'a triumph', as he said, of nearly two decades 'in catering for the public'.[82] Cook's passengers were given precedence on Scottish coaches. Scottish hoteliers, who had at first been inclined to snub him, now eagerly sought his recommendation and gave his tourists the 'best places'.[83] He was understandably proud of his achievement: 'We may subject ourselves to the charge of egotism, vanity, or any other foible, but we affirm . . . that there are no pleasure excursions that can compare with "Cook's Scottish Trips".'[84]

On the other hand, Cook's business was still run on a shoestring. He did almost everything single-handed, trying to cram a maximum of work into a minimum of time and exclaiming: 'How short and transient is this Excursion and Tourist season!'[85] Profits were small and they fluctuated alarmingly. Cook was quite candid about such matters:

> We were not a little amused the other day, in riding in a
> compartment with five hunting gentlemen, to hear a conversation
> about 'Cook's Excursions'. The general opinion of these gentlemen
> was that we made 'a good thing of it' by contracting for a number
> of carriages, at so much per mile, and then filling them at the best
> rates we could get . . . [In reality] we act but in the capacity of
> an Agent of Railway Companies. Our business is to suggest plans,
> and when they are adopted, find passengers to fill the trains,
> which is done by advertisement and all sorts of influence which
> we can devise and employ, receiving a commission for our labours
> and expenses according to the success of our projects. This
> necessarily narrows the sphere of our operations to certain lines of
> country, and sometimes great success is almost as prejudicial to us
> as failure would be.[86]

Cook depended on short-term agreements with the railway companies and on their long-term good will. Yet he was well aware that rivalry between the companies or resentment about his entrepreneurial position could ruin him at any moment. Many railway directors detested excursions, 'contending that all such income was drawn away from ordinary traffic, and was a practical loss'. When they were obliged to acknowledge that 'the mileage receipts for Excursion traffic were far in excess of [those for] ordinary trains', they objected to the excursion agent for taking a share of the profits.[87] In 1862, soon after Cook had celebrated his twenty-first birthday in the travel business – his 'coming of age' in a novel 'vocation . . . quite unpremeditated, and almost unparalleled'[88] – the Scottish railway companies refused to let him issue any more tourist tickets. On 24 May he announced dramatically: '*There shall be no Excursion Trains to Scotland this season!* This decision is fatal to all our cheap arrangements.'[89] At a stroke, the companies destroyed most of Cook's livelihood, and he blamed them bitterly for their 'lack of appreciation of our labours in early days'.[90]

Cook was crushed by the blow and for a year or so he almost lost heart. Yet adversity became the highway to opportunity. As the Scottish route closed the Continental one opened. Indeed, Cook was forced to look abroad at the very time when improved communications, rising incomes and the Pax Britannica were making tourism possible on a global scale. So his second great crisis led to a vast expansion in his tourist enterprise, beginning with the introduction of large numbers of his countrymen to the Alpine 'Playground of Europe'.[91] At the end of this eventful chapter of his life, with hope beginning to triumph over despair, Cook vividly described his mood:

> In the sadness of this disappointment we almost wish we could
> . . . give up all this anxiety, and toil, and risk, and quietly retire
> into some peaceful, noiseless occupation, away from the entreaties
> of friends and the cold influence of unappreciated finesse. But
> our inward nature rebels against this despondency; the memories
> of other days come back with urgent appeal; the surrounding
> associations of esteemed patrons and friends in every part of the
> kingdom re-animate the drooping spirit; the possession of health
> and vigour, and the hope and prospects of future usefulness impel
> us to renewed action, and we resolve to 'try again' to arrange
> and carry out some comprehensive plan of future labour and

interest . . . [After all the struggles and sacrifices,] to give up now would be almost like an issueless termination of the great aims of public life . . . There are feelings which prompt the mind to the wide grasp of objects and labours across the English Channel, and fix, as it were, the standard of hope on the mountains of Switzerland.[92]

The Napoleon of Excursions

In fact Cook had first contemplated taking tourists abroad at the beginning of the 1850s and it is to this time and to his other pioneering efforts that we must now return.

Most important was his contribution to the Great Exhibition of 1851, which first brought him onto the national stage. Just over six million people visited the Crystal Palace (a third of the nation, though of course many went more than once) and Cook conveyed 165,000 of them. Some who joined in the rush to Hyde Park were given time off and subsidized by their employers. Others pawned their watches, their clothes, even their beds, to see what Cook called this 'galaxy of splendour which has burst upon the world'.[1] Cheap excursion traffic made the Great Exhibition the astonishing triumph it was – the excess profits went to build the complex of museums in South Kensington then known, after the Prince Consort (who inspired the Exhibition), as Albertopolis. But in its turn the Exhibition gave an enormous impetus to the excursion movement. True, this was already growing apace. In 1850 *The Times* declared: 'Thirty years ago not one countryman in one hundred had seen the metropolis. There is now scarcely one in the same number who has not spent a day there.'[2] What the Great Exhibition did was to transform the excursion from a thrilling novelty into an established part of Victorian life. In this recreational revolution Thomas Cook played a notable part.

Cook's involvement with the Great Exhibition was quite fortuitous. In 1850 a clergyman suggested that he should conduct tours to the Holy Land, and he went to London to consult his temperance friend James Silk Buckingham about the proposition. Buckingham, who had travelled widely in both Asia and America, was 'just the man to sympathise with a movement for bringing together people of various nationalities and social distinctions, and he entered warmly into my project'.[3] But Buckingham also told Cook that North America, with over 8,000 miles of railroad track, was better adapted to tourism than Palestine, where there were 'no railways, coaches, or even public roads'.[4] Moreover, Britain was now much closer to the United States. In 1838 the first ship powered solely by steam, the *Sirius*, had crossed the Atlantic, confounding sceptics like Dr Dionysius Lardner who had expressed his willingness 'to eat' the vessel capable of this achievement.[5] Since that time speeds had increased significantly. In an article entitled 'Steam-Bridge over the Atlantic' (June 1850), *Chambers's Edinburgh Journal* reported that England was now only twelve and a half days away from the United States.

Thus, towards the end of the year, Cook took a train to Liverpool to see if he could obtain favourable tourist rates from the steam-ship companies. At Derby station he encountered Joseph Paxton, whose palace of glass was already being erected in Hyde Park to huge public acclaim, and John Ellis, the capable Leicester Quaker who was trying to revive the fortunes of the Midland Railway Company after the collapse of the 'Railway King', George Hudson, the previous year. Ellis, who well remembered the time when Leicester's coal supply had been 'brought on the backs of horses through Charnwood Forest',[6] had unbounded faith in the iron road. Anticipating that the Great Exhibition would generate enormous traffic, he had just ordered a hundred new third-class carriages, seating forty people each.[7] Paxton too had a strong financial interest in the railway – Dickens said that he was 'in it heart and purse'.[8] So between them the two men persuaded Cook to drop his American plans and organize excursions to the Great Exhibition.

Cook was immensely attracted by the prospect. Though an advertisement for British industry, the Exhibition was international in scope. Prince Albert considered that the progress of mechanical invention would lead to '*the unity of mankind*';[9] and its designer hoped that the Crystal Palace would become a Temple of Peace – wits quipped 'Paxton Vobiscum'.[10] Inspired by such idealism and never less than resolutely didactic, Cook told his excursionists that they should see the Exhibition 'not as a show or a place of amusement, but a great School of Science, of Art, of Industry, of Peace and Universal Brotherhood'.[11] The Exhibition also appealed to Cook because intoxicating liquor was to be excluded from its precincts; 1,092,337 bottles of Schweppes soda water, lemonade and ginger beer were sold instead, to say nothing of nearly a million

Bath buns. Indeed, in every way the Exhibition was a model of Evangelical sobriety: it did not open on the Sabbath, visitors were accosted by religious tract distributors and confronted by a large Bible depot, and Lord Shaftesbury covered up all the nude statues. Finally, Cook approved of the fact that the Exhibition was the 'coronation of labour',[12] honouring 'the working bees of the world's hive'.[13] It was, he considered, appropriate that the skilled 'operative classes' should receive such recognition, for England's industrial preeminence owed more to them than to the manufacturers, 'who may be mere noodles'.[14]

Cook agreed to advertise special trains and escort excursionists in his usual fashion. But he apparently contracted to receive a fixed sum of 'several shillings'[15] for each passenger instead of his normal 5 per cent commission on the fare charged. This arrangement would have satisfied the Midland Railway if it had been able to sell cheap return tickets at fifteen shillings, as originally planned. But it had reckoned without the competition of the Great Northern Railway, competition so fierce that it led on one occasion to the hijacking of a rival steam engine. The Great Northern had just constructed a direct line to London from Bradford and Leeds, which it now tried to make attractive by offering return tickets to the Exhibition for five shillings. If Cook had stuck to his agreement the Midland would have been unable to match these terms. So he tore up the contract and threw the pieces in Ellis's waste-paper basket. It was a dramatic gesture which probably owed as much to calculation as to magnanimity, a mixture of motives characteristic of Cook.

The fact was that he depended largely on the good will of the Midland Railway. There were now other excursion agents in business, notably H. R. Marcus, an able Liverpudlian who exhibited considerable 'push and energy in connection with the Great Exhibition',[16] and Cook himself was obliged to share the Midland region with a couple of rivals. So it was in his interest to accept present loss in the hope of future gain, and to compensate by drumming up additional trade for the Exhibition. This he did quite literally, employing as an assistant (not for the first time) his son John, then seventeen years old, one of whose tasks was to lead a band round likely towns in order to advertise the Exhibition excursions. Cook himself printed handbills, visited the major Midland centres, held meetings and encouraged the formation of savings clubs – a familiar device at the time – so that workers could pay for their trip to London in weekly instalments. Most important of all, on 3 May 1851, three days after the Great Exhibition opened, he published the first issue of *Cook's Exhibition Herald and Excursion Advertiser*. It sold for a penny. Though 'not designed to be a permanent periodical',[17] it became his firm's main vehicle for publicity and survived (in various guises) until the outbreak of the Second World War.

Cook's Excursionist (to adopt the title it bore for most of its life) soon began to thrive, despite the fact that its editor was travelling night and day throughout the summer of 1851. As he wrote,

> Notwithstanding the difficulty of conducting such a publication amidst multitudinous and exciting engagements betwixt town and country, our locomotive scribblings, cuttings and combinings, meet with the hearty appreciation of great numbers . . . Could we bring all the parts of publication machinery into active operation we should have no difficulty in disposing of 10,000 copies of each weekly number.[18]

The journal owed its initial success to the massive interest stirred up by the Great Exhibition. But Cook also imbued it with something of his own personal vitality. True, he sometimes fell into the unctuous style of the sermon or the flowery manner of the travelogue. Victorian critics, always apt to patronize the self-educated, 'doubted whether nature intended Mr Cook to attain literary distinction'.[19] They sneered at his high-falutin use of the editorial 'we' and mocked his '*mal-apropos*' references to the 'turbulence of Father Neptune'.[20]

However, Cook's prose had two qualities which none of his sophisticated detractors could match: candour and vigour. There was a rich vein of autobiography running through his pages, a secularized form of Evangelical witness. And, though not as combative as Cobbett, he wrote in a similarly spirited fashion. The journal *Fun* might poke fun at the crudity of 'our unstudied and unlaboured paragraphs',[21] but haste gave zest to Cook's writing. Witness this breathless vignette, designed to make the crowded thoroughfares of London seem less intimidating (but more intriguing) to country cousins:

> The other day, passing along Parliament Street, we caught sight of a slender-limbed man, rather tender in his gait, sharp-faced, his eyes red, perhaps with late watching, the collar of his blue topcoat turned up round his throat. The face was familiar – we looked

again, and it was – yes! – the Prime Minister of England! [Lord John Russell] – preceded by an errand boy, followed by a coal heaver, but not jostled.[22]

As Cook said in his opening number, the *Excursionist* aimed to be a 'practical worker rather than a sentimental traveller'.[23] He used the journal to advertise his arrangements, to promote new excursions, to publicize the opening of fresh routes, to foster the travelling habit. This involved giving circumstantial accounts of past tours and rosy intimations of future ones. It also involved boosting events which people might want to visit – fêtes, shows, memorials, galas, circuses, pageants, balloon ascents, royal occasions, music festivals, firework displays, opening ceremonies, anniversary celebrations. Notices of this kind were a staple feature of the *Excursionist*. So were advertisements relating to all aspects of travel, from temperance hotels to steamship lines, from trusses to portable fire engines, from Swaab's Universal Corn Plaisters to Seydel's Ashantee Pocket Hammock, from Keating's Powder to Beechema's Glycerine and Cucumber Skin Preservator, from Bailey's Air Cushion (mitigates the effects of 'vibration upon the nervous system') to Walter's Railway Convenience ('can be worn imperceptibly with the greatest comfort and security').

Despite his loathing of quack remedies Cook also printed puffs for such mountebank medicaments as Oldridge's Balm of Columbia which 'prevents baldness', Frampton's Pill of Health, and Amynterion, a patent remedy for sea-sickness through 'curative magnetism'.[24] Without revenue from sources like these, a pioneering periodical devoted to travel might not have survived. As it was, during the twenty-five years or so in which Cook edited it[25] the *Excursionist* went from strength to strength. By 1873 it was taken by London clubs and found 'as necessary to their patrons as "Bradshaw"'.[26] In that year an American edition was born and by the time of Cook's death there were several other foreign editions (French, Austrian, Indian, Australian) having a global circulation of one hundred and twenty thousand copies.

The first numbers of the *Excursionist* not only stimulated current enthusiasm for the Great Exhibition, they also reflected the mood of optimism about human and technological progress. Mechanical advances were particularly striking in the field of transport, typified by exhibits ranging from a vast broad-gauge locomotive to Franklinski's Patent Omnibus, which contained separate compartments for each passenger, thus avoiding the chance of 'robbery and infection, or annoyance of any kind'.[27] But while the 'moral grandeur'[28] of the whole enterprise was wonderfully appealing, the Exhibition was equally attractive as a huge fête. The Crystal Palace was surrounded by subsidiary exhibitions, panoramas, dioramas, hippodromes featuring equestrian marvels, temples of gastronomy, stalls, booths, sideshows, hawkers, souvenir-sellers, buskers, pugilists, pot-boys and all the fun of the fair. At its centre Paxton's palace, which was 'large enough to be a glass case for Versailles' and contained 38,000 separate exhibits, presented such an awe-inspiring spectacle that some were moved to tears by it. Thomas Cook, so busy that he filled the *Excursionist* by borrowing at length from other journals, reprinted an article from *The Times* which summed up the Exhibition's effect on the nation:

> The Great Exhibition has killed everything else. The Court,
> the two Houses of Parliament, the nobility, the gentry, the
> commonalty, the army, the police, carriages, cabs and omnibuses
> are all dancing attendance upon it. The shops are unfrequented.
> The places of public amusement are comparatively deserted. Even
> the railways lose their summer excursionists.[29]

Actually, before the cheap shilling tickets to the Exhibition went on sale, towards the end of May, *The Times* was worried that 'summer excursion trains will bring the artisans and mechanics of the north in upon London like an inundation' and that 'King Mob' would enthrone itself beneath Paxton's 'blazing arch of lucid glass'.[30] In the wake of the Chartist threat this was a widespread fear. The Duke of Wellington reckoned that 15,000 men would be needed to keep order in the capital. It took a cool calculator like Macaulay to declare on the opening day of the Exhibition: 'There is just as much chance of a revolution in England as of the falling of the moon.'[31] As it happened, the excursionists behaved impeccably and *The Times*, in a characteristic volte-face, explained what a tribute it was to British stability that 'well dressed, orderly and sedate' members of the 'industrial classes' could mingle so politely with those of higher rank.[32] So it was that the Great Exhibition won a wide measure of tolerance, even approval, for the excursion movement. Mass mobility was becoming acceptable.

This did not mean that there was less social discrimination. Partly from genuine indignation and partly as a form of self-advertisement, Thomas Cook wrote a public letter to Prince Albert protesting that the entry fee was too high for the working classes and advocating (since no one could take in the whole Exhibition on a single visit) the provision of four-day season tickets for a shilling. His plea was ignored. Yet Cook well knew that for provincial excursionists every penny counted. Not content with promoting and conducting tours, including a children's excursion, 3,000 strong, which was taken to and from the London terminus in an extraordinary array of omnibuses, vans and cabs, Cook organized accommodation for visitors. It ranged from bed and a substantial meat breakfast for two shillings (boot-cleaning a penny extra) at the Ranelagh Club, to dormitories at a shilling a night on board an emigrant ship moored at the foot of Vauxhall Bridge.

Cook once wrote that he tried to make his work 'remunerative as well as publicly beneficial; and we have yet to learn, that there is anything . . . hostile to true philanthropy in commercial success'.[33] While the Great Exhibition was open, he managed to combine organizing excursions with promoting 'a large and most successful temperance meeting, out of which grew the London Temperance League'.[34] And shortly after the Exhibition closed he found another opportunity to mix business with idealism. In the late autumn of 1851 Louis Kossuth arrived in England. Leader of the Hungarian revolt against Austrian domination, he was a hero to many English radicals and Cook went to Southampton to welcome the 'adored Kossuth' ashore in person. There the entrepreneur saw that he could capitalize on the Hungarian's immense popularity and he ran two excursion trains full of admirers from Leicester, one to London and the other to Birmingham. Seventeen years later, on his first trip to Hungary, still in the Austrian grip, Cook wrote that 'the heroic deeds of [Kossuth's] great struggle [for independence] seemed to be emblazoned on every object of tourist attraction'.[35]

What this proved was that tourism is the discovery of the well-known (whereas travel is the discovery of the ill-known and exploration the discovery of the unknown). So long as it was sufficiently famous, anything could become a tourist attraction – a man or a monument, a shipwreck or a waterfall, a mountain or a city. To some extent, as the *Excursionist* demonstrated, fame could be generated artificially, through advertisement. But fame had a pulling power of its own and over the next decade or so, as tourist horizons widened, Cook's clients began to urge him to visit new and famous places, so much so that many of them were bound to be disappointed. As he wrote, 'What a pity it is we cannot meet every desire, and gratify every travelling propensity.' But expectations had grown so large that some of his correspondents 'would not be easy without a trip to the Moon, if there were any possibility of such an ascension'.[36] (Only lunatics made this proposal in the Victorian age but today, interestingly enough, the firm of Thomas Cook has registered over a thousand lunar enquiries.)

Cook himself confessed to being 'moonstruck' later in the 1850s. This was when he initiated his 'first "Moonlight Trips" for the purpose of giving the working people of Newcastle a [cheap] day at the Manchester [Art Treasures] Exhibition' (1857). Actually, as Cook piously remarked, 'except where a great object is to be gained', he preferred '"Truth and Daylight" to night travelling'.[37] Still, this was a striking instance of his innovative tourist work during the decade after the Great Exhibition, the other elements of which must now be described.

Cook himself most valued his Irish enterprise, declaring that he would be not 'a little delighted if some future observer should be led to say that Ireland has become familiarised to the people of England by the *Hand Books* and other instrumentalities of "one Cook, of Leicester"'. Cook recommended short excursions and longer tours to Ireland in 1852, writing enthusiastically: 'From Derby to Dublin and back for 13s! is an astounding announcement; and the artizan and mechanic classes may now regale their spirits with the pleasurable libations of travel.'[38] The following year he took thousands to the Dublin Exhibition, part of an effort to stimulate industry and to revive the Irish economy after the Famine. Cook was optimistic about its effects – '"The good time coming" is the theme of every heart.' He particularly rejoiced about the expansion of the railway, writing in 1854 that 'the means of transit have reached a perfection never before attained'. But he also found it necessary to warn his clients about the impositions of 'Irish car-drivers . . . as jovial a set of Jehus as ever took a whip in hand'.[39] Subsequently Cook conducted a number of parties to Ireland. In 1856, for example, he filled sixty carriages in two special trains with about 1,500 people. However, in due course the rivalry of the railway companies frustrated his efforts, though his firm was later to wax lyrical about the beauties of the 'Emerald Isle' and to introduce many visitors, particularly Americans, to the lakes of Killarney and the mountains of Donegal.

By 1854, the year of his mother's death, Cook found himself so deeply engaged in tourism that he resolved to give up some or all of his printing business. Obviously he preferred the nomadic life, proud of being a pioneer, happy to make new friends, finding an 'inexpressible interest' in viewing 'the Monuments of the Mother Land'.

> We are never weary of pursuing the mouldering traces of the wall
> or aqueduct of the Romans and collecting the fragments of their
> hypocausts and altars. We love to muse amid the low-browed
> arches and ruinous cloisters of the Saxons.[40]

Cook was no mere antiquarian. He perceived modern lessons in ancient stones and eagerly imparted them to his tourists. He wrote, for example, of seeing the ruins of Welsh castles and monasteries with 'gratitude that the tyrannies they sheltered are no longer oppressing us, and regret that with all our increased facilities for amassing wealth, we have no charities in the present time, at all comparable to them'.[41] The world was indeed a book of which he who had not travelled had read only the first page.[42] Educational enthusiasm combined with commercial self-interest to convince Cook that travel was a duty as much as a pleasure: 'To remain stationary in these times of change, when all the world is on the move, would be a crime. Hurrah for the Trip – the cheap, cheap Trip!'[43]

The dear trip, as Cook discovered in 1855, when he made his first expeditions across the English Channel, was fraught with peril. Hoping to exploit pro-French feelings (generated, unhappily, by the Crimean alliance against Russia), he intended to repeat the success of London and Dublin at the Paris Exhibition. But he was almost totally thwarted. Cook made three expensive preliminary journeys to the Continent; but after 'a hard fight'[44] he was unable to persuade the French or Belgian railway authorities 'to make special terms'.[45] He could not even obtain a free conductor's pass from Strasbourg to Paris. So Cook ran no cheap excursions to the Exhibition, though he did manage to take 'large numbers'[46] as far as Calais, via the Midland and South Eastern railways, at a return fare of thirty-one shillings. Furthermore, having obtained a few grudging concessions on the Great Eastern route, he organized two circular tours, embarking from Harwich and including Antwerp, Brussels, Cologne, Mainz, Mannheim, Heidelberg, Strasburg and Paris.

They were eminently successful as far as the clients were concerned and three unpublished journals survive which bring the first trip vividly to life. The diarists were Lucilla, Elizabeth and Marian Lincolne, young schoolteachers from Norwich who supported the temperance cause and later became inveterate travellers. With their sister Matilda (who kept no journal) they went part of the way with Cook, whom they found 'most pleasant, kind and gentlemanly' and who endeared himself to them by his 'Christian manner'. With his expertise as a tour manager they were perhaps less impressed. At Heidelberg station, Marian recorded,

> Poor Mr Cook was in a fever of distress, having got too many tickets and could not make them understand so that [Matilda] went and explained matters. 'Ah,' said he, 'what a thing it is to have a tongue and know how to use it!'

The intrepid Lincolne sisters were even more inclined to make pitying remarks about 'poor nervous' Mrs Cook who, whatever her business capacity, seems at this stage to have been an indifferent traveller. On the German border she lost her cloak and at Heidelberg 'poor shiftless Mrs Cook' managed to lock herself in her hotel room and had to be rescued. If anything, such little adventures added to the sisters' enjoyment, and their accounts of the journey, which must be typical of hundreds of such diaries, are now of great interest.

On the steamer from Harwich, Lucilla recorded, she was 'not very ill' though the cabin was 'very hot and full of ladies'. A curious mixture of sophistication and naïveté, she found Antwerp a revelation. 'Everything looked so foreign', the 'men bearded like goats', the women wearing 'cap-bonnets' and gold ornaments, the children in wooden shoes, Madonnas and crucifixes on street corners, windmills in the distance. But during their sightseeing and shopping walks the Lincolnes were struck by the 'universal kindness and politeness . . . [shown] to ladies'. The twenty-five or so members of the party[47] were greeted with clapping in the market place at Brussels. The sisters found it a charming and 'magnificent city', with its gleaming white houses, its broad, clean streets and its pure air. However, they were shocked, while promenading in the beautiful park, that 'Young men as they pass a group of fine young ladies dressed as for a ball, use their spy-glass and make remarks.' And their first dinner at the Hôtel de France was overwhelming. It took two hours to serve and consisted of sixteen courses:

> Soup, fried eel, beef, brocoli [sic] and potatoes, veal, chicken, mutton, duck, peas, chicken again, tongue, salad, strawberry tart, brandy pudding, strawberries, cherries, sweetmeats, and to finish up a little dish of *toothpicks*! made of small quills.

Marian 'kept one as a curiosity'. She also noted, without adverse comment, the mealtime badinage of her fellow tourists: 'Mr Green our tall independent companion and Mr Mowbray the little dark-eyed good-natured man, made great fun by grumbling at the waiters for not speaking English. Mr G. thunders out his orders and frightens the poor fellows with his terrific frown.'

Before dawn the next morning (9 July) Cook bought the tickets and the party left Brussels in third-class open carriages for Cologne. The Lincolnes found themselves sitting next to a 'handsome, intelligent Frenchman whom Cook suspected of being 'a gendarme just put here to see what so many English can be about'. But the spy, if he was one, added to the excitement of a journey through 'rich, varied and lovely country'. 'There was nothing but "Oh, look here!" "do look there!" so that we could not see enough.' At Verviers, Lucilla continued, suffering from 'agonies of semi-starvation', they underwent the 'tiresome ceremony of weighing our baggage, such a contrast to our English order and business-like manners, for there was only one poor slow dawdle of a man to attend to it all'. The German train was much inferior to the Belgian one and Marian found herself in a carriage 'with a horridly dirty and disgusting set, who smoked and spat as much as any American, without regard to any ladies present'. In Cologne the people were polite and the city was 'picturesque'. But the cathedral was 'disappointing', the streets 'narrow and dirty' with 'open gutters' and one tourist claimed to have identified seventy-three different smells.

All that was forgotten when the tourists boarded their Rhine steamer. This romantic river voyage was the high point of the trip and 'most thoroughly did we enjoy it'. As they passed the 'wild rocks' and 'castled crags' of the Drachenfels Mr Green read aloud from Byron's *Childe Harold*. On deck the tourists held 'patchwork conversations' in 'Babel-language' with foreigners. Among themselves they discussed literature, education, 'geology, astronomy, and the paralax' [sic]. Below they played charades and 'twenty questions'. They also enjoyed the sensation which their combined presence caused on the steamer: 'the under-steward . . . got so hot and excited at having such an influx of company that he broke 3 plates, 2 tumblers, a butter boat and a tureen full of cauliflowers'.

At Mainz the arrival of so many English at the Hôtel Angleterre caused similar 'bustle and confusion', as Marian recorded: 'landlord sending waiters flying on all sides, servants standing agast [sic] at the sudden increase of company, while porters were hauling luggage to the various rooms'. These were found to be dirty and uncomfortable, with sanded floors, 'pie-dishes instead of basins to wash in' and hard beds full of small intruders which prevented sleep. At Mannheim, where the party finally left the steamer, 'porters swarmed' and then 'the cab and bus drivers would not accede to our terms'. So the tourists shouldered their luggage and set off in an ungainly procession for the hotel, which proved to be a good one. As emerges from the Lincolnes' diaries, Cook's early tours were haphazard affairs. Much was left to chance, tourists came and went of their own accord, plans were made on the spur of the moment. Thus at Mannheim members of the party debated whether they should stay for a while and explore the town. Cook was obviously consulted but apparently it was a majority of the ladies who decided that they should go straight on by train to Heidelberg.

Here, Lucilla wrote, 'we ladies waited while Mr Cook ran to secure lodgings'. They turned out to be the best of the entire trip. The Lincolnes had a 'splendid room' with Brussels carpet, chairs of crimson velvet, 'almost gorgeous' curtains and *'glorious* views'. As usual the tourists saw the sights. Cook rode up to the castle on a donkey and the Lincolne sisters performed their role of interpreters in response to the invariable cry: 'Where are the ladies who know French and German? Forward please – and say what this man is jabbering about!' Some of the group also visited a gaming room; but the Lincolnes left quickly, finding the atmosphere 'morally unwholesome'. It was the antithesis of what tourism should impart. As Lucilla wrote,

I would hope and desire that this trip will not be fruitless in good
results but that the glorious sights that have filled my mind with
such ideas of natural beauty, have also in some degree, purified
and refined my thoughts and given me higher concepts of the
Creator.[48]

Thomas Cook could hardly have expressed his own purposes better. But before parting company with the Lincolnes at Heidelberg
he did not scruple to take advantage of their literary as well as their
linguistic skills. He solicited a testimonial from them to publish
in the *Excursionist*. Apparently this was his normal practice and
other members of the party also obliged. One wrote: 'We found
the greatest comfort in having such a friend as Mr Cook to whom to
look in every perplexity of selecting hotels, arranging with landlords,
procuring railway tickets, exchanging money, or learning the times
of trains.'[49] Other correspondents thanked Cook for his 'personal
attention and uniform kindness'.[50] Several of the letters were 'full
of enthusiastic fire, animated by the pleasant recollection of sights
and associations of the most instructive and cheering character'.[51]

Despite these tributes Cook must have been aware that Continental tourism involved him in more awkward compromises. He
himself hated war enough to denounce the annual Waterloo banquet
at Apsley House as 'a blot upon this bright era of peace'.[52] But on his
second trip he could not avoid taking his party to the most famous
battlefield in the world and he reported the 'very graphic account'
given to the tourists by Sergeant Munday, who had himself fought
at Waterloo and acted as the resident English guide. Similarly,
Cook entered a somewhat disingenuous defence of those among
his party who had visited the casino at Baden-Baden: 'when the
danger is known it is easy to avoid and . . . [there is] little fear of
our tourists being caught in the meshes of the gambler's web'.[53]
On this occasion such agreeable flexibility, though doubtless an
asset in any tourist manager, profited Cook nothing. Indeed he lost
money on both these long tours. Nevertheless, the following year he
proposed another one, provided that fifty people put down deposits
of a pound. Only ten did so and the project was cancelled. Not until
1861 would Cook again venture outside the British Isles.

Still, although 'dearly purchased', he did now have invaluable
experience of foreign travel. He could advise English tourists to
equip themselves with soap and tea. He could pronounce on the

need to arrive at railway stations an hour early in order to secure the registration of baggage. He could talk with authority about sights to see and routes to take, about passport regulations and customs declarations, about the 'unceasing vigilance' required 'to keep on the "right side" of hotel keepers, money changers, booking clerks and others with whom we had pecuniary transactions', about the 'sudden changes of currencies, the wretched and uneven appearance of coins and notes, the conglomeration of francs, centimes, thalers, gold and silver groschen, florins and kreutzers'[54] – in short, about all the circumstances of Continental travel calculated to perturb anyone rash enough to travel abroad without his personal chaperonage.

That Cook did not exaggerate is well illustrated by a contemporary *crie de coeur* graphically entitled *Cautions for the First Tour or the Annoyances, Short Comings, Indecencies and Impositions Incidental to Foreign Travel*. Its pseudonymous author, Viator Verax, was particularly eloquent about the terrors of Continental railways, where bewildered English travellers were often mobbed by avaricious porters ('tobacco or onion-scented, blue-frocked varlets') and laughed at or bawled at by 'low *caste*' officials. When luggage was weighed there were 'bear-garden scenes of rude and rugged contact, vociferation and vulgar grossness'. These were succeeded by a 'tumultuous and disorderly rush' for carriages when passengers, clutching 'hand-parcels and umbrellas, biscuit bags and bird-cages', were released from waiting-rooms three minutes before their train was due to depart. Viator Verax recommended travelling with a courier.[55] Cook himself certainly proved able to overcome the worst railway hazards – many a traveller found that 'the magic name of Cook seemed to clear away all difficulties'[56] – and in due course he helped to eradicate them altogether.

At this stage Cook evidently reckoned that his Continental experience entitled him to attack his rivals, though before the 1860s Henry Gaze and others actually knew more about foreign tourism than he did.[57] However, Cook resented their false claims to have anticipated him in the management of cheap excursions. So he dismissed them as 'bustling upstarts' whose 'puffery' was 'laughable' and whose pretensions were 'bosh'.[58] Less amiably still, Cook sought to undermine his competitors by denigrating the Continent as a tourist destination. In particular, he suggested that France was less attractive than Scotland because it was a police state: 'Those who think well to battle with suspicion and surveillance – who are content to be dodged by gens-d'arme and scrutinized by spies, may cross the English Channel.'[59]

If Cook's charity did not extend to his rivals it was much in evidence, throughout the 1850s, closer to home. And, as usual, it somewhat impeded his work. During the winter of 1855–6, for example, Cook intended to write a book about his travels. But distress among the Leicester poor was so acute that a public subscription was raised to help them and Cook personally supervised the feeding of some fifteen thousand. He bought the raw materials and saw to the making and distribution of thousands of gallons of 'very strong superior soup'. Coining one of the earliest puns on his own name, he wrote: 'Our "Cookery" was that of the soup kitchen instead of the editorial table.'[60] In the same spirit of philanthropy, when Leicestershire was subsequently afflicted by a potato famine he purchased hundreds of tons of potatoes from as far afield as Scotland and sold them to the needy at cost price.

Cook himself probably considered that his most signal service to Leicester was in promoting the construction of the Temperance Hall. A stuccoed, neo-classical pile, this temple to sobriety was opened in 1853. At the opening ceremony tributes were paid to Cook, 'to whom the honour of the whole design was due'. In reply he spoke of having 'concocted' a scheme for their 'magnificent hall' with 'higher motives than pecuniary' and of being determined that it should display the 'chaste and beautiful ornamentation and design' which had hitherto been 'confined to gin palaces'. Appropriately, the hall was the first building in Leicester to receive pure water from the new Thornton reservoir. Seating 1,700 people, it became the venue for many improving leisure activities in the city. Cook himself was adept at filling it. As the *Leicester Chronicle* later wrote, 'With what raptures he used to tell the story of his travels to crowded audiences at the Temperance Hall. But the people were as delighted to listen as he was to speak.'

Cook insisted, however, that 'no man who was not a moral man should ascend their platform',[61] and freethinkers were rigorously excluded – they retaliated by putting up a Secular Hall, where the bust of Christ stood in equality with those of Socrates, Voltaire, Tom Paine and Robert Owen.[62] Quick to see the advantages which proximity to the Temperance Hall would bring, Cook himself built a new hotel next door to it, at 63 Granby Street. 'Cook's Commercial

& Family Temperance Hotel' cost £3,500 and was another imposing monument to his principles, though once again he made a shrewd commercial compromise – he provided a smoking room. Ironically the two edifices to temperance were sandwiched between a couple of pubs, The Nag's Head and The Waggon and Horses. Still, Thomas Cook could take much credit for the fact that Leicester was unique among large British towns in never having a licensed hotel close to its principal railway station.[63]

Cook's ability to raise the sum of £3,500 showed how far he had travelled, in every way, since his bankruptcy. His efforts did not slacken as the 1850s progressed. In 1857 he not only sent four tours to Scotland (a total of 4,107 passengers, 1,000 of whom he conducted personally), he also helped to save the Manchester Art Treasures Exhibition from serious loss. Having been opened to great éclat by Prince Albert, it initially drew few visitors. The Board of Commissioners then requested Cook to act as its agent. Urging his countrymen to 'feast in the glorious noon day of Art's finest representations and richest treasures',[64] he organized a series of trips to the Exhibition, travelling by moonlight to extend the cheap day return to its fullest possible limit. All told, Cook conveyed some 26,000 people to Manchester, mainly from the north and east. During these years he also arranged an increasing variety of trips, short and long – to Scarborough, Hull, Birmingham, York, Wales, the Lake District and other places of interest and recreation. Some of them attracted literally thousands of people. One local paper expressed astonishment at the sight of a train of 100 carriages passing through Uttoxeter 'under the management of the leviathan excursion promoter, Mr Cook of Leicester'.[65] Of course, the lengthier tours were considerably more profitable than the briefer outings. But throughout the Victorian age Thomas Cook and his firm set a high value on the excursion train, recognizing that it was 'the first link in the chain of cheap travel'.[66]

All the same, by 1859 there were ominous signs that Cook should seek a greater diversity of longer tours. Most of his eggs were in the Scottish basket and in that year the railway companies tried to run their own trips over routes that he had made popular. Their efforts were unsuccessful and he was able to improve and extend his own arrangements the following year. But he feared that as the railways perfected their system his kind of agency would be less needed. So, undeterred by 'a serious failure and loss' which he had experienced in the West Country 'some dozen years ago', Cook organized a large expedition to Land's End.[67] Cornwall was now more accessible because the rail link between Plymouth and Penzance was completed in 1859 via the Saltash Bridge. This was one of Brunel's final achievements and was itself a great tourist attraction – Cook extolled it as 'a fairy-like marvel of engineering skill'.[68] But tourism was still such a novelty that every station on the narrow-gauge railway from Truro to Penzance 'was lined with spectators' eager to see Cook's train of twenty-eight carriages. The last lap of the journey to Land's End was completed by horse-bus. Then the party split up, some going to the Scilly Isles, others to St Michael's Mount, Plymouth and Torquay. This tour was so successful that Cook ran two more in 1860. The following year he was 'besieged with enquiries about other West Country trips'[69] and his endeavours helped to make tourism what it eventually became – the staple industry of the South-West. Interestingly, the guides who showed Cook's first party to Land's End foresaw the development, declaring that 'this would "be the making of Cornwall"'.[70]

Hoping to change his Continental fortunes as well, Cook now made another foray across the English Channel. Once again he was prompted by Joseph Paxton, who was President of a Committee of Working Men which planned to hold a demonstration in Paris in the summer of 1861. The project appealed to Cook, not least because in that year British subjects were no longer required to have passports to enter France, and he set about organizing a large 'International Excursion'. The railway companies were less enthusiastic: the Midland and South Eastern Railways demanded guarantees 'so onerous' that he would eventually make a loss of £120 on the enterprise.[71] The French Northern Railway, 'a very aristocratic line',[72] proved equally obstructive. Nevertheless, with Paxton's help, Cook was able to offer the lowest fares to Paris ever obtained – £1 for a third-class return from London (including a maximum of 28 lb of luggage). Cook also went in advance to the French capital, where he met the British ambassador, who proved helpful, and investigated the hotels, which offered rooms for two francs (one shilling and eight pence) and dinner for the same.

Cook advertised heavily and 1,673 people (including wives and children) bought tickets for the six-day Whitsun tour. Most came from the North (including a contingent of 200 from Titus Salt's cotton works in Bradford) but not all were working class, or did not seem so to the sensitive social antennae of the *Illustrated London News*'s correspondent. However, as the tourists embarked from Folkestone there were apprehensions about this daring foreign adventure and 'notwithstanding the promise of interpreters and guides, something like misgiving was felt touching the lingo'. On landing they were encouraged to see a triumphal arch on the quay bearing the words, 'Welcome to Boulogne'. It was surmounted with a French eagle and decorated with tricolours and Union Jacks, which led the tourists to give 'three cheers for the red, white and blue'. Then followed the usual contretemps over food: a long French loaf was passed from hand to hand in amazement, experiments took place with vin ordinaire and bifteck, a Yorkshireman expressed indignation about the vermicelli worms in his soup. After an overnight train journey, the tourists, travelling in three separate 'divisions', arrived in Paris.

Here the hoteliers were initially suspicious and uncooperative. However, though there were cases of exploitation, they soon warmed towards their guests and on their departure gave splendid bouquets to the ladies. Cook had arranged to meet his entire 'muster' under 'the umbrageous canopies of the Champs Elysées' but here he encountered a snag. The English party fell foul of the French law against unauthorized gatherings and the police ordered them to disperse. According to the *Illustrated London News* reporter, Cook was responsible for an 'excusable want of organisation' but made up for it by being 'unceasing in his attentions' to his 'forces'. He now divided them into groups of ten or a dozen, led by 'Captains' (some of whom could speak a little French), and they saw the sights in their own way. Apart from the opening of the Hôtel de Ville, no special facilities were granted to them and Cook blamed himself for not having thought to ask. But, assisted by the 'admirable and economical omnibus and cab system', the tourists travelled around Paris without undue difficulty.

Cook wrote:

The Louvre, the Palace of the Luxembourg, the Hotel Cluny,
the Invalides, the tomb of Napoleon, the Corps Législatif, the
Churches, the Garden of Plants, the Gardens of the Luxembourg,
the Monuments, the glorious walks and drives of the Champs
Elysées, the Gardens of the Tuileries, the Bois de Boulogne,
the Gobelin Tapestries, the promenades of the Palais Royal, the

solemn yet tasteful and deeply interesting Père la Chaise, and
perhaps surpassing all else, the Galleries and walks of Versailles;
– these and a hundred other attractions . . . excited the wonder
and admiration of the visitors.[73]

Despite their boisterous enthusiasm for the roundabouts and other
amusements in the Tuileries Gardens, the visitors themselves
impressed everyone (except the mocking Paris *Charivari*) by their
'gentlemanly and orderly conduct'.[74] Apparently even the Emperor
and Empress approved, for on their drives through the Bois they
responded to English cheers with 'affable smiles and grateful rec-
ognitions'. So, at least, Cook recorded, nothing loath to exploit
Napoleon and Eugénie as tourist attractions. Casting off from
Boulogne on the way home, Cook's steamer was 'a scene of
enthusiastic excitement, expressed in song, speech, and hearty
cheers'.[75] Cook's own delight in the success of this notable early
experiment in foreign travel for the masses was doubtless tempered
by frustration that the railway companies would not permit him to
recoup his loss by conducting more trips on the same lines.

Restricted to his thriving but vulnerable Scottish business, he
received a further blow in the autumn of 1861, delivered from no
less a quarter than Printing House Square. In a single issue *The
Times* printed a leading article denouncing 'excursion mania', and a
report of an 'Eagle Murder' in Iona for which Cook was responsible.
The leader pronounced that the modern craze for 'rushing about
in crowds' was not only exhausting in itself – better a peaceful
holiday at the seaside – but it was exhausting the country's admittedly vast 'locomotive means'. 'We cannot put all England upon
wheels at once, and accommodate simultaneous flights of the whole
Anglo-Saxon race.'[76] Cook quickly dismissed this criticism, saying
that people found touring in Scotland profitable and invigorating,
whereas 'every watering place on the English coast has been glutted
with gossipping [sic], flirting, listless indolence'. As for the rest of
the argument: 'Bosh! such thunder will never terrify anyone who
understands what it is to travel in the Highlands.'[77]

However, Cook found it more difficult to justify having had the
golden eagle shot, all the more so because he acknowledged that 'the
feathered monarch of the hills . . . was never before remembered to
have settled on the Island of Iona'. His defence – that the bird was
'to form the centre of a case of ornithological specimens from Iona'

for visitors to see if a hotel was built on the island[78] – was not persuasive. Indeed, the whole episode might be interpreted as an early instance of the ecological blight that tourism so often brings in its wake. Perhaps Cook's uncharacteristic act of vandalism can be understood in the context of a time when shooting was turning from a casual field sport into an organized massacre. Certainly his firm later became sensitive to the charge that natural and man-made attractions were being spoilt by the very agency that enabled them to be widely appreciated. His son John, for example, contributed generously to the conservation of ancient Egyptian monuments – doubtless reckoning that he was making an indirect investment in his own business.

Cook felt able to brush off *The Times*'s strictures as he contemplated his achievements over the previous twenty-one years. Others had imitated him and had even done better locally, but no one had thrown himself into the tourist system as he had, no one else had treated this 'novel' work as a 'vocation'. 'We have not only arranged Excursions and Tours, but have gone and travelled with parties from day to day, and from week to week until sympathies have been awakened and friendships created that live and move in hundreds of happy spirits.' A million people, Cook claimed, had made journeys under his arrangements, without fatal accident. He personally had been to the Highlands nearly sixty times, to Ireland and north Wales often, twice through Belgium and up the Rhine, and several times to the West Country – not counting hundreds of shorter excursions. Some of his tourists had now 'gone to "That bourne from whence no traveller returns"'. Others were enjoying the 'happy life unions created and cemented' on his tours. Cook himself had helped to give the revolutionary 'lessons of locomotion' their present 'practical results'. But if he looked back with pride, he looked forward with trepidation. 'The thought of twenty-one is pregnant not only with sentimentalism, but also with deep and anxious solicitude.'[79] Perhaps he had some inkling, even then, of what the Scottish railway companies would give him for a twenty-first birthday present.

Actually, Cook was not only prevented from running cheap excursions to Scotland, he also suffered a serious setback south of the border in 1862. As he wrote in September,

> We began the season in great uncertainty as to what our course
> might be: a thick Scotch mist overshadowed our Northern

prospects; in England it was doubtful if there would be sufficient
local traffic to justify the running of provincial Excursions;
the Railway companies we usually served resolved to keep
the London Trains under their own management, and not to
employ agency.

But as Cook was gloomily contemplating the wreck of his whole
enterprise, 'another course of usefulness presented itself'.[80] This
was the second Great Exhibition (again inspired by Prince Albert,
who this time did not live to see its opening) at Kensington in
May. Unable to arrange excursions to what was variously called
the 'Palace of Puffs' and 'a gigantic joint-stock show-room',[81] Cook
drew on his experience in the temperance hotel business and provided accommodation instead. His original plan was to put up
'country visitors' in 'one good-sized House'. But despite a severe
depression in the cotton industry caused by the American Civil
War, the Exhibition proved so popular that he soon found himself
boarding and lodging on a much larger scale. He accommodated
the 'humbler classes' in a new block of tenements at 147a Fulham
Road and 'the select class of visitors' in a further 'half-a-dozen good
Houses' over which he acquired 'command'. True to his temperance
principles, he even provided them with milk from his own cows
(though where they came from history does not relate). All told
he catered for about twenty thousand people, some of them from
France, Germany and Italy. As Cook wrote in an abbreviated
Excursionist, the arrangements involved him in a 'vast amount of
mental and physical labour, and the editorial fire waned'.[82]

Cook's fires burned low altogether in 1862. Yet he was already
preparing for a new and revolutionary burst of tourist activity
abroad. When rebuffed in Scotland he had initially planned to
'confine my operations for a few years' to the West Country,
regarding designs of trips further afield, to Sicily or even Jerusalem,
as 'pleasant fancies and illusions'.[83] His forays to France had all
been disappointing, including a recent one in the summer of 1862.
But thanks to Paxton's intervention with the London, Brighton and
South Coast Railway, Cook was given favourable terms to take his
tourists to the Continent through the small port of Newhaven. Cook
had also provided himself with a London base in 1862, a 'private
family house' at 59 Great Russell Street, Bloomsbury. This he
discreetly advertised as 'Cook's British Museum Boarding House',

though the lease stipulated that he could not display any trade signs apart from his own name on the door. From this new office Cook set off in May 1863 on a further 'reconnoitring trip' to Paris.[84] He was astonished by what he saw.

In the ten months since his previous visit the city had been transformed:

> Whole streets of close-crowded houses are gone, and not a trace
> of them can be found; whilst, as by the wand of some mighty
> magician, have sprung up on their sites lines of buildings –
> mansions or shops of great magnificence. Where old faubourgs of
> revolutionary notoriety once stood – houses towering up towards
> the clouds, with but a few feet of narrow street betwixt them,
> where a barricade could be thrown up in a few minutes, have
> been razed – expensive Boulevards now exist – streets of great
> width, with deep causeways, on the margins of which flourish
> beautiful chestnut and other ornamental trees.[85]

Such a description was well calculated to whet the appetite of English tourists. But Cook could offer them something more. He had reached an agreement with the Western Railway of France to give low rates, thus opening up the Newhaven–Dieppe route to Paris. This was not the quickest way to reach the French capital, though Cook insisted that it was the most picturesque. However it gave him a cheap entry to the Continent, something which was to change the nature of his business as dramatically as Haussmann was changing the face of Paris. Within five years Cook conveyed seventy thousand tourists over this route.[86] The ports of Newhaven and Dieppe were virtually made by the traffic he generated, and in 1872 their harbours were deepened to eradicate tidal delays.

Cook himself was a bad sailor. Although he liked to describe the waters of the English Channel as being 'alive with the emotions of fraternity and cordiality',[87] on at least one previous occasion they had given him a 'most unpleasant tossing and sousing . . . quite sufficient to set all the bile of the system in motion'.[88] His return journey in May 1863 was marked by such fierce squalls that he was six hours at sea. But a 'mutton chop and cup of tea at M. Bosson's excellent Station Hotel [in Newhaven], assisted to repair the damages of a dilapidated "interior"'.[89] Even more comforting must have been the thought that while his Scottish hopes, 'fragile as a spider's web',[90] had been dashed he could now take the flood tide to fortune.

Without delay he advertised two trips to Paris, himself conducting one and the other being taken by an assistant, John Ripley, formerly a temperance missionary in Leicester. Some 1,600 excursionists made the journey, most of them paying £1 7s. 6d. for first-class returns but some as little as 17s. 6d. for second-class tickets. As Cook was quick to point out, it was now possible to get from London to Paris as quickly as from London to Edinburgh, and at half the price. Having demonstrated the demand for cheap Continental holidays, Cook rushed off to prepare the way to Switzerland, which was now more accessible because of new rail links. And at the end of June he took his first party there, over sixty tourists paying a minimum of four guineas for second-class returns. They travelled 388 miles by rail from Paris in seventeen hours; went from Geneva to Chamonix in diligences and two-horse carriages; had 'a most magnificent' drive to the foot of that 'mountain monarch', Mont Blanc; made an eleven-hour trek to Martigny on mules; and everywhere found ample confirmation of the 'morality of the Swiss character'. The 'good-natured Mr Cook', as one of the company called him,[91] was so elated by his first Swiss tour that in describing it for the *Excursionist* he went so far as to 'cast off the flimsy veil of the editorial "we", and in my own proper, first person, unblushingly avail myself of the often odious singular pronoun I'.[92]

By September 1863 Cook had taken 2,000 visitors to Paris, of whom 500 had gone on to Switzerland. Most of the tourists travelled in personally conducted parties but about 100 of them took their own time and selected their own routes. On average the cost of an eighteen-day tour, including all travelling and hotel expenses, was £15 12s. 7d. It was possible to go more cheaply but Cook only chose 'first-class establishments', trying to make them adapt their cuisine to the appetite of 'a thorough roast-beef-and-pudding-eating Englishman'.[93] John Bull wanted to 'see his dinner before him' and disliked fancy dishes such as sauced pig's ears resembling, one Briton complained, 'a pair of brown kid gloves cut into short strips'.[94] If a lunch menu for Cook's first tourists at Geneva is typical, hotel keepers endeavoured to oblige their guests. It consisted of ten courses: vegetable soup; salmon with cream sauce; sliced roast beef with brown potatoes; boiled fowl served on rice; sweetbreads; roast fowl with salad; artichokes; plum pudding steeped in brandy;

sponge cake and stewed fruit; two varieties of creams and ripe cherries.[95] En route, too, sterling efforts were made to satisfy the voracious English: Cook reported that at Dijon, where the train stopped for ten minutes, 'a dinner of some eight or nine courses was well served and well eaten'.[96]

These Swiss tours did indeed mark 'a new epoch in our labours and adventures'.[97] Not only was their success phenomenal, so was the rapidity with which it was achieved. While blowing his own trumpet as loudly as possible, Cook himself sounded a note of surprise: 'That which took *teens* of years in Scotland seems to have been acquired at a single bound in Switzerland, where "Cook's Tours" already rank among the Institutions of the Confederation.'[98] Yet the logic of the package tour was becoming increasingly plain to him, and he came within an ace of formulating what later became known as 'Cook's Law', namely that the largest profits came from 'intensive use by the greatest number of people at the lowest cost'.[99] At the time Cook wrote:

> I now see no reason why a hundred may not travel together as easily as a dozen, and I guess that the day is not distant when a Centurion's corps may march through some of these Alpine passes, as the first Napoleon crossed the Alps with his grand army.[100]

Within a few weeks Cook himself crossed the Alps – in a diligence drawn by thirteen mules – and opened up northern Italy to mass tourism. Within a few months he was being hailed as 'the Napoleon of Excursions'.[101]

John Bull Abroad

The Alps had only become fashionable in the last generation or two. In the sixteenth century Benvenuto Cellini had crossed the mountains protected by a cavalcade and a suit of mail. In the seventeenth century the diarist John Evelyn had been appalled by the 'strange, horrid & firefull Craggs'.[1] In the eighteenth century the novelist Richardson called the Alps 'these great excrescences of nature',[2] the poet Gray said that Mont Cenis carried 'the permission mountains have of being frightful rather too far',[3] and Horace Walpole had his pet dog snatched up by an Alpine wolf before his very eyes. But the Romantic movement transformed such antipathies into feelings of awe and delight. Everyone paid homage to what Byron called, in *Childe Harold's Pilgrimage*, these 'palaces of nature'.

In the Victorian age John Ruskin became high priest of the Alpine cult, rhapsodizing about the 'pure and holy hills . . . link between heaven and earth',[4] 'the seen walls of lost Eden'.[5] As these words suggest, Ruskin believed that the Alps were there to be venerated by the aesthetic elite, not desecrated by the philistine multitude. He deplored the craze for mountaineering, the formation of the Alpine Club in 1857, Whymper's conquest of the Matterhorn in 1865. And in a characteristic jeremiad, written the year after Cook first came to Switzerland, he denounced the spread of tourism:

> The French revolutionists made stables of the cathedrals of France; you have made race-courses of the cathedrals of the earth. Your *one* conception of pleasure is to drive in railroad carriages round their aisles, and eat off their altars . . . [There is no] foreign city in which the spread of your presence is not marked among its fair old streets and happy gardens by a consuming white leprosy of new hotels . . . the Alps themselves, which your own poets used to love so reverently, you look upon as soaped poles in a bear garden, which you set yourself to climb and slide down again with 'shrieks of delight'.[6]

But Ruskin could not kill the Alpine appetite which he had done so much to stimulate. Thomas Cook arrived on the scene at the moment when ever larger numbers of the English middle class, buoyed up by the mid-Victorian boom, could afford to satisfy the appetite.

That they often did so in a Ruskinian spirit is evident both from the pages of the *Excursionist* and from the various diaries still extant which were kept by early tourists. Cook himself was enthralled by the mountains, preferring the 'white canopies and glaciers' to 'all the gorgeous and glittering splendours' of Paris.[7] In her account of Cook's first Swiss tour Miss Jemima Morrell quoted both Wordsworth and Ruskin on the beauties of the Alps (though she also recorded an encounter with a lackadaisical Englishman who remarked: 'Doing Switzerland jolly').[8] Two years later, in a similar journal, Edward Miell wrote that 'these mountains seem to enwrap the very soul' and he rejoiced to have seen 'the great and glorious works of the mighty Creator'.[9]

All the same, there was something in Ruskin's criticism. For Cook helped to domesticate Switzerland. Hotels did spring up to cater for his tourists. Moreover they were clean, commodious establishments, a different species from the romantic little inns which had formerly made Swiss travel such a challenge, inns where fresh meat was often unobtainable, where 'the bread and wine were alike sour' and where 'vermin abounded',[10] inns like that described by Leslie Stephen where the bugs walked downstairs arm in arm and 'the fleas sat on the chairs and barked at you'.[11] Furthermore, as Frederic Harrison said, organized tourism brought to the snow level those 'cardinal British institutions – tea, tubs, sanitary appliances, lawn tennis, and churches'.[12] By making Switzerland more comfortable Cook contrived to make it less exotic. By making 'the tourist ticket a passport to all that is civil and obliging'[13] he made travelling in the Alps more prosaic. By ensuring that 'even delicate persons may, with tolerable ease, reach the famed scenes of Geneva'[14] he turned what had once been an adventure into an institution.

Yet for those new to it even the most cosseted experience of foreign travel was an adventure. Some novices were so nervous that they clung to Cook, competing for his company and following him 'through doors and round corners, as if he might suddenly dissolve into thin air'. As a journalist who went on one of the Swiss trips sardonically remarked, 'It reminded me of a string of pet dogs going to be fed.' The same writer observed Cook in Paris 'answering questions and swallowing coffee with a rapid dexterity worthy of a Chinese juggler'.[15] The tourist's question, like the proletarian's pronunciation, became a stock joke among people who considered *Punch* witty: 'Where are the four horsemen of the Acropolis?'[16] 'The Koran: by Rameses, I suppose?'[17] Cook was inundated with less pretentious questions: 'How many Napoleons do you think I shall spend in a month, Mr Cook?'[18] 'Is this suit of clothes good enough for Florence, Mr Cook?'[19] Commenting on the 'incessant inquiries addressed to him, many of them needless', one visitor to Switzerland remarked that Cook 'was a perfect Job in the matter of patience'.[20]

So he had to be, for questions were not the only tax on his temper. Abroad he became all things to all tourists. Yet another journalist wrote:

> Unprotected females confide in him; hypochondriacs tell him of their complaints; foolish travellers look to him to redeem their errors; stingy ones ask him how eighteenpence can be procured for a shilling; would-be dandies ask his opinion about dress; would-be connoisseurs show him the art treasures they have picked up; the cantankerous refer their quarrels to him, and the vacuous inflict on him their imbecility; but the great conductor never flinches.[21]

Cook doubtless comforted himself with the thought that he was introducing Switzerland to people who could not, or would not, have seen it without him. Most of them were pathetically grateful. By 1864 Cook had received enough tokens of thanks – watches, chains, paintings, pencil cases, ornamental caskets, silver-topped canes, snuffboxes ('never dirted by the pungent powder') and other articles – to stock a small museum.[22] Some tourists were positively awed by the Napoleon of Excursions. One young lady who travelled to Geneva with a 560-strong party wrote:

> It really is a miracle. Everything is organised, everything is catered for, one does not have to bother oneself with anything at all, neither timings, nor luggage, not hotels. And, do you know, I have met the man who arranges it all. I have even said 'Good morning' to him. He is named Mister Cook and they say he is a Saint![23]

However, most of those who went on Cook's early tours were by no means sheep, let alone milksops. Although initially two-thirds of those visiting Switzerland on a Cook's ticket joined one of his parties, an increasing number (over 90 per cent by 1865) travelled independently. Even those who were personally conducted found themselves deserted when their leader had to attend to other business; partings were such sweet sorrow and once, as his charges drove off in a crowded omnibus from the Hôtel de la Ville in Milan, Cook remarked: 'we could most heartily have thrown an old shoe after them, had we possessed a spare one'.[24] Nor was it all plain sailing for those who, as one tourist put it, 'choose to place themselves under Mr Cook's immediate guidance'.[25] Jemima Morrell noted that, despite his presence, 'The troubles of hotel life, the bargaining for guides and mules, and [other] arrangements . . . set anxiously on the male members' of her group.[26]

Cook could not always protect his parties against predators, who were active even in the high Alps. As he wrote 'wherever the "carcase" is, the "Eagles" of prey are ever ready to pounce',[27] and he had a number of 'very unpleasant skirmish[es]' like that in 1864 'with an impertinent, drunken hotel touter'. He was also surprisingly prone to error. He sometimes got lost or fell asleep or mislaid his luggage. His arrangements often went awry. Once when he telegraphed ahead requesting an omnibus for ten and twenty-four beds, the guide translated it wrongly and ordered ten beds for twenty-four persons. Tired and hungry tourists soon grew impatient with romance and demanded a good dinner and a comfortable billet. They indulged in so many 'petty jarrings and paltry ebullitions of temper' that Cook had to insist that 'any who cannot accompany us in a genial, sociable and confiding spirit' should not apply to join his parties at all.

Cook did 'not intend to conduct' tourists 'to the summit of Mont Blanc'[28] – Murray's *Guide* had recently commented on the 'remarkable fact that a large proportion of those who had made the ascent of Mont Blanc had been persons of unsound mind'.[29] But the Napoleon of Excursions did expect his charges to be extraordinarily energetic. Thus the expedition from Geneva to view the glaciers of Chamonix, which when first made by an English party in 1741 had taken the best part of a week, was accomplished by Cook's tourists in a single day. Certainly the stereotype of the Victorian lady – given to a fit of the vapours if obliged to rise from her chaise-longue – is

1 Thomas Cook –
'the Napoleon of Excursions'

2 *left* 9 Quick Close, Melbourne – Thomas Cook's birthplace
3 *right* Marianne, Thomas Cook's wife

4 Leicester Temperance Hall and Cook's Temperance Hotel –
sandwiched between two pubs

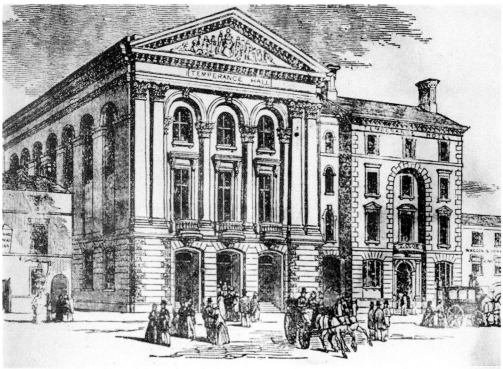

5 *left* Rational recreation with Thomas Cook

6 *right* Great Exhibition excursionism

7 A train of 'tubs' like that used
on Cook's first excursion of 1841

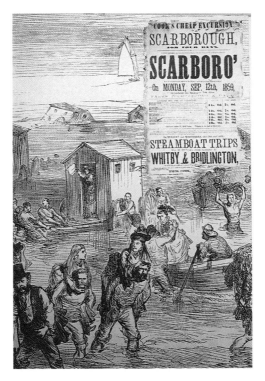

8 Beside the seaside

9 Royal tourist attraction

HER MAJESTY, EN ROUTE FOR SCOTLAND, AT DUNBAR STATION.

10 Miss Jemima Morrell's party
on Cook's first Swiss tour, 1863

AN INNOCENT ABROAD

A PHILOSOPHICAL EXCURSIONIST

Elderly Gentleman (politely to middle-aged Spinster opposite, evidently one of Cook's Tourists). "AND WHERE, MAY I ASK, ARE YOU GOING NEXT?"
Middle-aged Spinster. "OH! LET ME SEE!—I'M GOING TO GENEVA!"
Elderly Gentleman. "GOING TO GENEVA! WHY, YOU ARE IN GENEVA!"
Middle-aged Spinster. "AM I REALLY? OH, THEN I'M GOING TO MILAN!"

11 Cook's tourists according to *Punch*

12 Alpine equestriennes sans crinolines

13 A Cook's party crossing the Mer de Glace

14 Cook's excursionists at the Gare du Nord, Paris, 1861

15 A Cook's party at Pompeii during the 1860s –
Thomas is seated in the centre

contradicted by the female members of Cook's parties. As one of the males recorded,

> the amusing part of the business was to see the ladies, destitute
> of their steel armour (the anti-crinoline movement is very
> general, and in fact a necessity here) mounting their mules, and
> endeavouring to look perfectly at ease, when I could well see that
> a rocking-horse in their nursery days had constituted their sole
> equestrian performance; biting their lips and telling big fibs about
> being perfectly at ease and it was just like sitting in the armchair
> at home etc, etc.

Despite the mockery he was genuinely impressed by the courage such women displayed in the mountains, concluding: 'some would I believe face the Matterhorn . . . of course I am writing of a certain class'.[30]

Englishmen are always writing of a certain class, and the question arises, what class of persons went on Cook's Swiss tours in the 1860s? The answer, it has been suggested, was the middle class. But this begs any number of further questions. As Bulwer Lytton wrote, 'the middle class cannot be called a class, because it comprises of all classes, from the educated gentleman to the skilled artisan'.[31] To be specific, then, the sort of people who visited Switzerland with Cook were, as he said, 'clergymen, physicians, bankers, civil engineers, and merchants'.[32] They were 'tradesmen, manufacturers, professional gentlemen, and others'.[33] Among others, mention is made of booksellers, literary men, chemists, shopkeepers, theatre book-keepers, lawyers, professors, schoolmasters, scientists, architects. In the 1920s *The Observer* printed a ribald description of Cook's early tourists (by then as extinct as their grand precursors): the Englishman with

> the long, lean face, the hook nose, the lank, sandy side-whiskers,
> the deerstalker cloth cap, the Inverness cape, the large pipe and
> the hob-nailed boots . . . the Englishwoman with the pince-nez,
> the prominent front teeth, the wisps of hair escaping from a
> ridiculously misshapen hat, the skirt which droops amorphously
> at the back, and the feet as flat as her chest.[34]

But this was a caricature. Most of them would have had an income of between £300 and £600 a year. Nearly all were 'genteel': the men of one party were doubtful about taking alpenstocks to the Mer de Glace because they were 'rather a Cockney addition'.[35] As Cook stressed, nearly all were people of the 'highest respectability',[36] some wearing this bourgeois badge upon their sleeves.

A few, indeed, were so puritanical that they regarded Cook himself as lax. For example, he recommended Paris on the specious grounds that Englishmen could learn to 'emulate its excellences' and 'shun' its 'vices'. But he somehow managed to make the 'open scenes of folly' sound rather alluring. Thus he advised gentlemen to 'avoid low neighbourhoods after dark'.[37] He told ladies that they could 'without impropriety' sit inside or outside the 'best cafés' but that they should 'on no account enter the cafés on the north side of the Boulevards, between the Grand Opera and the Place St. Denis'. And he informed gentlemen that 'the "Can-Can" is danced by paid performers, and is altogether of an unnatural and forced abandon. Nine-tenths of the company consist of men, attracted by simple curiosity.'[38] At least one of his tourists was less tolerant (or less naïve). He was shocked by being taken to a Grand Bal in the Mabille Gardens off the Champs-Elysées, where there seemed to be a 'dreadful rivalry . . . between the sexes as to which can excel the other in indelicate gesture, attitude and position'. 'Surely Sodom in its worst days or nights never equalled this,' he exclaimed, roundly rebuking Cook for exposing tourists to such corruption. 'An excursion agent might with as much propriety, and even more, make it part of his programme to conduct his patrons to the night houses of the Haymarket, at midnight, as to the Mabille Gardens at Paris.'[39]

Such censoriousness was untypical. Cook himself warned his clients that other countries had other customs and that 'not Monsieur, but John Bull, will be the foreigner when we have landed on French soil'.[40] And as one Victorian wrote, the Englishman abroad enjoyed himself 'in great measure because he never loses the sub-consciousness that he has left Mrs Grundy behind'. He was consequently 'the principal patron of the artistic nudities of the Rue de Rivoli'. In Switzerland his inhibitions relaxed in different ways. The result was that sometimes, for all his pipe and flannel shirt, he seemed like a pale reflection of the arrogant English milord of former times:

He rejoices in rowdyism and the smashing of restaurant windows,

and is the terror of waiters whom he abuses or knocks down,
and, with a lordly air, throws them a napoleon wherewith to buy
plaster.[41]

'United Englishmen who travelled for fun', Anthony Trollope
noted, all too often indulged in 'energetic buffoonery and wild
effrontery'.[42]

Most of those joining Cook's parties were serious-minded persons
who consulted their Baedekers and took notes on what they saw.
But some were rumbustious, notably 'the high-spirited Cockneys
who carry London everywhere about with them'.[43] And more were
facetious. At Lucerne one wrote: 'Had some glorious fun in the
lobby of the hotel, Lord Dundreary (Webb) being chaffed by two
or three fellows.'[44] Another, who went to Switzerland with Cook
in 1864 ('May he long live to "pilot" my countrymen abroad'),
was agreeably surprised to find that there was no 'Quaker-like
taciturnity' at their dinner table.[45] Instead there were larks and
japes – as a young lady wrote, 'I am exploding with laughter.'[46]
Sometimes the jokes were at the expense of the benighted foreigner
who, as Cook himself lamented, could not 'understand our good
old Saxon tongue'.[47] But most parties produced butts of their own:
a certain Mr Law became one when he tried to obtain a penny
'rebate' from a waiter whom he had tipped a franc, eventually giving
up either because he 'thought the thing hopeless or [because] the
ridiculousness of his position dawned on him'.[48]

That such people were visiting the Continent in such numbers
shocked fastidious contemporaries. Watching the arrival of a body
of Cook's tourists in Berne, Henry James wrote: 'It is like the march
past of an army' whose recruits were 'rarely, to judge by their faces
and talk, children of light in any eminent degree'. They choked the
transport, filled the hotels ('I was lucky it seems to discover an
empty cot in an attic') and obscured the view with the smoke of
their pipes. Despite the instinctive snobbishness of his first response,
James had characteristically refined second thoughts about Cook's
tourists:

> They have rather too few h's to the dozen, but their good-nature
> is great. Some people complain that they 'vulgarise' Switzerland;
> but as far as I am concerned I freely give it up to them and offer
> them a personal welcome and take a peculiar satisfaction in seeing

them here. Switzerland is a 'show country' . . . and its use to the world is to reassure persons of a benevolent imagination when they begin to wish for the drudging millions a greater supply of elevating amusement.[49]

Other sophisticated critics were less generous, though their assault on tourism was part of a wider campaign against a worthier target, British philistinism. 'That brutal, ignorant, peevish bully of an Englishman is showing himself in every city in Europe,' exclaimed Thackeray. 'One of the dullest creatures under heaven, he goes trampling Europe underfoot, shouldering his way into galleries . . . more ignorant about Art than a French shoeblack.'[50] In more temperate and more classical vein, John Henry Newman warned that travel was no substitute for education, as so many ignorant tourists seemed to assume.

They sleep, and they rise up, and they find themselves, now in Europe, now in Asia; they see visions of great cities and wild regions; they are in the marts of commerce, or amid the islands of the South; they gaze on Pompey's Pillar, or on the Andes; and nothing which meets them carries them forward or backward to any idea beyond itself. Nothing has a drift or relation; nothing has a history or a promise. Everything stands by itself, and comes and goes in its turn, like the shifting scenes of a show, which leave the spectator where he was.[51]

As Cook began to go further afield, Newman's view was widely echoed. Emerson said that no man could find in travel anything he did not carry with him. W. H. Mallock wrote: 'as for the excursionist, who in the course of a single holiday is "personally conducted" through India, Japan, and America, it can hardly be said that he has ever left home at all. He has virtually sat still and looked at a moving peep-show.'[52] Of course, people do need learning to get the best out of their leisure, especially when it is spent abroad. But what Victorian social critics found it difficult to see from their intellectual eminence was that tourism could be part of the learning experience. As appears from the diaries of so many of Cook's followers, travel stimulated curiosity, fostered enthusiasm for the arts and opened a university for those without the advantage of more formal instruction. Such, indeed, was tourists' eagerness to assimilate foreign culture that it became a subject for satire and, as a recent historian has written, 'the general charge of philistinism' is difficult to sustain. [53]

Most commentators expressed their hostility to tourism more crudely than James or Newman. They referred to 'Cook's Circus', [54] 'Cook's Hordes', 'Cook's Vandals'. [55] Any number of disobliging descriptions were applied to the invaders of Switzerland. They were a 'low, vulgar' mob, [56] 'an irregular procession of incongruities', [57] a 'swarm of intrusive insects'. [58] The Rev. Francis Kilvert called British tourists 'noxious animals . . . vulgar, ill-bred, offensive and loathsome . . . No wonder dogs fly at them and consider them vermin to be exterminated.' [59] Neatly combining social and racial slurs, the *Pall Mall Gazette* said that the tourist had 'the same passion for bright and gaudy hues as the wild negro, who is ready to commit murder in order to possess an orange cravat'. It proposed that Cook should dress his flock in uniform. [60] *Punch* suggested that Cook's tourists were mental patients. And, in the most celebrated onslaught, the Irish writer Charles Lever said that they were convicts who could no longer be sent to Australia. Once they had been dispersed over the Continent 'the fussy little bald man' in charge of them would 'return to England for more'. [61]

Lever was both the British vice-consul in La Spezia (though he had no high opinion of the office, calling himself 'Her Majesty's Flunkey' [62] and carrying out his duties from his home in Florence) and a professional wag whose brand of humour amused Victorians, Shaw included, though it has failed to travel beyond his own age. Cook's clientele and his system provided Lever with a perfect target. This 'enterprising and unscrupulous man', he wrote,

> contracts to carry [tourists], feed them, lodge them, and amuse them. They are to be found in diet, theatricals, sculpture, carved-wood, frescoes, washing, and roulette. In a word, they are to be 'done for' in the most complete manner, and nothing called for on their part but the payment of so many pounds sterling, and all the details of the road or the inn, the playhouse, the gallery, or the museum will be carefully attended to by this providential personage, whose name assuredly ought to be Barnum. [63]

Of course, as Lever acknowledged when he accused Cook of swamping Europe with 'everything that is low-bred, vulgar and ridiculous', his essay was more of a jeer than a joke – once again in the patronizing manner of *Punch*.

However, Lever's example as well as Cook's prompted similar public attacks during the mid-1860s. Cook himself complained that he was 'frequently assailed by the pelting missiles of a portion of the metropolitan press'.[64] He especially resented the *de haut en bas* tone of *The Times* 'and his faithful cur, *Mister Punch*'.[65] But perhaps the worst offender was the fashionable new evening paper, the *Pall Mall Gazette*. This supported Lever and ridiculed the increasing number of tourists who only wanted 'to "do" certain sights and scenes', thus exhibiting their 'ignorance, stupidity, and incapacity for enjoyment with the utmost *naïveté*'. To such a person 'the grand attraction is that he can qualify himself cheaply and quickly for talking glibly about places and things, familiarity with which he fancies confers some kind of distinction'. Here the evident social snob was ranged against the aspirant travel snob. But, in the *PMG*'s view, Cook's tourist system itself was really to blame. It encouraged people to travel above their station, to climb socially by climbing the Alps, to 'go abroad on the principle on which a kitchen-maid distends her Sunday petticoat with a barrel-hoop because her mistress wears a crinoline'. However, the *PMG* indicated, geographical mobility was no way to social mobility. Indeed, promotion via locomotion was a fraud. Cook's organization was to the traveller

> what the ingenious deceptions of the cheap haberdasher and tailor are to the gent. who wants to make himself look like a gentleman at the lowest possible figure. By availing himself of the facilities offered by Mr Cook he can get up a kind of continental experience which is to that obtained in the regular way precisely what a 'dicky' is to a shirt.[66]

Such supercilious comments had their effect, and many were deterred from travelling abroad on Cook's tickets. As one writer warned, there was a danger of becoming 'more or less inoculated by the tone of your acquaintance and his "bad style". You get yourself shunned by people of greater knowledge of the world, who judge you by the company they see you keeping.'[67] These considerations weighed even with people who did book with Cook. One wrote: 'I had read and heard so many playful things about this gentleman's tourist parties, that it would be affectation on my part if I did not claim a certain kind of moral courage in forming the resolution to avail myself of this form of travel.'[68]

A journalist named J.C. Parkinson reported his own experience in detail. When he first announced his intention of travelling with the famous 'advertising trip-conductor', Parkinson provoked ribaldry at his club. He was nicknamed 'Young Captain Cook' and told that he would be driven from pillar to post 'with a herd of fellow-excursionists'. As the news spread 'genteel people . . . asked me meaningly whether I was really going abroad with "a mob of people", grinning acquaintances stopped me to inquire whether "I knew Cook was a teetotaller" and that all travellers with his tickets are compelled to take the pledge'. Some humoured him but most treated him 'as a zany of hopeless vulgar tendencies'. However, Parkinson had the last laugh:

> Now for my triumph. I have boldly run every risk spoken of
> by my impertinently-anxious friends. I have journeyed with
> a 'tourist-ticket' from England to France, from France to
> Switzerland, from Switzerland to Italy; and whether it please you
> to regard me as a travelled Thane, or a monkey who has seen the
> world, I know full well I have had a thoroughly enjoyable month;
> that it is my own fault if I have not added to my stock of ideas;
> and that from the moment of departure to that of return, there
> has not been a single incident to justify the prophetic strictures of
> my censors; that such provision was made for my comfort as few
> ordinary travellers obtain; that my dignity was never ruffled, nor
> my gentility flyblown.

Nevertheless, during these early days many people were so affected by the scorn of others, or by their own apprehensions, that they would travel abroad on Cook's tickets only when they learnt that they could go independently. It was for this reason that so many writers stressed the versatility and acceptability of the tickets in Cook's little green wallets, the fruit of his laborious negotiations with the transport companies:

> There was neither limit nor restriction connected with the
> tickets we took out. They were eligible by any train within the
> month, and were apparently as popular and well known on the
> diligences of the Alps and Apennines, and the mail-steamers of
> the Mediterranean, as between London and Newhaven, or Dieppe
> and Paris.[69]

Of course by travelling alone tourists deprived themselves of Cook's 'society and guidance', about which the Napoleon of Excursions spoke so 'sternly' to Edmund Yates, who interviewed him for Dickens's journal *All the Year Round* in 1864, that the writer forbore to question him further on the subject.[70] However, they rebutted the charge of timidity and they lessened the chance of being forced into uncongenial company, especially that of their inferiors.

This was the crux of the matter. Victorians feared social contamination almost as much as sexual contagion. Tourism, even more than travel, had egalitarian tendencies. As the *Pall Mall Gazette* grimly remarked, 'The tweed and the wideawakes bring about signs and tokens of levelling up in some directions and levelling down in others.'[71] Tourism broke down the carefully constructed barriers which inhibited the promiscuous mingling of classes. This was especially true of journeys by train, despite the three-class division, and some sought further segregation. The Duke of Portland, for example, had a special railway carriage built to accommodate his own barouche. Augustus Hare's family travelled to London by train but disembarked at some station near the capital and completed the journey in a post-chaise – his mother did not want it known that she had sat opposite strangers in a railway carriage, considering it 'so excessively improper'.[72] Railway travelling abroad further obscured the familiar landmarks by which social position was determined and defined. This often led to embarrassment. Holidaying on the Continent in 1865, a Cook's tourist named George Heard found himself sharing a compartment with a man

> who I took to be a well-to-do mechanic honeymooning with his
> young wife. He was very talkative, and seemed desirous to make
> himself friendly. Judge my surprise, when on turning over one
> of his books, I accidentally discovered his name with a prefix of
> 'Major'. I saw my error at once, and changed tactics altogether.[73]

Not all social signposts were obliterated beyond England's shores. In 1866 Trollope wrote of English ladies abroad who knew the value of men's every tone and every stitch. Voyaging to America in impoverished circumstances in 1879, Robert Louis Stevenson discovered to his chagrin that the polite ladies of the first class simply looked through him and he was curious to know 'exactly at what stage of toilette a man becomes invisible to the well-regulated female eye'.[74]

But it was all too easy for a patrician Englishman to find himself hob-nobbing with a tailor. Worse still – Victorians spoke of the prospect with horror – he might meet his own tailor. Cook's efforts made such painful encounters more likely. As one writer noted, 'We talk glibly of leaving England but England is by no means an easy country to leave.' Europe was being annexed by little Englands, which were springing up all over the Continent. 'During the summer indeed England is everywhere.'[75] Unfortunately, too, tourist emotions could embrace people as well as places, investing them with a charm which often proved all too temporary. Even upper-class English people were less reserved abroad and, as one observer noted, 'They easily fell into travelling friendships, though naturally snobbishness would occasionally assert itself, and people who were glad to know you abroad might ignore you civilly if they met you in Pall Mall.'[76]

In his efforts to take tourists overseas Thomas Cook was thus contending against that supreme British institution, snobbery. He did so vehemently if not always coherently. He first complained to the Foreign Secretary about Charles Lever (whose duty it presumably was to assist, not insult, Britons abroad), justifying tourism as 'breaking down the barriers of prejudice'.[77] Later he issued a shilling pamphlet containing a xenophobic assault on the man and a democratic assault on his argument.

> He would reserve statue and mountain, painting and lake,
> historical association and natural beauty, for the so-called upper
> classes, and for such Irish doctors with German degrees as choose
> to be their toadies and hangers-on. I see no sin in introducing
> natural and artistic wonders to all.[78]

By doing so Cook was perhaps dispelling something of their esoteric magic. But he was on good ground when he protested against atavistic class prejudice and condemned 'the odious and offensive stench of exclusiveness'.[79] Many contemporaries sympathized with him, including influential newspapermen like G. A. Sala, and several journals entered the lists on his side.

By far the most eloquent was the *Morning Star* – no relation to the present Communist sheet, but a newspaper inspired by Richard Cobden and 'conducted as a London outpost of Manchester radicalism'.[80] It objected to the 'lofty, lordly, genteel, and grumbling tone'

adopted by 'our literary brethren' when they discussed the vogue
for taking holidays abroad:

> The one theme perpetually harped on is the vulgarity and
> impertinence of people who presume to travel by excursion
> trains, or with cheap return tickets, or in companies, or in any
> way that is not grand, expensive and solitary. Every one (that is,
> everyone who writes) is indignant at the insolence of such people
> in daring to invade the sacred Continental haunt which, by virtue
> of a previous sojourn of a fortnight's duration, he has come to
> regard as his own exclusive possession. He cannot any longer
> enjoy the mountains or the castles, the picture-galleries or the
> glaciers, the cathedrals or the lakes, since these Cockney people or
> manufacturing people will persist in coming to look at them. You
> would fancy, to read his indignant sarcasms, that the Louvre was
> his private residence, that the Mer de Glace was his birthright,
> that the Cathedral of Milan was built by one of his noble
> ancestors, that Lago Maggiore was a pond in his own demesne.

The *Morning Star* went on to criticize the way in which other
periodicals disdained the manners, the pronunciation, even the
sea-sickness of such as Cook's tourists. Moreover 'great writers'
had joined in the chorus, Wordsworth bemoaning the proposed
introduction of a railway to Grasmere, Macaulay scorning 'clerks
and milliners' who had the effrontery to enjoy Loch Katrine, Ruskin
lamenting 'the British desecration' of Lake Geneva, 'which he possibly thinks ought to have been left undisturbed to himself and the
ghost of Rousseau'. It was all snobbery and affectation, a far cry
from the satire of former days which, though overdone, was at least
more 'manly'.

> Then the joke was to show up silly Lord Foppington on his
> travels; coarse Sir Stentor Stubble doing the grand tour; the
> Hon. and mischievous Captain Fribble making his collection of
> marble noses from the sculpture galleries of Europe; and such like
> specimens of the stupidity and vulgarity of the British aristocracy
> let loose upon the Continent.[81]

Naturally this was the line Cook himself took as the great tourist
debate continued. He lambasted 'purse-proud younglings who
affect to treat with disdain those who occupy a lower sphere than
themselves'.[82] He declared that "boorish travellers" are generally

those scions of wealthy families who are too mentally weak or morally unamiable to shine in home circles'. He announced that the arrogance of such 'rakes and prodigals'[83] and the insolence of 'the hirelings and witlings of a very small section of the London Press' were obliterated by the 'grateful appreciation of hundreds of delighted travellers'.[84] He made much of his defenders – one had called him a 'locomotive magician', another a 'public benefactor' – and prophesied that they would soon demolish critics who seemed to be 'affected by a mania of discontent at the idea of anyone, save the privileged few, being provided with the means of tourist enjoyment'.[85] He claimed that 'The best of men, and the noblest of minds, rejoice to see the people follow in their fore-trod routes of pleasure.' In short, through writing as well as touring Cook indefatigably promoted himself as the peripatetic people's champion.

However – briefly to pursue this theme – as the 1860s shaded into the 1870s a new note began to creep into Cook's apologetics. The last time he contrasted 'wealthy and aristocratic' travellers unfavourably with 'economical and industrious' tourists was in 1871, when he printed John Ripley's burlesque on an effete sprig of the nobility visiting Cairo:

> Adolphus, who was at the opera last night, and who is so *vewy* little *wefweshed* with his night's sleep, that he can't make up his mind to join 'Fwed and the girls' for a drive to Suhorba Gardens, the *woad* is so dusty, the sun is so hot, and *fwowers gwow* just as they do at home.[86]

Such ridicule was now inappropriate because Cook was extending his appeal from the masses to the classes and he looked on Adolphus as a potential customer. Instead of trying to beat the aristocracy he wanted it to join him. As early as 1865 Cook had claimed that he could mention 'the names of hundreds of the Nobility, Clergy, men of science and of the the highest social distinction' who had expressed approval of his work – a claim which would have been more plausible if the two names he did mention, John Keble and Bishop Blomfield, had not both been misspelt.[87] But as Cook's tourist system spread further afield it really did begin to attract a socially superior clientele. Indeed, like other Victorian organizations which started life as forms of philanthropy designed to benefit the working class (building societies, for example), Thomas Cook &

Son grew to a prosperous maturity by catering for the middle and upper classes.

Admittedly Cook's tourists could still be a pretty mixed bag. Travelling with a party to the Holy Land in 1874, Edwin Hodder, Lord Shaftesbury's biographer, recorded that:

> Amongst them were representatives of all sorts and conditions of men, from the light and frivolous idler to the devout and earnest student. They came from all quarters of the globe; they included four out of the seven ages of man, and of course they represented every phase of character. No educational test had been applied to them before starting by any school board; and while one spoke of the Arabs as a 'premature' people, meaning primitive, and of three houses being 'contagious' to one another, when he meant contiguous, another could discourse with the Arab in his own tongue, and read the monumental histories with almost as much ease as he read the newspaper.[88]

But proletarians hardly ever made such long journeys. When a solitary working man joined one of Cook's parties for Palestine in 1877, he caused amazement and consternation. He had spent thirty years saving up the requisite £100 and because he was 'dragged up from the lowest dregs of society' some of the tourists feared he would be 'a bore', which happily proved not to be the case. In the same year Cook could claim among his patrons '11,000 names of distinction'. Three hundred of these names were displayed at Cook's office, 'all of whom bear titles of different degrees', and the catalogue was headed by the Emperor of Brazil and Queen Victoria's grandson Prince Heinrich.[89] By 1892 the printed 'List of Royal and Distinguished Persons who have travelled under the Arrangements of Thomas Cook & Son' read like the *Almanach de Gotha*. It included not only the cream of European society but some of the most famous names in the world – the Duke of Connaught and the Shah of Persia, the Queen of Denmark and the Empress Eugénie of France, the Archbishop of Canterbury and the Viceroy of India, General Gordon and General Grant, Mr Gladstone and Lord Randolph Churchill.

In response to all this the press naturally changed its tune. Even by 1867 Cook noted that the newspapers were giving him much 'kindly recognition'.[90] The following year they expressed further 'sympathy with our exertions'. Even the satirists were muted. *Fun* was more friendly (if not more funny):

The Channel is now but a brook,
The journey to and fro no bother,
For thanks to friendly Mr COOK,
We *daily* visit one another.

Tomahawk was less wounding, though Cook found its proposal
that he should put on a grand Cook's Tour 'here, there and
everywhere' 'slightly impracticable'.[91] In 1871 he had even more
reason to be 'thankful for the general tone of the London press'.
Typical of the 'pleasant banter' to which he was now subjected
was the *Saturday Review*'s suggestion that 'all raw tourists should
be "Cooked" before they leave for the Continent'.[92] Formerly a
critic, the *Saturday Review* also paid tribute to Cook as 'a man of
practical genius' who had 'done something towards organizing the
means of locomotion, and making easier the mere mechanical part
of travelling arrangements'.[93]

Admittedly there was still sporadic sniping, and as late as
1905 an American newspaper could refer to 'the much abused
and ridiculed Cook's'.[94] But, Cook's many defenders being quick
to retaliate, criticism was often couched in somewhat apologetic
terms. During the late 1870s Fanny Kemble, who abominated the
'enormous mass of restless humanity' in Switzerland, '*endeavour[ed]* to
rejoice in the increase of the pleasure of "travelling for the million,"
while I do really rejoice that my travelling was done under far other
conditions'.[95] By the 1880s Cook was becoming an institution. As
the *Illustrated London News* wrote, although it 'used to be the fashion
to sneer at and disparage "Cook's Tourists"' the firm was now
'so widely known and their system . . . has gained such universal
acceptance that no public notice of their work can be looked upon
in the light of a . . . puff'.[96] Other journals echoed this opinion:
'People do not sneer at Cook's tourists now – they are only too ready
to be numbered of that happy band.'[97] Even *Punch*, which declared
in the 1890s that 'too many Cook's tourists spoil the Continent',[98]
was simultaneously paying backhanded tributes to the omniscience
of the organization that took them there. It featured a lady asking
a booking clerk:

Could you inform me if the 1.55 train from Calais to Basle stops
long enough for refreshments anywhere, and when they examine
the luggage, and can I leave my handbag in the carriage, and

whether there is an English service at Yodeldorf, and is it held in
the hotel, and Evangelical or High Church, and are the sittings
free, and what Hymn Book they use?[99]

All this is to anticipate. In 1863, when the Napoleon of Excursions first crossed the Alps, he had no idea of metamorphosing his
'unprecedented and unique vocation'[100] into a commercial empire.
He still looked on Henry Gaze, for example, as more of a collaborator than a competitor, recommending his Paris Guide as 'a good
shilling's worth'.[101] In the spirit of Richard Cobden, he regarded
tourism as a kind of free trade in people. It was an extension of the
laissez-faire ideal to human beings, a form of social enlightenment
and a means to international harmony. Furthermore, like his clients,
Cook enjoyed travel for its own sake.

When, to take up the thread of his story again, Thomas Cook
first entered Italy in the autumn of 1863, he was ecstatic. 'What a
scene was witnessed' from the 'lofty and glorious elevation' of the
mountains, he wrote, as his diligence began its lumbering descent.
Having negotiated 'fearful zigzags' like 'the Devil's Elbow', it finally
crossed the border and Cook breathed with rapture air that 'was
the inspiration of a famous land of patriots, painters and poets'.
However, he was less preoccupied than were his contemporaries
by classical culture and by notions that the British empire was the
successor to the Roman. What chiefly interested him was the current Italian scene, over which he experienced 'mixed emotions'.[102]
He deplored 'the power of the Papacy',[103] pitying the victims of
'priestly domination and besotted superstition'. But he delighted
to walk forth 'in the pure air of political freedom'[104] and he felt
'joy for the resurrection of Italy'.[105] In due course Cook himself
gave a modest fillip to that resurrection. For there was at least a
grain of truth in the claim (advanced in a letter to *The Times* in
1891) that by making it easier for Italians to visit one another via
his tourist railway tickets, Cook helped to remove 'petty jealousies
and hereditary feuds', thus doing 'more to bring about the unity of
the Italian nation than any military or political influence'.[106]

Having visited Turin, Milan, Florence and other north Italian
cities, Cook returned via Leghorn, Genoa, Nice, Cannes, Marseilles
and Paris. He was therefore able to act as an experienced cicerone
the following year, when he took his first tour to Italy. The party consisted of about fifty people, enough to astonish the Milanese. They

were an energetic lot who had a snowball fight on the St Gotthard and bathed in the Mediterranean at Leghorn. And they completed the 3,000-mile journey, the longest Cook had ever undertaken, 'with scarcely a single hitch',[107] presenting him at its conclusion with a 'mosaic casket of Florentine workmanship' plus a testimonial.[108]

Although Cook had thus established his 'social travelling arrangements' in Italy as well as in Switzerland by the end of the season,[109] his whole enterprise was still in a shaky position. The Italian tours of 1864 (consisting of 140 people in all, as opposed to 1,200 to Switzerland and 3,000 to Paris) ran at a 'pecuniary loss'.[110] Yet he remained optimistic. Cook believed that the Continental countries offered him 'new and almost unlimited fields of tourist labour'.[111] And in 1865 he conveyed so many people to France, Switzerland and Italy that they were able to present him with a pianoforte costing £50. Nevertheless, as his son John later wrote, the cash books proved that even then the entire 'business was being conducted without profit – if not at a loss'.

Cook's profit margins were always tiny. But the real trouble was, as John pointed out, that his father liked to sacrifice commerce to altruism. He sometimes allowed Baptists or teetotallers to travel at cost price. He often listened to hard-luck stories and occasionally failed to drive a hard bargain. As John afterwards complained, 'actual business arrangements have constantly to give way to personal, whereas I have *never* allowed my family or private matters to affect my business labours or duties for one hour'.[112] John particularly objected to the fact that his father made concessions to friends – and tourists often became friends. This is not to suggest that Cook was an incompetent entrepreneur, merely that he was not just an entrepreneur.

An interesting glimpse of the benevolent businessman at this time emerges from the journal of Alfred Miell, who went on a Cook's tour to Switzerland in August 1865. It was a particularly congenial party. Miell noted that 'such an intimacy had grown up amongst us that we seem'd all one family'. At the end of their journey the tourists held a meeting, under the chairmanship of W. Bates Esq., a Justice of the Peace from Stalybridge, who invited anyone to volunteer a 'spontaneous effusion of the heart'. J. Cockran Esq. of Dublin obliged, proposing

a vote of thanks to Mr Cook who had travelled the whole distance from Paris with us and by whose good management this excursion had been brought to so successful a termination . . . He never enjoyed a journey better and this was in great measure to be attributed to Mr Cook's supervision and general management.

Mr Brown of Belfast seconded the motion, commenting on the unexpected ease with which the ladies had made the trip and concluding that 'Mr Cook had cook'd them up a good dish.' There was general praise for Cook's 'uniform kindness and urbanity' and hopes were expressed that he had made a profit.

Amid cheers, Cook thanked them warmly and said that he had been engaged in the business of 'pleasure journeys' for twenty-five years, meeting rough and smooth, 'sunshine and storm'. But when asked whether he was 'not tired of getting about so' he always answered: 'No, I delight in it; to me it is a pleasure. And I can safely say that the tour we have this night completed has been preeminently so.' He finished by outlining his future plans, which included Italy, Scotland, the United States and, eventually, the Holy Land. Miell was impressed. He wrote: 'Mr Cook is one of the most cool men I ever met with. Nothing seem'd to disconcert him, or put him out of his usual tract. He is also a very intelligent man, in fact a man more suited for the part he occupies would be difficult to meet with.'[113]

As it happened, a figure who was in certain respects even better equipped to play that part had just stepped into the centre of the stage. This was John Mason Cook, who in 1865 began to work with his father on a full-time basis. Since his Scottish rebuff Thomas Cook had opened up the Continent to tourism and become the impresario of the Alps. But despite his combination of vision and energy Cook's one-man band was still not vastly superior to those of 'piratical imitators'[114] such as Florian & Co., whose 'bubble excursion schemes' he always condemned.[115] It took a man of outstanding ability and ruthless determination to transform 'a perfect chaos', as John Cook described his father's organization in 1865, into a 'business which is the Conductor of the World'.[116]

Cook & Son

John Mason Cook was a victim of his father's philanthropy. He took second place in Thomas's affections to his temperance and travelling mission. Indeed, John was early enrolled as a missionary. He was a teetotaller from birth and stuck to the principle until his dying day (though he did become a smoker, with a special fondness for cigars). Only once, a friend recorded, was 'the iron will . . . forced to bend': when John entertained the Prince of Wales to luncheon he was informed that he could on no account offer him ginger ale or Zoedone, a simulated champagne.[1]

From the start, too, John was involved in the business of travel, being (in the words of an admirer) 'broken to harness almost as an infant'.[2] Aged seven he went on the first journey from Leicester to Loughborough and he was soon officiating on his father's juvenile excursions, marshalling troops of his contemporaries and solemnly wielding the sceptre of his authority – a white teetotaller's wand. As John himself later recorded, his career as a personal conductor commenced in 1844 when he helped to guide '500 other small children from Leicester to Syston by special train' for a picnic.[3] What with travelling, attending temperance meetings, distributing tracts and helping to print them, John had little time for his lessons and did not shine at them. He did attend a dame school at Market Harborough and a preparatory school in Leicester, but at the age of fourteen, in 1848, he was sent to work for a printer in Derby. As an obituarist wrote, 'What he knew in after life (and he knew much) he had acquired for himself.'[4]

John mainly acquired facts. If his upbringing smacked of Mrs Jellyby his adulthood was redolent of Mr Gradgrind. As a young man he became an expert on railway timetables. Later he kept a diary in which he recorded that between 1865 and 1873 he spent 100 nights a year out of his own bed and travelled between 42,000 and 53,000 miles annually. John enjoyed collecting statistics about the progress of the firm. He filled the *Excursionist* with the sort of information that became the stock in trade of Ripley's *Believe It or Not*: the leaves of the South American Inaja palm are sometimes over fifty feet long;[5] all 1,400 million people in the world could fit onto the ice of Lake Constance and if it broke the water level would only rise six inches.[6] It was later said that John was 'a voluminous reader' who perused every line of *The Times* with religious attention, busily scanned other journals and 'missed none of the best books and novels'.[7] In the years of his prosperity, too, he acquired a library of ten thousand volumes. All the same, it is difficult to avoid the conclusion that John's chief concern with books was to balance them. He was not an autodidact like his father and he once confessed to his assembled staff that many of them were better educated than he was. Indeed, John reacted against Thomas's humane interests as well as his liberal ideals. Despite the piquant snippets, under his editorship the *Excursionist* became prosaic. He possessed none of his father's flair as a writer, none of his verve as a speaker. Late in life he was clearly more fond of cards than culture. And until that final, fallow period he devoted nearly all his waking hours to business. In fact, he laboured with such dogged, inexorable, Gladstonian persistence, as almost to make his father seem a sluggard.

In Derby, where he lived with his grandmother, John often worked eighteen hours a day. Considering the wage inadequate, he soon returned to serve in his father's printing office, where he preferred to do the hard physical labour of operating the press instead of the finicky job of setting the type. Ever strong rather than subtle, he could apparently run off posters more quickly as an apprentice than any journeyman in the business. In addition John travelled all over the Midlands distributing and displaying advertisements for his father's trips and otherwise soliciting trade. And in the summer months he worked as a precocious personal conductor. His father recorded that when, aged fourteen, John arrived at Bishopsgate Station in London to take a party of tourists to Scotland, the railway officials 'looked with astonishment and merriment at the stature of our youthful representative'.[8]

What Cook's clients made of him is not revealed, but further trips followed. Thus in 1849 he conducted the first excursion from the Potteries to North Wales and Dublin. As a pioneer of tourism John learnt to use his initiative. In 1850 Cook 'entrusted a party of a hundred tourists to his care in the Trossachs'. It was a complicated journey, involving trains, coaches and boats, and almost everything that could go wrong did. Some of the tourists, who had missed the steamer on Loch Katrine, were nearly drowned when a squall struck their open boat. As one of John's obituarists wrote, the journey was 'only completed through that unconquerable resolve to keep faith with the public which has ever since been one of the best traditions of his firm'.[9]

John's efforts at the Great Exhibition have already been mentioned. Like Thomas he was so busy shuttling between London and the Midlands that he spent five nights in seven out of his bed, snatching what sleep he could on trains. For the next five years he continued to assist his father, never slackening the pace of work even in the winter, when Thomas himself sometimes confessed to feeling exhausted. Such a team should have pulled together perfectly, Thomas providing the inspiration and John the dynamism. But in practice, as John later wrote to his father, 'we never had worked well together and . . . our notions of business were so opposite that I did not believe we ever could'.[10] The truth was that, far from complementing each other commercially, the high-minded father and the hard-headed son were temperamentally at odds. Theirs was not just the perennial clash between idealism and pragmatism or even between age and youth, it was also a personal disagreement. Thomas could never really bring himself to trust his son's judgement, giving him responsibility but denying him power. As one observer wrote, 'To the last the senior often demurred to and differed from his junior's opinions.' This discord was probably aggravated by John's feelings of resentment about his toilsome youth. Although there was no doubting his parents' affection for him, John could scarcely have failed to contrast their indulgence towards his sister Annie, born in 1845, with the severe treatment to which he had been subjected. Subsequent conflict between father and son suggests that their differences were long-standing and deep-seated.

In 1856 they virtually parted company. John accepted an invitation from Ellis to become superintendent of the Midland Railway's excursion traffic. This was a post for which he was ideally suited. He had the experience of promoting trade, marshalling trains and managing passengers. And he had the energy: once again, in the summer months, he found himself working for eighteen hours a day. Unfettered by his father, whom he nevertheless continued to help when necessary, he must have enjoyed directing the Midland's special operations. John also found scope for an unusual talent.

'From his earliest days he had a strong bent towards the detection of crime.' He got much pleasure from the 'analytical processes' involved, could have 'won renown as a police-officer'[11] and later became an ardent fan of Sherlock Holmes. On at least one occasion he tracked down a thief and recovered stolen goods. Such satisfactions did not compensate him for the fact that his salary was only £75 a year. In 1859, reckoning that he could do better at his old trade, John set up on his own as a printer in Leicester.

What persuaded him, five years later, to become 're-united with his father' is not known, but he was probably influenced by several factors. Competition among Leicester printers was fierce, as Thomas himself had discovered. In 1861 John married a local girl called Emma Hodges, daughter of a prosperous elastic-web manufacturer, and the following year his first son, Frank Henry Cook, was born. John realized that (as a contributor to the *Excursionist* wrote in 1867) Cook's tourist system 'is still in its infancy' and that with the Englishman 'bursting the bonds which have hitherto confined him to the shores of his native island' its potential for growth was immense.[12] Another consideration might well have been that his father offered him some kind of independent authority in the firm, perhaps holding out the promise of a full partnership (which materialized in 1871). Certainly Thomas was keen to be 'relieved from office duties' for he wanted to give 'increased vent to his travelling propensities'.[13]

As it happened, no clear separation of powers and duties took place, a source of much future trouble. Far from sitting behind a desk all the time, John was soon spending so many hours of the day and night in trains that even his stalwart frame began to suffer. 'Certain alarming symptoms' suggested that he was developing a spinal complaint, but happily they disappeared when he ceased to sit with his back to the engine.[14] However, in April 1865 John did establish a new office, at 98 Fleet Street. Appropriately situated at the hub of London's communications industry, this was a vast improvement on 59 Great Russell Street, where Thomas had carried on his business in an old conservatory. The ground floor of the leased Fleet Street premises was in effect a shop, not only issuing tickets but forwarding parcels and selling guide-books, maps, bags, waterproof knapsacks, hat-cases, telescopes and Alpine footwear – Cook always stressed the need for proper 'understandings . . . boots with good firm soles'.[15] There, in 1865, John personally 'answered all letters, booked nearly all the passengers, and kept all the accounts'.[16] The upper floors became a temperance boarding house presided over by Marianne Cook. And to Thomas's delight he was also able to accommodate the Freedman's Aid Society of America. What is more, after a busy summer season, he himself was now free to carry out a long-cherished plan – to visit the United States and open up a new world of tourism.

Needless to say, transatlantic pleasure travel was by no means unknown at this time. By now there was an annual exodus to Europe of some 40,000 Americans and, although far fewer Britons went in the opposite direction, fifteen years before Cook's arrival Niagara Falls was said to be as crowded with English tourists as those at Schaffhausen had been a generation earlier. The expense was enough to prevent most people from crossing the ocean, but even those who could afford it were deterred by the discomforts and dangers. Steamers were small, cramped and noxious; bed-linen was not changed throughout the voyage; cockroaches were abundant and baths unknown. The *City of Boston*, on which Cook sailed in November 1865, sank without trace in 1869. Seasick but unbowed, Cook struggled through the customs which, much to his indignation, charged him a heavy duty on some advertising pamphlets he proposed to give away. Then he took the first steps on a 4,000-mile journey which 'immensely added to our stock of travelling experience, and has opened up to us an entirely new class of travelling facilities'.[17]

Cook found New York 'a combination of the great features of London, Liverpool and Glasgow'. He heard many English voices there, and many Irish ones. When he asked to be taken to 389 Broadway, headquarters of the *American Phrenological Journal* which was directed by Messrs Fowler and Wells, sometime Cook's tourists and his agents in New York, the driver replied: 'Yes, yer honour, and Mr Wells will soon tell you what's amiss with your head.'[18] Luckily Cook's cranium had already received his friends' authoritative endorsement:

> You are the king and father of Excursions . . . Having been
> with you to Scotland and to Switzerland, we have found you
> a gentleman in every respect – gallant, polite, good-natured
> and successful in planning. You understand your business
> perfectly and your Phrenological developments are favourable

for just such an Excursion as you contemplate to make to America.

Cook bore with him less unusual testimonials from eminent figures in Britain, notably John Bright. Most of them stressed the value of tourism in promoting Anglo-American understanding in the aftermath of the Civil War, a time when Fenian troubles posed a continuing threat to good relations. Cook himself publicized his mission with characteristic energy. In letters to the press he described how he had pioneered the development of cheap travel, work 'appertaining to the great class of agencies for the advancement of Human Progress'. He told Americans that a million people had made use of his arrangements in Europe and that he would have visited the 'Great Republic' earlier but for its 'disorganization'. Now the United States and Canada provided him with 'a field of operation of unparalleled scope and interest'. The time had come for 'a great attempt to harmonize extensive schemes of American and European travel' and to spread his system over two continents.[19]

From New York Cook went to Montreal, Toronto ('well situated in the midst of rich farms, and in the enjoyment of a tolerably brisk trade') and Hamilton. He found Niagara Falls 'most wonderful and sublime',[20] ignoring entrepreneurs who tried to charge for the view or to obscure it with advertisements – 'Lovell's worm powder was never known to fail.'[21] He visited Detroit, Chicago, Springfield (where he paid homage to the 'martyred President') and St Louis. Here he put up at the Great Southern Hotel, 'a vast and gorgeous edifice', and witnessed an anniversary parade to celebrate the abolition of the 'great curse' of slavery. About '1,000 coloured people march through the city in the finest order, with three bands of music, marshals on horseback with swords drawn, a fine regiment of coloured militia' and so on. In the 'great Quaker City' of Philadelphia Cook spent a 'marvellously quiet' Sunday. In Germantown he stayed with a friend who vainly commended 'the "sinless wine of his own grapes"'. He was affronted in Baltimore by recent demonstrations against blacks and did not tarry long, for 'our free spirit could find no rest there'. In Washington he admired the 'fine Capitol, with its magnificent dome', just completed. A 'visit to Ford's Theatre brought back painful memories of the deeply mysterious tragedy, by which one of the best of lives [President Lincoln's] was terminated'.[22]

All told, it was not only an exciting trip but a congenial one. Cook met many old friends, among them a judge in Cincinnati who had left their native village of Melbourne forty years earlier. He heard a 'stirring' sermon from Henry Ward Beecher. He was delighted by the American habit of serving iced water at table. He thoroughly approved of Pullman sleeping cars, introduced in 1863. He found that the 'vogue' for internal pleasure travel, which had been increasing since 1825,[23] made North America an agreeable destination for foreign tourists. He publicized his own agency so effectively that within weeks the Fleet Street office was crowded with Americans booking tours of the Continent. And he obtained such favourable terms from the railroad companies that he was able to run the first 'package' tour to North America in the spring of 1866, only a couple of months after his return home.

This was conducted by John and it proved to be anything but straightforward. There were delays caused by interference from jealous local agents of the steamship companies. Eventually concessionary rates were secured – return tickets from £16 to £25, depending on class, line and port of embarkation – and in April several groups set sail independently on a journey which would take them 10,900 miles in nine weeks. After some delay they met in New York, where John found that the agreements which his father had reached with the American railroad managers (who were unfamiliar with the concept of tourist tickets) had come unravelled. John stitched them up again with such speed that not a day was lost. Altogether, while in America, he met or corresponded with at least a hundred railroad officials, as well as dealing with the details of the journey – baggage, reservations, bills – and acting as guide, philosopher and friend to the sixty or so tourists. John thought that 'even our American friends must admit that nobody but a "Britisher" would have been able to successfully cope with such difficulties'.

Following in his father's footsteps, the members of John's party were particularly fascinated by scenes of the recent conflict. They crossed the Gunpowder and Bush rivers on temporary bridges and were 'astonished at the still vivid picture of the effects of the war'. Near Richmond 'we saw skulls, arms, legs, etc., all bleaching in the sun' and brought away mementoes 'productive of sad and strange thoughts'. Otherwise, according to John's account, they considered Kentucky's Mammoth Cave the 'greatest treat', they delighted in the view from Lookout Mountain, admired the Capitol (though not the shops) in Washington and found it 'impossible to say too much in the boasting line respecting [the] wonderful city of Chicago'. For John personally, seeing Niagara Falls was the 'realization of a day and night dream from childhood'. He only regretted that his 'unpoetical pen' could not do justice to the spectacle.[24]

As it happened this was not only the first American Cook's tour, it was also the last one for seven years – though Americans visiting Europe increasingly resorted to what Thomas now grandly called his Chief Tourist Office, in Fleet Street. John did cross the Atlantic again in the winter of 1866 with a view to promoting their arrangements for the Paris Exhibition the following year. But once again he was thwarted. Others were inspired by, and benefited from, his advertisements. Among them were tourists on the first luxury cruise ever to leave American shores, its adventures graphically chronicled in Mark Twain's *Innocents Abroad*. Thomas Cook complained that the 'jealousies of agents and the rivalries of competing lines frustrated my plans and my precious American bantling was stifled in infancy, and died a lingering death in 1867'. It was not resurrected until Cook acquired an American partner, proved that 'we have a power to move English travellers in a Westerly direction' and established 'systems which nearly cover the entire Republic and Canada'.[25]

While John was trying to gain a foothold in America, Thomas was breaking new ground in Italy. He took a party of fifty tourists to Rome for Holy Week. Once again his emotions must have been mixed. Italy was on the brink of full unification and while in Venice Cook not only observed 'the throbbings of the people for emancipation from Austrian bondage', he also joined in the 'Vivas' to King Victor Emmanuel in St Mark's Square.[26] But the gorgeous Papal pageantry of Rome, while being a superb tourist attraction, he regarded as a form of idolatry. Cook was also beset by more mundane concerns. As usual Rome was packed with pilgrims, and the hotel at which he had made reservations refused to honour them. Cook's response was to hire Prince Torlonia's palace (in Henry VIII's time it had been the English embassy and Wolsey had resided there) for the sum of £500. Although Cook charged his tourists an extra £4 each, he still made a slight loss on the trip. Extortion was standard practice in the Eternal City during Holy Week and he was subjected to much additional 'commercial brigandage'.[27]

Like Hazlitt before him, Cook was revolted by the prevailing squalor of Rome, disease-ridden alleys and filthy courts 'where the smell of garlick prevails over the odour of antiquity'.[28] Doubtless this was an outward sign of an inward lack of grace. But Cook was indignant on behalf of tourists who, as Mark Twain opined the following year, might survive the cholera only to succumb to the crude methods of 'Italian purification'.[29] Cook later wrote to *The Times*:

> Myself and friends often felt it to be a terrible farce to be closeted and fumigated in Montalto, Civita Vecchia, Ceprano and other frontier stations, until almost suffocated with the disagreeable vapour, and then, when we got into the city, to see and inhale the stench of heaps of decaying vegetable matter in many of the streets, the walls of side streets black with filth and coated with cobwebs, revealing a state of offensive and dangerous stagnation.[30]

Still, Cook reckoned, the Rome trip, augmented with a visit to inspect the excavations at Pompeii, marked a 'memorable epoch in the lives of all members of our party'.[31]

The return journey was equally memorable. There were dangers from brigands in the hills and avalanches in the mountains. At the best of times, as one tourist wrote, negotiating a Swiss pass by diligence felt like 'trying to pull the town [of Turin] over the Alps'.[32] The hazards were multiplied for Cook's huge cavalcade: to take a party of seventy over the St Gotthard he had to employ nine diligences (warmed by hot-water footpans similar to those used in English trains), 432 horses besides bullocks which assisted at some of the heavier stages, and 108 men.[33] Only the previous year the Cooks' own diligence had overturned on the Mont Cenis pass – recovering from this 'gentle capsize', as John called it, father and son were approached by a St Bernard dog, complete with barrel, whose intemperate ministrations they sternly rejected.[34] Now, in 1866, Cook's party became separated by a terrific avalanche in the Simplon and one of the diligences had to turn back. Cook could hardly be blamed for that, but he was bitterly criticized for other difficulties on the tour. He would not be browbeaten. Refusing to 'succumb to unworthy feelings, or bend to an inferior position', he insisted that people should not travel with him unless they could do so in his own spirit of 'universal brotherhood'.[35]

Despite the initial problems Cook was clearly satisfied that Rome was one of the world's prime tourist resorts. Even when the Papacy lost its temporal power in 1870, with a corresponding diminution in pomp and circumstance, the city still had a wealth of classical remains to attract visitors. Cook made the most of this in his advertisements and he soon began to employ the archaeologist and *Times* correspondent, Shakespere Wood, to act as a guide. 'We learned and saw more in three hours with him,' wrote one tourist, 'than we should have got out of our guide books in three months. For me the palaces of the Caesars first rose from their ruins as I listened to Shakespere Wood's eloquent words.'[36] Within a few years Thomas Cook was conveying so many of his countrymen to the Eternal City that Americans improved the ancient maxim thus: 'When in Rome do as the English do.'[37]

Rome, or rather his experience at the Palazzo Torlonia, taught Cook another valuable lesson. This was that paying hotels on a single bill benefited everyone. It saved hoteliers work and made it easier for tourists, through their agent, to secure rooms by block bookings. And by allocating rooms in advance Cook could avoid the unseemly scramble (whereby the fittest tourists secured the best berths) which had hitherto followed the arrival of his parties at their destination. Cook declared: 'We shall not shrink from the responsibility of again catering for the entire accommodation of a travelling party.'[38] Here was the nucleus of the modern package tour. Here too was the germ of that crucial innovation, the hotel coupon, bought in advance from Cook and accepted by establishments approved by him, which he first issued in 1868. And here was a reminder, if Cook needed it, that he would do well not only to convey tourists to the International Exhibition of art and industry at Paris in 1867, but also to house them.

In his efforts to outshine the earlier British Exhibitions Louis Napoleon transformed Paris 'into a veritable fairyland'.[39] He also extended, through his private secretary M. Leplay, every assistance to the Napoleon of Excursions. In practice this did not amount to much. As Cook complained, 'coils of red tape [had] to be unrolled before gas and water' could be supplied to the large house, previously a school, which he rented at 15 Rue de la Faisanderie in Passy and renamed Cook's Anglo-American Exhibition Hotel.[40] Furthermore when Cook brought over a shipload of furniture, bedding and china from England part of it was mistakenly diverted to the Exhibition, where it was almost put on display beside the 7,000lb. cheese from Toronto and the vast Meerschaum pipe from New York. Eventually Cook and his wife did open the hotel, providing a 'liberal supply of all *necessaries* of life, but not an atom of luxury'. But this 'quiet, practical, thorough, unpretending, middle-class' couple (as a visiting clergyman in charge of a party of eighty schoolchildren from Liverpool described them)[41] soon discovered a concealed 'enemy to the peace and good government of the house'. It took the form of dozens of brandy bottles smuggled in from a 'low wine shop' opposite by the porter, a sixteen-stone professed Jacobin nicknamed Prince Murat, who sang incessantly and dispensed cognac to the other servants at two sous a glass.[42]

After a teetotal purge matters ran more smoothly. Indeed Cook expanded his accommodation to meet a huge demand, taking more apartments in the Rue de la Faisanderie and erecting temporary buildings in the grounds of No. 15, thus housing 250 people a night. This was the cheap end of his operation. English working people, busily recruited by John, could make a four-day excursion to Paris, including board and lodging as well as return tickets, for as little as thirty-six shillings. Even this proved too much for some of them and Cook was accused of overcharging. He vigorously denied it, asserting that 'our prices are ridiculously moderate', a view substantiated by the *Daily Telegraph*'s Paris correspondent:

> In the interest of classes not so effectually protected as Mr Cook's
> Tourists, who ought to think themselves too fortunate in having
> such a Palinurus at the helm, I will state I never in my life
> witnessed such extortion as is now practised in Paris.[43]

Probably most of Cook's profits came from catering for higher society, which he did with surprising panache. In the Boulevard Haussmann he rented a spacious, six-storey mansion, once occupied by Benjamin Franklin, and equipped it (according to the *Morning Star*) with a 'degree of luxury and comfort' surpassing that of the Grand Hotel.[44]

Unhappily Thomas's success in Paris – he accommodated about half of the twenty thousand people who travelled under John's arrangements – was an early cause of dissension between father and son. Worse, it helped to start the family feud which ranged John against both of his parents and his sister Annie. Ten years later the episode still rankled with him. Then John protested that he had spent over a hundred nights out of his bed 'in obtaining passengers for Paris' in 1867 while his mother, by her own admission, had 'cleared and banked to her private account £2000' earned from the Paris hotels.[45] For Thomas the firm was little more than an extension of the family; for John business was business. It was a curious reversal of the usual pattern whereby the founder of a commercial dynasty tends to be ruthlessly single-minded while his successors are magnanimous dilettanti. Maybe Thomas was sad over the intrusion of financial wrangling into what he still saw as a personal crusade. Or perhaps he was just mindful of the arrival of his sixtieth year. But in the autumn of 1867 he penned some uncharacteristically pessimistic remarks, reflecting that his 'much-loved labours in the cause of human progress are dying out, and the last long journey to the "last home" will soon be completed'.

In fact Cook was soon cheerfully off to Venice. He was glad, after a residence of eight months, to get away from the 'brilliant and bewitching' French capital, remarking grimly that 'philosophers and physiologists are terribly at fault if Parisian tippling is not a "quick march" on the highway to a state of ruinous dissipation'.[46] He was pleased to take his party over the direct rail link to the 'Queen of the Adriatic'. And he was thrilled that the sea-girt city was now incorporated into Italy. Indeed, he seemed to think that the lifting of the Austrian yoke was responsible not only for industrial progress and a free press but for improved bathing arrangements at the Lido and a decrease in the number of mosquitoes. Admittedly an outbreak of cholera – the 'terror-inspirer'[47] – somewhat marred this success story. But the following year, when Cook entered Italy through the newly completed Mont Cenis tunnel, he was even more enthusiastic about emancipated Venice. His party was met by the manager of the Hotel Victoria, who took them down the Grand Canal on board two large boats (lashed together and decorated with Chinese lanterns) escorted by a band and a choir. Cook noted that the beggars had disappeared from the city and that 'the gondoliers sang merrier songs'. Venetia thus presented an idyllic contrast to the Austrian empire which Cook now visited for the first time. He found that Budapest was full of 'feather-bedecked riflemen' and that the Viennese Sunday was a 'carnival of folly and vice'.[48]

While his father was abroad John expanded the business at home, enjoying, as he put it, few moments for revelling in the gleams of his own fireside. In 1866 he took an important part in promoting the Midland Railway's excursions. The following year he established an office in Manchester to exploit the Midland's new Derbyshire route to London, where St Pancras Station opened in 1868. That year the Great Eastern Railway appointed him to manage its Continental passenger traffic by way of Harwich. He succeeded brilliantly, lowering prices and achieving the quota which the Great Eastern had set him – 500 first-class passengers a year – within a single month. Soon afterwards he opened offices in Brussels and Cologne to help 'dovetail' the Rhine and Swiss tours.[49] In the British Isles he continued to push the usual variety of trips, from brief excursions to extended journeys, some of them to Scotland. But since 1863 arranging for parties to visit the Highlands had resembled, as Thomas said, 'a game of chess, in which attempts have been made to carry out competing operations without that regular sanction which the united English and Scottish Railways gave to previous arrangements'.[50]

However, other tourist attractions duly appeared: a Grand Gala at Ashby de la Zouch; a Workman's Conference in Brussels; new discoveries at Herculaneum; an incognito visit by the Queen to Switzerland; the changing face of London as a result of the construction of Blackfriars Bridge, Holborn Viaduct and the Thames Embankment, 'the finest river promenade in the world'.[51] When the Earl of Shrewsbury began to exploit, in the modern manner, his stately home at Alton Towers, Thomas Cook acted as his agent, extolling the place as 'a kind of earthly paradise'[52] and conveying as many as ten thousand people there at a time. The Earl occasionally protested about litter and rowdiness. But he must have been pleased when, in 1872, John conducted a special train taking the Duchess of Cambridge, the Tecks and assorted aristocrats to Alton Towers. John received not only their thanks but assurances that 'our system was perfectly understood and appreciated by our own Royal Family'.[53]

By the beginning of 1868 Thomas Cook claimed to have organized the travel of some two million people. The firm's three English offices were dealing with thirty thousand letters and fifty thousand enquiries each year. Thomas himself seemed almost surprised by the 'increasing and extraordinary interest and weight of our public obligations'.[54] But John was not satisfied. In that year he introduced the system of hotel coupons which gave a further boost to the business. Charging a small fee (though not taking a commission from hotels in the scheme), Cook sold eight-shilling coupons which entitled tourists to bed, two substantial meals, lights and attendance – but not alcohol. Hoteliers benefited from the increased custom and, according to a modern authority, resorts which were not part of Cook's network 'by and large failed to develop on the scale of those that were'.[55] Tourists benefited from the knowledge that they could not be overcharged, that they would have no difficulties over changing currency or disputes about tips, and that they could obtain a refund for unused coupons from 98 Fleet Street. Cook benefited from a favourable 'cash flow' – he received tourists' money before he had to pay hoteliers – and from the growing number of people attracted to his offices as a result of the system. By 1872 he had sold 120,000 sets of coupons, worth £20,000 to the 150 Continental hotels which had joined the scheme. In fact the coupons proved so popular and provided such a comprehensive service that Thomas thought they had 'to a very great extent done away with the necessity of any personally conducted tourist parties'.[56]

Although John established a 'vast department' to dispense coupons, snags did occur. In Switzerland, for example, the English were not content with rolls and honey for breakfast. According to that 'scale of gluttony which so mysteriously sets in as we land on the Continent', a journalist wrote, they demanded steak.[57] John made his coupons more flexible and issued a $1^{1}/_{2}$ franc supplement to cover it. This 'international dispute' provoked mirth in the columns of the *Saturday Review*.[58] But tourists were lavish in their praise of the system. One described the coupons as 'better than gold'.[59] *The Graphic* explained that through 'a Gladstonian flash of intellect' Thomas and John Cook had pierced the fallacy that hoteliers could not be systematized. It prophesied that the 'sagacious' new scheme

> must by-and-by supersede all others . . . Largely as travelling has been placed within reach of the multitude it is not half developed . . . A time will come when vast numbers of the population . . . will be carried enormous distances for ridiculous sums.[60]

This was a prescient forecast, for the hotel-coupon system helped to expand tourism until the 1920s when it perished, mainly as a result of fluctuating exchange rates. But *The Graphic* was wrong to attribute the invention of the system to Thomas and John Cook, something they never claimed themselves. John had in fact copied it from the scheme successfully introduced in 1865 by their arch-rival, Henry Gaze.[61]

Gaze also anticipated by a year Thomas Cook's arrival in the Middle East, which took place in 1869 and will be described in the next chapter. This one must conclude by appraising John Cook's contribution to his father's enterprise, a contribution acknowledged by his being made a full and equal partner in 1871.

During these years, in effect, John created the business. Or rather, he transformed his father's rickety mission of good will into an efficient and profitable commercial organization. Only someone of extraordinary resolve could have accomplished this, and John had that quality in abundance. As one commentator wrote, 'An iron will in an iron frame best describes John Cook in his prime. His tenacity of purpose was extraordinary: when he had once set his mind on anything nothing would shake him.'[62] Not least of his triumphs was, when confronted by the multitudinous frustrations of the tourist business, to exercise control over himself. Patience, his father's trump card, was not one of John's virtues. Fierce passions seethed beneath his dapper exterior and one observer fancifully suggested that not only time but 'the exasperating questions of the thousands of tourists whom he has piloted have worn the top of his shapely head as bare as a billiard ball'.[63] Once, John told his father, during protracted negotiations with Continental railway companies: 'I almost killed myself by suppressing my feelings, tongue, and feet.'[64]

Where his family and his staff were concerned, John sometimes did lose his temper. Tall, thick-set, abrupt, with flashing eyes and bristling beard, he was an intimidating figure. He was capable of physical as well as verbal violence: on one occasion he threw an insolent dragoman into the Nile; on another he did the same to a recalcitrant steamboat captain. However, in dealing with customers, hoteliers and transport managers he was calculatingly impassive and remorselessly persevering. He possessed organizational ability on a grand scale but, more than anyone, he appreciated that travel was a matter of detail. None was too small to escape his attention. He was an inveterate fusspot, meticulous to the point of obsession. Indeed, his infinite capacity for taking pains over the minutest circumstance of business was the key to his success. Yet if John was narrow-minded he was not mean-spirited: in a paternalistic way he looked after the interests of his employees. Honour was a duty as well as a commodity and he regarded agreements, verbal or written, as sacred obligations. But he was rightly described as 'a hard man at a bargain, shrewd and keen and persistently resolute to buy in the cheapest market' – and, it must be said, to sell in the dearest.[65]

This meant appealing to a richer section of the market, which was much more John's policy than his father's. When John entered the business in 1865 he was assisted at Fleet Street by a single clerk and an office boy, while Thomas recruited teetotal friends like John Ripley to help him conduct tours as necessary during the season. By 1871 his growing staff was finding it so difficult to attend to the daily influx of 250 letters (John insisted that they should be answered by return of post) and the hosts of callers (who at times had to queue for two hours) that he was urgently looking for larger and better premises. The firm also now employed four permanent 'travelling assistants', men like August Plagge, formerly manager of the Cockburn Hotel in Edinburgh, who were distinguished by their 'great suavity of manners and deportment'.[66] Such couriers were the gentlemen's personal gentlemen of travel and John increasingly tried to demonstrate that they performed a smart, expert and indispensable personal service. His case was greatly strengthened in 1870 when, paradoxically, Thomas Cook's business of peace was invigorated by the Franco-Prussian war.

At first, it is true, prospects looked black. The conflict interrupted the Passion Play at Oberammergau, where Cook's first parties were establishing a tradition which has prevailed ever since, namely that 'the British have been in an overwhelming majority among foreign guests'.[67] The war also revived those enemies of travel, the passport and the visa. Most seriously, from the Cooks' point of view, it disrupted regular traffic and provoked a 'panic' among tourists all over Europe. They returned home 'helter-skelter', leaving fashionable resorts like Baden-Baden empty. Cook was presented with a mass of unused tickets and 'unhesitatingly' refunded their cost though, as he noted, 'Our own risks and losses are very heavy.'[68] However, the crisis enabled the Cooks to demonstrate as never before their mastery of the travel scene. Their Fleet Street office was 'besieged with personal and written enquiries as to the safety of coming here or continuing on the Continent' and Thomas went on several 'tours

16 John Mason Cook – 'the Augustus Caesar of modern travel'
17 John, Emma and Frank Cook

18 The 'Cookii' in Egypt

19 Tourists climbing the Great Pyramid

20 Shepheard's Hotel, Cairo –
its style was 'Eighteenth Dynasty Edwardian'

21 Cook's office in the grounds of Shepheard's Hotel

22 Navigating the rapids during the Gordon Relief Expedition, 1884

23 Cook's first great steamer, *Prince Abbas*, at Abu Simbel

of observation' in order to answer them.[69] He also issued a 'Daily Bulletin of Continental News' containing the latest telegrams from his agents abroad. John arranged for tourists to go to and from England around the battle zone, notably to Brindisi via the Brenner Pass – Thomas initiated through tickets on this important route to the east. To give their service even wider publicity Thomas wrote a number of letters to *The Times*. He insisted, for example, that in spite of price rises in Switzerland 'my coupons retain their full value'.[70]

Although deploring the resurrection of the 'War Demon',[71] Thomas was not above exploiting it. In the summer he took a party of tourists down the Rhine, earning a magisterial rebuke for his 'doubtful taste' from *The Observer*.[72] (It had no effect, since the habit of regarding war as a spectacle, in the Crimean fashion, had not entirely passed away: later John conducted a group of tourists to within half a mile of the front line near Metz.) However, in September Cook paid another visit to Paris where he found 'the Rue d'Amsterdam blocked with baggage-laden cabs' and witnessed 'the exodus of frightened inhabitants'. On his return journey he also saw French preparations to 'blow up both [Seine] bridges and Prussians'.[73] By the end of the month, when Paris was under siege, even Cook acknowledged that 'France had ceased to be a country for tourists'. It was everywhere dominated by 'invincible, cigar-loving, fearless Teutons'.

Yet this situation gave him an even greater opportunity to shine. When the Archbishop of Canterbury, A.C. Tait, was told by his doctors that he must recruit his health by spending the winter on the French Riviera, Cook volunteered to organize the entire journey. He accompanied the Archbishop's party of sixteen down the Rhine, through the Brenner Pass, and from Genoa to San Remo. Everything went smoothly and when the Archbishop's sister set eyes upon 'the magician who wrought these wonders' she was surprised to see 'a quiet, middle-aged man, very much like a home-staying, retired tradesman' who spoke not 'a word of any language but his own'. Without his 'magic wand', she noted, they found the return journey far less easy – and not significantly cheaper.[74]

Even more than Thomas, John appreciated the prestige that accrued to the firm from such quasi-official missions. The younger Cook himself took part in a similar enterprise immediately after the Franco-German armistice and the consequent raising of the siege of Paris at the end of January 1871. His commercial object was to see if it was possible to take tourists to the French capital, but he also assisted with the transporting of 75 tons of provisions sent by the Lord Mayor of London's committee for the relief of Paris. The French railway service being in disarray, John travelled from Dieppe by coach, cart, horse and 'Shanks's Naggie'. En route he met Mr Challis, at his death in 1923 the oldest member of staff at Cook's, who acted as his interpreter and helped him through the Prussian cordon. In Paris John took food to M. Chardon, whose London and New York Hotel at 13 Place du Havre the Cooks used as their French headquarters, but he refused to eat it until he was assured that it had not been bought from the Germans.[75] During his forty-eight-hour stay John lived like the beleaguered citizens. He even sampled the horse-flesh soup, which he found 'excellent . . . but then it was not being forced down me at the point of the bayonet'.[76]

On his return John reported to the Lord Mayor, and to the press, that British gifts were being dispensed 'in the proper channel' though Paris was still 'closed'.[77] The firm's status was so enhanced by this expedition that before long 'members of the Royal Household' were applying to Cook's office 'for assistance to send provisions to their friends in Paris', though John himself advised that what was really required was money. Furthermore, when, in the summer of 1871, a member of the Legislative Assembly at Versailles expressed hostility towards the English excursionists (whom Cook had been taking 'to see the ruins of the city' since March) and proposed a heavy tax on passports, Thomas was in a good position to damn this 'mad ebullition of frenzy and mistaken policy'. Writing to Jules Favre, the Foreign Minister, he claimed that, like his son, the tourists were moved to visit Paris not so much by curiosity as by sympathy.[78]

By 1871, then, the firm of Thomas Cook was becoming, under John's aegis, both respectable and prosperous. People 'from the heir to the throne to the humblest greengrocer' were indulging in what one journalist called the 'good wholesome practice' of taking summer holidays.[79] And, as another wrote, Cook's tourists were 'pervading the whole globe'.[80] Cook's own organization was 'carried to a pitch of perfection' that was, in the *Daily Telegraph*'s view, 'really wonderful'.[81] Despite Continental troubles Cook arranged the travel of 105,000 people in 1871, including a large party of American Freemasons known as Knights Templar, the most influential and 'delightfully harmonious party' John had ever conducted.[82] By the autumn Thomas could see 'new and enlarged prospects of public service' opening up for their enterprise.[83] He 'repeatedly urged' his son to come into formal partnership with him. Indeed, he went so far as to offer John more than a half share in the business. But the younger man resisted, fearing that their disagreements could only increase. Eventually, no doubt persuaded by the glittering commercial prospects, he capitulated. But he insisted on an equal partnership and only for a fixed term of seven years: the deed would lapse at the end of 1878. Thus the firm acquired its full name – later perhaps the most famous trade name in the world – Thomas Cook & Son.[84]

Egypt and Beyond

In 1869, two years before the partnership was agreed, Thomas Cook embarked on what he called 'a great event in the arrangements of modern travel'.[1] He took his first tourists to Egypt and the Holy Land. As usual he somewhat exaggerated his own originality. Gaze had organized three small expeditions to the Middle East before Cook even went on his reconnaissance to Turkey, Syria, Palestine and Egypt, in the autumn of 1868. And as early as 1835 Murray's initial *Handbook* for Egypt was published, precursor of 165 different guides printed in England and America over the next eighty years. Soon the first steamers appeared on the Nile and by 1843 the British consul in Cairo was complaining of a 'flood' of tourists into Egypt, though it consisted of only about fifty people.[2] Over the next couple of decades many more visitors came, attracted by the climate, the antiquities, the natural life and beauty of the Nile valley or, as Flaubert's erotic odyssey suggests, by the dancing girls. The affluent lotus-eaters often took a Nile detour in the course of a longer journey. The more serious-minded visitors made it part of a pilgrimage to Palestine and Syria. Cook spoke for them when he said that it marked an epoch 'in one's life to be able to come and see these wonderful places and countries, and with the Bible in one hand and Murray in the other, to trace out sites and scenes immortalized by imperishable events'.[3]

Until Cook's time, however, these Middle Eastern journeys were fraught with dangers, difficulties and discomforts. The experience of a party making a forty-day camel trek from Jerusalem to Petra during the 1850s was typical: one lady died from disease and the rest were almost buried by a sandstorm and then robbed by Bedouin.[4] In his first guide to Syria and Palestine (1858) Murray advised that although travellers did not need compasses and sextants in the desert they should go armed and accompanied by an escort. But even Murray could provide no protection against smaller marauders, the voracious and ubiquitous insects. It is true that Harriet Martineau found Mr Levinge's patent sleeping-bag 'an inexpressible comfort',[5] but most people seemed to regard it as a kind of mummification. Nearly all travellers were bitten and some were moved to extraordinary flights of eloquence by their sufferings. In Tiberias a frenzied Kinglake imagined the Jews returning to the Promised Land had assembled a cosmopolitan convention of fleas:

> The smug, steady, importunate flea from Holywell Street – the pert, jumping 'puce' from hungry France – the wary, watchful 'pulce' with his poisoned stiletto – the vengeful 'pulga' of Castile with his ugly knife – the German 'floh' with his knife and fork, insatiate, not rising from table – whole swarms from all the Russias, and Asiatic hordes unnumbered – all these were there, and all rejoiced in one great international feast.[6]

Travellers in the Holy Land were vulnerable to assaults of all kinds because like 'the patriarchs of old', they had to be 'dwellers in tents'.[7] At least in Egypt there was Shepheard's Hotel, built by its John Bull owner on a site adjoining Cairo's Ezbekiyah Square, which he was said to have acquired from Abbas Pasha, Muhammad Ali's grandson, for the price of two whippets called Bess and Ben. But though Shepheard's was the best hotel in Egypt Mark Twain described it as the second worst on earth.[8] Staying there in 1867, Edward Lear likened Shepheard's to 'a pigstye mixed with a beargarden',[9] and it certainly left much to be desired in the way of comfort and cuisine until improvements were made during the 1870s. The Nile steamers were worse, stifling, cramped, sordid and verminous, though even they were preferable to the dahabeahs, sailing craft which Murray said should be sunk before a voyage to rid them of rats and 'other noxious inhabitants'.[10]

Finally, whatever perils he avoided in the Middle East, the traveller could not escape his Nemesis, the dragoman. This guide, interpreter and general factotum was as essential as he was execrated. Murray cited a contemporary's 'terse and humorous description' of the dragoman, who came in 'four species': 'the Maltese, or the able knave; the Greek, or the cunning knave; the Syrian, or the active knave; and the Egyptian, or the stupid knave'. Murray acknowledged that there were 'many exceptions'.[11] But often the dragoman did look upon travellers as 'so many well-fledged geese' which it was his 'bounden duty . . . to "pluck"'.[12]

Their exactions were the stuff of Victorian tourist tales. With some justification visitors regarded 'Baksheesh' as 'the national anthem of Egypt',[13] and while the dragomans kept beggars and touts at bay it was clear that they usually did so in order to funnel all available tourist cash into their own pockets.

Yet, even more than this exploitation, visitors hated being dependent on these exotic cicerones. The typical dragoman, dressed in light blue robes with a velvet jacket, gold chain and black silk scarf, made the most of his indispensability and sometimes lorded it over his white employer with what Cook himself called 'unbearable hauteur'.[14] Reflecting the feelings of his readers, Murray waxed hysterical about this dire inversion of the cosmic order. He advised against 'constant use of the stick'[15] but he insisted that visitors should not allow themselves to be humiliated by these dirty and ignorant 'rogues'. 'Above all,' he urged, 'keep the *dragoman* in his place.'[16] This, in effect, was what Thomas Cook accomplished over the next few years, part of his general policy of cushioning tourists against the rigours, even the realities, of Middle Eastern life. As early as 1874 a group of Egyptian dragomans wrote a letter to the London *Times* protesting that 'our living has been almost taken from us by the English agents monopolizing the conveyance of tourists to this country in large companies'.[17] Cook replied with asperity, contradicting most of the dragomans' assertions, citing the case of a Belgian count whom he had rescued after his dragoman had gambled away all his camping equipment, and grandly declaring that he (Cook) was looking after the interests of both regular customers and 'Archdukes of Austria and other States, and . . . English noblemen'.[18] He employed the best Egyptian guides. That the worst should suffer was a just reward for 'the overbearing conduct, the cupidity, and the non-reliability of the much-dreaded dragoman'.[19]

Cook could scarcely have expected such a speedy success after the problems he encountered in 1869. Luckily his first Middle Eastern venture is well documented, notably in the unpublished diary of one of the tourists, Miss Riggs. In her ingenuous fashion she conjures up the novelty of the Victorian travelling experience and gives an intriguing insight into the nature of early tourism. Over Mont Cenis, she records, 'great excitement and fear owing to the difficulty the engine had in working us up the winding and precipitous incline, sometimes stopping entirely and gasping dreadfully – fear lest we should all go backwards'. In Bologna some of the party grumbled because there were too few carriages at the station and they had to walk to the hotel. But Cook smoothed matters over, showing himself to be concerned about their comfort and a hard bargainer when they were over-charged for meals. He also arranged a special church service in English for them. By the time they boarded the Mediterranean steamer all were 'in good spirits', agreeing that 'we were a very harmonious party'. The cabins were stuffy and cramped, but the voyage was uneventful. When they reached Alexandria, however, Cook's thirty tourists had their first taste of the East, a riotous experience on which almost all visitors commented with varying degrees of indignation and amazement. A host of porters and hotel touts swarmed on board and besieged Cook's party. As Miss Riggs wrote, 'our luggage was seized by main force, very nearly falling into the sea, with vociferations beyond all description, by men of all colours and castes – never to be forgotten'.[20]

After this baptism of fire, Alexandria proved to be rather an anti-climax; Cook called it an 'Oriental-European agglomeration'. Cairo, too, thanks to the extravagance of the Khedive Ismail, had 'Parisian innovations', 'modern pleasure grounds, opera-house, theatre, circus, and *cafés chantants*, in the style of the *Champs Elysées*'.[21] But Miss Riggs found the bazaars 'most wonderfully Oriental'. The spectacle really was like something out of the Bible or the *Arabian Nights*: a sea of green palms, white roofs, turquoise domes and brown minarets; a jungle of antique streets filled with dirt, dust and dilapidation, strings of camels and asses carrying bundles of sugar-cane, flocks of sheep and goats, fly-ridden market stalls, men in flowing gallabeahs and red fezzes or white turbans, and veiled women revealing their submissiveness, according to Miss Riggs, in a land 'where all is tyranny and oppression'. With its 'capacious lounge' and dining room – Miss Riggs found the 'table d'hote tolerable' – Shepheard's Hotel was a refuge from all this. But once embarked on the tourist round – Cook's party climbed the Great Pyramid and admired the Sphinx – they were exposed to the full blast of the Cairene cacophony: whining beggars, howling dogs, screeching buzzards and braying donkeys. These last were a striking feature of the city's life. If the hansom was the gondola of London, the donkey was the cab of Cairo. Colourfully decorated, some with red, white and blue stripes, others with maroon brocade saddles and blue and silver necklaces, they bore names like Lord

Palmerston, Billy Button, the Prince of Wales and Champagne
Charlie. The donkey boys, 'lithe as lizards' and mischievous as
monkeys,[22] delighted to prod their sure-footed, long-suffering beasts
into a gallop when foreigners were aboard and Cook's party suffered
quite 'a few donkey tumbles'.[23]

In Cairo Cook hired two English-built steamers, the *Benha*
and the *Beniswaif* at a cost of £40 each. Miss Riggs found the
'commisariat' acceptable, with its daily routine of coffee at 8
o'clock in the morning, breakfast at 10, lunch at 1, dinner at 6.30
and tea at 8.[24] But the boats were not very clean and the tourists
suffered from what Cook delicately called 'F. sharps' though not 'B.
flats' – Victorian euphemisms for, respectively, fleas and bugs. Also
'captain, doctor, mates, pilots, stewards, engineers, stokers, cooks
and sailors of every grade, all look for backsheesh'.[25] On the same
errand, naked monks swam out to the steamers. Miss Riggs was
no more abashed by this (though Cook's brochures later advised
ladies to stay in the saloon when their boat passed the monastery)
than by the 'dancing girls . . . which the gentlemen patronized'.[26]
However she did note signs of resentment aboard the *Beniswaif* that
Cook chose to travel with Miss Riggs's group on board the *Benha*.

As for Cook himself, he was delighted 'to be conductor of a party
of intelligent enquirers to this wonderful land, and to this astonishing river'. But he felt a characteristic ambivalence about Egypt. He
admired the temples, 'mighty even in ruin', and he found the birds
that haunted the river as 'elegant and beautiful as they were in the
days of Egyptian glory'.[27] Indeed, his imagination was captured
by the magical experience of sailing on the Nile, itself 'as great a
wonder as its surroundings . . . the life of all that lives in Egypt'.

We seemed to be literally living amongst the Pharaohs and the
people of 3000 to 4000 years ago: their history, their lives, their
habits of work, play, and devotion being all delineated by colours,
incisions, reliefs of hieroglyphics, symbols, and inscriptions on the
walls, pillars, ceilings, tombs and other monuments of their art
and greatness.[28]

Yet mindful of the sufferings of the children of Israel before the
exodus and of the poor fellahin now at work under the blazing
sun, Cook concluded that Egypt had always been sustained by
'the prostrate and abject life of . . . slaves'. 'Owls and bats

occupy the dark recesses of the temples and tombs,' he wrote, 'and everywhere the curse of Omnipotence seems to be written in legible characters.'[29]

By chance the *Benha* and the *Beniswaif* were sailing in the wake of Edward, Prince of Wales. His party, a day or two ahead, was going up the Nile in a fleet of six blue and gold steamers each one towing a barge full of 'necessities and luxuries', among them 3,000 bottles of champagne and 4,000 of claret.[30] Although the Prince took time off to shoot large quantities of wildlife, lizards included – he had brought his own 'stuffer', or taxidermist, on the voyage – Cook did not catch up with him. The *Benha* first broke a paddle-wheel and then ran aground. But the coincidence of the two Nile cruises became a source of controversy. For William Howard Russell, the famous *Times* war correspondent who was in the royal entourage, afterwards asserted that Cook's party, some wearing 'eccentric head-dresses', had been 'in full cry up the river after the Prince and Princess'.

> Respectable people – worthy – intelligent – whatever you please,
> but all thrown off their balance by the prospect of running the
> Prince or Princess of Wales to earth in a Pyramid, of driving them
> to bay in the Desert, of hunting them in the recesses of a ruin.[31]

Actually there was little chance of this because the Prince displayed a sterling aversion to 'tumbledown' old temples.[32] Nor is there any solid evidence that Cook's party were engaged in a royal lion-hunt. Miss Riggs mentions missing the royalties a couple of times but she was apparently sorrier to have missed the illuminations in their honour at Karnak.

Like Cook himself, the members of his party were to be incensed by Russell's slurs, and they contributed to the grand remonstrance which the Napoleon of Excursionists subsequently addressed to the Prince of Wales. One, who considered that Russell was 'dizzy with Royal Patronage' penned a middle-class tourist's manifesto:

> It is not from the ranks of the associated tourists that the gaming-
> houses of Baden are supplied with frequenters, that the leading
> continental haunts of vice and dissipation procure much of their
> funds, or that we have those examples of silly snobbishness
> which have done so much to render the name of Englishmen
> contemptible on the Continent. No; we must look for these among

the crowd of purse-proud, independent, and selfish tourists, who
love to play the Grand Seignor.[33]

Arthur Sketchley's comic Cockney, Mrs Brown, was equally outspoken in her fashion. 'Fiddle-de-dee. Impertinent,' she cried.
Anyway she was sure ''is Real Ighness' would have been pleased
to fall in with some 'good honest Hinglish faces' after all those
'Turkey Blackamoors'. Maybe they all protested too much. Cook
later claimed that he had wanted to steer clear of the royalties
because prices in their vicinity would be higher, and it is true that
he did see the little donkey boys gloating 'over the *backsheesh* they
had drawn from the Prince of Wales'. But at the time he seemed to
regret having been unable to overtake the 'Royal tourist party' and
to give it 'a really English cheer on the Nile'.[34]

Perhaps Cook was chiefly piqued by Russell's patronizing description of him:

> The energetic gentleman who has incurred so much opprobrium
> for his organizing tendencies to lead tourists all over the world,
> inspired me with the notion that he is an honest outspoken
> bustling man, with a good deal of tact in his business, and
> considerable power of management.[35]

When Russell attacked 'bear-leaders', said Cook, he 'opens a
menagerie and cannot be surprised if Bruin should attempt to
retaliate upon his tormentor'. Cook therefore accused him of
'falsehoods', 'illiberal imaginings', even of eavesdropping, or as he
put it, 'earwigging'.[36] But Russell deserves to have the last word in
this period squabble, for his comments on the new phenomenon of
tourism indicate that it was reaching a watershed. It was still the
subject of artistocratic prejudice, yet on democratic grounds it was
reluctantly becoming accepted as inevitable.

> That it is a nuisance to the ordinary traveller to have his peace
> broken, to have a flood of people poured into a quiet town, to
> have hotels and steamers crammed, to see his pet mountain
> peak crested with bonnets and wideawakes, to behold his
> favourite valley filled up with a flood of 'mere English, whom
> no one knows,' I am not prepared to deny; but what are we to
> say to 'the greatest good of the greatest number?' Let us reflect
> and submit. The people at Alexandria were, as far as I could

judge, very respectable – it was only in the concrete they became disagreeable. Mr Monpensier Brown and Miss Clara de Mowbray may be capital companions as individuals, in the abstract, but as 'Cook's Tourists' they become an aggregate of terrors.

As Russell acknowledged, though, there was no stopping the advance of the 'enterprising contractors' of tourism. 'The Rocky Mountains, Japan, the Great Wall of China – "rien n'est sacré" from these vigorous sappers of travel for the million.'[37]

Actually the Nile almost put paid to the leading sapper on his maiden voyage. This was not because Cook drank the water; he did so 'with impunity', spurning the wine and bottled Bass which others took. (Indeed, glorying in his principles, he even drank water from the Jordan although he regarded taking it home for christenings as 'superstitious and ritualistic'.[38] Unhappily Jordan water contained 'a little too much substance and flavour' and it may well have caused the 'small annoyance of physical derangement' that Cook experienced in Palestine.)[39] No, while taking a Sunday bathe in the Nile Cook was carried off by a current and nearly drowned – the Arabs who rescued him thought that he had been grabbed by a crocodile. Cook soon recovered but the river, which was exceptionally low, caused further problems on the return journey. The steamers kept grounding and the captains, said Miss Riggs, grew 'very passionate'. For a time one of the steamers actually sailed off and 'left us in the lurch' and some of the passengers threatened to return to Cairo by train unless matters improved. Apparently they did improve, but when the *Benha* and *Beniswaif* at last reached the city everyone had to stay on board. So many people had come to attend a 'grand ball' in honour of the Prince of Wales that there 'was not a bed to be had'.

The second stage of Cook's first Middle Eastern tour was even more hazardous. Miss Riggs's party, now reduced to twenty-four, including eight ladies, travelled to Beirut by steamer. Here they chose horses for the 'long and arduous journey through Palestine. Most amusing scene, some ambitious for horses with spirit, others looking for quiet, sober ones.'[40] Then, accompanied by a dragoman, thirty-three servants and seventy animals, Cook's caravan set off down the coast to Caesarea before venturing into the unknown. For Cook had found it impossible to obtain much definite information about Palestine which was, the dragoman indicated, more a land of promises than the Promised Land.[41] Covering twenty to thirty miles a day, which meant spending up to eight hours in the saddle, left them 'all *stiff*'. But Miss Riggs's party were so 'delighted' with the camping arrangements that 'we thought ourselves in clover'. The sleeping tents were furnished with iron bedsteads, woollen mattresses, mosquito nets, carpets, tables and chairs. There were also tin baths and, according to Miss Riggs, '2 closets', though it is not clear whether this was the grand total. It would certainly not have been an excessive number for the whole party. But perhaps the ladies had equipped themselves with that traveller's friend, the Inodorous Standard Pail, which was disguised as a bonnet-box and sold by Fyfe's Repository of Scientific Inventions for Sanitary Purposes at 46 Leicester Square. Camping proved to be a splendid adventure. There was 'great amusement' when people fell over the guy ropes. Reveille at 4.30 a.m., with the tents coming down almost before the tourists had got up, involved a 'great scurry'.[42] The food was good and it was served in a saloon tent large enough to hold twenty-five people. A typical menu for breakfast (at 6 a.m.) offered : tea or coffee and milk; boiled eggs or omelettes; hot chicken; cutlets. Dinner might consist of hot soup followed by mutton or lamb; then goose or wild boar; then chicken or turkey; and finally a 'capital pudding' with fruit for dessert.[43] Lunch was usually a picnic on an equally lavish scale.

Nobody molested Cook's party en route, though at one 'cut throat place' the men felt it necessary to fire off their guns 'to let the Arabs know what customers we were'. However, in Jerusalem they were robbed. Earlier Cook had left Miss Riggs's group to visit one of their number who was ill in Jaffa (she later died and they 'all felt the solemnity of the event') and to bring up another lot of tourists. When the two parties camped together just outside the walls of Jerusalem they presented a tempting target. During the night £450 in gold was stolen from Cook's portmanteau and the tourists lost another £200. The Arabs responsible were soon caught and much of the money recovered. In further compensation the Turkish authorities confiscated a house at Bethlehem belonging to one of the thieves and gave it to Cook, who donated it to the Society for the Promotion of Christianity among the Jews. This was one of several proselytizing missions he supported in Palestine, for Cook was profoundly moved by the country's Biblical associations. So were his tourists. Miss Riggs declared that 'all Jerusalem is *Holy Ground*' and described it as 'the desire of my heart'.[44] Cook himself wrote:

It is from the summit of the Mount of Olives that Jerusalem, once 'the joy of the whole earth' is best seen, and my plan was to let as little of it, on the west side, be seen as possible, until the glorious sight of walls, domes, minarets, flat and dome roofed houses, burst at one view on the astonished beholder; and a glorious view we had on the bright day that we encamped under the walls of the city.[45]

The remainder of the journey, back to Beirut via Bethlehem, the Dead Sea, the Jordan (where they bathed separately), Jericho and Damascus, was uneventful, though at one point Miss Riggs noted: 'The Sheik has charge of us or we might be murdered.'[46] All the members of her party signed a testimonial to Cook thanking him for the 'honourable, efficient, and straightforward manner in which he has fulfilled his engagements'.[47]

Cook himself told the *Leicester Journal* that this Middle Eastern trip was 'the greatest event of my tourist life'[48] and he gave a lecture about it to 2,000 children and teachers in the Temperance Hall. He spoke in personal terms. Yet within three years, by 1872, Egypt and Palestine had become so commercially important to his firm that he could regard them as 'the two greatest features in our present programme'.[49] This was because the Middle East was a winter holiday resort. So, of course, was the Riviera at that time but visitors to the south of France had little need of Cook's agency. 'Personal supervision', as Cook said, was advantageous on tours to Egypt and Palestine (often continued to Turkey and Greece) which were difficult to manage even for the better-off traveller who had been accustomed to touring Europe independently.[50] At the same time, thanks to the forging of new European rail links, the eastern Mediterranean was more accessible to Cook's regular clientele, a class 'more serious intellectually ... and more comprehensive socially' than any which had gone before.[51] From Cook's point of view Middle Eastern tours were invaluable because they provided full-time work in what had hitherto been a seasonal business. This transformation was vital to its growth. As Cook wrote in 1873, now 'it is summer with us all the year round'.[52]

The Cooks immediately set about incorporating the Middle East into their system. They established through tickets to Alexandria at a cost of £20 (this figure, for first-class returns, soon fell to £18). To avoid the 'attacks of Eastern kleptomaniacs' and the exactions of a people 'utterly indifferent to every moral obligation', they extended their scheme of pre-payment via hotel coupons to the Middle East. Thomas wrote a guide-book containing everything from advice about dress – gentlemen should wear 'light tweed', ladies 'good woollens' – to maledictions on dragomans, 'haughty, imperious, dogmatic, violent, selfish'.[53] John Ripley promoted trade by giving lectures wearing Eastern costume – he dressed as both an Arab sheik and a Turkish lady. He and both Cooks conducted further parties to Egypt in 1869–70. John, who had to pay £1,848 in gold to charter the large new steamer *Beherah* for a party of forty-four tourists, was 'impressed with the idea that the traffic of the Nile might be considerably developed'.[54] On his return to Cairo he obtained the agency for the passenger service of the Khedive's Nile steamers. Soon these boats were smartened up, became known as 'Cook's steamers' and began to operate at a profit instead of a loss.[55]

Even though Thomas Cook could only muster a party of ten 'owing to the uncertainty in which I had been held by a Steamboat Company',[56] he was determined to witness the opening of the Suez Canal. This took place in the late autumn of 1869. Cook and his tourists sailed from Venice aboard the Levant Line's paddle-steamer *America* which had been fitted out as a 'floating hotel' for the occasion. On 16 November they found a state of high excitement at Port Said, with guns being fired off to welcome the visiting dignitaries, chief among them the Empress Eugénie of France. All the buildings were 'ablaze with gas, oil, and candles' and, Cook recorded, the ships' mastheads were 'covered with fantastically arranged lights and coloured fires'.[57] What he did not record was that the opening ceremonies were even more spectacular than planned because the fireworks dump at Port Said blew up and 'very nearly demolished the town'.[58] Next day an imposing procession of seventy ships, led by the imperial yacht *Aigle* (with the *America* lying thirty-sixth in line), steamed through the Canal. After mooring for the night they arrived in Ismailia, a new town which owed its existence to Ferdinand de Lesseps, architect of the Canal. Here the 'festive arrangements' were 'conducted on a scale of the utmost prodigality'. Cook noted severely:

> champagne and other costly wines flowed like water; thousands
> met at the Palace of the Khedive to dance, talk and sup together;
> a wild military exhibition of Arabs and Bedouins was arranged for

the gratification of the visitors; fireworks and illuminations closed the night, and thousands slept in tents specially provided for the occasion.

After four days most of the ships had passed into the Red Sea and many of the spectators returned to Cairo by rail. Cook himself was content to repose 'at a point evidently not very far from that spot where the persecuted Israelites rested from the pursuit of their oppressors'.[59]

His mind soon turned to the moral consequences of what was plainly a 'great triumph of science and persevering energy'[60] – even *Punch* could no longer ridicule de Lesseps's great excavation as an 'impossible trench'.[61] No one appreciated better than Cook that vice travelled as well as virtue, and he believed that the revolutionary new thoroughfare posed a fresh missionary challenge. For

> greedy and reckless speculators and a race of avaricious
> adventurers have taken their positions at the terminal and
> intermediate stations of this new highway of the seas, and
> these have been accompanied by a race of harpies of the vilest
> composition, who pander to the worst passions of corrupt
> humanity. Corruption assumes the worst features of unblushing
> merchandise, and souls as well as bodies, priceless virtues as well
> as substantial realities, are imperilled at the shrines of filthy lucre.
> Conspicuous in Port Said, Ismailia, and Suez, are pictorial and
> living representations of vice, whilst it is next to impossible to find
> a good book of any kind.

But while such jeremiads fell easily from Cook's lips, he was confident that good would conquer evil in an open encounter. By carrying 'the Commerce of the world' and by easing the passage of 'Cook's Tours to the Four Quarters of the Globe', the Suez Canal could become, so to speak, a channel of grace. The vital waterway, which the British soon came to regard as the jugular vein of their empire, captured Cook's imagination. 'Africa is converted into an island,' he declared, and the joining of the Mediterranean and Red Sea was 'a fact of immense importance'.[62] He described his own passage through the Suez Canal as 'one of the red-letter days of my tourist life'.[63]

While in Egypt on this occasion Cook gathered more information about tourism throughout the Middle East and soon he and his son improved the service in Palestine. They imported vast quantities of provisions, including English ham, Yorkshire bacon, potted salmon, tinned sardines and jars of marmalade, as well as an improved stock of camping equipment. In 1873 they established an office in the grounds of Shepheard's Hotel and an agency in Jaffa. Gradually, too, the Cooks built up a reliable team of dragomans, couriers, porters and boatmen, poaching some of Gaze's staff if he is to be believed. Tourists benefited from all this in many ways, not least when they landed at Jaffa or Alexandria. The 'rude and clamorous' greeting was soon reserved for those unfortunates who were not travelling on Cook's tickets. When Thomas arrived at Alexandria in 1877 he recorded:

> Under our own bright flag, representing the Union Jack and 'Cook's Boatmen', eight or nine fine boatmen, clad in scarlet jackets with 'Cook's Tours' on the breast, came and took possession of passengers and baggage, and at the Custom House another set of porters, in blue jackets, with the same words on the breast took possession of baggage, none else presuming to touch it. The conquest over an excited rabble has been triumphant.

Cook's agent said, 'I will put you through like a shot' and he was as good as his word. The whole procedure, from boat to carriage, took twenty minutes.[64]

However, taming the Middle East in the interests of tourism was no easy matter. Despite every effort some journeys went disastrously wrong, amid bitter recriminations. As Thomas wrote, 'We have all too often seen parties in sunshine all joyous and complimentary, who, under the influence of storm and inundated pathways, are too prone to complain and murmur.'[65] He himself conducted just such a party of 'Cookii' (as the Arabs called them) through Palestine in the spring of 1871. According to Isabel Burton, the explorer's wife, who encountered them in Beirut, they were an 'incongruous assemblage', so much so that 'the enterprising Mr Cook' must have advertised for them and then picked 'the queerest'. Certainly they were dogged by every sort of problem, atrocious weather, illness, stampeding animals, collapsing tents, falls from horses. They were delayed in Damascus because one of their number insisted on being supplied with beer and, as Cook noted with grim satisfaction, en route some of the bottles exploded. A lady known as 'the Sphynx' had an equally alarming adventure, as Isabel Burton recorded: 'It appears that her bower falling at the stroke of 6 disclosed the poor thing in a light toilette, whence ensued a serious quarrel.'[66]

After further difficulties, Cook recounted disgustedly, 'one of the sagacious grumblers of the party suggested the formation of a *Committee* to superintend the travelling arrangements of the next four days, over roads of which not an inch was known to any of the Tourists save myself'. Eventually the grumblers insisted on cutting short their trip and returning to Beirut, at some cost to Cook. He felt sorry about the disappointment, sorrier still that he had accepted such temperamental tourists 'into our ranks', and sorriest of all for himself. Anyone could see 'how much personal annoyance I had to endure', including 'undeserved imputations of inattention and distrust'.[67] Isabel Burton, at least, was sympathetic:

> Mr Cook is obliged, with a large caravan, to make certain rules which must be kept with military precision. Every now and then some one who is unused to any restraint resents, and quarrels about it. Mr Cook takes it all so quietly and good-humouredly, never notices or speaks of it, nor loses his temper, but goes quietly on his way, carrying out the programme, as a nurse should act towards a fractious child. I have often thought, What a knowledge of human nature he must have acquired, and what curious experiences he must have had![68]

Other visitors had equally unhappy Eastern experiences. 'Gyppy tummy' was as prevalent then as it is now and tourists sometimes recorded that most of their party were 'more or less ill'.[69] Sunstroke and heatstroke were also common in spite of, or because of, the elaborate Victorian precautions taken against them – Murray recommended wearing wool next to the skin since linen 'checked' perspiration and 'fever or diarrhoea is the result'.[70] Tourists' health was not improved by the dragomans' habit of keeping to 'the beaten track',[71] with the consequence that campsites became filthy and fly-ridden. Many visitors to Palestine found the long rides a form of torture. W.H. Leighton, who kept a journal of his tour in 1874, wrote that he 'arrived at the camp in a state only to be envied by one just broken on the wheel'.[72] (In the 1870s John Cook provided English saddles and side-saddles in place of the excruciating Arab ones and in the 1880s he imported specially built private landaus.

They were 'the *only* comfortable carriages to be found in Palestine' and a notable improvement on the earlier conveyance from Jaffa to Jerusalem which was described as 'a compromise between the ancient ark, a modern dray and a threshing machine'.)[73]

Many tourists suffered from what is known, in the cant phrase of today, as 'culture shock'. They were horrified by ragged slum-dwellers, importunate beggars, mangy dogs and decrepit donkeys. Cook received frequent pleas to ameliorate the cruel lot of Egyptian donkeydom. He could do little, but he and his clients did a great deal in the way of charity towards the human inhabitants. It is recorded, for example, that 'At one place the Cook's tourists fed 1,000 people with bread.'[74] On the other hand some were given to crude forms of racial prejudice. One American wrote to the New York *Observer* complaining about 'the Officers and crew' of the Nile steamers 'being natives', to which Thomas Cook feebly replied that his firm only acted as agent for the Egyptian government.[75] Yet foreigners were shocked by the condition of women and slaves in the Middle East. After visiting a slave market in Constantinople John Ripley wrote: 'We left the dirty den with our hatred of Eastern abominations very much intensified.'[76]

It is difficult to say how far male tourists took their patronage of the dancing girls, who dispensed with 'all outer adornment of person – except noserings and necklaces' and tattoos[77] – and whose performances were 'indecorous to a degree'.[78] But, the opportunity for sexual adventure being so much a part of the allure of travel, some may have formed fleeting liaisons like that described by a British officer who went up the Nile in 1884:

> I bought a very lady like little girl for £16. I kept her en pension
> and gave her the best of everything. A brougham, champagne,
> the finest gowns and bonnets, of the Dongola standard. This all
> ran to 2 piastres a day. I wept over her on leaving and sold her
> for £10.[79]

The bolder men certainly visited the hashish dens and the red-light districts of Cairo, and at the beginning of the twentieth century one excitable moral reformer claimed that tourists 'scarcely ever leave the land of the Pharaohs' without calling at a licensed brothel known as Madame Fatima's.[80] Furthermore, according to Sir Sidney Low, who wrote a chapter called 'The Clients of Cook' in his book about

Egypt, lurid stories circulated 'in Cairo of the relations of some European lady-visitors towards certain of the picturesque Arab ruffians who swagger about in the capacity of dragomans'.[81] But many tourists were apparently more repelled than attracted by what they took to be Asiatic sexual decadence. At Damascus one of the Cook's diarists saw a marionette display 'which represented beastliness beyond any you would even credit a Turk with'.[82]

Despite all the drawbacks, Middle Eastern tourism under Cook's auspices flourished during the 1870s. Stray statistics survive. By 1872 the firm had taken 400 passengers to Egypt and 230 to Palestine. In 1873 another 200 went up the Nile. From Palestine alone during the mid-seventies Cook made a profit of £800 in one year and £1,500 in another. In 1879, John Cook claimed, more than three-quarters of British and American visitors going to the Holy Land travelled under his arrangements. By 1882 Cook had conducted 5,000 visitors to Palestine.

Cook's advance can also be charted in the changing responses of tourists. Early in 1877, for example, Captain John Ardagh joined a party on board one of the Khedive's mail steamers, 'now virtually in the hands of the enterprising Mr Cook', going from Cairo to Aswan and back at a cost of £46 (to include everything except liquors and gratuities). In his unpublished account Ardagh confesses that he was hesitant about embarking on the voyage:

> The enjoyment of such a trip depends in a very high degree on
> the individuals forming the party, and Cook's Tourists in general
> do not possess a very high character among travellers. Enquiries
> tended to prove that the parties who had previously gone up
> under the auspices of Cook were neither happy nor contented.

However Ardagh could not afford the time or the money to make the journey by dahabeah and he found that his thirteen fellow passengers, all male, 'pulled well together'. They consisted of three clergymen, the Hon. Fred Wynn (son of Lord Newborough), a manufacturer, a 'very intelligent' Scot, a 'deeply religious' philanthropist from Manchester, two Italians (one of them a parliamentary deputy), an ex-infantry officer, an 'inveterate traveller' and two men who had no 'ostensible means of livelihood, and [were] therefore according to polite logic – gentlemen'. With this congenial company the voyage proceeded smoothly, if not quietly

– as the steamer passed by 'the whole riparian population of the Nile shout *backsheesh* with one accord'. The 'feeding and service were good'. They enjoyed the sightseeing. Because there were no ladies on board they could stay up late and smoke everywhere in the boat, which they found comfortable and spacious. Ardagh concluded: 'The result was a very agreeable surprise, for I have never spent such an interesting and pleasant time elsewhere.'[83]

It was an experience shared by more and more voyagers on the Nile.[84] Yet the old-fashioned habit of disparagement survived. The English in Egypt had a saying that 'we had four seasons, which we distinguished as follows: First, flies; second, mosquitoes; third, flying bugs; fourth, Cook's tourists'.[85] From Amelia Edwards in 1877 to Marie Corelli twenty years later, women were particularly liable to sneer at Cook's cheap Nile trippers and as late as 1914 a writer like Sir Sidney Low, who hailed Cook as a 'man of genius', could still be found referring to 'strange cohorts of the personally conducted'.[86] Still, the Khedive was impressed by John Cook's progress and with the several hundred thousand pounds a year which, it was estimated, his tourists spent in Egypt. At high Nile in 1875 he gave John permission to take a small steamer over the first cataract and initiate a regular passenger service between Aswan and Wadi Halfa. He also appointed Cook to be the sole agent for the mails.

Thomas did not share the Khedive's confidence in John, who in 1876 spent 'a lot of money' to improve the steamboat service and to open a hotel in Luxor where a physician would be stationed, thus 'realising the idea of a sanatorium'.[87] This was the beginning of John's dominance of tourist traffic on the Nile. It was also the origin of Luxor as a health resort, especially for people suffering from pulmonary diseases who were thought to benefit from the dry air. However Thomas so disapproved of this investment that it became a major cause of dissension between them. It was reported that 'when the son embarked heart and soul upon the great scheme of Egyptian passenger traffic which has produced such splendid results, the father gave him formal notice through his solicitors that he would not permit any of the capital of the firm to be engaged in the undertaking'.[88]

Evidently they reached some compromise. For the Luxor Hotel's second season, in 1878, John added a new wing, doubling its capacity to about forty-five bedrooms. But two years later Murray's

Handbook roundly criticized the hotel. Although set amid beautiful gardens about 350 yards from the Nile, its accommodation was 'not good', it cuisine was 'poor and unsuited to invalids', its board and lodging, at fifteen shillings a day plus extras, were 'very dear'. In 1880 John made significant improvements. The hotel was so transformed that Murray soon described it as 'excellent'.[89] John also signed a ten-year contract with the Khedive which gave him complete control over the Nile steamers, fittings and appointments as well as day-to-day running, though the hulls, machinery and crews (but not waiters or servants) remained the responsibility of the government. These vessels were now over twenty years old, and in Europe they would have been sent to the scrapyard. But John refurbished them and operated all departments with meticulous efficiency. For instance, he controlled their coal consumption to 'prevent us being robbed in the same manner that we know the Government has been robbed'.[90] Murray was soon reporting that the steamers were 'fairly comfortable and the food good',[91] whereas previously he had recommended travelling by dahabeah.

In 1882, when the nationalist revolt of Arabi Pasha was crushed in what Sir Garnet Wolseley regarded as 'the tidiest little war ever fought by the British army',[92] John took the wounded from Cairo to Alexandria at cost price. He also visited the battlefield of Tel-el-Kebir exactly seven weeks after Wolseley's victory and arranged steamer trips up the Nile for the General and his staff and for soldiers convalescing from enteric fever. Two years later John offered to buy the 'whole fleet of steamers' from the Khedive Tewfik (who had replaced his bankrupt father in 1879), making payments by annual instalments from fees he charged the government for postal, towage and other services.[93] But the Gordon relief expedition intervened, finally wearing out the existing steamers and giving John the opportunity to build a new fleet of his own. By that time – the mid-1880s – John had, in the words of a friend, 'fallen under the spell of the Nile and it became his darling hobby to exploit its possibilities, and by means of its attractions to charm into his net the big fish who so far had disdained to be classed in the category of Cook's tourists'.[94]

Before he attained this position in Egypt, however, his greatest coups occurred in Palestine. In 1881, for example, John arranged what he modestly described as the most gigantic travelling enterprise 'since the days of the Crusaders'.[95] This was to transport a party of some thousand French pilgrims on a round trip from

Marseilles to Jerusalem. The French consul in Jerusalem actually tried to stop it, telegraphing that: 'The thing cannot be done; if attempted it will prove a disastrous failure.' John replied: 'We will undertake the work and agree to make it a success.' Everything was arranged on the largest scale: horses, mules, donkeys and camels, 1,500 in all at a cost of £4,000, were collected, some from as far afield as Aleppo; 50 dragomans, 150 cooks and waiters and hundreds of muleteers and other servants joined the throng; a mass of camping equipment was acquired, including two huge dining marquees each capable of seating five hundred people.

Although the party included 356 priests, 185 ladies and 100 'people of rank' some of them 'acted at first more like a rabble than a company of pious pilgrims'. However piety set in once they reached Jerusalem. The long procession, 'to solemn chanting . . . filed through the narrow gate and streets to the church of the Holy Sepulchre, the important goal of the pilgrimage'. All were 'more than satisfied with the general management' and they returned to Marseilles without accident save for, according to a brusque American account, 'an elderly gentleman who lost his life simply by his own carelessness'.[96] John Cook himself was much less than satisfied. The advertisement was all very well but the reward was not. Kicking himself for having, like his father, mixed business with religion, John declared that the French pilgrimage committee were 'simply a set of Jesuitical thieves'. He told a member of his staff: 'I have made up my mind never to have anything to do with another French Pilgrimage without seeing my way to a good profit.'[97]

Much more gratifying, thirteen years after William Howard Russell's supercilious attack on his father, was the commission to conduct the Prince of Wales's two sons, Prince Albert Victor and Prince George, on a forty-day tour of the Holy Land. John's son Frank took charge of the party and John himself received a letter from the Princes' tutor, Canon Dalton, thanking him 'for the energy and promptitude with which each difficulty as it arose was always faced and overcome'.[98] During the royal progress, incidentally, the future King George V, envious of the 'luxuriant beard' sported by one of Cook's staff, Mr Aquilina, sought his advice about cultivating a similar growth.[99] Hence the famous royal beaver.

John's achievement in the Holy Land, though less conspicuous (and less profitable) than his achievement in Egypt, was perhaps even more impressive. In 1858 Murray had insisted that travellers in the region '*must* employ' the Bedouin as 'guides and guards. No foreigner can traverse their territory except under their protection.'[100] Thirty years later all talk of escorts and dangers had disappeared from his handbooks and the country presented relatively few difficulties to tourists. John contributed signally to this state of affairs.

Not the least of his problems was a vicious feud with a former employee called Rolla Floyd, which dragged on until the end of the century. Floyd was one of the few remaining members of an American colony of 'Latter-Day Saints' who had come to Palestine a few years before. He began to work for the Cooks as a superior dragoman in the early 1870s, finding both of them 'sharp business men', especially in their dealings with him. By 1877 they had committed their 'entire local arrangements' to his care and the following year they signed a short-term contract giving Floyd a third share of their profits in Palestine. In 1880 he acknowledged that Cook's was 'the best business I can do in this country' but there were so many tourists that 'it may be too much for me'. In particular he could not cope with the book-keeping. That year John Cook came to Palestine and asked Floyd to sign a new long-term agreement. This the American, who hankered to return to his native land, refused to do. Then John discovered that Floyd had apparently stolen $7,000 from the firm, dismissed him from its service and induced him to sign a paper admitting the theft. Floyd later maintained that he had signed unknowingly, that any peculation had been due to incompetence not dishonesty, and that Cook had only got rid of him because he would not commit himself to manage the business. Being discharged, said Floyd, was 'so unexpected that if one had tied & thrown me into the sea it could not have surprised me more'.

Floyd now set himself up in competition with Cook. Only his side of the story survives, but it is clear that their rivalry turned into a full-scale vendetta. In December 1881 Floyd wrote: 'I have had the good fortune to take 4 passengers away from Cook, and made a small profit, also gained a great victory in doing so . . . . I will beat Cook in all kinds of business.' In 1882 John came to Palestine for three weeks and, according to Floyd, 'went away like a *Dog*'. But, he added, Cook had offered to pay the Bedouin $5,000 for his head. Although he believed a 'barking dog will never bite . . . I am sure Cook would give twice that sum if some one would get me out of the way'. In 1883 Floyd managed to inveigle General Gordon away from 'Cook's brutes' and several skirmishes followed.

Once Cook's boatmen hit Floyd over the head and threatened 'to cut me in pieces'. Floyd charged 25 per cent less than Cook. He also tried to monopolize the best places to eat. Cook retaliated by hiring all the draft animals in Jaffa, by bribing officials and by entering into a partnership with Alexander Howard, who had been the dragoman on Thomas's first tour of Palestine in 1869. This partnership eventually triumphed, though the struggle was long and bitter. By 1898 Floyd was writing dispiritedly: 'Tourist business has become so bad, that there is nothing to be made out of it.'[101] In the same year John Cook personally conducted the German Emperor to Jerusalem.

Floyd's account of all this, though always partial and sometimes unbelievable, does convey a vivid impression of the difficulties that John had to overcome in Palestine. Yet the Middle East was just a small part of his steadily ramifying concern. As early as 1869 Thomas Cook told a Scottish audience, with considerable hyperbole, that he 'had now accomplished the immense object of having tours in the four quarters of the globe'.[102] In 1872, when Cook conducted the first party of tourists ever to travel round the world, the firm's ambitions really did extend to the ends of the earth. As a contemporary exclaimed at about that time, 'The world belongs to Thomas Cook.'[103]

Around the World

Taking a tour round the world was the last great challenge facing Thomas Cook. Such a record-breaking voyage would set the seal on his claim to be the creator of modern tourism. Cook was not a vain man but he was proud of his pioneering achievements. And he would scarcely have been human if he had ignored the blandishments of a press that was now tending to compare him to the eighteenth-century circumnavigator whose name he shared. The *Daily News* for example, said that Cook was 'regarded by thousands as a greater man than the Captain, his famous namesake'. For useful though it was to 'discover Botany Bay, and to cause its adoption as a criminal colony', to become the means of transporting 'your honest countrymen and countrywomen to the most elevating scenes and associations in the world, of lifting them out of the dull round of everyday life, and of bringing them back heartier, happier and better, is a higher and more useful discovery still; and this is the position Cook, the excursion agent, fills to-day'.[1]

Cook also had a commercial motive for girdling the globe. Improvements in communications, notably the opening of the Suez Canal, now made it a relatively straightforward operation, at least in theory. Cook was anxious to see how easy it was in practice so that other tours could follow. But most of all he wanted to satisfy his high-minded curiosity, both about the United States, where he was starting again with a new office and a new partner and hoping to bind the two English-speaking peoples together in 'harmony and fraternity', and about the Far East and India, where he wished to gauge the success of efforts to stop the heathen in his blindness bowing down to wood and stone. As Cook wrote just before his departure in the autumn of 1872, he aimed to inspect the

> great Railway work of the vast American Continent, the
> connecting lines of steamboat communication, and to test the
> practicability and safety of recommending others to follow in

our march. We also wish most heartily and have long desired, to see once more the Americans at home, and to learn from actual observation the social condition of the thousands who have left old England and other lands for the vaunted new world of Mormondom; and hoping to steer safely through the reported rowdyism of California, it is worth a long voyage to witness the changes in favour of liberty and truth that come to us from Japan. We wish to get a glance of John Chinaman at home, and to see the intermixtures of English settlers and traders in the Chinese ports. British India has many attractions for an English traveller, and our desire is to see how the influences of Anglian society, government, and Christian and philanthropic efforts, show themselves in Calcutta and Bombay, and other places.[2]

John, too, was eager for his father to be gone. It did not matter that his party was a small one – eight people initially – for he might pick up more in the United States. John wrote: 'It is a journey you *ought* to make and you will never have a better opportunity.'[3] It is plain that John had an ulterior motive, that he felt he could run the firm more efficiently in his father's absence. Better management was particularly vital at this time because the business was being plagued by the problems of 'unparalleled success'.[4]

New offices such as those opened in Birmingham and Venice increased custom dramatically. France abolished her passport regulations and a flood of English tourists swept into Paris, where traces of the siege were being removed and the Commune was, in the words of the *Excursionist*, 'beginning to be regarded as a hideous dream'.[5] Switzerland enjoyed the 'greatest season ever known', with 'universal crowding'.[6] Other Continental holiday resorts were equally full for, as the *Saturday Review* said, those who swarmed abroad 'to spend their brief leisure in conscious or unconscious submission to the will of Mr Cook' viewed those who stayed at home 'as a kind of social monstrosity'.[7] Everywhere, Thomas wrote, 'demand for personal assistance, or companionship, seems to increase with the facilities for travel'.[8] The firm of Thomas Cook was becoming ever more of an institution: it was 'generally approved' and the 'highest and best in the land acknowledge its utility'.[9]

In August 1872 receipts at 98 Fleet Street amounted to about £1,000 a day and the office was overwhelmed. Anyway, the lease was soon due to expire. John was determined to find larger and smarter premises. The trouble was that his father still did not trust him. In 1870 Thomas had actually accused his son of 'manipulating the cash for [his] own purpose', whereupon John left work in a dudgeon and did not return until fetched from home by his father two days later. Before the partnership deed was signed Thomas admitted that the business needed a bigger London office but he refused to take the responsibility for acquiring it. However, he gave John permission 'to build on [his] own speculation' and to take what money he needed so long as the business was not affected – a singularly vague injunction.[10] The matter remained in the air, but John was clearly determined to settle it while his father was travelling round the world. Thomas himself was so anxious to be off that he neglected to say farewell to his half-brother, James Smithard, who was seriously ill and died before his return. For this failure Thomas 'reflected most bitterly on myself'. From the other side of the globe he wrote to his wife Marianne: 'I do remember my faults this day. May God implant deep on my heart the sad lesson.'[11]

The first and worst stage of a journey that would take Cook 25,000 miles in 222 days was made on the White Star Line's *Oceanic*, which left Liverpool on 26 September 1872. Storms battered the ship and though Cook 'strove against the enemy' he was terribly seasick. When the Atlantic at last subsided he was able to inspect the vessel (which was carrying many 'rational-looking' emigrants) and to address his fellow passengers on 'THE BUSINESS OF PLEAS-URE'.[12] In New York Cook went sightseeing, conferred with his new American partner, the Knight Templar E.M. Jenkins, and heard Henry Ward Beecher deliver a 'marvellous sermon'. Then he proceeded, via Niagara, Detroit and Chicago (rising 'phoenix-like' from its own ashes), to Salt Lake City. The trip was a lively one: 'Prairie fires on all sides, antelopes, wolves, and Indians kept us in a state of almost constant excitement.' But the Sioux, though 'armed to the teeth', waved and whooped in a friendly manner. Cook found the open Pullman cars a vast improvement on 'boxed-up' English carriages, as was the streamlined system of baggage handling. In sleeping cars, however, 'the admixture of strangers and sexes is very repulsive to English travellers' and emigrant trains were markedly inferior to the European third class.[13] American hotels, where '*Iced Water* is *The Beverage of the Tables*'[14] and 'great attention is paid to the privacy and comfort of ladies', he considered to be the best in the world.

In Utah Cook saw 'the great Temple' slowly rising from its foundations and met a number of Mormons. But in the letters he sent home, which *The Times* and other journals were happy to print, he refused to discuss questions such as polygamy and 'celestial marriages', sticking to safe topics like the impressive agricultural achievements of Brigham Young's followers.[15] His party was disappointed with the Rocky Mountains but its members found the Sierra Nevada, though scarred by the gold-diggings, 'grand beyond description'. After 170 hours on board trains they reached San Francisco, 'a fine city of noble streets and fresh business – wonderful as a *new* place'. As he inspected the markets of the 'golden gate of the West', which were 'teeming with the richest and most delicious fruits, including fine strawberries, grapes, apples, pears, plums, &c', Cook could hardly believe 'that we are entering upon a Californian winter'.

Apart from a single bout of 'mad turbulence'[16] the Pacific lived up to its name, and Cook was only 'once or twice a little sickly'. The service aboard the paddle-steamer *Colorado*, provided by pig-tailed Chinese, was equally smooth; Cook had never seen 'more industrious and attentive waiters and berth porters'. However, his party's European servants 'complained of their being located close upon the Chinese steerage passengers' (one of whom was taking home his father's bones in a bag which he used as a pillow). So Cook allowed a white servant to share his cabin.[17] Nothing else occurred to mar the twenty-four-day voyage (except for the puzzling disappearance of twenty-four hours) and Cook reflected airily that 'this going around the world is a very easy and almost imperceptible business'.[18]

Cook was enthralled by the 'wonderful empire' of Japan. This was largely because it was fast emerging from what he took to be an obscurantist seclusion and seemed to be modelling itself on Western civilization, particularly on that of liberal, Christian England. In Yokohama his party (now amounting to ten) stayed in a 'thoroughly English hotel' and ate the 'best beef' he had tasted since he left home.[19] English notices were common and the English language predominated on the new railway. Yet Cook was also fascinated by Japan's native culture. He took his party to the Temple of Shiba and the Tombs of the Tycoons in Yedo (only just made accessible to foreigners) 'which for richness in carving, gilding, and decoration surpass all that I have seen in any land'.[20]

He was delighted, too, by the friendly reception where two years previously Europeans would have needed a military escort. He told his wife that their line of thirteen rickshaws (a novel invention – Cook bought two and sent them home, giving one to John's children) pulled by coolies, caused 'as much sensation as there would be in Granby Street if thirteen Japs were carried in procession' through Leicester.[21] All through the clean streets they were greeted by laughing and cheering people, who crowded in on them whenever they stopped at a shop, exhibition or temple. At Osaka and Nagasaki where, Cook said, the feared daimio warlords had mostly settled down and opened bazaars, his party enjoyed the same kind of reception. They were tempted to buy lavishly from the marvellous display of figured porcelain, embroidered silks, ebony and japanned goods.

The Inland Sea of Japan 'surpassed all [Cook's] dreams of beauty of that island and mountain-studded lake'. He went into raptures over it.

> I have seen almost every lake in England, Scotland, Ireland, Switzerland, and Italy, but this surpasses each of them, and combines the best features of them all in one. Such clusters of grotesquely-formed hills and mountains, and all so richly clad with brushwood, trees, and open carpets of the most brilliant verdure, encircling the windings of narrow passes, running into creeks and bays in seeming defiance of all geographical observations, that there is a perfect bewilderment of ever-changing but never-ending beauties.[22]

Though muddy, the Yellow Sea of China was equally serene. But sailing over it Cook suffered 'a little from constipation'. This was a disorder which must often have afflicted Victorians abroad, to judge at least by their revulsion to alien lavatories, overflowing chambers of horrors full of abominable effluvia and 'pencilled obscenities', not to mention the 'moustached foreigner ... with his waistcoat unbuttoned, cigar in mouth, and his hands fumbling at his braces'.[23] Cook at once 'took a couple of Mr Turner's family aperient pills which had the desired effect'.[24]

China proved a sad contrast to Japan. In Shanghai 'narrow, filthy, and offensive streets, choked and almost choking bazaars, pestering and festering beggars in every shape of hideous deformity; sights, sounds, and smells all combined to cut short our promenade of the "native city"'. Owing to a miscalculation over steamer times

Cook and his party missed seeing Canton altogether and could only glance at Hong Kong, 'another edition of English life'. They then went on to Singapore where they liked the charming botanical gardens, coconut groves and pineapple plantations, and found in the strange mixture of races 'a prolific theme for Ruskinesque dissertation and discrimination'. Cook was also delighted to see a signboard advertising the *Temperance Star*, than which, he quipped, no constellation in the sky blazed more brightly. After visiting Penang, which was 'close and hot',[25] the tourists celebrated an incongruous Christmas on board the *Mirzapore* in the Bay of Bengal. As Cook told his wife, they had 'decorations and mottoes in evergreens but no other sign of Christmas – no Yule block, no snow falling, no skating, no midnight orgies, no hot elder wine or other cordials to stimulate and madden the drinkers'.[26]

Cook was thrilled at the prospect of inhaling 'Ceylon's spicy breezes'. But while paying dutiful tribute to the 'odours of delicious fragrance' emitted by the cinnamon groves, he seems to have been rather overcome by 'the close muggy atmosphere'. Also 'an inevitable war with mosquitoes robbed us of our peaceful slumbers'. On New Year's Day they landed at Madras, experiencing less trouble with the surf than many visitors and becoming the first organized tourist party ever to set foot on Indian soil. But the city was celebrating both Hindu and Roman Catholic festivals and after promenading the principal streets and inspecting the unkempt gardens, Cook was glad to return to the ship. Four days later it sailed up the Hooghly to Calcutta, then the capital of India and the City of Palaces, where the season was in full swing. Cook spent five days of what he called 'hard labour' 'doing' Calcutta – 'the fashionable drives, the public gardens, the botanic gardens, the great banyan tree with its 300 stems, covering an area of 1,000 feet in circumference'.[27]

However, India excited him less as a field of tourist enterprise than as one of missionary endeavour. He had made it obvious throughout the trip that, like John Wesley, he took the whole world for his parish. It was clear, too, that he considered the East especially ripe for conversion. But in the subcontinent he was particularly inspired by the work of a trio of Baptist missionaries with Leicester connections: William Carey, Joshua Marshman and William Ward. For him 'the red letter day of the tour' was a visit to Serampore, a Danish trading enclave just outside Calcutta where the Baptist

Mission had been established (the East India Company opposed missions) and where the 'three immortals' had 'lived, laboured and died'. Cook so venerated these men that, while disclaiming any ideas of superstition, 'I felt interested in leaning on Carey's crutches, which are in the Library'.[28] He also sat in Carey's 'neat and prim elbow-chair', stood in his 'decaying pulpit' and plucked leaves and fruit from the mahogany and tamarind trees he had planted in the college gardens. And Cook visited nearby temples where he was pleased to see two huge Juggernaut cars being destroyed by white ants.[29]

The same pattern was repeated throughout India. Cook hired a private railway carriage with 'sleeping berths, baths and closet', and kept it for over three weeks, 'attaching and detaching it where we liked for the whole 2,300 miles'. But so engrained were his prejudices that he could not appreciate the colourful scenes and cultural riches which have attracted tourists to India ever since. In Benares Cook only cared to see one of the city's 5,000 temples and shrines, and that contained abominations 'which exceeded all my conceptions of idolatry'. He was 'conducted through centres of filth and obscenity, combining bull, peacock, monkey, and other nameless objects of worship'. He observed priests dispensing holy water to eager drinkers from what looked like an open sewer and 'leering dancing girls, calling out from upper windows and inviting strangers to their wretched abodes'.

> From the deck of the boat on the Ganges we saw the crowds of bathers trying to wash away the 'filth of the flesh;' others shaving the heads and washing dead bodies, previous to laying them on the funeral piles, which were burning on the banks of the river. The whole of those heathen scenes were revolting in the extreme, and we turned with pleasure to see the contrast of 200 or 300 intelligent youths being educated in Queen's College.

In Agra not even Cook could withhold his admiration from the Taj Mahal: 'This exquisite tomb of white marble, inlaid with precious stones in great variety of ornament and inscriptive memorial, stands on the high bank of the Jumna, and is surrounded in the quadrangle by a beautiful garden of tropical plants, trees, and flowers, interspersed with a profusion of richly-tinted English roses, the whole surrounded by a massive and lofty wall, with a magnificent central gateway.'[30] But, as his letters to Marianne reveal, Cook was even more enthusiastic about the retreat from alcohol – generally regarded as the cement of the Empire – being conducted by the British garrison in Agra. Hearing that 400 out of 950 red-jackets were teetotallers, he gave them a lecture, apparently well received, on his own 'experience of nearly 40 years of abstinence'. In Delhi, too, he passed quickly over the Red Fort, 'the rich marble structures of the Palace, baths and harem, the pedestal on which stood the famed Peacock Throne; the Great Mosque, the Cashmere gate', the Qutb Minar and the monuments of the Mutiny. Then he concentrated on 'spiritual, sanitary, and social affairs', native Bible classes, zenana missions and the like.

At Lucknow and Cawnpore his thoughts were naturally dominated by the Mutiny, an event he interpreted as the slaughter of Christians by infidels. In Allahabad he was less interested in Brahmin shasters than in Baptist tracts. Hindu fakirs he contemptuously likened to the mendicant friars of Rome, though he was reluctantly impressed by the fact that most Indians were forbidden by religion to touch alcohol. However, during an 'evening ramble' through Bombay he observed 'lewd women' and drink sellers plying their trades in the same narrow streets and reflected that 'the worship of the Lingam and the worship of Bacchus and Venus are alike destructive to the native Indians in one case and thoughtless Europeans in the other'.[31]

What Cook's tourists made of his preoccupations is not entirely apparent. Four of them were teetotallers and they seem to have accompanied him on his various religious and temperance excursions. Another two, Chief Justice Slade of Hong Kong and one of the ladies on the party, had eyes only for each other and later got married. But Cook's relations with at least one tourist, Mr Wicks, were evidently strained. As they steamed through the Red Sea in the beautiful P & O liner *Hydaspes*, Cook commented that Wicks was prone to 'what he calls bilious affection, which I strongly suspect to be alcoholic affection as he drinks wines of various characters'.[32]

However, John believed that his father had sacrificed tourism to his religious and philanthropic interests. This exacerbated family differences, for John evidently felt that his own efforts were being used to subsidize his father's hobby. Thomas, whose return home was delayed because he had to help with the busiest tourist season Egypt and Palestine had ever known, received a 'painful letter'

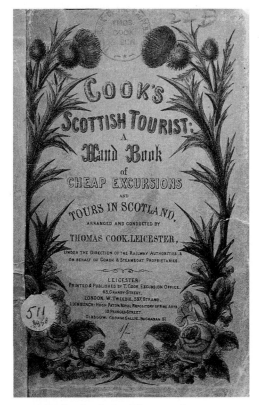

Tartan tours – the basis for Thomas Cook's early success

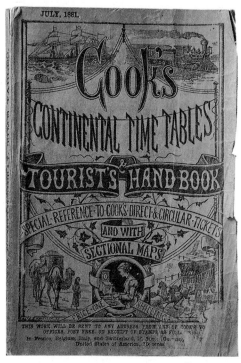

The European traveller's bible

Cook's tours celebrated in song.
The bearded figure doing the
'Excursion galop' is John Mason Cook

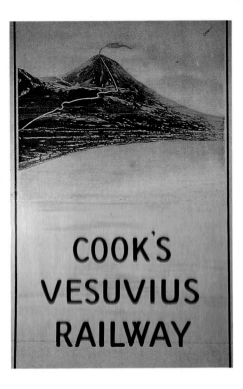

**COOK'S
VESUVIUS
RAILWAY**

Cook's transports of delights

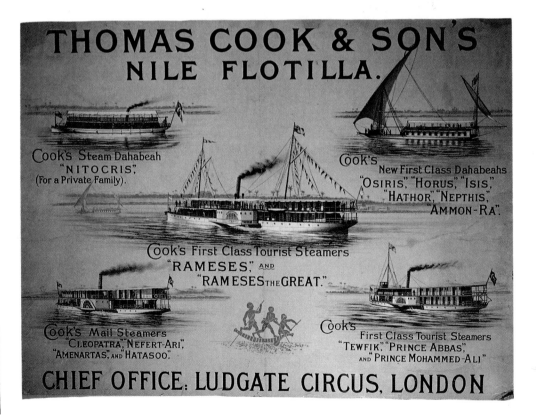

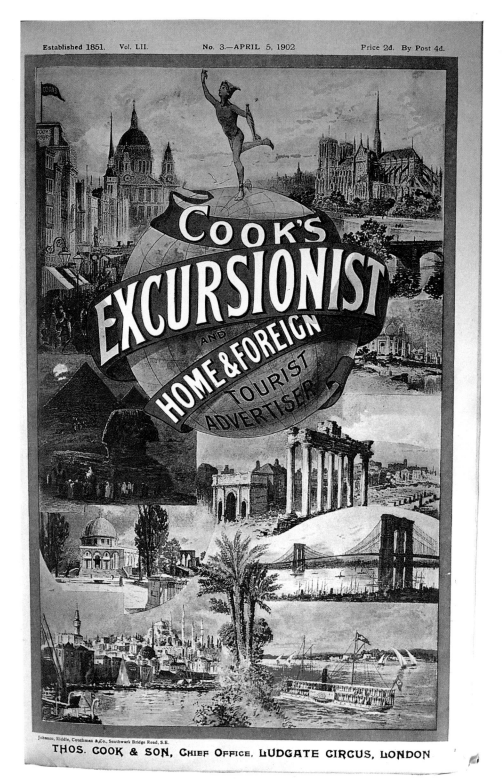

Established 1851.   Vol. LII.   No. 3.—APRIL 5, 1902.   Price 2d. By Post 4d.

Cook's EXCURSIONIST
AND HOME & FOREIGN
TOURIST ADVERTISER

Johnson, Riddle, Couchman & Co., Southwark Bridge Road, S.E.

THOS. COOK & SON, Chief Office, LUDGATE CIRCUS, LONDON

Cook's Excursionist was published
in many foreign editions

from him while he was in the Mediterranean. But, as he told Marianne,

> I am not going to distress myself. I know my heart is right
> towards him and towards yourself, and my dear girl [Annie] also,
> and I shall not be moved from the path of Duty to either Division
> of my family. He does not like my mixing Missions with business;
> but he cannot deprive me of the pleasure I have had in the
> combination; it has sweetened my journey and I hope improved
> my heart without prejudice to the mercenary object of my tour. I
> shall neither be expelled from the office nor stifled in my spirit's
> utterance, and I have told him so very plainly.[33]

The Cook family was thus already divided against itself and the rift was made wider by John's having read some of his mother's private correspondence. It seems, too, that the son was already thinking in terms of removing his father from the business.

Yet on this occasion Thomas was probably correct in believing that he had in no way harmed the firm. On the contrary, for eight months he had kept out of John's way, so far from 'the pressure of current events' that he seemed 'in retrospect, to have been living in dream-land, inhaling the soft breezes of Eastern climes, surrounded with the luxuries of the tropics, listening to the warbles of fairy songsters, and watching the motions of swarthy and nearly nude semi-barbarians'.[34] Moreoever, he had gathered a mass of tourist information. He could justly write:

> I have learnt the way to circumnavigate the globe; have seen
> what may be done and what should be avoided; what time is
> required and the best season for making the tour; what détours
> may be made to the best advantage; what are the respective
> denominations and the proportionate values of moneys of all the
> states and countries visited. In a word, I think I comprehend the
> whole of this 'business of pleasure' around the world.[35]

In a letter he wrote soon afterwards to a clergyman in Lincoln, Cook showed that he could indeed give copious advice to anyone wanting to go round the world – about costs, hotels, routes, means of transport and places to see. He had also appointed a number of local agents and representatives, even in places as remote as Jubbulpore, 'where the Thugs of India are held in confinement and may be seen manufacturing carpets under military supervision'.[36] Furthermore, Cook had made proposals to the transit companies about cheap rates which enabled him to offer round-the-world tickets (including accommodation) for about 300 guineas. So this grand circular tour became a regular feature of Thomas Cook's programme.

In the Victorian age such a complicated journey could not be entirely a routine matter, but Cook's global tours were certainly a far cry from Jules Verne's fantastic extravaganza, *Around the World in Eighty Days*. Actually this book (which was written fast and published at the end of 1872) may well have been inspired by Cook's first tour (which had been advertised in May of that year). It is true that others, notably *Le Magasin Pittoresque* in 1870, had earlier demonstrated that the Suez Canal made the sort of itinerary which Phileas Fogg would adopt a practical proposition.[37] But according to Verne's niece and biographer, Marguerite Allotte de la Fuÿe, who alone had access to all the family papers, her uncle happened to see a Cook's tourist leaflet while he was strolling along the boulevards of Paris. One paragraph

> pointed out that, thanks to the speed of new methods of transport, and the linking up of international time-tables, a complete voyage round the globe had now become no more than a holiday excursion, a mere jaunt taking no more than three months at the most. The idea immediately took shape in the novelist's mind. The trains and buses and steamers of Cook's and other tours began to whirl faster and faster in his head, describing an uninterrupted circle round the globe.[38]

Whatever the genesis of Verne's classic, it is interesting to note that he chose a phlegmatic Englishman as its hero. As Cook's *Excursionist* sometimes complained, 'The French are not a travelling people.'[39] But it observed smugly in 1879 that a French attempt to duplicate Cook's round-the-world tours had collapsed and that the organizers were reduced to buying tickets from Cook's New York office.[40]

It was not quite true, as the *Excursionist* added, that only Cook had carried out round-the-world tours successfully – the Stangen agency of Germany organized one in 1878. But without doubt the firm of Cook became preeminent in the field and Thomas could justly claim to have established the 'most comprehensive Tourist system in the world'.[41] Its growing team of couriers acquired unrivalled expertise.

Its network of agents, which expanded with time, could give tourists local assistance wherever they went. Many globe-trotters paid tribute to Cook for having fulfilled every obligation 'to the entire satisfaction of all concerned'.[42] Cook's fulsome advertisements, which puffed these tours as the supreme travelling experience, attracted affluent customers.

Probably no person can hope to enjoy more than once in a lifetime so grand and instructive a tour, to perform which is a liberal education in itself. The most indifferent are rendered enthusiasts by a familiarity with the varied aspects and captivating forms of nature presented in new and distant regions. The pages of history become illuminated, and the mystery of ages is plucked from the vivid story of past centuries for those who thus sail in foreign seas and become familiar with many lands.[43]

By the time of Thomas Cook's death in 1892 over twenty parties – nearly 1,000 people according to John's (perhaps exaggerated) estimate – had circumnavigated the globe under his arrangements. As G.A. Sala wrote, 'Cook at present pervades the whole civilised world'; and, addressing the shade of Thomas, he declared: 'If there ever was a public benefactor you were one.'[44] But not everyone was happy about the expansion of Cook's enterprise. Writing in *Macmillan's Magazine*, Violet Paget declared that she had not the 'faintest prejudice' against tourist agencies like Cook's:

I fervently desire that these gentlemen may ever quicken trains and cheapen hotels; I am ready to be jostled in Alpine valleys and Venetian canals by any number of vociferous tourists, for the sake of the schoolmistress, or clerk, or artisan, or curate, who may by this means have reached at last the land east of the sun and west of the moon, the St. Brendan's Isle of his or her longings. What I object to are the well-mannered, well-dressed, often well-informed persons who, having turned Scotland into a sort of Hurlingham, are apparently making Egypt, the Holy Land, Japan, into *succursales* and dependances (I like these good Swiss names evoking couriers and waiters) of their own particularly dull portion of London and Paris and New York.[45]

However, this was scarcely a logical objection and the improvement in communications made global touring inevitable. In 1894

Cook's organization broke Nelly Bly's round-the-world speed record (seventy-four days) when one of their clients, George Griffiths, made the journey in sixty-five days. And in 1908 Cook broke another record, conducting the first Japanese tour round the world. These visitors, forerunners of today's enormous annual exodus from Japan, caused a sensation in England, where they were entertained to tea on the terrace of the Houses of Parliament by Lord Northcliffe. (He found the Japanese very inscrutable, though not so inscrutable as the Chinese.)

This, then, was the bright future for which Thomas Cook's global tour of 1872–3 had blazed the trail. Thereafter he could optimistically hope to be 'pioneering the way for the golden age when "nations shall learn war no more"'.[46] In view of such aspirations it was ironic that the simultaneous construction of the new office in Ludgate Circus should have caused such strife within the Cook family, particularly at a time when Thomas's letters home (assisted by Phileas Fogg's serialized exploits) gained the firm such favourable publicity. John might be driven distracted by his father's missionary and temperance obsessions, but the *London Echo* hailed Cook as

> Grand Courier Extraordinary to the human race. Prince – we may, perhaps, more correctly say Emperor – of Tourists, he rules a kingdom . . . which is ever on the move. Like a comet, he flies through infinite space with his tail – of sight-seers – behind him. He is building a mansion in Fleet Street, but he has, in truth, no particular place of residence. He is domiciled in ubiquity, he is the incarnation of perpetual motion.[47]

On reaching London Thomas paused long enough to have a full-scale row with John. As usual he was morbidly suspicious about his son's financial dealings. Having said that John must have robbed someone to pay off the mortgage (£1,100) on the Leicester hotel, he accused him of applying 'the partnership assets' to carry out 'speculation of [his] own' in Ludgate Circus.[48] He also condemned John for having borrowed money to complete the new office, which cost about £30,000. John retorted angrily that the business was doing so well that he could afford to liquidate one mortgage and incur another, that his actions were wholly proper and that he was empowered to take them under the deeds of partnership. Probably

John had been rather devious on a personal level, but from a financial point of view he was certainly right. Not long afterwards he told his father triumphantly that 'the Ludgate Circus premises has done more to increase the business of the firm than anything' since the move to London in 1865.[49] In proof he could cite the fact that before the office had been open two years he had paid back every penny of the loan raised to build it. For some time, however, Thomas refused to set foot in the new office.

What were to be the headquarters of Thomas Cook & Son for just over half a century rather resembled the elaborate edifices of Haussmann's Paris. There were five floors and four frontages, Ludgate Circus, Fleet Street, Farringdon Street and St Bride Street. Inside was a branch post office and a telegraph office, a free waiting and reading room, and a large ground-floor booking hall decorated with engravings of travel scenes. There was no smarter building in the neighbourhood, which was still a Dickensian rookery pullulating with life, a network of alleys congested with huge horse-drawn drays carrying great rolls of paper to Fleet Street, a crush of pedestrians dodging through the traffic, sweepers with their brushes and pans, crowded bars and shops with onions and sausages frying in their windows. The office was, in fact, on the edge of what Jack London called 'the Abyss', the East End, the one area of the globe to which, he claimed, Thomas Cook could not be his guide.

O Cook, O Thomas Cook & Son, pathfinders and trail-clearers, living sign-posts to all the world, and bestowers of first aid to bewildered travellers – unhesitatingly and instantly, with ease and celerity, could send me to darkest Africa or Innermost Thibet, but to the East End of London, barely a stone's throw from Ludgate Circus, you know not the way.[50]

As a matter of fact, Thomas Cook later ran sightseeing tours to the East End of London, no small tribute to its ghetto-like state.

At first the Ludgate Circus premises were too big for Cook's needs and space on the second floor was let to Professor and Mrs Dr Fowler for their Phrenological Consulting Rooms. In 1880 John thought of converting two or three upper floors into a first-class restaurant, run on temperance lines – 'no features of the liquor trade' were to be visible on the building. In the event he started a temperance club which, situated in Fleet Street, undoubtedly represented a triumph of hope over experience.[51] It attracted a few inky eccentrics, among them George Bernard Shaw, W.T. Stead and T.P. O'Connor. But as a committee member said, 'teetotalism was incompatible with club life and financial success', and John disbanded it in 1884.[52] Apparently he was then anxious to let it 'to someone who will turn it into a regular club, selling wines &c.' The prospect of opening Ludgate Circus to 'the enemy of everything that is noble and grand in man' and 'licensing it for the sale of liquid death' appalled at least one member of staff, Arthur Faulkner.[53] But, for a time at least, John's commercial instincts overcame his temperance principles. The *City Press* reported that 'beers and wines' did find their way to the tables of the new club.[54]

Soon, though, Cook's business expanded so much that nearly all the building was required. This was not just because Thomas Cook & Son 'go everywhere and carry everyone everywhere',[55] though Harry Furniss's *Punch* cartoon of 1889 showed the booking hall of Ludgate Circus crammed with famous faces.[56] It was also because other departments had developed, notably Banking & Exchange and Shipping & Forwarding. By the turn of the century Cook was overflowing into adjoining premises and the main building was a warren of offices linked by 'an intricate series of speaking tubes'[57] – as yet there was only one telephone, a daring innovation situated under the stairs. In the basement, which was 'pitch dark, damp, smelly, musty and alive with rats', office boys conducted gang warfare, flicking bent pins at each other with rubber bands.[58] Above, decorum reigned. The busy staff – wing-collared, frock-coated managers, clerks in their prescribed dark suits (a bowler was obligatory out of doors), well groomed 'typewriters' (i.e. typists, all male) – were organized into a strict hierarchy along Civil Service lines. Imperious and meticulous, John dominated the organization by sheer force of personality. Even during the 1870s he was more patriarchal than his father. Thomas was not one to insist on military discipline in the office whereas John was a martinet. He imposed rigorous work practices: employees toiled from 8 a.m. until 6 p.m. during the winter, from 9 a.m. until 9 p.m. (very often) during the summer. He would not tolerate inefficiency: all letters were answered by return of post. He fretted about the tiniest details, from dirt on the windows to the quality of his managers' top hats. Anyone suspected of malingering, he referred at once to a Dr Green across the road. Younger members of staff (those under twenty-five) had to ask his permission to marry. Older ones were made to wear blue uniforms with gold buttons when on outside duty. For a short time during the imperial heyday the uniform included a singular variant of the pith helmet – which proved so unpopular that it had to be replaced by a peaked cap. Yet among his staff at Ludgate Circus John built up a genuine *esprit de corps*.

This was because he was a benevolent despot. He had a rough tongue but a surprisingly soft heart. He took on as general factotum an old man called William who had worked at the grocer's shop demolished to make way for the new office and who could remember Nelson's funeral procession passing down Fleet Street on its way to St Paul's on 21 January 1806. He was also generous to the lady, Mrs Bestley, who provided the teas for employees working late in the summer. These were gargantuan meals of bread, butter, jam and cake, brought in on trays and served on china with gold and green bands round the edge. They were free, obtained in exchange for halfpenny-sized tokens marked 'Thomas Cook & Son', a forerunner of the luncheon voucher. In November 1873 John also encouraged the formation of a staff Mutual Improvement Society, which held meetings in the reading room at Ludgate Circus. He himself sometimes attended, listening to addresses on subjects like phrenology or Oliver Cromwell, and recitations such as 'The Pig Imitator', and joining in the songs: 'Little Nell', 'Married to a Mermaid' and 'Woodman Spare that Tree'. There were also debates, one, inevitably, on 'Total Abstinence versus the Drinking Customs of Society'[59] – since many members of staff came from temperance backgrounds (and all knew better than to embrace intemperance anywhere near their place of work) the argument must have been distinctly one-sided. This association was the harbinger of others – a Sports Club, an Operatic Society, 'the Ludgate Singers' and so on. It was probably at this time, too, that the long tradition of staff stamp collecting began – the firm later devised an elaborate scheme to share out stamps received in the mail among its philatelist employees. (In the cost-conscious 1970s management decided that the stamps should be sold to dealers, but staff found ways of circumventing this decree.)

Altogether, then, a somewhat Pooterish atmosphere seems to have prevailed at Ludgate Circus, though by 1884 John remarked on 'the considerable number of young men, well educated and powerfully connected, hanging about this place seeking employment in the various offices'.[60] Arthur Faulkner, the Chief Accountant, was a typical representative of the older breed. By the 1880s he was probably paid, like other senior men, £250 a year. This was a higher salary than he could have earned working for a railway company and, John said, 'quite as high, if not a little higher, than I am justified in authorising'.[61] It also compared favourably with the annual income of ordinary clerks, which was around £70. So Faulkner was content. He wrote to a colleague, Cates, 'Give me my little *nest at Highgate* and my hard and complicated work at Ludgate with the calm sense of security, before a great splurge, a rapid and gilded run, and a collapse at the end of it.'[62]

Faulkner could hardly have been a more conscientious worker. He told Cates that 'no one can succeed as head of the Accts. Dept. unless his whole soul is in the work and that is backed by a resolute will and a dogged perseverance; and that I say from hard experience'.[63] Yet John harried and abused Faulkner unmercifully, accusing him of a '*a want of business system*' in keeping the accounts and demanding improvements.[64] Despite all this Faulkner evidently respected – even revered – his chief. Discouraging another colleague, H.H. Spiller, from accepting an attractive post which he had been offered elsewhere, Faulkner said: 'I think we know enough of the disposition of JMC to feel sure that those who stand by him and do their uttermost for the firm and its success – he will reward in proportion as he himself prospers.'[65]

This optimism was not entirely justified. At his death in 1899 John's estate was valued at £663,534, hardly the sort of sum which any of his employees could amass. Some of them, indeed, reckoned that they could do better by using the expertise they had gained working for Thomas Cook to set up in business on their own. This was to become a perennial problem for the firm, which by the twentieth century would sometimes claim to have trained everyone in the travel industry. But there was no solution to it. As John wrote, 'Unfortunately we cannot patent our ideas . . . [and] every new arrangement we inaugurate at great expense is pounced down upon and copied by unprincipled imitators.'[66]

One of them, named Caygill, added insult to injury by not only deserting Thomas Cook and establishing himself as an independent travel agent, but by enticing away some of Cook's couriers. However, the tourist business was much more complicated than it seemed, and what Thomas called the 'mushroom schemes' of 'copyists and pirates' seldom did last long.[67] Within a few years Caygill suffered a 'frightful collapse', which John greeted with undisguised relish.[68] He recorded gleefully that Caygill's Egyptian agent was selling the fixtures and signboards of his Cairo office in lieu of pay. He doubted reports that Caygill 'is in a lunatic asylum', believing them to be rumours spread to avoid his being served with legal papers.[69] He had 'no regrets at Burnley or any others of our old associates losing any amount of money through their connection with Caygill'. Obviously John regarded their actions as a form of apostasy – he called Burnley 'such a cur'[70] – and he took measures to protect the firm against any future betrayal. Some of these were self-defeating. In 1884, for example, John wrote to Lany, his manager in New York, about their new agent in Chicago: 'I am rather impressed with the idea that Rollins contemplates doing business on his own a/c, and I certainly should not let him know more than is absolutely necessary of the basis of our business arrangements etc.'[71]

Needless to say, Cook's enterprise could only function properly if its employees were taken into its confidence and taught the tricks of the trade. So it was desirable that they should be bound to the firm by ties of interest as well as loyalty. This John attempted to achieve, notably by demanding fidelity guarantees, a standard practice in banking and railway companies: in 1892 men earning a salary of £120 a year had to post a bond worth £1,500. As a matter of fact neither this nor Faulkner's best efforts in the accounting department prevented occasional dishonesty among Cook's staff. One instance, in the early 1890s, was so bad that John feared it would damage the firm's reputation for efficiency. In most cases, however, the relatively generous financial incentives which John also offered seemed to work. In 1892, for example, employees received a quarter or a half per cent commission on ticket sales, 1 per cent on the sale of hotel coupons and 10 per cent on guide-book sales, which became an increasingly prominent feature of Cook's business after 1875. There were other perquisites too. At the jubilee dinner, when the staff presented John with some monumental silver figures of Bedouin in the desert, he told them that he believed in 'working men sharing the profits'. In 1891, he said, Thomas Cook's employees all round the world had received £10,000 more in salaries, percentages and bonuses than in 1890.[72] Such benefits helped to create a tradition whereby able men made a career in the travel business. Many stayed with Cook's for life, working their way up the promotion ladder as though they were in the Civil Service. Thomas Cook was not being unduly vainglorious when he claimed to have created a new profession.

That profession grew in dignity as it became associated with the expansion of British influence around the globe at the end of the nineteenth century. Such official prestige was largely acquired by John who, unlike his father, had no Gladstonian reservations about British imperialism. But John also endeavoured to uphold the dignity of his profession in a more personal fashion, and his style of leadership is well illustrated by the curious affair of Dr Mattson which occurred in 1873. Mattson, an American, came into the Ludgate Circus office and applied to join a Cook's tour to the Middle East. He told the booking-clerk that he proposed to travel with a certain Miss Hughes, adding that if her parents made enquiries the tourist agency should explain that he had been advised by other medical men to take a companion 'for the purpose of administering . . . appliances'. At this point John was called. He advised Mattson 'plainly', but 'as delicately as I could', that it was not advisable for him to go on the tour. 'I shall never as long as I live,' John later wrote, 'forget the demoniac manner in which Dr Mattson turned on me and with a volley of oaths demanded an explanation.'

In the ensuing argument John first maintained that Mattson was 'not a proper person to travel with a personally conducted party'. Then he agreed that the doctor could be booked, though he must leave the party if Thomas Cook or his representatives thought it desirable. 'I regretted it as soon as I had given the decision,' John recorded. 'I am quite sure that Mr Thomas Cook would have taken a stronger stand that I did.' No doubt he was right and, in any case, Mattson was not to be mollified. He afterwards engaged in a long wrangle with the firm about payment and he published a pamphlet in the United States giving his version of the 'the wonderful "serio-comic-Cook Drama"' and advising his fellow countrymen not to book with Thomas Cook. John threatened to sue if it were reprinted in Britain, claimed that he could prove Mattson had been 'assisted in the compilation of that pamphlet by our imitators' Gaze & Son, and wrote a forty-seven-page refutation of the charges contained in it. Perhaps as angry about his own capitulation as about Mattson's 'scurrilous and libellous attack', John beat the Cook drum with more than usual vim. He quite agreed with Mattson's assertion 'that I should have made a superb president of the Erie Railroad and there is no doubt that had I been in that position, I should have kicked out Jay Gould much sooner than he was kicked out'. As for Gaze, John dismissed his competition as trifling and his pretensions as ludicrous. Only the other day John himself had signed cheques worth £20,000 for the Continental railway companies alone. Furthermore:

> It is well known that there is scarcely a tourist or cheap excursion ticket in operation in this country at the present time that does not owe its origin to the brain of Thomas Cook. It is well known that he is the originator of the system & that I am now engaged in carrying out our combined ideas & in extending our system to all parts of the globe.[73]

Considering his father's circumnavigation, press praise for a comprehensive travel system that was 'among the marvels of the age',[74] the 'thousands of new patrons'[75] obtained by the opening of the Ludgate Circus office, and the exciting new American initiative, John could, by 1873, reasonably regard the world as Cook's oyster. Thomas, too, could declare that although his work had taken a generation to consolidate, its 'International and Cosmopolitan advantages' were now beginning to be realized.[76] He was particularly optimistic about the resuscitation of his American enterprise, which was proceeding as a result of their partnership with that 'trustworthy, intelligent and thoroughly practical co-adjutor', Mr Jenkins of Alleghany.[77] But Thomas's hopes in that direction were to be largely disappointed. His partnership with Jenkins helped to undermine his partnership with John and success in North America proved as elusive as ever. In fact, the world proved easier to conquer than the New World.

Cook, Son & Jenkins

Ever since Thomas Cook's 'precious American bantling'[1] had been stifled in 1867 he had nursed ambitions to make a new start in the United States. By 1872 conditions seemed right. More and more of the tens of thousands of Americans who crossed the Atlantic each year used his agency, and his reputation stood high among them. As one American journal declared, 'If Livingstone's expedition had been arranged by the great English manager, the Doctor would have been home long ago.'[2] Among Cook's most satisfied clients were the fifty or so freemasons, known as Knights Templar, whom John had conducted on a comprehensive European tour for the modest sum of £90 a head. Initially they had all expected to be 'hocus pocussed' by Cook. So, as E.M. Jenkins wrote,

> imagine our surprise and satisfaction when we found ourselves treated, in a measure, as a royal party, having special carriages, and in some cases special trains, at our disposal, and in finding the best staterooms kept for us in boats. We domiciled in such houses as the Shelbourne in Dublin, the Inns of Court in London, Metropole in Geneva and Victoria in Venice. When we left our heavy baggage in our rooms in the hotel in one city, we found it, as if by magic, in our rooms in the next as soon as we arrived there; in fact we had nothing to do but to 'laugh and enjoy ourselves,' as expressed by a clergyman of our party.[3]

The Cooks were equally delighted with the Knights, an amiable and high-minded company. Jenkins, in particular, struck them as capable, honest and energetic. He was a bank cashier from Alleghany, Pennsylvania, earning $2,500 a year, and he seemed the ideal person to become their American partner. As such he would stand a good chance of overcoming the jealousies and rivalries to which they attributed their previous failure. Probably they broached the subject with him during his European tour. Almost certainly some sort of arrangement was in train by May 1872, when Thomas

Cook described Jenkins as their 'co-adjutor'.[4] So it must have been with a stab of surprise as well as delight that Jenkins opened *The New York Times* the following month and found an editorial urging the domestic development of tours designed to suit the needs and purses of Americans.

> In England there is a beneficent being named COOK, of whom many of our readers have doubtless heard, and whose grateful mission it is to meet just such wants as these. Mr COOK's business is to provide suitable excursions for people who have not the originality, or the time, or the patience to think them out, and attend to them in person. For example, a London tradesman or attorney decides to spend his three weeks or a month in a trip on the Continent. He goes to Mr COOK, he mentions his limit as to time and money, and selects from a long list of tours to Madrid or to Malta, to Copenhagen or to Constantinople, the one which takes his fancy. He pays a stipulated amount; he has his baggage sent on the stipulated day, and from the moment he gets into the railway car or the steam-boat until he returns home he has not an atom of care, or responsibility, or expense. His hotel bills are paid for him, his luggage looked after by some good-natured invisible sprite; all the trials and mishaps that vex and worry the ordinary traveler are carefully smoothed from his path. He dines at the best hotels; he sees all the places of interest; he knows what to admire and what to despise; he travels, in a word, like a Prince of fairy tale with Mr COOK as his tutelary genius. Is it any wonder that all traveling England gratefully puts itself under the guidance of this accomplished man, whose combinations now embrace the entire world, or that Peers and Archbishops last year, were glad to travel under his protection?
>
> If we only had an American Cook, how much of the troubles of our tourists would be simplified. The field seems to offer a legitimate opening for American enterprise, and we trust before long to see it filled[5]

If *The New York Times* had not been above suspicion this might have seemed like a paid advertisement for the incipient firm of Cook, Son & Jenkins. Jenkins himself was quick to pen a puff of his own. Signing himself KNIGHT TEMPLAR, he wrote to the *Times*:

> No, Mr Editor! Instead of wishing for an 'American Cook,' stop the English 'COOK' when he reaches your City [on his

round-the-world tour]. Ask him to establish in New York a house like he has in London, to open routes for pleasure travel in our country like he has in Europe, Asia and Africa, and to show us cheap methods of spending our summer vacations. Tell him, Mr Editor, that we have mountains, lakes, and forests grander than they have in Europe. Tell him that if he does this he will find that the American people will patronise him, and perhaps you can induce him to give this country the benefit of his thirty years' experience.[6]

It is just possible that *The New York Times* editorial actually precipitated the formal Cook–Jenkins alliance. But if, as seems almost certain, it was already in the making, Jenkins's letter was thoroughly disingenuous. This hardly boded well for such a tricky transatlantic partnership. Nor was the financial arrangement promising. The firm's capital of ten thousand dollars was all provided by the Cooks, who lent Jenkins half of the sum on a note of hand so that he could have an equal share.

At first, however, prospects looked good. In the summer of 1872 Jenkins personally conducted his first party to Europe. In the autumn he set up a smart (and expensive) head office at 262 Broadway, New York. In the spring of 1873 he began to publish an American edition of the *Excursionist*. In that year Cook, Son & Jenkins took about 1,400 Americans to Europe (including a party of 200 public school teachers) and 'nearly mapped out' the North American continent itself 'for a universal system of tours'.[7] Jenkins scouted the familiar tourist haunts – Niagara, the Mammoth Cave, the White Mountains, Colorado, the Grand Canyon, Yosemite, the Rockies ('the Alps of America') – and discovered the 'best, cheapest, and pleasantest routes'.[8] He opened branch offices in Boston, Philadelphia and Washington. In due course he fostered new resorts, from Bermuda in the east to islands like Hawaii ('Paradise of the Pacific')[9] in the west, from Jamaica in the south to Alaska in the north. He negotiated with the railway companies and obtained their consent to issue 'tickets capable of being used in thousands of combinations throughout the country'.[10] He issued such enticing brochures that the *Minneapolis Tribune* cried: 'Enough! We fling Cook's blandishments resolutely aside. Were we to linger with their attractions we might, some evening, insanely desert our post, and be advertised for next morning in the *Tribune* column of "Lost."[11] As well as adopting Cook's hotel coupons, Jenkins inaugurated, on an experimental basis, a new system of Circular Notes in 1872. Such letters of credit had been in use since the late eighteenth century, but they could normally be cashed only with the foreign agents of the issuing bank. Cook's Circular Notes were more versatile, being exchangeable at any of the hotels, banks or ticket agents in his scheme. They were the immediate descendants of travel vouchers which John had successfully initiated on his first trip to the United States in 1866. They were also the ancestors of modern traveller's cheques, whose development in the 1890s by American Express owed much to Cook's pioneering enterprise.

Not surprisingly the advent of the firm was widely and favourably noticed in the American press. The *Springfield Republican*, for example, remarked that Cook was a 'guardian angel to the traveler's interests' and forecast that the firm 'will soon come to be a kind of traveler's Lloyds'.[12] Ironically, amid a chorus of praise, the one discordant voice was that of *The New York Times*. Less than a year after calling for an American Cook, it damned him and 'his numerous imitators' for reducing their clients to a 'condition of tutelage':

> If the tourists only marched through streets and museums in a
> solemn procession, headed and flanked by clerical-looking ushers
> with stout sticks, the resemblance would be complete. So strongly
> is the average COOK's tourist impressed with the feeling that
> he has been suddenly put back into his school-boy days, that it is
> rumoured that tourists have abstained from smoking, except by
> stealth, and have even run away by night from the hotels to which
> they have been committed, with vague ideas of working their way
> back to London and appealing to the charity of prosperous uncles.
> Remonstrances have also been openly made against the parsimony
> of COOK in not supplying his tourists with pocket money, and
> in instructing the Continental shop-keepers not to give credit for
> pastry and new boots to any tourist under his care.

In fine satirical vein, and presumably quite unconscious of its own fickleness, *The New York Times* proceeded to inveigh against the kind of people whose company the gregarious traveller would have to endure – the pessimist 'who has private reasons for suspecting the integrity of all steamboat boilers'; the earnest man 'who insists that everyone should take an interest in the spiritual condition of the Slavic races'; the invalid who sees life as a conspiracy to expose him to 'drafts and damp sheets'. 'The bitterness and misanthropy, the lasting hatreds and the permanent ill-temper which Mr COOK has been the innocent means of fostering, cannot be calculated, but by the gloomy faces of a party of COOK's tourists at a railway station.' These remarks, *The New York Times* added, had been suggested by the news that a party of Cook's tourists were shortly to embark from San Francisco for a tour of the Cannibal and Christian Islands of Polynesia. It concluded with a flourish:

> When the moment arrives that the excursionists are led into the
> Fijian kitchen, and made ready for boiling and roasting, the joy
> with which one-half of the company will witness the cooking of the
> rest, will more than atone for the horrors of the earlier part of the
> tour, and will stand out in striking contrast to the uninterrupted
> gloom of the sharers of Mr COOK's European miseries.[13]

These were entertaining sallies (though Thomas Cook was not amused) but they lacked originality as well as consistency. The name of Cook had always proved irresistible to punsters and when his system began to embrace far-flung regions they enjoyed playing with the notion of cannibals cooking, or failing to cook, his tourists. One verse saga along these lines, dating from about 1870, ended thus:

> Which means – 'Unhand this kindly gentleman,
> Observe those coupons! Note that small green book!
> Put out the fire – hang up the frying-pan!
> We musn't eat him. He belongs to Cook!'[14]

The most celebrated variation on this theme was a cartoon of the 1920s which featured a cannibal chief, complete with grass skirt and a bone in his nose, untying his victim and saying: 'Why didn't you say before that you were from Cooks? – I'm their Local Agent.' This so caught the firm's fancy that they adopted it as a poster, though it is now taboo on racial grounds.

It was, indeed, merely a continuation of the kind of publicity which the first two Cooks had encouraged. In the 1860s Thomas promoted the business through the writings of 'Arthur Sketchley', whose Gampish heroine 'Mrs Brown' engaged in antics, verbal and slapstick, which made Victorians laugh. In the 1870s John evidently fostered various more or less deplorable effusions, including a panegyric from 'the Poet Close', one of William McGonagall's rivals, and a popular song from G.W. Hunt entitled 'She Played Rink-a-Tink':

> Of course you have heard of that Mister Cook,
> The Tourist's Cook, the Fleet Street Cook;
> Who takes out excursionists to have a look
> At Switzerland, Egypt or Rome.[15]

In the 1890s John even went so far as to pay Seymour Hicks £200 for favourable mentions in his musical comedy *The English Girl*. This included the immortal refrain:

> Oh, follow the man from Cook's,
> The wonderful man from Cook's;

to which *Punch* responded acerbically,

> Oh, murder the man from Cook's![16]

Obviously Thomas and John did not regard all publicity as good publicity and they felt it necessary to counter attacks on the firm. John was particularly sensitive to snobbish sniping and he went out of his way to do little favours for journalists – to some effect. At the firm's silver jubilee he toasted 'the Press', who 'have said a great deal about me sometimes, and in later years always in my favour'.[17]

This is to digress. We must return to America, where sound public relations were especially important for a foreign firm. Jenkins did his best to build up what is now called the image of the business. He advertised frequently in the *Trans-Continental Tourist's Guide*, whose owner, George A. Crofutt, responded with editorial puffs: 'Thomas Cook is an enterprising Englishman with Yankee ingenuity.'[18] Jenkins also stressed that it was possible to travel independently and in style under his arrangements. Buying Cook's tickets was not a matter of '*economizing*', for 'this idea, to some Americans, is simply horrible'. The truth was that 'it *is* fashionable to travel in Europe or America, or in any place, on Cook's tickets'. Somewhat inconsistently, Jenkins cited many touching letters of thanks from clients who could not have travelled without Cook's reduced rates: 'it was through you that the fondest dream of my life was realized.'[19] At the same time, in democratic America, he listed noble and high-class persons who patronized Cook's agency and he made much of the fact that the firm conducted the Emperor and Empress of Brazil to the Philadelphia Centennial Exhibition in 1876 and on a subsequent tour of the United States.

Thomas Cook himself spent most of that year in the United States helping to promote the Exhibition. It was, he said, 'the biggest of all the "Great" Exhibitions of London, Paris, Vienna and other big shows' and 'such a scene as the world never before saw'.[20] It was therefore also an excellent tourist attraction, offering a huge range of artistic, industrial and agricultural exhibits. Among the 200 buildings, erected on a site so large that a five-cent railroad trip around it took half an hour, was Cook's own 'World Ticket Office'. This ornate pavilion stood near the lake and Cook presided over it in person for most of the summer. Its display included tourist tents and camping equipment from the Holy Land (brought over by Rolla Floyd) and other Palestinian artefacts such as wooden goods from the Mount of Olives. But what most intrigued the crowds was the mummy of an Egyptian princess. One young lady remarked: 'See, there is one of the Cook's tourists who has fallen out.'

Despite attracting half a million visitors, the 'World Ticket Office' only managed to break even financially, though a small profit was realized when the building was sold for $525, to be re-erected and used for Methodist camp meetings. This poor result was caused, Cook reported, by the formation of 'an American "ring" against us'. Earlier in the year a convention of ticket agents meeting in Louisville had resolved that firms like Cook's, which obtained 'transportation rates' from railroads and issued tickets under their own names, should no longer be tolerated. Cook, Son & Jenkins already had contracts with 150 companies, who received much business as a result, and only a few of them bowed to this pressure. But at the Philadelphia Exhibition the 'World Ticket Office' was faced by a rival 'American Railroad Ticket Office' and, despite previous assurances, certain railroad and steamship companies did refuse Cook's tickets.[21]

Naturally Cook resented this kind of protectionism, but not just for financial reasons. He loved America, regarding it, paradoxically, as the land most inclined to prohibit alcohol (President Rutherford Hayes had banned liquor from the White House and his wife was known as 'Lemonade Lucy') and the land of the freedoms he cherished. Freedom of movement was not the least of these. As a nation immigrants with an open frontier, Americans knew more about travel than any other people on earth. Mobility was part of their heritage. It was an impulse that found expression in everyone from the coonskin-capped pioneer to the top-hatted tourist. As the New York *Evening Telegram* wrote, referring to the latter:

> 'Travel' is the catchword of the hour. Everybody in the gay world seems to be impelled by an irresistible impulse to go somewhere. The cry of the restless globe-trotter, 'Anywhere, anywhere – but here!' is echoed by hosts of people who are starting on journeys to Scandinavia, Venice, Paris, London and Japan.[22]

Cook identified passionately with this spirit, though it distressed him when American tourists patronized their vegetative European cousins. Often, indeed, Americans expected to impose the New World on the Old. In European hotels they frequently demanded à la carte breakfasts at table d'hôte prices, refused to pay extra for iced water and coffee, and indulged in 'high airs and tall talk'.[23] The London *Daily News* went so far as to declare that 'the "Hotel American" is, assuredly, one of the most offensive products of modern civilization'.[24] Cook himself was not above issuing a gentle rebuke:

> may we say without offence? –many of our Republican visitors evince much of the spirit of the old Republics of Rome, Venice, and other powerful states. Mighty in enterprise and dollars, great in mechanical skill, rich in Educational provision, boundless in territorial grasp, revelling amongst the varieties and fertility of natural supplies, free in religion and politics, brave in arms . . . there is no wonder that our visitors should come among us with confidence.

But, he continued, their actions and attitudes sometimes shocked sensitive observers. And the English press was critical because it had 'America on the brain'.[25]

John was clearly delighted that his father became so heavily engaged in the United States after 1872, saying at one point that no business required Thomas's attention save the American. John himself was thus left free to expand their enterprise in other directions, which he did with characteristic energy. He opened new offices almost every year: in Geneva (1872); in Cairo (1873); in

Liverpool, Dublin, Edinburgh and Rome (1874); in Regent Circus, Piccadilly (1875); in Bradford, Leeds and London's Strand (1876). He began to issue *Cook's Continental Timetable* in 1873 and in 1875 he expanded the *Excursionist*. In 1878 he established the Banking & Exchange Department which was soon 'extensively patronized by our own friends and the general public'.[26] He drummed up new kinds of trade, anything from organizing the transport of Queen Victoria's cattle to arranging the travel of the first Catholic pilgrimage to leave England since the Reformation. This went to the shrine of St Marguerite Marie Alacoque at Paray-le-Monial in September 1873 and the five hundred pilgrims were led by the Duke of Norfolk (already an old client) and other noble and distinguished Roman Catholics. But, as the *Annual Register* commented, on Victoria Station 'the presiding genius was Mr Cook, inquired for on all hands by good Catholics, come by night train from Manchester and other places, and anxious at the last moment about their vouchers. Archbishops and bishops may have their day, but on the railway platform the tourist agent must reign supreme.'[27]

John engaged in a constant struggle with the transport companies and his negotiations increasingly bore fruit. In 1872 the Irish railways accepted Cook's tickets for the first time for seventeen years. In 1873, as passenger agent to the Vienna Exhibition (where Queen Victoria's cattle were shown), he fully integrated German and Austrian railways into his system. A year later he came to an agreement with the London, Chatham & Dover Railway which gave him access to the shortest Channel crossing and led to an 'enormous increase' in his business.[28] In 1875 he wrung a revolutionary concession out of the Continental railway companies, enabling passengers to send their luggage in advance – before that time they had to accompany their bags and claim them laboriously at the station when they stopped or changed trains. In 1876, when the Midland opened a new direct route from London to Scotland (via Settle), John re-introduced the tourist system to the Highlands and the Western Isles. This line also made the Lake District more accessible to Cook's tours.

The most important international travel facility that John pioneered during the 1870s (justifying the telegraphic address for all Cook offices for a hundred years – 'Coupon') was the introduction of railway coupons. These were paper tickets, bound together in a long string, which enabled passengers to book their entire train journey in advance and pay for it in the currency of their country. The system spread quickly thanks to its own simple merits as well as John's energetic persuasiveness. It was a boon for travellers eager to explore an expanding global rail network but anxious to avoid the myriad inconveniences imposed by its maddening bureaucracy. It was also a boon for Cook, since most railway companies accepted payment on a monthly basis, leaving a handsome cash balance permanently in the firm's coffers.

Simultaneously John was opening up new tourist destinations abroad, such as the Black Forest and Algeria. In 1872 the first Cook's tour went to Spain, then a virtual *terra incognita* to foreigners. After an interruption caused by the Carlist wars, this service was resumed in 1876 and the following year John personally conducted the largest party which had ever visited Spain and Portugal. In 1875 he extended his programme to include Scandinavia, previously 'beyond the pale of tourist haunts' according to the *Excursionist*, though in fact an Englishman named Thomas Bennett had been running a travel agency in Oslo since 1850. Clients who wanted to escape the 'over-crowded' European countries were introduced to the 'varied charms' of Norway and to the 'Land of the Midnight Sun'.[29] Within a couple of years, John claimed, he had secured 'facilities for travel . . . as good as those for any other part of the Continent'.[30] In 1878 Britain's new acquisition of Cyprus was investigated as a holiday resort. John also initiated a series of educational tours for boys; they visited the South-West and travelled aboard the 'Flying Dutchman' coach to places like Bude 'where the billows of the Atlantic break with a force and fury that seem to threaten the submersion of our tight little island'.[31]

All his ventures (except, at first, Scandinavia) were immediately profitable. In 1875, despite the 'greatest number of financial disasters' John could remember, the firm had never had a more successful season – 'our patrons have increased by thousands'.[32] In November 1876 he told his father: 'Our receipts keep up wonderfully – over £1,000 on Tuesday.'[33] In 1878, John recorded, Cook's June takings showed an increase of £32,780 over the previous June and all other months were up proportionately. This was largely due to the success of the Paris Exhibition, which included the Cook display first shown at Philadelphia, which saw Thomas's final venture in arranging 'cheap and popular [accommodation] facilities for all classes',[34] and which attracted over 12 million visitors, 400,000 of whom travelled on Cook's tickets, 20,000 buying Cook's guide-books. The London *Times*, reporting Cook's results, reflected that the depression seemed to have no effect on the holiday traffic.[35] All the same, the combination of low margins and high investment meant that net profits were modest. During the 1870s the business only made, on average, about £5,000 a year.

John refused to let anything distract him from his programme of expansion. When, in 1875, he was invited to join a company for the purpose of introducing Pullman sleeping cars into Britain, something he had actually proposed a decade earlier, John wrote: 'my time is too valuable in my own peculiar business to justify me being connected with any Company unless I am well paid for my services'. In any case, he remarked, George Pullman and his New York manager 'Mr Grey have taken upon themselves to *talk* in America against T.C. & Son'.[36] John did dabble in related commercial concerns. Interestingly, in view of his firm's subsequent relationship with Wagons-Lits, he bought stock in George Nagelmackers's International Sleeping Carriage Company, a 'good' business in which he 'took a great interest'. But, he added, 'our business is so very extensive that I have many better modes of investing my money'. Similarly, when E.M. Jenkins proposed that they should enter a joint speculation in coal in 1875, John refused out of hand:

> I am equally anxious as yourself to make money but I cannot see how it is possible for me to take hold of anything like the Cameron Estate simply because I have not time to spare from this awfully worrying business to enable me to visit . . . half my own friends.

Never one to beat about the bush, John went on to remind Jenkins that their partnership deeds called 'for the whole of your time and energies being directed to our legitimate business'.[37]

This was an early indication that all was not well with Cook, Son & Jenkins. It is true that the firm had successfully established itself in the United States despite adverse conditions following the financial panic of 1873. In the words of Crofutt's *Trans-Continental Tourist's Guide*: 'Cook's has grown to be one of the indispensable institutions of the present day.'[38] The compliment seemed justified by an increase in Cook's clients and a dramatic rise in turnover, from $14,000 in 1872 to $500,000 in 1878. But not until the end of this period did the American business show a profit, and then it was only a few hundred dollars. Early in 1875 John threatened to dissolve the partnership if the losses continued. But Thomas had faith in Jenkins. As a young member of the firm, H.H. Spiller, said, Thomas Cook was 'a quiet, easy-going man who trusted everybody and that was why he was taken advantage of by the man with whom he became associated in America'.[39] In February 1875 Thomas took upon himself the responsibility of Jenkins's promissory note for $2,740, which was due for repayment that month. And in April he praised their American partner in the US edition of the *Excursionist*, saying that in three years he 'has learnt as much as I learnt in thirty-three'.[40] Across the Atlantic John waxed furious as he watched the American business grow 'worse and worse'. In July he wrote Jenkins a long and intimidating letter. It had

> for some time been *my impression* that you are trying your utmost to bring matters to an unpleasant issue; and that you are doing your utmost to complicate [accounts] and work the business of Cook, Son & Jenkins in everything possible to the apparent benefit of that firm without the slightest regard to the position or interest of Thomas Cook & Son.

The Cooks had now put in £7,000, whereas Jenkins had 'drawn all you could out'. In particular, John accused Jenkins of incurring 'enormous expenditure' over the Philadelphia Exhibition and 'acting clearly upon the principle of crediting the N.Y. firm with *all* receipts and debiting Thos. Cook & Son with all the expenses, so making us find all the capital'. Having previously agreed to delay matters in deference to the wishes of his two partners, John now insisted that 'unless the whole of the [accounts] are at once adjusted . . . I shall be reluctantly compelled to place our own cashier in your office and . . . to wind up the business'.[41] This threat was not carried out for over two years, during which Jenkins clearly used his friendship with Thomas to thwart John. The latter told his father in 1877:

> You ought not to write [to Jenkins] *personally* upon any *business* matters but send his letters to the office to be dealt with instead of destroying them. All his personal letters are written with a *motive* and as long as you recognise them he will write them.[42]

By this time John was so disgusted with the whole Jenkins affair that he not only wanted to break with their American partner, but 'I wish most sincerely Christopher Columbus had never found that western shore.'[43]

Furthermore, the American débâcle strengthened John's determination to end the partnership with his father. Of course, it was not his only grievance: during the mid-1870s old ones rankled and new ones accumulated. In 1875 Thomas built himself a large house, called 'Thorncroft', on the outskirts of Leicester. Rather impractically, he proposed to pay for it by raising a loan at 5 per cent interest, until John pointed out that it would be cheaper to draw funds from the business. But when he did so John complained of having to subsidize the firm himself – 'any business man would feel aggrieved'.[44] Again, despite his son's protestations, Thomas insisted on giving concessionary fares to Baptist parties – one to Rome in 1875, another to the United States in 1877. Thomas went his own way literally as well as metaphorically. In November 1877 John complained that 'as you have not *given me the slightest idea* of your movements I do not feel disposed to ask any of the staff for information which ought to have been given to me personally'.[45]

John was further angered because their Granby Street premises in Leicester had got into a 'wretched state', Thomas having allowed himself to be 'misled . . . entirely' by his nephew, Mason, who was the lessee.[46] Then there was the matter of a property in Jerusalem which Thomas had bought and which John described as 'nothing but a millstone around us'.[47] It is not clear what this property was, though it may have had a religious as well as a tourist purpose. However, Thomas claimed that John had sanctioned the purchase, something he vehemently denied. And this dispute was exacerbated by accusations of a more personal nature which so poisoned relations that the partnership could not possibly survive.

Again, it is not clear from John's letters, all that remains of the correspondence, exactly what these charges were, though evidently Thomas expressed renewed suspicions that his son was misappropriating the firm's funds. At any rate, John was enraged by them: 'I tell you,' he wrote to Thomas in November 1877,

the future of our peace and the continuance of this business under the firm of Thomas Cook & Son depends entirely on you taking steps to bring about such a meeting and a settlement of the abominable lies which are being stated against me and my actions in the management of the business. [48]

John blamed his father for these 'outrageously false statements', though his mother and sister had repeated them, and he declared in December that he would 'hold no family intercourse' until they were withdrawn. [49] In January 1878 John's anger poured out in the kind of 'volcanic eruption' which Thomas had feared. He swore that he would not cooperate or communicate with his father until he had received satisfaction.

> I may simply add that your whole action and letters prove clearly that you think only of *self*. I am branded as a rogue of the blackest die [sic], have had to bear up under the libels until everybody can see that both [body] and mind are suffering so that I cannot bear it longer and I tell you *I will not mince the matter longer*, I will have it cleared up or *you* leave this business – I don't intend to leave it. I have placed it in the high position it is in and if I have health and strength will keep it there.

John then repeated what he had told his father three years before: '*I want you to rest . . . and leave me to work it out.*' [50] A few days later John returned to the fray. In a long memorandum, which had taken him nearly two months to compile, he rehearsed the entire history of his grievances. The conclusion was plain: his father did 'not understand what is due to a partner' but

> allows *travellers* to think he does everything in the business, when everybody *connected* with the business knows that for several years he has actually done nothing of importance or taken any responsibility except in connection with America or Americans or personal friends. [51]

Thomas should therefore retire and John offered him £1,000 a year or half of the firm's profits to do so.

The entire family was now involved in the quarrel. Marianne and Annie took Thomas's side, thus adding 'fuel to the fire'. [52] According to John, his parents had criticized him in front of his own thirteen-year-old daughter 'apparently for the special purpose of poisoning her mind against her father, who if he has been guilty of half the charges brought against him is one of the most unnatural scamps not yet brought to justice'. John asserted that his own wife and children rejoiced in all he did and that he had to protect them 'in the event of the matters in dispute having to be settled by "Executors"'. (This was a rather heavy-handed reference to his father's age, though, John added, 'I am as like to be called as *you*.') Thomas complained that John's family held aloof from his; John emphatically denied it.

> It is your family that persistently turns their backs upon us. What would your religious and teetotal friends say if I were to tell them that your only son knew nothing of your special parties, held with such apparent sanctity, until he was told of them by those who were astonished at not meeting him at those parties.

As appears from the context, John was not suggesting that Thomas Cook was a secret drinker, something inconceivable in view of his private as well as his public avowals. He was commenting on the great gulf fixed between father and son.

Thomas was anguished by the rift, but John brusquely dismissed his feelings as a mixture of self-delusion and self-indulgence. 'As to your remarks . . . respecting the agony you have suffered through my treatment of *you*, I say the whole is a fabrication and hallucination.' It was characteristically selfish of his father to speak of 'his heart-rendings &c, &c, entirely ignoring the fact that I am made of flesh and blood'. Then John heaped coals of fire on his father's head: 'no son or brother can have been more cruelly and wickedly treated'; 'the nearer you approach death the more are you determined to embitter the relations existing between all concerned'; 'can it be possible that such wicked injustice can emanate from my parents, *for whose present position they have to thank me*?' John proceeded to deny 'most indignantly' his father's statement that 'I want to kick you out of the business'.[53] But this does indeed appear to have been his intention and throughout 1878 he harped on the theme. John declared that he certainly would not enter a new partnership and would meanwhile work according to conscience. He hoped that they could 'dissolve amicably' when the deed of partnership lapsed at the end of the year. He proposed that his father should receive 'full monetary benefit' of the business. But he insisted that 'I must be left unfettered as the sole manager' with 'sole legal and monetary responsibility'.[54]

Thomas resisted these pressures and tried to cement his alliance with Jenkins. This was doomed to failure. In September 1878 John finally lost patience with the Knight Templar and sent over a 'financial commissioner', probably Faulkner, to investigate matters in New York. A month later John wrote to John Allport, General Manager of the Midland Railway:

> I have obtained clear and undeniable proof that our American partner has robbed the firm of over £3,000 . . . The worst feature of the affair is that my Father will not assist me in prosecuting Jenkins but on the contrary wants me to sell my share and interest in the goodwill [so that] Jenkins may be reinstated with the power to use the name of 'Cook' or 'Cook's Tours'.[55]

To impede this move John asked Allport to make him personally the Midland's General Passenger Agent in the United States as well as Excursion and Tourist Agent in Britain. In the event, John did not need Allport's help for his father capitulated.

Doubtless Thomas was worn out by the quarrel and anxious to bind up the family's wounds. But apparently he also became persuaded of Jenkins's guilt. The American had not only gone off to Europe with $15,000 of the firm's money but, according to John, he had sent Thomas letters convicting himself of dishonesty. So John was victorious on two fronts. The partnership of Cook, Son & Jenkins was dissolved. And, with his father's acquiescence, lawyers made the necessary settlement at Thomas Cook & Son. Thomas subsequently retired to Leicester, where he busied himself with Baptist and temperance work, probably receiving £1,000 a year plus free travel from the firm. In 1879 John became its 'sole managing partner'[56] and 'holder of all the capital in the business'.[57] The process was not without its traumas. John informed his sister Annie that one interview with his father caused him 'mental and physical suffering' not to be repeated. He also said that Thomas had told 'menial servants, strangers . . . and others the whole history of my life' including '*frightfully* exaggerated misstatements'. One acquaintance had actually referred to John as Thomas Cook's 'wicked son'.[58]

What is one to make of this dispute? Clearly it was the outcome of a personal incompatibility which had expressed itself in lifelong

dissension. Clearly, too, it was the product of particular circumstances and there were rights and wrongs on both sides. From a
commercial point of view John's judgement was unquestionably
sound. The embodiment of the Victorian entrepreneurial spirit, he
had put the firm on a solid business footing and was in the process
of making it a famous global concern. And these achievements were
hardly assisted by the idealistic ventures and haphazard methods
of his prodigal father. John had to be ruthless, though there is no
evidence that Thomas's corrosive suspicions about his son's financial
integrity were justified. Yet morally speaking there is much to be said
on Thomas's side. He had founded the business as a form of philanthropy and was surely entitled to preserve its altruistic character. It
was reasonable for him to resent being usurped by his son. John's
behaviour was often tactless and inconsiderate, sometimes arrogant
and aggressive. Thomas actually accused John of killing him by the
horrible things he said and the parent must have found it bitterly
ironical that the child signed even his most vitriolic letters 'Your
affectionate son'. Altogether it was a tragic schism, the result of
an inexorable clash of temperaments and an inveterate conflict
of values.

The tragedy was soon compounded. Annie Cook became secretly
engaged to one of the clerks at Ludgate Circus, a man named
Higgins. John was furious and insisted that Higgins should resign,
asserting that 'I could not have a brother-in-law a member of my
staff.'[59] But there was to be no marriage. At Thorncroft, in November, 1880, Annie was evidently overcome by fumes from a new gas
water-heater while she was taking a bath. She fell back into the
water and drowned.[60] Her parents were 'prostrated with grief'.[61]
Marianne never really recovered from the 'shock'. She suffered from
'frequent physical exhaustion and depression', seeking to restore her
health in places like Bath, Bournemouth and Worthing. Cook gave
'almost unceasing attention to her desires and to her weaknesses'
but, as he recorded after Marianne's death in 1884, her last year
was a 'time of extreme trial'.[62]

Cook himself sought refuge in faith and charity. He found comfort in his favourite hymn, 'Forever with the Lord'. And to Annie's
memory he built, at a cost of £7,000, a hall and classrooms for the
Archdeacon Lane Church Sunday School (attended by over 900
children) at which his daughter had long taught. Cook's smaller
good works were legion: he brought green figs from the Holy Land

for the Sunday School children, provided treats for the Mothers'
Meeting, took his pastor on foreign trips and kept open house
for his friends at Christmas. Nevertheless his final years were sad
and lonely. He adored his grandchildren but saw little of them.
His relations with John were nominally affectionate but actually
distant. And although he continued to take an interest in the business he was rigorously excluded from it, for John would brook no
advice, let alone interference. It says much for Thomas's charitable
nature, then, that between 1881 and 1885 he personally deposited
securities with the Leicestershire Banking Company (which later
became part of Midland Bank) to enable the firm to raise a loan.[63]
After 1888 frailty and increasing blindness added to his 'personal
isolation'. By then Thomas had little to cherish but 'a vivid and
true memory' of the events of his personal history. This, he told
John poignantly, formed 'a good part of my present enjoyment, and
especially incidents which constitute the luxury of doing good, which
is now my highest earthly life'.[64]

Meanwhile, in the United States John Cook carried on a relentless
vendetta against Jenkins and took 'upon ourselves the entire and
sole management of the American portion of the business'.[65] His
tactics afford a revealing insight into his character. Partly to assert
his control and partly to vent his spleen on Jenkins, John began by
publicly accusing him of dishonesty. This was a blunder, for it gave
Jenkins the opportunity to enter a libel suit against John for $50,000.
In the case that followed, Jenkins's counsel referred to the wealth
and power of John Cook 'whose branches extended from one end of
the civilized world to the other, wherever there was travel'. But, he
continued, without Jenkins's work Cook could not have succeeded in
the United States. This was 'because Americans never liked English
manners', which were too 'domineering' and not as 'free and easy' as
their own. Jenkins was therefore justified in drawing on the partnership's assets as he had done.[66] However, under cross-examination
Jenkins admitted that he had purchased government bonds with
$10,000 taken from the business – on account of 'probable earnings'
– because 'he did not wish Mr Cook to get the advantage of him
by securing all the firm['s] funds'.[67] Nevertheless, in the summer
of 1883, the case finished inconclusively, Jenkins being awarded six
cents damages and six cents costs.

Despite this result and the fact that Jenkins was reported to be
fatally ill with dropsy, John pursued his own action for damages. The

stricken Knight Templar tried to settle out of court, as recommended by the referee in the case who wrote: 'Mr Cook impressed me very strongly as a man who when believing himself in the right would fight to the bitter end, but he also impressed me as a kind hearted man who would listen to and be moved by an appeal.' Cook's American lawyer considered that 'it was a waste of time and money to go on for he felt sure Jenkins would die and that it was cruel of us to press the case on with Jenkins in that condition'. Even Faulkner, who was acting for John in New York and had 'no sympathy' for the 'impenitent' Jenkins, advised John to drop the case,[68] because 'it seems like hitting a man when he is down'.[69] But John was implacable. He insisted: 'I must have justice at any sacrifice.' Faulkner replied, *'What a terrible sacrifice it is, you are making to obtain justice.'*[70] A week later, on 17 December 1883, Jenkins duly died, thus putting an end to this protracted, rancorous and unsavoury episode.

By then John had remodelled the American business and placed it on an entirely 'new footing'.[71] It was still, as Faulkner noted, 'a very insignificant affair' compared to its British counterpart. So 'we have got an uphill battle' to make it 'a success', particularly in view of the emergence of its first major rival, the Boston firm of Raymond & Whitcomb. John increased the number of branches to thirty and put capable, well paid men in charge. He kept a scrupulous eye on finance, insisting that local agents should immediately account for the slightest decrease in profits. He paid for his American clerks to go on an 'educational run' to Europe, a wise investment and not a large one thanks to the free rail and steamship passes which the company received.[72] He used his bargaining power to extort favourable terms from railroads and hotels. He also fostered new tourist resorts.

In 1880 the first advertisements for winter visits to Florida, 'Land of Flowers', appeared in the American edition of the *Excursionist*.[73] The following year the American office planned an Arctic cruise to Greenland and Iceland. It also issued, along with other guides, a new *Handbook to the Health Resorts*. Less delicate Americans visited the stockyards of Chicago which were, amazingly enough, a popular tourist attraction by the end of the 1880s. In 1883 John's son Frank, then aged twenty-one, went on a pioneering trip to witness the opening of the Northern Pacific Railroad to the west coast and to explore Yellowstone Park, 'The Wonderland of the World'. He spent five days riding through the wilderness on horseback equipped with little more than a spare flannel shirt and a toothbrush. At night he wrapped himself in a blanket; by day he shot grouse, caught trout and admired the marvellous 'natural curiosities', canyons, lakes, waterfalls, 'weird' geysers and 'fantastic' rock formations.[74]

Actually Frank considered that Yellowstone would never draw many tourists because it was so remote. But steam was shrinking the American continent rapidly. In 1888 a new record of four days seventeen hours was set for the journey between New York and San Francisco. In the same year the American edition of the *Excursionist* noted the 'stupendous growth of southern California', which was becoming 'the great sanatorium of this country' thanks to its 'superb climate' and to thousands of miles of new railway.[75] By 1891 half the world's track was in the United States, and wherever the iron road went dusty frontier towns were transformed into bright new cities and inaccessible mountains acquired a *'commercial value'* – as the *Canadian Gazette* put it, 'We have our Interlaken at Banff.'[76]

Other developments fostered the growth of internal tourism. At the beginning of the 1880s hotels had been thin on the ground. And, despite Cook's earlier encomiums, most were thoroughly 'primitive',[77] little better than nineteenth-century versions of Fawlty Towers. Witness this announcement, not wholly tongue-in-cheek, from the Desert House Hotel, Green River City, Wyoming:

> The proprietor will take it as a personal affront if any guest on leaving should fail to dispute the bill, tell him he is a swindler, the house a barn, the table wretched, the wines vile, and that he, the guest, 'was never so imposed upon in his life, will never stop there again, and means to warn his friends.'[78]

Within a few years, however, the United States, and particularly California, could boast 'some of the finest hotels in the world'. They included places like the Hotel del Monte, a 'veritable paradise' set in vast, beautifully landscaped grounds at Monterey, 'Queen of American Watering Places'.[79] It was built by the Southern Pacific Railroad in 1880 (and later enlarged), partly in order to accommodate the hosts of Cook's tourists. For, unlike Raymond & Whitcomb, John did not build his own hotels in the United States. But by 1888 his thirty American offices were selling over 135,000 dollars' worth of hotel coupons a year and spearheading the growth of domestic tourism. The American *Excursionist* quoted an investigation which found that 'for every *one* person who traveled for pleasure forty years ago, *one thousand* traveled in 1882'. It attributed the increase to the improvement in railways (though the Tourist Pullman Car was not introduced until the late 1880s) 'combined with our unceasing efforts in teaching people how to travel and railway companies how to encourage traffic'.[80]

This was not too extravagant a boast, and it might also have applied to foreign travel. According to a contemporary newsman, James E. Scripps, the majority of Americans venturing abroad in 1882 took advantage of Cook's services in one way or another. According to a modern scholar, Foster Rhea Dulles, the establishment of Cook's agency in the United States 'was perhaps the most important innovation in the field of foreign travel since the introduction of the steamship and the railroad'.[81] Of course, these steam-powered engines of transport were encouraging the trans-atlantic voyager throughout this period, so much so that (as the US edition of the *Excursionist* noted) 'A trip to Europe is an every-day occurrence with thousands – not thought as much of as a journey to Chicago would have been a generation ago.'[82]

In 1850 the average crossing between Liverpool and New York had taken fifteen days; by 1875 it was down to eight and a half days. Propeller-driven, iron-built 'ocean greyhounds' like those of the Cunard and White Star lines also offered a wholly different sea-board experience from that of the leaky old paddle-steamers: gilt chandeliers replaced smoky lanterns; marble bathrooms superseded an upper-deck douche; and other refinements proliferated – orchestras, coal fires, ship's newspapers, French gastronomy and public rooms like film sets designed by Cecil B. De Mille. The railways followed suit, introducing upholstered seats, dining and sleeping cars, lavatories, steam heating, electric light. In 1883 the Midland, always in advance of its competitors, ran Pullman cars 'at ordinary first-class fares'. This was a 'revolutionary' step which the London *Standard* reckoned would effect the 'gradual approximation of the English Railway system to that in vogue on the other side of the Atlantic . . . [which is the] best conducted in the world'.[83] A couple of years later the *Excursionist* described the de luxe wagon-lit as 'a nineteenth century realization of the legendary palace of Aladdin'.[84] And a new British magazine called *The Tourist and Traveller* reported that to add to the 'dining-rooms, drawing-rooms, parlours, and bedrooms on wheels . . . travelling pianoforte saloons are the latest railway novelties'.[85]

24 A Cook's party in Palestine

25 Camping in the Promised Land

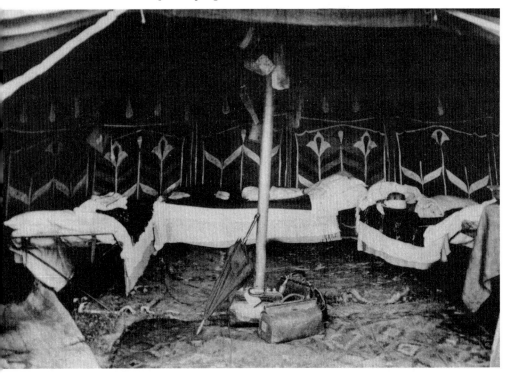

26 The 'much-dreaded dragoman'

27 Frank Cook in Oriental dress astride 'the cab of Cairo'

28 The Reise Kaiser enters Jerusalem in 1898

29 *above* Imperial Appreciation. 30 *below* Imperial Calculation

The firm of Thomas Cook tried to emulate this sort of sophistication with its uniformed interpreters at principal railway stations (from 1881), its urbane couriers and its smart personal service. Much to John Cook's annoyance, however, even in the United States his enterprise was still hampered by its humble origins and lowly associations. At a public lecture in New York 'Cookites' were described as 'generally very ancient maids, and still more antique bachelors'.[86] Some people were converted by the experience of travelling with Cook's help. Moncure Conway confessed in 1880 that he had earlier 'written disparagingly' of Cook but had found his tourist tickets and hotel coupons 'very satisfactory' on a recent trip to Italy. Cook was 'a benefactor . . . [who] has enormously increased the foreign travel of Europe . . . [and] is assisting to fulfill the prophecy that "many shall go to and fro, and knowledge shall be increased"'.[87] But often Cook's arrangements and his tourists still proved an irresistible butt for American writers, though the ridicule was increasingly alloyed with respect. In 1890, for example, a contributor to the *Chautauquan* described how newly prosperous Americans who wanted to go to Europe would probably 'take refuge in that harbor of the intellectually destitute – Cook's nearest office, where a highly competent and obliging official maps out the whole thing, counts the cost, and assures them that he will see them safely through the whole adventure'.[88]

As a client from St Louis observed, the prejudice against the firm was 'a legacy of the time when Messrs. Cook issued tickets only for "personally conducted tours"'.[89] John did what he could to counter this misapprehension, and the US edition of the *Excursionist* frequently reported that while only a few hundred Americans were going on Cook's conducted tours of Europe, many thousands were travelling independently with Cook's tickets and coupons. Within a generation the fashion really had changed. The firm became a status symbol, perfectly illustrating the aphorism coined by that arbiter of fashion Lucius Beebe: 'How you travel is who you are.'[90] As the historian of the Paris edition of the *Herald-Tribune* recently wrote, when its American readers went abroad they used Louis Vuitton luggage, took photographs with Kodaks, stayed at the Hotel Meurice on the Rue de Rivoli, wore Walkover shoes, used Houbigant perfume, washed with Cuticura soap, shopped at the Grands Magasins and made their travel arrangements with Thomas Cook.[91]

King of Egypt

By the time John Mason Cook became sole controller of his father's firm, the habit of tourism was spreading quite far down the British social scale. As a factory inspector reported in 1865, 'The working class are moving about on the surface of their own country, visiting in turn exhibition after exhibition, spending the wealth they have acquired in "seeing the world" as the upper class did in 1800, as the middle class did in 1850.'[1] The change was largely due to a rise in real standards of living. This enabled the aristocrats of labour, skilled craftsmen, prosperous artisans, small shopkeepers and the like, to take advantage of new opportunities for leisure, notably the August Bank Holiday (introduced in 1871 and soon 'the most popular holiday of the year')[2] and the Saturday half-holiday (becoming more common by the 1870s). More people were also receiving paid vacations (bank clerks usually got a week or two each year) which they liked to spend at the seaside. Here resorts grews and flourished, hotels and boarding-houses sprung up, piers and promenades were built, jellied-eel stalls and picture-postcard booths proliferated, a bucket-and-spade culture was born.

Even so, a modern historian estimates, more than half the population had never set eyes on the sea.[3] And although the masses became more mobile towards the end of the nineteenth century, a process that accelerated during the Edwardian age (when, for example, Southend boomed), the pace of change was anything but uniform. In the countryside, particularly, the static way of life was slow to alter. As late as 1895 Thomas Hardy, in *Jude the Obscure*, could plausibly represent a villager who lived only twenty miles from Oxford as never having visited the city and being vague about its exact location – just as the travel-writer Colin Thubron recently discovered a Chinese peasant who lives twenty miles away from the Great Wall but has never seen it.[4] Other literary evidence, such as Laurie Lee's *Cider with Rosie*, illustrates graphically that it was the motor-bus that finally brought mobility to rural England.

Still, each generation believed that it was witnessing a revolution. Much concern was expressed during the 1870s and '80s about the new travelling propensities of the 'great unwashed', not least the fact that they were liable to spit on the floors of trains, steal the leather straps which pulled the windows up and down, smoke foul pipes, make ribald comments to female passengers and cook herrings in waiting-rooms.[5] Thomas Cook naturally rejoiced in the new mobility of working people; he regarded it as a form of emancipation and extolled his own part in achieving it. Though he appreciated the value of having smart clients, his mission had been essentially a popular one: in 1873 he had proclaimed flatly, 'We have gone in for numbers.'[6] Ever since 1865 John had always pushed in a different, more exclusive direction, sometimes pulling Thomas in his wake. But once John assumed sole command he definitely reversed his father's policy. While doing his best to cash in on the increased domestic traffic – by 1884 the cheap excursion business was producing receipts in six figures – he simultaneously tried to suggest that his firm had little or nothing to do with mass tourism.

John moved away from the practice as well as the ideal of democratic travel. In July 1879 he announced that 'we have decided to reduce the numbers of our parties and keep them more manageable than they have hitherto been' since at present they 'cause a certain degree of dissatisfaction by crowding steamers, trains, and especially hotels'.[7] His advertisements reflected the new policy: 'Select First-class Party of Limited Numbers'.[8] So did his brochures: parties were 'select and private'; they were conducted by 'gentlemen of experience and culture'; members were 'uniformly of the most intelligent, refined and cultured class' and they enjoyed 'practically the freedom of an individual traveler without the responsibility'.[9]

With more vehemence than ever John emphasized that personally conducted tours were only a small percentage of his business. The French edition of the *Excursionist* (begun in 1881) explained that, 'having been patronised by the middle class, we now count among our clientele the royal family and the highest aristocracy of the land'. It also forecast that France would soon follow England on this 'voyage from vulgarity'.[10] It was a long voyage and Thomas Cook's firm did not complete it until after the turn of the century. Then, in a splendid irony, the *Excursionist* could be found disparaging Brighton because it was 'much frequented during the summer by trippers'.[11]

Unlike Thomas Cook, John had social pretensions. His employee H.H. Spiller later recorded that John 'rather looked down upon the business which his father had founded'.[12] By 1896 it had reached the ears of the Empress Frederick of Germany (Queen Victoria's eldest daughter and the mother of Kaiser Wilhelm) that 'young Cook is rather a snob'.[13] But what was a personal foible was also a matter of commercial expediency, for John well understood that he could only attract rich patrons by investing the business with social prestige. This involved transforming it from a retail trade, whereby leisure was packaged and sold over the counter, into a professional service ministering to the requirements of eminent Victorians.

It was for this reason that John tried to establish a more formal relationship with his clients, especially through the medium of the *Excursionist*. In its pages at the beginning of 1880 he issued a declaration which was as illuminating as it was illogical. A new generation of travellers was arising, he said, most of whom 'know very little of the origin of our system and have very little personal knowledge of the originator'. Therefore, 'it is fortunate that the necessity for personal articles, letters, or reports of progress of events advertised, does not now exist' and nothing more of a 'personal and friendly nature' would be printed. Thanks to the 'rapid and enormous growth of the business', which had quite changed its nature since the days of 'cheap excursions, tourist tickets, and personally conducted parties', there was in any case no room to include more than a programme of Cook's worldwide travel arrangements. John concluded that he was only retaining the title of the *Excursionist* because 'the whole of our business has sprung' from it.[14]

What emerges from this pronouncement is John's determination to break with the past, to reject the undignified methods of his father and to establish a business of irreproachable respectability. This starchy, impersonal policy was so strictly adhered to that by 1888 it gave rise to the rumour that 'there was no Mr Cook'. What purported to be a family firm was said to be an anonymous corporation. John was quick to kill this canard, explaining that his father was still alive though he had 'taken no part in the business' for a decade. With the assistance of his sons, John himself was fully in charge of an organization then consisting of some three hundred employees working in fifty-one offices all round the globe.[15]

To have achieved this measure of success within ten years of becoming sole head of the firm represented a triumph of energy and ability. For although business expanded during the first half of the 1880s, competition was fierce and profits small, still only about £5,000 a year. New rivals were emerging, many prompted, like Thomas Cook, by high-minded impulses. They included Dean & Dawson (founded in 1871 and an effective partnership by 1878), John Frame's tours in 1881 (Frame was such a fanatical teetotaller that he asked his customers to sign the pledge), Quintin Hogg's Polytechnic tours in 1886 and Sir Henry Lunn's tours in 1893. More serious was the advance of Cook's oldest competitor, Henry Gaze. In 1879 Dickens's *Dictionary of London* noted that though Gaze & Son had 'not achieved so wide a notoriety' as Cook & Son, they divided the tourist business between them, their prices were virtually identical and they provided the same facilities for 'those joint stock journeyings known as "personally conducted parties"'.[16] Gaze issued hotel coupons and tourist tickets, published his own travel gazette, had uniformed interpreters at the principal Continental railway stations and later even a fleet of steamers (much inferior to Cook's) on the Nile. By the time Henry Gaze retired in 1890 his organization was seriously challenging Cook: he had ninety-four offices scattered round the world (as against Cook's eighty-four offices and eighty-five agencies) and claimed to be the 'universal Tourist Agents'.[17] As it turned out, Gaze's three sons proved much less capable than their father and in 1903 their business went bankrupt. However, during his early years as head of the firm John had to keep a wary eye on Gaze, countering his every move and struggling to stay ahead.

This involved John in taking several new commercial initiatives, which he was curiously reluctant to do. His uncharacteristic ambivalence is well reflected in two letters sent to his Bombay agent within a few days of each other. In the first John said: 'I am quite prepared to receive any ideas or suggestions you may have respecting any business that can be done in India during the summer months, in fact any business which you think we can conduct to profit.' In the second he stated that he did not want any 'forwarding business' and that 'Thos. Cook & Son have made what reputation they have by adhering exclusively to their one business in connection with the movement of passengers.'[18] It was one of John's great strengths, however, that for all his refractoriness he could take advice.

Thus in 1878 he had adopted the suggestion of H.H. Spiller (who had chosen to enter his service rather than go into partnership with Gaze) that he should establish the Foreign Banking and Money Exchange Department. Admittedly he had done so 'as a great favour', allowing Spiller 'to carry out an idea which he considered was no use'.[19] But by 1882 John saw the possibilities of the new department, recognizing that moving people involved moving money, something which could be done at a profit. However, he was short of capital to develop this financial enterprise. He even considered taking Spiller as 'a "special" partner to participate in the B & E dept. only' (brusquely rejecting Spiller's own proposal that he should 'become a general partner . . . [sharing] the profits of the total business of T.C. & Son').[20] Nothing came of this, probably because Spiller could not raise the £10,000 that John considered necessary. Spiller himself considered that the Banking & Exchange Department was still treated as a poor relation of the tourist business and in 1883 he almost accepted a 'brilliant' offer to work elsewhere.

He was dissuaded by Faulkner, who said that it would cause him 'some pain' to lose a colleague who had 'pulled shoulder to shoulder for the benefit & glory of Thomas Cook & Son' and expressed boundless 'faith and hope' in the future of the firm and in their own prospects with it.

> Thomas Cook & Son's Tourist Business I think has only *just entered* upon its career of prosperity. It has taken these forty years to lay the solid foundations & rear the superstructure, and it has now arrived at that point when success and *material* prosperity are certain . . . . You some times complain that during my absence there is little or no interest taken in the B & E – well it is a pet child of ours & other people don't seem to think it such a beautiful and promising creature as its parents, but by & bye [sic] when it passes from infancy to youth & from youth to manhood they will think it a prodigy.

Faulkner added that although John Cook was busy with tourism he saw the Banking & Exchange Department 'in the right light'. He intended to put someone in charge of it in Paris, which was a 'good sign'. Better still, he was bringing his son Ernest into that side of the business.[21]

The following year John's faith in Spiller's banking abilities was momentarily shaken, for one of his clerks incurred losses by lodging some of the firm's balances in a 'speculative business', an American railroad company. John was furious. He insisted on a 'clear and distinct' explanation, damned as 'perfect nonsense' Spiller's 'rambling letter' full of excuses, refused to 'allow the money of the firm to be dealt with in such a loose and careless manner' and asserted that 'we are simply to act as dealers in exchange' (though he did not mind safe investments).[22] This was a temporary setback. In both the short term and the long, Faulkner's predictions proved marvellously accurate. In 1884, a poor year for tourism (partly because of a cholera scare), the Banking & Exchange Department accounted for £861 of the firm's total profit of £2,379. Twenty years later Thomas Cook & Son were known as 'the Bankers of the World'.[23] By 1924 the banking section of the tourist business had grown to such proportions that it 'became necessary to form a special company under the title of Thomas Cook & Son (Bankers) Ltd.'[24] Today Thomas Cook forms an important part of a massive financial conglomerate and issues (to quote just one statistic) 18 per cent of the world's traveller's cheques.

As Faulkner suggested, John's slowness to appreciate the worth of the Banking & Exchange Department was caused by his obsessive involvement in the tourist side of the business. This was expanding so rapidly that even he could scarcely keep abreast of it. In 1879 he began advertising tours to Australia and New Zealand. In the following year he was deeply engaged at Oberammergau (taking 75 per cent of all British and American passengers); he inspected the new St Gotthard tunnel; he helped to make a success of a number of special events, such as a Fine Arts Exhibition in Turin and a Piscatorial Exhibition in Berlin. Exhibitions, ever more varied and more far-flung – in Melbourne (Australia), Calcutta, Budapest, New Orleans – became an increasing source of revenue during the 1880s. But John arranged travel for events as mundane as Kennel Club meetings and as exalted as eclipses of the sun. He was also willing to make money in ways that must have scandalized his father. He took people to the races at Epsom. He even ran excursions to abattoirs and, on at least one occasion, to a public execution. At the height of the celebrations marking the centenary of the French Revolution, the Paris office filled seven forty-seater horse-buses with people eager to see Allorto and Sellier guillotined, a spectacle which attracted more visitors than the Eiffel Tower.[25]

During these years the pace of John's work never slackened. In 1881 he visited India for the first time. In 1883 he spent 99 nights in trains or steamers, 160 nights in hotels (130 different ones) and travelled 50,000 miles. Twice in that year he visited Greece and Turkey, hoping to open up these countries to tourism as he had done Palestine and was doing, with his first tour, Iceland. He received optimistic assurances from the British consul that 'such a thing as brigandage did not now exist in Greece' and he set up branches in Athens and Constantinople.[26] By then he had established thirty-seven offices and for the first time there was substance to the firm's claim that 'our arrangements are of so universal a nature that we are meeting the wants and requirements of all classes wishing to visit any part of the Globe'.[27]

John's efforts and the growth of his business helped to encourage the whole tourist movement, which was all the rage during the 1880s. The Channel Tunnel became a live issue and a comedy called *Three Continents' Express* opened in 1882 with a guard at Victoria Station saying: 'Any more for New York, St. Petersburg, Paris, Jerusalem, Moscow, Berlin, the North Pole, Hong-Kong, Honolulu, Kamschatcha, or Clapham Junction?' In 1884 *The Alps* appeared – a magazine of 'light literature and useful information for summer tourists' – one of a spate of publications devoted to travel that poured from the presses during the decade. In 1886 a Travellers' Exhibition was held at Liverpool illustrating the spectacular advances that had been made in the 101 years since the introduction of the mail coach. The following year the editor of *The Tourist and Traveller* put forward a proposal for founding 'a national tourists' union' to protect the interests of the 'vast numbers of intelligent and respectable persons who indulge in . . . pleasure travelling'.[28]

Needless to say, this was a visionary scheme. Far from wanting to consort together, British tourists made strenuous efforts to avoid each other abroad.[29] Indeed, they were anxious to avoid being considered tourists at all, adopting more or less elaborate stratagems to disguise their state. The pretence was often satirized, a character in one Edwardian skit remarking: 'It's funny, isn't it, how every traveller is a tourist except one's self.'[30] The best way to preserve the illusion of being a traveller was to shun the tourist haunts, and those who could afford it increasingly went further afield or took their holidays out of season. In Egypt they did both, one reason why the country became such a fashionable destination. There were other reasons, of course, as the 1880 edition of Murray's *Handbook* pointed out: 'for lovers of all that is luxurious in travel, of all that is glorious in memory, of the grand, the beautiful, the picturesque and the strange, Egyptian travel is the perfection of life'.[31] As we have seen, no one did more to discover and promote Egypt as a tourist resort than John Cook. It was said in Egypt that the Sphinx first broke her eternal silence to congratulate Cook on his Nile excursions.[32]

During the first half of the 1880s, however, the work was interrupted by two major upheavals. These were Arabi Pasha's revolt and the expedition to rescue General Charles Gordon, besieged in Khartoum by the forces of the Mahdi, self-proclaimed Messiah and leader of a Holy War against aliens and infidels in the Sudan. Yet, with his usual astuteness, John managed to gain something from both campaigns. Publicly he held rather aloof during the 1882 uprising, announcing that 'Ours is a "business of peace" as well as "pleasure" and it is not for us to express any opinion on the cause or the probable results of the recent troubles.' Perhaps because of this none of Cook's property in Egypt was pilfered or damaged and he did not have 'the slightest difficulty with the natives'.[33] Yet John also maintained his popularity with the British. The *Egyptian Gazette* reported that he arranged for tourists on board his newly refurbished steamer the *Masr* to give an entertainment for the convalescent soldiers he was taking on the Nile, who were duly grateful. After a concluding firework display and a rendering of 'God Save the Queen' they 'gave three hearty and stentorian cheers for their entertainers, and one round more for Mr John Cook'.[34] John revelled in the 'prestige we obtained . . . through the part we took in the movement of the sick and wounded'.[35] He was to gain vastly more prestige, and a significant financial reward, from the role he played in the Gordon relief expedition, one of the most notable episodes in the firm's history.

In 1883 the Mahdi annihilated an Egyptian army led by Hicks Pasha which had been sent to crush him. This defeat in the desert endangered Khartoum. It also sent ripples of alarm to Egypt, which exercised nominal suzerainty over the Sudan, and to Britain, now the real ruler of Egypt – the Khedive had to do what he was told by Sir Evelyn Baring, whose official title of Consul-General gave less clue to his powers than his nickname 'Over-Baring'. As far as John Cook was concerned, the Mahdi had ruined tourist prospects in Egypt, prospects that were already bleak because of the cholera epidemic. John did his best to play down the crisis. He insisted that the disease was 'purely local', caused by and confined to 'Black Troops . . . [who] are the most filthy in their habits and the most degraded of the Egyptian army'.[36] He also wrote to *The Times* ridiculing the idea that the Mahdi 'may be in Cairo at any moment', a 'misconception' attributable to 'the want of even ordinary geographical knowledge by the very great majority of those who, at home, are considered well educated'.[37] Such pleas were ineffective and Cook's Middle Eastern business fell off in an unprecedented fashion. John became so worried by the 'very serious' decrease in receipts that his health suffered.[38] Having spent the whole winter season of 1883–4 in Egypt, he told one of his staff that he proposed not to hurry home by train but to take a restful sea voyage – which would enable him to inspect the new Malta office. He added gloomily:

> I cannot see what is going to be the end of the present troubles
> and I am satisfied it will be some time before the travelling
> public have sufficient confidence to visit this country again in the
> numbers they did up to and including 1882.[39]

John was in a much better position than he realized. The Nile was the vital link between Egypt and the Sudan. So the evacuation of thousands of (mainly) Egyptian troops and civilians from Khartoum, the task with which Gordon was charged, was bound to involve the firm of Thomas Cook. As John later wrote, 'we had a monopoly of the passenger traffic on the Nile by steamer, therefore the Government must either buy us out or they must give us the work'.[40] In January 1884 Cook's steamers took Gordon from Asyut to Aswan and then on to Korosko. The voyage began with a sharp contretemps, as the General evicted the gorgeously bedizened Sultan of Darfur and his twenty-three wives from the main-deck cabin and installed himself in their place. The imperturbable Gordon later thanked John for 'the admirable manner in which we have been treated while on your steamers' and said that Cook's agents had been 'kind and obliging, and have in every way assisted us to the best of their ability'.[41] When he reached Khartoum Gordon began the evacuation and the military authorities in Egypt told John that 'every boat will be required'.[42] In addition to moving about 2,000 refugees north he was employed to ferry men and matériel south. One convoy of three steamers towing four barges transported 1,426 soldiers, 20 field guns, 2 gatlings, 20 mules, 8 horses and 20 tons of ammunition from Cairo to Aswan in three weeks. However, as the Mahdi tightened his noose round Khartoum, in March 1884, military and civilian movements up and down the river became, as John said, 'uncertain and erratic'.[43]

The mood of the British government was also uncertain throughout that spring and summer. Gladstone was infuriated by Gordon, believing that in confronting the Mahdi he had deliberately disobeyed orders and that he was trying to engage Britain in an imperialist war in the Sudan. Determined to prevent this, the Prime Minister temporized and procrastinated in his unique fashion, arguing, for example, that Gordon was not so much surrounded as hemmed in. But Gordon's plight caught the national imagination. Members of the Cabinet were also mindful of the Victorian domino theory, which was used (especially by those with small-scale maps) to justify Britain's 'grab for Africa': if the Sudan fell Egypt might follow, and then the Suez Canal, and then India, and then the empire itself. So in August Gladstone was obliged to sanction an operation to relieve Gordon. Wolseley was the obvious man to take command. The War Office had already consulted John Cook about navigation on the Nile and his firm tendered to transport the entire expedition from Alexandria to Wadi Halfa, aptly known to the troops as 'Bloody Halfway'. Cook's offer was accepted on the day it was made and he received formal instructions on 2 September. For the only time in history a private firm arranged the transport of a British army.

Here was a commercial and imperial venture that really appealed to John, and he threw himself into it with more than usual energy. He initially contracted to carry 6,000 men, 10,000 tons of stores and 400 light, open boats known as 'whalers'. (These were Wolseley's chosen means of transport on the upper Nile, where they brilliantly proved their worth, though beforehand British experts, John Cook included, had dismissed them as 'an unfloatable flotilla'.)[44] However, the expedition inevitably expanded and in the end John moved 18,000 British and Egyptian troops, 130,000 tons of stores and 800 whalers. To accomplish this he employed a fleet of 28 ships running between the Tyne and Alexandria, 6,000 railway trucks, 27 steamers and 650 sailing boats on the Nile itself, and a private army of 5,000 men.

Unfortunately the contract, which stipulated that Cook was to receive £21 for every passenger taken from Cairo to Wadi Halfa, was drawn up with such haste that many details were left unresolved. For example, there was no agreement that the army should continue to use Cook's Nile steamers after they had made their specified deliveries. Although Cook contracted to take the whalers from Alexandria to Wadi Halfa nothing was said about the accompanying gear – masts, sails, rowlocks, rudders and so on. The result was friction, confusion and delay.

Much more seriously, it was not made clear who was responsible for supplying coal for the Nile steamers. Before the expedition was even authorized Wolseley had asked John Cook to lay in 10,000 tons of coal. John complied, but the War Office then gave Wolseley to understand, quite wrongly, that Cook was already under contract to the army in Egypt to supply coal as far as Wadi Halfa. Once the expedition was approved the Admiralty and Wolseley's Chief of Staff, the bulky and rubicund General Sir Redvers Buller (who required forty camels to convey his personal supplies and equipment), only managed to order 12,000 tons of coal. John then purchased 20,000 tons on his own responsibility, trying to insure his firm against loss by writing the General a formal letter saying what he had done. He risked having to pay for it himself, but probably he also hoped to make a tidy profit, since he was part-owner of three Tyne colliers.[45]

In the event, a total of 70,000 tons of coal were to be required. By autumn supplies began to run short, though Buller was slow to appreciate it. He wrote on 18 October:

> It appears that no contract has been made for the delivery of any given quantity of coal above Assuan. Cook says that he undertook to deliver 300 tons at Korosko at £4 a ton, and 800 tons at Halfa for £4. 8s. a ton. This has been delivered. All that at Korosko has been used and about 500 tons remain at Halfa. Cook wants 10/- a ton more for future supplies.[46]

The reason for this increase, John said, was that he proposed to pay the Egyptian boatmen double wages and allow them to carry half cargoes in order to make them sail and deliver more quickly. When signing the new contract on 22 October the army commander remarked: 'Mr Cook, the Government ought to be thankful that they have an honest firm to deal with, because you might just as well have had ten pounds as ten shillings.'[47] Nevertheless, between 28 October and 10 November the steamer relay came to a full stop.

The whole situation, as Buller wrote at the time, 'I confess took me by surprise.'[48] The fundamental fault was poor staff work in an unreformed army. But Wolseley wrote in his journal, 'Buller is of course to blame for not having made certain that all was right on this most vital point.'[49] This delay, added to others, would prove fatal to Gordon.

Still, by the end of October 1884 John had managed to take much of Wolseley's force to Wadi Halfa, and in reasonably good order. Officers had been pleased with their floating accommodation and with their rations on board. In fact there seems to have been only a single complaint, from the eccentric Lord Charles Beresford, who claimed that one of Cook's steamers, the *Fersaat*, had 'the appearance of a boat and the manners of a kangaroo'. Beresford's account of this unusual vessel is so lively that it deserves to be quoted at length:

> She was loosely concocted of iron and leaked at every rivet; she squealed and grunted, her boiler roared like a camel; she bounded as she went. Her Reis (captain and pilot) was a sorrowful old Mahommedan, whose only method of finding out if the shoals and sands were in the same place was by running upon them; and his manner of getting off them was to cry 'Allah Kerim!' ('God is great!') and to beat his poor old forehead on the deck. In the meantime one of his Arabs, tastefully attired in a long blue night-gown, an enormous pair of drawers, and decorated elastic-sided boots, stripped and jumped overboard and pushed the boat, and while he pushed he chanted a dirge. As the boat began to move, he made sounds which suggested that he was about to be violently sick but could not quite manage it satisfactorily, although encouraged thereto by the loud objurgations of the two stokers. When he climbed back on deck he put on the decorated boots and walked about in them till he was dry enough to dress; while the Reis gave thanks to his Maker, and the two stokers, men who knew nothing and feared nothing, piled wood on the furnaces and drove the boat along again.
>
> If anyone walked from port to starboard or touched the helm, the boat rolled over, and until the next roll maintained a list of ten degrees, so that I was frequently shot off the locker upon which I was trying to sleep, landing upon the top of José, my Maltese interpreter, and followed by field-glasses, filter, sword and boots. The mosquito curtains carried away, and the mosquitoes instantly attacked in force, driving me nearly mad with loss of blood, irritation and rage. My only comfort was a pneumatic life-belt,

which had been sent to me by Lady Charles Beresford, and which
I used as a pillow.[50]

Behind steamboats rather bigger and better managed than the
Fersaat Wolseley's men were towed upriver in long lines of whalers. John Cook personally supervised the process, assisted by his
tough, ubiquitous deputy Rostovitz, whom Colonel Furse, Director
of Transport on the Nile, described as 'the main spring, the motive
power of the embarkation at Assiout'.[51] On the journey the soldiers were protected by awnings and fattened by the sweets that
Wolseley provided to compensate for alcohol, which he had banned
(something to help reconcile the aged Thomas Cook, perhaps, to
the fact that his business of peace had become an agent of war).
Cook's steamers had also deposited vast amounts of matériel at
Wadi Halfa, including 1,6 million tins of bully beef from Chicago,
1.3 million pounds of ship's biscuit (a third of which went bad) and
30,000 tons of cereal. The scene that greeted John, when he arrived
there accompanied by his youngest son, was one of indescribable
confusion. Sir William Butler wrote:

> Soldiers, sailors, black men and yellow men, horses, camels,
> steam-engines, heads of departments, piles of food and forage,
> newspaper correspondents, sick men, Arabs and generals, seemed
> to be all thrown together, as though the goods station of a London
> terminus, a couple of battalions of infantry, the War Office, and a
> considerable portion of Woolwich Arsenal had been all thoroughly
> shaken together, and then cast forth upon the desert.[52]

In heat so terrific that Wolseley felt his blood turn to liquid fire, a
canvas city had sprung up beside the mud huts of Wadi Halfa. It
was soon infested with a rich variety of insects: mosquitoes, lice,
weevils, scorpions, 600 types of fly, white ants that could eat the soles
off a man's boots in a single night, and (in Lord Charles Beresford's
tent) 'a stag beetle big enough to carry me to hounds'.[53] Under these
conditions disease spread rapidly and Wolseley's force became a prey
to typhoid, smallpox, scurvy and cholera, not to mention blisters
and boils.

John Cook's third son, Thomas Albert (known as Bert), then aged
seventeen, was infected only by a desire to push on up the Nile. He
was 'fired by the idea that if any Englishman went to Khartoum,
he would go also'. Moved by Bert's enthusiasm, John agreed that

they should go as far as Dongola, some 250 miles south. John later gave the impression that he had volunteered for some sort of official mission, seeing 'what the real obstacles to navigation were' and putting his sixteen years' experience of the Nile at the army's disposal by scouting the easiest channels.[54] But it seems that he really wanted to explore on his own account and to meet the powerful Mudir (or Governor) of Dongola. Perhaps John had visions of taking tourists to the Sudan, though the country was a wilderness so desolate that even the inhabitants regarded it as a cosmic sick joke – as the Arab proverb said, 'When God made the Sudan he laughed.' Certainly this was travel rather than tourism, as the Royal Geographical Society implicitly acknowledged when it afterwards invited John to give an address on the subject.

Anyway, in November John and Bert, each nearly six feet tall, embarked in a borrowed dahabeah which they christened the 'Dog Kennel' because its saloon was so tiny that they had to crouch on entering and could not stand upright inside. The vessel was stifling, leaky, rat-infested and fly-ridden. John wore 'full dress of cricketing shirt and trousers' but although, as he told his wife,

> I protect and ornament my bald pate with a pocket
> handkerchief, still I cannot keep the flies from the attractions
> surrounding my 'best feature' and the brilliant sparkle of my eyes,
> nor off my suntanned hands and fingers.

The captain, called Diab, had such a 'peculiarly fiendish and gorilla-like' appearance that Bert nicknamed him Diable. And the crew looked so villainous that John brought in several of his own men, including his leading Egyptian dragoman Mohammed. The voyage, which lasted three weeks, proved exceptionally dangerous and difficult. John said that it taught him the virtue of patience in a way never experienced by 'Job and all the Saints of the Calendar'.[55]

The riverine sheiks were unpredictable – some spurned as a form of evil John's usually popular gift of needles – and there was no telling whether they had thrown in their lot with the Mahdi. More perilous still was the Nile itself. Nothing downstream had prepared John for the fierce torrent of water swirling through narrow, rock-strewn gorges – it poured over the Second Cataract so loudly that British sailors had to communicate by semaphore.

Actually, like travellers before him, John discovered that the numbered cataracts meant nothing; they were just extended rapids between which lurked many other obstacles just as fearsome. (Wolseley wondered who had first invented the romantic term 'cataracts' and added, 'If Messrs. Cook had been in existence then I should have said it was started by the firm to increase the number of tourists and add zest to the desire to come here.')[56] John's dahabeah struck 3,000 rocks, he said, and frequently had to be bailed out and repaired. In one accident many of their supplies were spoiled. In another their filter was destroyed and they had to drink the Nile neat – the water was so brown that it hid snags inches below the surface. It was seldom possible to sail in these conditions and most of the journey was accomplished by pulling and poling. In five difficult places the craft, though only 24 feet long, 6$^{1}/_{2}$ feet across and drawing 20 inches of water, had to be hauled by 170 men (once assisted by 75 Dongolese).

At the beginning of December the Cooks reached the large mud town of Dongola, theirs being the only boat apart from the whalers to complete that journey. Wolseley entertained them to dinner. And John had a tense colloquy with the Mudir, who was a 'dervish of the most fanatical description' and 'one of the most powerful men from the brain point of view that I have ever been in the presence of'. This verdict may have reflected the fact that the Mudir offered him an 'enormous bribe to wreck the most valuable cargoes on their passage through the Cataracts'.[57] John only stayed at Dongola a couple of days, for he was determined to be back in England by the New Year. After his experiences on the river he proposed to return across the desert. However, he was persuaded to entrust himself and Bert to a whaler piloted by one of the skilled 'voyageurs' whom Wolseley had brought over from Canada. To his amazement John passed through the rapids feeling 'as much at his ease . . . as he did when sitting in his own easy chair in his library'.[58] He accomplished in eleven hours what had taken him thirteen days on the upward journey, a feat which was all the more remarkable because the Nile, which was exceptionally low and still falling, kept changing its course and exposing new hazards. The state of the river, John said after his return, was 'one of the secrets of the delay' in Wolseley's advance.[59] Despite every exertion it often proved impossible to tow whalers through the rapids and they had to be portaged round – sometimes the boats carried the expedition, it was said, and sometimes the expedition carried the boats.

The result of this toil is so well known that it hardly needs rehearsing here. The advance guard's trek across the desert from Korti; the bloody action at Abu Klea, where (in Kipling's words) the Fuzzy-Wuzzy 'bruk a British square'; the fall of Khartoum and the death of Gordon on 26 January 1885; the arrival of the relieving force two days later: the story became one of the great epics of imperialism, a kind of Mafeking in reverse. The news of Gordon's death, even more than of the dervish victory, shocked and outraged Victorians. Gladstone became more unpopular than at any time in his career – the GOM (Grand Old Man) often became the MOG (Murderer of Gordon). To sustain his government he briefly compromised with 'the Fiend of Jingoism', ordering Wolseley to smash the Mahdi.[60] But the General's hopes of salvaging even this triumph from the wreckage of the expedition were thwarted in the spring of 1885 when trouble blew up in Afghanistan. The Prime Minister believed that it had been inspired by God to enable him to abandon the Sudan, which he promptly did. Wolseley, who taught his dog to growl at the name of Gladstone, never forgave him.

Like any stiff-upper-lipped imperialist John Cook was personally modest about the part he had played in the expedition. Referring to his exploratory efforts, he said only that in all his experience nothing had pleased him more than working with the soldiers, especially those of the Staffordshire Regiment, who pioneered the army's route south from Wadi Halfa.[61] However, he did consider that his firm was entitled to official gratitude. It had done a highly professional job. And its normal tourist trade had suffered accordingly. Of course John had tried his best to sustain it, in August 1884 advertising trips from India to Egypt, with arrangements if desired 'to pay a visit to Khartoum',[62] in October taking forty passengers from the SS *Orient* on an excursion to the Pyramids, and continuing to hire out dahabeahs throughout the campaign. Thomas Cook & Son did indeed receive official thanks – of a somewhat equivocal kind – for having 'strenuously endeavoured to carry out this transport in an efficient manner'.[63]

True, the War Office later vouchsafed a formal 'opinion that great credit is due to you for the satisfactory way in which your contract was performed' but it did so grudgingly and only at the prompting of the firm.[64] Others were much less stingy with their plaudits. More than one journalist went so far as to say that if the travel agents had been responsible for taking the expedition all the way to Khartoum,

Gordon might well have been saved, a view echoed by at least one contemporary historian.[65] (This was pure speculation: there is no reason to suppose that Cook's organization, anyway non-existent south of Wadi Halfa, could have overcome the difficulties that beset the army.) Much to John's annoyance, however, the praise was mixed with blame. In particular the military authorities criticized his firm for having made 'a very large profit indeed' out of the expedition,[66] an assertion he categorically denied.

The dispute was a sharp one, exacerbated by the bitterness of failure, by the army's disposition to seek civilian scapegoats and by all sorts of incidental wrangles. For instance, Cook had lent the army linen which was returned unwashed. Some of Cook's barges proved unsatisfactory. There was a disagreement about whether the army could terminate Cook's contracts before all troops had been brought down the Nile. A more protracted argument occurred over who was responsible for the severe 'wear and tear' suffered by the steamers. About this John wrote to Colonel Ardagh (whose account of a Cook's tour up the Nile has already been quoted and who was now commandant of the base in Cairo): 'I decline to render our account in the manner you suggest. I have yet to learn that HMG have anything whatever to do with the actual cost of war carried out by any contractor under a contract.'[67] As usual there were wrongs on both sides.

Victorian governments were cheese-paring to the point of sharp practice over military expenditure. After the Gordon relief expedition, for example, Britain dealt Egypt a 'crushing blow' by reneging on its financial commitments.[68] On the other hand, John clearly exploited loopholes in his contracts with the army. He also found enterprising new ways to squeeze money out of his official pay-masters and was not unduly scrupulous about using them. The fact that he reduced his rates by 20 per cent when contracting to bring the army down the Nile in 1885 (admittedly a cheaper operation) suggests that he had overcharged in the first place. And in July 1887 a financial committee of the Egyptian government reported to the Ministry of War that Thomas Cook & Sons had already made 'a very considerable profit' out of the army's operations. Their additional demands were 'exorbitant'. John 'exceedingly' regretted and firmly rejected this conclusion, saying that it left him with no alternative to 'bringing an action against the Government'.[69] But he quickly thought better of it and renounced his claims.

This was an unheroic epilogue to what had been an exciting, if also a tragic, adventure. John's firm gained much public prestige from being involved in it. But his private relations with some of the army chiefs, notably Wolseley and Buller, were soured for the rest of his life, though the former maintained a façade of friendship and later entrusted his travel arrangements to Cook. The antipathy, aggravated by the two soldiers' resentment that John had conjured not only profit but acclaim from a national defeat over which they had presided, may well have cost him the knighthood he craved. George Royle (a friend who lived in Egypt) later wrote to him:

> Major-General Dormer . . . told me he had sent through Baring and the Foreign Office direct to Lord Salisbury the strongest possible recommendation for you to get the K.C.M.G., that his former attempts had been foiled by the jealousy of Buller and Wolseley so this time he went on a new tack . . . . [Dormer] says, [illegible] Quartermasters and the rest put together but a Bushel has been put over your light.[70]

As this suggests, the state had reason to thank John, despite his ruthless acquisitiveness. And the glass-eyed Dormer was not the only soldier to think so. Buller himself acknowledged that Cook's contract had been fairly executed. Colonel Francis Grenfell said that it was not too unfavourable to an army weak in transport, since beggars could not be choosers.[71] In his unpublished diary Colonel Furse noted that John had proved 'invaluable' to the authorities in Egypt, who were 'fortunate in dealing with a man with an established reputation and name, enterprising and prepared to render every assistance the Government needed'. Furse continued:

> He was the real Quarter Master general of the expedition. To those who came privately into contact with him he endeared himself by his amiable manners and readiness to answer every question put to him, which coming from a lot of griffs [i.e. greenhorns] must at times have taxed his patience and equanimity. Here was the man who in anticipation of work to be done on the Nile had on his own hook sent to Egypt some thousand tons of coal, asked by the War Office, when in the midst of his work for some guarantee for the fulfilment of his contract; this was really quite in keeping with the traditions of the Supply and Transport Dept. What a laugh we had when Cook told us.[72]

According to Buller, the evacuation of the expeditionary force went 'as smooth as clockwork'.[73] But it was a lengthy affair and it finally exhausted Cook's steamers, leaving them quite unfit for further tourist work. The winter of 1885–6 was thus a frustrating one for John. People were clamouring to come to Egypt and he was unable to provide them with a 'first-class passenger service'.[74] He thereupon decided to build a Nile fleet of his own. This was to be the most ambitious enterprise of his life. Its scope can be gauged from a letter which Faulkner sent to one of Cook's Egyptian agents in August 1886. The new steamers, he wrote,

> will be floating palaces and will be finer than anything that has floated on the grand old river since the days of Cleopatra. They will cause a sensation and I hope will prove a great attraction.[75]

With his usual attention to detail, John oversaw the design, construction, equipping and staffing of the new steamers. He personally subjected the first of them, the *Prince Abbas*, to trials on the water. Then, in December 1886, he directed its maiden voyage. This was a spectacular affair, as the Egyptologist E. Wallis Budge recorded. Various dignitaries came as John's guests, among them the Sirdar (Commander-in-Chief). The boat was decorated with bunting and hundreds of flags. Crowds of Egyptians ran along the bank as it passed, beating drums with 'appalling vigour'. At Aswan guns were fired, nominally to greet the Sirdar. But, according to Budge, the salute was primarily intended to welcome the largest steamer ever seen there, 'symbol of many tourists' and 'much *bakhshîsh*', and to hail John Mason Cook '"King of Egypt," as the natives called him'.[76]

Booking Clerk to the Empire

Egypt was quickly to provide Thomas Cook & Son with its most flourishing and profitable business. In building it up John Cook was enormously helped by the prestige his firm had gained from its involvement in the Gordon relief expedition. John had always fostered and exploited official connections. During the 1880s he behaved increasingly as though Ludgate Circus was an integral part of Whitehall, as though Cook's organization was a subsidiary of the great imperial enterprise. In 1881, for example, he wrote to Earl Granville at the Foreign Office requesting an introduction to the British ambassador in Germany. John wanted to bring pressure to bear on the German government because it had taken over several main railways with which he had contracts. He stressed the international 'importance of our business' and the fact that 'we have our own offices with our own salaried staff in every capital on the globe'.[1] John assumed too much too soon. Yet he was not being unduly fanciful in hoping that the men from Cook's would be seen as a kind of informal diplomatic corps. Before his death they were indeed styled, 'not inaptly' according to the *Daily Telegraph*, the '"unofficial consuls" of Great Britain'.[2]

Oddly enough, Thomas Cook & Son initially established itself in India, a development which did much to strengthen its position as an adjunct of empire, because it received overtures from the Italian, not the British government. Italy wanted to encourage travellers to take the overland route from Brindisi instead of sailing through the Strait of Gibraltar. So in 1880 Cook was offered a fixed commission on all passengers booked from India to Italy. The firm had initiated through tickets to Brindisi a decade earlier and the Italian offer galvanized John into further action. He at once solicited the British government's support, writing directly to the Prime Minister.

Gladstone had 'frequently expressed admiration for [Cook's] system',[3] regarding it as one of the 'humanising contrivances of the age'.[4] Cook's tours were 'wonderful things' he declared, for through their agency

> thousands and thousands of the inhabitants of these islands
> who never would for a moment have passed beyond its shores,
> have been able to go and return in safety and comfort, and with
> great enjoyment, great refreshment, and great improvement to
> themselves.[5]

On the other hand, the GOM was unusual in resisting the allure of the brightest jewel in Britain's imperial crown. Indeed, it is scarcely an exaggeration to say that he felt enthusiasm for India only at the prospect of sending Cook's tours there. With exuberant verbosity Gladstone therefore commended John's plans to the India Office: 'the proposals deserve the most favourable consideration that circumstances will permit on account of the real public value which attaches to your successful efforts for promoting intercommunication of countries through increase of facilities of travel'.[6] Incidentally, the GOM made two other small contributions to the advance of tourism: he suggested an improvement to *Cook's Continental Timetable*, which John adopted;[7] and in 1883 he helped to set a fashion for cruising by taking a holiday on board the *Pembroke Castle* with the owner, his friend Sir Donald Currie. The voyage gave rise to this notable quatrain:

> The Grand Old Man his place has booked
> And off to sea has hurried;
> Plain travellers are only 'cooked',
> But G.O.M. is curried.[8]

Thanks to Gladstone, John received the blessing of Sir Louis Mallet, Under Secretary of State for India. His scheme was also endorsed by the great Conservative grandee Lord Salisbury, formerly Secretary of State for India, shortly to become a Cook's tourist himself and subsequently, of course, Prime Minister. He said that to get wealthy Britons and Indians to visit one another's countries would be to perform a 'great service from a social and international point of view'.[9] So, early in 1881, John visited India. His reputation preceded him, to judge at least from this tribute, penned by the recently departed Viceroy, Lord Lytton:

> We may live without poetry, music and art,
> We may live without conscience and live without heart,
> We may live without friends,
> We may live without books,
> But civilized man cannot live without Cooks.[10]

Yet at this time, John said (with pardonable exaggeration), 'India was a sealed book to tourists.' He actually found more American visitors there than Britons.[11] Determined to create new trade, he met all the chief government and railway officials. With their help he arranged cheap travel facilities 'never before afforded to the tourist'.[12] He then established an office in Bombay, which lost no time in organizing Cook's first Indian excursion. It took place during the Easter weekend of 1881 when a hundred members of the native 'artisan and middle classes' went from Bombay to Poona, courtesy of the Great Indian Peninsular Railway.[13] On his return home John issued a shilling brochure entitled *Cook's Indian Tours*, setting out an extensive programme. It contained a helpful glossary of Hindi phrases, such as 'Take my boots off' and 'Are there alligators in this river?' And it proudly displayed the legend, 'Under Special Authority of the Government of India and the Secretary of State for India'.

John hoped that India would attract 'a very large number of well-to-do travellers'.[14] After all, Britons were becoming increasingly conscious of their imperial destiny and increasingly fascinated by their dazzling Indian possession. Books with titles like *Picturesque India* proliferated, aiming 'to interest holiday people in our greatest dependency'.[15] Undoubtedly Indian tourism made some progress during the early 1880s. After John's initiative there was, according to the *Times of India*, 'a constant and steady increase in visitors',[16] who could travel first-class from London to Bombay via Brindisi for £74. It was £6 cheaper to go all the way by Peninsular and Oriental steamer. On these fares, incidentally, Thomas Cook & Son received a 5 per cent commission (rising to 10 per cent if they sold over £30,000 worth of tickets), at a time when rival agencies were only getting 3 per cent. This was a recognition, P & O managers said in 1881, of Cook's 'speciality – the tourist traffic' and of 'the entirely new business we expect you to bring'.[17] That some of it materialized appears from the fact that in 1883 Cook opened a branch office in Calcutta. The following year Indian Railways, which already gave concessions to Cook's clients, approved the firm's proposal 'for putting into operation a system of circular tickets for tours in India whereby we might book both Europeans and Natives'.[18] Soon afterwards Rudyard Kipling, sweating out a laborious apprenticeship on the *Civil and Military Gazette* in Lahore, wrote:

> Cook's tourist comes and goes –
> He is but a rover,
> While I watch the burning sun
> Turn over and over.[19]

However, Cook's tourists were still exceedingly thin on the ground in India for the first few years after John's initial visit. They were doubtless put off by the catalogue of warnings contained in Murray's *Handbooks* for India. The first edition (1859) emphasized the dangers of intense heat, malaria and other diseases, wild beasts, leeches and snakes. It stressed the fact that much of India was uncharted territory, partly because there was no agreement about the spelling of place names. It also suggested, two years after the Mutiny, that the British were merely a white froth on a brown tide. Subsequent editions were less alarming but they continued to dwell on the 'poor food' and the 'indifferent' accommodation – as late as 1891 visitors were advised to take their own bedding.[20] By 1882, of course, the few reasonable hotels had been brought into Cook's system, his coupons (costing six shillings and ninepence) being accepted in exchange for a bedroom with bath, lights and service, chota hazri (early tea with toast), burra hazri (meat breakfast), tiffin (lunch) and dinner. But it was not until 1889 that the *Excursionist* could boast: 'By our coupon system the whole of India has been opened out to tourists.'

Cook's slow start in India also reflected the fact that John himself was too busy elsewhere to pay proper attention to the subcontinent. Thus, for example, one of his staff, G.E. Howse, reported in 1884 that the traffic agent of Indian Railways

> received from time to time from our opponents a copy of 'Travel', an American publication, which he said is most elaborately got up, together with pamphlets of tours in America and on

the Continent, and expressed surprise that we do not go in for something of this kind.

Howse gave out copies of the English *Excursionist* but found it 'of little or no use'. He wanted 'a good quantity' of publicity material 'of an attractive nature'.[21] The Bombay and Calcutta offices were therefore allowed to produce their own publications, and in 1889 these were amalgamated into *Cook's Oriental Traveller's Gazette*. But it was not advertising which promoted Cook's cause in India so much as further official commissions.

At the end of 1885 the Prince of Wales appointed Thomas Cook & Son General Passenger Agents to the Colonial and Indian Exhibition in London. This was an attempt to celebrate the imperial connection through a huge show of art, culture and commerce. Indian wares, for example, were displayed in long arcades put up by craftsmen from the Punjab, who also created model agricultural and village scenes. The Prince was keen that everyone from Indian maharajas to British workers should see all this and Cook helped to fulfil his wish. The firm established a reading room and a rendezvous point next to its office at the Exhibition. And it began the profitable business of acting as travel agents for many of the rulers of India's 600 semi-independent states. Actually, it was not quite the beginning. In 1882 a number of Indian princes had travelled with Cook. And as early as 1870 one of Cook's couriers, Frank Buckley, had conducted the Maharaja of Kolhapur on a tour of Britain. It had been no easy matter, for in addition to shooting birds out of season the Maharaja brought with him an entourage of Indian servants and twenty-two packages of boxes, bags, hampers and parcels 'containing such like heavy materials as Rice, Iron, Coppers, Stones for grinding curry powder, patent fuel stoves, etc', which provoked quite a 'few Oaths' from the railway porters.[22]

This was a prelude to much more elaborate princely journeys later organized by Thomas Cook & Son. Of greater importance in 1885 was a request by the government of India that the firm should help improve the arrangements for transporting Moslem pilgrims to Mecca. Every year during the monsoon season eight to twelve thousand pilgrims made this journey, mostly from Bombay to Jedda. Some of the pilgrims, who were usually poor, came from as far away as Central Asia or Afghanistan, and at every stage they were mercilessly 'fleeced'.[23] At Bombay they became the victims of unscrupulous brokers. They were crammed into insanitary and often unseaworthy vessels. During the voyage to Jedda conditions, as the *Madras Mail* said, 'recalled the horrors of the slave traffic in "the middle passage"'.[24] Disease and death were rife. At Jedda the pilgrim business was, as Frank Cook later reported, 'a complicated system of trickery' and extortion. He was shocked to discover that pilgrims who could not afford to return home were simply left to starve.[25] The government of India, though it had laid down detailed regulations and severe penalties for their infringement, was ultimately responsible for these evils. It was widely criticized, not least by the Sultan of Turkey.

On his first visit to India John had become aware of this situation. Government officials had then requested him, as he later wrote, 'to consider whether we were not in a position to take up this Pilgrimage question and protect Pilgrims from crimps, low lodging-house keepers, and sharpers, who were not only living upon the Pilgrims, but overcharging and defrauding them at all ends'. John had replied that as soon as he had inaugurated 'our legitimate business' he would be prepared to help. So, in October 1884, after protracted negotiations with the government of India, John offered to undertake the pilgrim traffic himself. The Viceroy, Lord Dufferin, persuaded the India Office that the state's problem could best be solved by private enterprise. In November 1885 John was already en route to India 'for the express purpose of completing the arrangements', when Dufferin sent a personal letter urging him to 'come out and settle the business'.[26]

In India John conducted a rapid investigation and came to clear conclusions. These were that Thomas Cook & Son should become official pilgrim agents, assisted at every turn by government officers; that return rail tickets should be issued (with passports where possible) at fixed prices from the chief Moslem centres through to Bombay; that the cost of a deck passage from Bombay to Jedda should be reduced from fifty to thirty rupees; that ticket-brokers should be licensed; that improved steamers, each with a Cook's courier aboard, should embark pilgrims at the docks instead of in the roads, thus making medical supervision easier and overcrowding more difficult; that at Jedda a better quarantine system should be imposed, Cook's tickets should be accepted and a set tariff charged for disembarkation. Here were the first comprehensive and practical recommendations ever made for regulating the pilgrim traffic along humane lines. When John presented them to the government in Calcutta (then the Indian capital) they were immediately accepted and Thomas Cook & Son were appointed pilgrim agents for the whole of India.

As usual, John was in a hurry, and perhaps it was all done too quickly. The authorities in Bombay were not consulted and they took umbrage at being presented with a *fait accompli*. The firm later encountered a 'degree of enmity' there which was to hamper its operations severely.[27] However, both the Pilgrim Department itself and the police liked John's scheme. The Moslem community was delighted: as a response to Cook's initiative one of its richest members, Coumoo Suleman, built a large rest-house in Bombay for the free accommodation of pilgrims. The Viceroy, who had personally discussed the whole matter with John in Calcutta, was also pleased. He wrote, not without a touch of irony, 'I have got the great Mr Cook to personally conduct the pilgrims to the Prophet's shrine and the new arrangements are very much appreciated.'[28]

What remained was to put the arrangements into practice, for John had no illusions about the task. Indeed, he said that it would be the most difficult he had ever undertaken, not excluding the Gordon relief expedition. John refused to be pressed into premature action in 1886. He tried to persuade the government of India to tighten up various regulations, notably that concerning medical supervision on board pilgrim ships, but though, as one official minuted, his 'suggestions appear well worthy of attention' some of them apparently proved too expensive to adopt.[29] John sent out representatives of the firm to make detailed preparations. Chief among them was his eldest son Frank, aged only twenty-four, to whom John gave a list of instructions running to nineteen pages. Frank was told to travel round the subcontinent, using a saloon carriage as his headquarters. His task was to explain the plan to local government officers, railway officials and Moslem leaders, and to obtain their cooperation. He was also bidden to meet some of John's friends: 'At Lahore, of course, you will introduce yourself to Mr [Lockwood] Kipling, the head of the School of Art – his son is the Manager or Editor of the chief newspaper of that district.'[30] Actually Rudyard was only 'fifty per cent of the "editorial staff"'. But he admired 'the great J.M. [Cook] – the man with the iron mouth and the domed brow'[31] – and esteemed his agency, often using it in later life and singing its praises.

When, in January 1887, Frank arrived in Lahore, one of twenty-one Indian cities he visited in five weeks, Rudyard penned a characteristic report of his mission in the *Civil and Military Gazette*. Faith in 'the great tourist firm' was such, he said, that

> on one occasion a leader of the Mahommedan community suggested, among other reasonable things, that the firm should put an end to sea-sickness. But Thos. Cook & Son do not rule the waves as yet, and were forced to admit that they could do nothing.

Still, Kipling opined, Cook's arrangements would save 'much unpleasantness'. The 'only pity is that the firm cannot work beyond Jedda, and impose some sort of check on the tribes who, for generation after generation, have lived solely by plundering the pilgrims on their way to Mecca'. Perhaps, though, Cook would obtain concessions from the Turkish government, 'in which case the world may witness the astounding spectacle of the Infidel piloting the True Believer through the dangers that beset the former's path to salvation'.[32]

Actually John Cook well appreciated the offence such imputations could cause and sent two of his experienced Egyptian dragomans on the Haj itself. They joined 800 pilgrims crowded on board the *Adowa*, surprisingly a P & O ship, and experienced a hair-raising succession of adventures. First a storm extinguished the engine-room fires. Then the drinking-water ran out and the captain said that the vessel could not last more than twenty-four hours, whereupon 'the ship's doctor retired to his cabin and got dead drunk'. With the help of some English sailors picked up from an open boat, they eventually managed to start the engines and limped into Aden. After further delays they proceeded to Jedda where they were subjected to a series of unwarrantable exactions. As Mohammed Elewa (the dragoman who had accompanied John to Dongola) concluded in his report, 'A pilgrim in the Hedjaz lands is just as grass and a nice piece of meat: everyone likes to take a piece of it.'[33]

Armed with all this experience, Frank Cook began to implement his father's system of conveying pilgrims in 1887. He established special pilgrim offices in Bombay and Jedda. He ensured that Cook's through tickets (which also covered baggage) were acceptable everywhere, from the government-controlled lines to the Nizam of Hyderabad's Guaranteed State Railway. He saw that the firm's representatives travelled with the pilgrims and secured decent conditions. These included, as his father had insisted, 'good food at non-extortionate rates on voyages'.[34] Initially pilgrims were attracted by these high standards and the whole enterprise looked set for success. In 1887 Cook carried about 20 per cent of the traffic and this figure rose to almost 45 per cent by 1891. But the pilgrim trade proved anything but plain sailing and thereafter the numbers fell sharply. In 1893 only 10 per cent of pilgrims were travelling with Cook (in two chartered steamers) and, much to John's relief, the government terminated the arrangement.

What had gone wrong? The answer – replete with warnings for the future – was that although Thomas Cook & Son had provided a good service, it cost so much that competitors were able to undercut them. As *The Times* said, Cook gave 'more than the pilgrims were willing to pay for'.[35] Once the long-established operators had got rid of the worst abuses of their trade they were able to offer a cheap, basic passage from India which most pilgrims found acceptable. Not that Cook's rates were unduly high, for John never expected the pilgrim traffic to yield a direct dividend. He had told Frank to make it clear to everyone on his Indian travels that

> in this matter we are simply acting as Govt. Agents, and that we have no profit or direct benefit from the transaction at all, that the Govt. simply pay us costs out of pocket with a maximum amount stipulated.[36]

In fact the indemnity, £2,000 in the first year and half that sum subsequently, was never enough to make up Cook's losses. After the usual unedifying wrangle, however, the government reimbursed John fully, in recognition of 'the good work done by the firm in improving the conditions under which Indian pilgrims during the last few years proceeded to the Hedjaz'.[37] This was a somewhat hopeful conclusion. That the evils of the system were almost ineradicable becomes clear from an official report on the Haj written in 1931 which mentions, among other things, that the pilgrim guides had 'a fine old tradition of extortion inherited from their fathers and grandfathers'.[38] Nevertheless, Thomas Cook & Son had carried some 25,000 Moslems to Mecca, setting such a high standard that

The Times could reasonably proclaim in 1895 that they had achieved an 'amelioration of the pilgrim traffic'.[39]

Despite philanthropic appearances, John's prime purpose had always been economic. He was intent on building up a subsidized network of offices and contacts throughout India, on advertising the omnicompetence of his firm, on endowing it with the prestige of a quasi-official institution. The governmental accolades and the public recognition translated into a much richer trade than anything the poor pilgrims could provide. Thus in 1887 it was not the firm of Cox & King, which had been taking military men to India since the eighteenth century, but that of Thomas Cook & Son which was officially invited to conduct British notables and Indian princes to and from their own countries to attend the celebrations marking Queen Victoria's Golden Jubilee. This spectacular set of pageants was designed to mobilize the loyalty of all imperial subjects round the throne. In London the glittering array of maharajas (themselves disappointed that their Empress wore a widow's bonnet instead of a crown) added a magnificent blaze of colour to the proceedings.

Unfortunately the more official business Cook undertook the more the firm became infected by the official disease of secrecy. And the more elevated Cook's clients became the more reticent the firm grew on their behalf. As Princess Alexandra remarked at the opening of Thomas Cook's Peterborough headquarters in 1977, the adventures of Edward (VII), Prince of Wales, when he was 'travelling incognito with Thomas Cook escaped the eagle eye of the press, largely due to the skill and tact of the Company's representatives, who were masters of discretion'.[40] The firm's archives are equally discreet and they contain little about its dealings with the maharajas. In 1887 Cook not only brought them to England but also made arrangements for some of them to go on Continental tours after the Jubilee. Later the most powerful prince of all, the Nizam of Hyderabad, thanked John personally for his pilgrim work. In 1893 Cook conducted the Maharaja of Kapurthala round the United States. In 1897, at the request of the Foreign Office, Cook again organized travel for the maharajas and their suites who were attending Queen Victoria's Diamond Jubilee as guests of the government. Acknowledging the importance of this business, John set up a special Indian Princes Department during the 1890s, which lasted until well after the British Raj had disappeared.

Never were there more exotic or extravagant Cook's tourists.

One maharaja proposing to visit Europe asked the firm to convey 200 servants, fifty family attendants, twenty chefs, ten elephants, thirty-three tame tigers, 1,000 packing cases and a small howitzer – presumably for acknowledging the salutes with which so many of the princes were obsessed.[41] Other Indian rulers were accompanied by doctors, secretaries, musicians, court jesters. Often they would occupy whole floors of hotels, where their behaviour was, to say the least, unconventional. The Maharaja of Baroda once took over the entire Hotel Royal in Naples, removing all the beds and pictures, supplying some of his own furniture and kitchen equipment as well as cows and sheep, which were respectively milked and slaughtered in the garden. The Maharaja of Patiala instructed a servant to light a charcoal fire on one of the Hyde Park Hotel's most expensive carpets.[42] The Maharaja of Jaipur came to London with fifty enormous jars of Ganges water in which he bathed.

The men from Cook's whose job it was to escort these unpredictable rulers abroad, and to satisfy their sometimes bizarre whims, had to combine monumental tact with superhuman enterprise. G.M. Piccoli, who served in Cook's Rome office between 1905 and 1951, was a model courier to royalty. In answer to a request by the Nawab of Rampur, he managed to persuade Italy's Cavalry School to put on a special riding display – all the officers (and Piccoli himself) were rewarded with Mappin & Webb gold watches. And when (in 1939) the Maharaja of Mysore demanded not only to meet the Pope but also to have his orchestra perform in front of him, Piccoli arranged it. He also shepherded the Maharaja through further European adventures, featuring a performing parrot, a banished relative and assorted chorus girls. Acting on the orders of the British government when war broke out, Piccoli at last got the Maharaja home, together with his sixty tons of baggage. There, no doubt worn out by his exertions, he promptly died – to the sincere regret of his sorrowing subjects.[43] James Maxwell, later General Manager of the firm, had some equally remarkable experiences. When a prince whom he was chaperoning died at sea Maxwell had to pack his corpse in a bath full of ice so that he could be buried on land.[44]

We must return, though, to late Victorian India, to the high noon of the British Raj, where the firm of Thomas Cook had now secured itself a favoured place. Its unique position was best indicated in the 1891 edition of Murray's Indian *Handbook* which simply said: 'The intending traveller cannot do better than to apply to Messrs. Thos. Cook & Son for advice.'[45] Cook's organization was ubiquitous. Travellers booked their passage with Cook, had their itineraries organized by Cook, insured their baggage with Cook, were met by Cook's steam launch *Victoria* at Bombay, relied on Cook to hire their Indian servants, used Cook's tickets and coupons wherever they went or stayed in the subcontinent. Cook could arrange all forms of transport away from the railways – bullock carts, tongas, dak gharries, palanquins, jinrickshaws, elephants. Cook had command over every type of accommodation, from the humblest dak bungalow in the jungle to India's premier hotel, the Great Eastern in Calcutta. One visitor for whom Cook obtained rooms there when others were having to sleep on the roof in tents or in twelve-bed dormitories thanked 'that beneficent providence of modern travellers' and remarked: 'It is always a pleasure to have any transaction with this enterprising firm, who attend to the smallest and most trifling wants of clients as readily, cheerfully, and as thoroughly as they would if you wanted a ticket for a voyage round the world.'[46]

Cook's Banking Department found wide scope for its operations in India and even dealt with its customers' stocks and shares. Cook's Agency Department served Indian army officers and civil servants in other ways, collecting their pay and pensions, keeping regimental accounts, making remittances to families at home. Cook covered the whole Indian empire. The firm opened offices in Rangoon and Colombo, describing Burma as a 'charming country' so far 'comparatively little explored by tourists'[47] and billing Ceylon as 'a land of exquisite beauty and romance'.[48]

By the turn of the century Thomas Cook's firm had laid the foundations of tourism throughout India. It had helped to tighten the imperial bonds and had earned the title, 'Booking clerk to the empire.'[49] The *Excursionist* is full of proud allusions to 'the Queen and the Empire on which the sun never sets', so John Cook was obviously pursuing a deliberate policy. Empire-builders like Lord Curzon appreciated its worth. In a speech delivered shortly after his resignation as Viceroy, Curzon pleaded

the cause of travel as one of the supreme duties of an Imperial race. It seems to me that no man has any right to be a citizen of this great Empire unless he knows something about it, and the only way to know it is to take advantage of the opportunities for

Edwardian escapism

Tourism for 'the gods with very long purses'

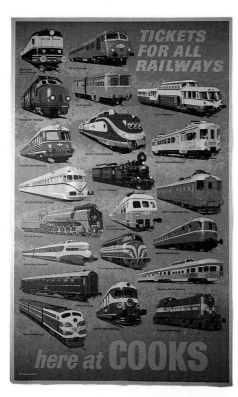
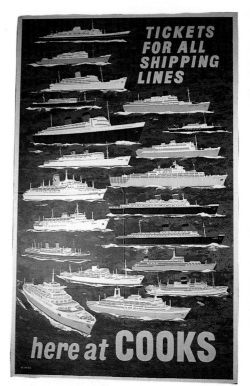

Trains and boats and planes

travel, which, formerly the monopoly of the rich, are now brought within the reach of the relatively poor.[50]

This was true even of more remote outposts of the empire than India. In 1880 John had been able to offer the first tours of Australia and New Zealand at 'moderate cost', having obtained very 'liberal' concessions from the steamship and railway companies. Initially, though, the firm was dogged by misfortune 'down under'. Cook's first agent, H.B. Smith (employed in the summer of 1879), turned out to be a 'perfect fraud'; he simply used his position to get free travel. Smith's successor made 'an attempt to blackmail us' into paying him for obtaining railway concessions. The third appointee, named Byron Moore, was equally unsatisfactory; he 'issued drafts for money upon us at a time when he held money for us'. John regarded all this as 'only another proof of what I have repeatedly said, viz. that if the business is worth doing at all we must have our own salaried representatives to do it'. He suspected that it was worth doing, noting that 'every year the number of well-to-do and wealthy Australians desirous of travelling increases considerably'. So in 1887 he sent Frank Cook to investigate, saying: 'I have every confidence in you giving me such a report as will enable me to settle conclusively the point as to whether we open out in Australia or not.'

Following his father's copious instructions, Frank visited New South Wales and Victoria, and saw 'all the chief objects of interest'.[51] Frank also met the chief rail, coach and steamboat administrators, demanding and obtaining the terms Cook enjoyed in India, namely a 10 per cent commission on tickets sold and a 10 per cent reduction in fares charged to the public. His report was so encouraging that at the end of 1887 John 'decided to appoint one of our most competent representatives to the position of Agent' in Melbourne. This was the 'experienced and energetic' A.A. Higgins, late of Bombay and Calcutta. He was soon followed by other men from Cook's, who went to Adelaide and Sydney.[52] The following year John told Frank to 'secure the best possible advertisement we can' at the Melbourne Exhibition, perhaps by running excursion trains.[53] This was done and the firm also pioneered the tourist trail into the Blue Mountains. By the end of the 1880s Cook's system was fully operational in Australia. Uniformed representatives greeted visitors in Sydney harbour. A larger office was needed in Melbourne. The firm offered a whole range of internal excursions and external tours – to New

South Wales, Victoria, Tasmania, the South Sea Islands. And an Australasian edition of the *Excursionist* began publication.

This also dealt with New Zealand, which Frank visited in 1888. He was delighted with the place, reckoning that it contained more tourist attractions within a limited area than any other country. He reported:

> In the South Island there are fjords rivalling those of Norway in solitary grandeur, waterfalls higher than those of the Yosemite, and lakes that will bear comparison with those of Switzerland or North Italy, with mountain ranges and peaks which test the powers of the best Alpine climbers. In the North Island is the wonderful Hot Lake district, as interesting as the far-famed Yellowstone Park, though the geysers are not so fine or so numerous. It is commonly thought that since the frightful eruption of Tarawera, which destroyed the pink and white terraces, there is nothing of interest in the district, whereas nothing can be further from the truth. The awful scene of desolation caused by the eruption is quite as interesting in its way, if not more so, than the terraces can ever have been, and the hot springs and geysers and the extraordinary mud volcanoes still remain uninjured. Then, again, beyond the region of Tarawera is the 'bush' or forest-land, which never ceases to charm with its endless variety of trees and ferns. The Maoris, too, though almost as degenerated as the Red Indians, maintain their old habits and habitations, and are worth the journey from England to see.[54]

Frank at once opened an office in Auckland. As the *New Zealand Herald* said, the event 'marks an epoch. It is the closing of the last link in a chain of communication encircling the world.' Cook was 'the creator of the system of travelling made easy' and despite his many imitators he 'still holds the premier place'. The *Herald* catalogued the 'wonderful achievements' of the firm and looked forward to 'shoals of tourists and globe trotters'. Cook's office 'largely removes the terrors of distance, giving tourists the certainty of trustworthy information and guidance'. All told, Cook's enterprise was 'one of the most startling developments of the age we live in'.[55] Just over a year later Cook's agent in Auckland, E. Bilborough, wrote to Frank forecasting that 'we might very shortly be able to do a lucrative business'.[56]

In the latter half of the 1880s the business was proving lucrative 'all round'. As John told Frank in 1888, 'Egypt is splendid', the

United States had produced £2,000 and France £700.[57] Total profits were running at an average of nearly £20,000 a year. So many people were booking with Cook that John was paying 'millions sterling annually to the chief companies carrying passengers to and fro in all parts of the globe'. His interests were 'greater now on the Continent of Europe than in my own country'.[58] Naturally John attributed the 'very large growth in travel' chiefly to his own organization, which now had a global chain of six journals 'entirely devoted to the promotion of travel'.[59] Cook's English *Excursionist* was selling over 100,000 copies a month and its foreign editions about half that number, all of them bursting with advertisements, not just for shipping lines and hotels but for Epps's Cocoa (grateful, comforting), Lithia Water (for gout and rheumatism), Mëen Fun ('Celebrated Chinese Skin and Toilet Powder') and Eno's Fruit Salt, which won the battle of Kandahar.

In August 1888 Ludgate Circus was 'literally besieged' by people wanting to escape the English summer and, at *The Times*'s suggestion, Thomas Cook & Son gave a daily weather report from European tourist centres.[60] It had become axiomatic that, as the *Fortnightly Review* said, 'The high pressure of our keenly competitive modern life has made at least a yearly holiday not a luxury of the wealthy, but a necessity of the workers as much to be reckoned with as the universal need of food and clothing.'[61] Everywhere, it seemed, people were on the move and requiring Cook's services. In Britain new recreations were becoming popular, such as watching professional football or sailing on the Norfolk Broads. Elsewhere the building of railways, in places as remote as Mexico and China, opened up novel destinations for the tourist. New European lines had the same effect: in 1888 John Cook travelled as 'an ordinary passenger' on the recently inaugurated Calais to Constantinople route. It was still a difficult journey, taking ninety-four hours, with many carriage changes, passport controls and customs checks – despite his 'fear and trembling' at the Turkish border, John reported to *The Times*, he was 'agreeably surprised to find . . . a very polite and gentlemanly Custom-house officer'.[62]

In the absence of trains, enterprising travellers sought adventure by other means. Probably encouraged by the Shah, whom Bert Cook brought to England in August 1889 (for which he was awarded the Order of the Lion and the Sun), Frank and Ernest soon afterwards went to Persia. Exploring the country's tourist possibilities, they covered 1,000 miles on horseback and brought back much arcane lore: Baku was the place to stock up with tinned soups and meats; English camping kit was essential because the post houses were 'usually little better than mud hovels, with no furniture, but plenty of dirt'; Tehran had 'very little to interest the traveller'; Isfahan was 'thoroughly oriental' with 'very fine' bazaars; this was no trip for ladies.[63]

In the same year the *Daily Telegraph* remarked:

> Like Puck, Mr Cook has drawn a girdle round the earth and
> enabled the Briton to 'do' the Pyramids with as much ease as he
> could 'do' Paris; but it is in the French capital that the veritable
> guide, philosopher and friend of all the pilgrims from Putney
> to Pimlico, or other parts of the British metropolis, has his
> hands full.[64]

Here, during the summer months, Cook's office in the Rue Scribe proved quite unable to cope with the crush of clients and elegant new premises were shortly found at 1 Place de l'Opéra. The reason for all this excitement was, of course, the centenary celebrations of the French Revolution. For several months Paris was '*en fête* day and night'.[65] The 'Universal Exposition', almost a city within a city, attracted 25 million visitors. As the *Excursionist* wrote,

> On no former occasion has the word 'Universal' been so
> applicable, both as to the cosmopolitan variety and extent of the
> exhibits illustrating the triumphs of science, art and industry, and
> as regards the comprehensive nature of the musical, theatrical,
> and other amusements to be met within the precincts of the
> Exhibition. The Gardens of the Palace and the Horticultural Show
> of the Trocadero present the appearance of a City of Flowers.[66]

Needless to say, the pièce de résistance of the 'grandest Exhibition the world has ever seen' was the Eiffel Tower – between 15 May and 31 July it took £100,000. With such attractions so easily accessible Thomas Cook & Son could hardly go wrong. The firm took 200,000 visitors to Paris, nearly half of all those who went from England. It made elaborate arrangements to board and lodge them, offering rates which varied between 4s. 6d. and £1 for bed and breakfast. A hundred horses a day were kept busy taking parties of Cook's tourists on sightseeing excursions. Profits that year were a record £22,819.

Meanwhile John Cook was inaugurating another enterprise, an unlikely but not an illogical extension of his tourist business. This was the funicular railway up Mount Vesuvius. Its history sheds an interesting light on both the man and his organization. The funicular had been built in 1880 by a Hungarian tramway promoter named E. Obleight and it inspired the Neapolitan song 'Funiculi, Funicula'. John first saw it in 1882, when his friend William Bemrose recorded: 'the toil of climbing up on the loose ashes is so great, that we decided to avail ourselves of the railway notwithstanding the unpleasant look it had'. They boarded a car taking fifteen people; a bugle sounded and at an angle of 65 degrees they travelled 1,000 yards in twelve and half minutes, pulled by a wire rope driven by a stationary winding engine.[67] On a busy day the funicular could transport 300 people. But costs were high – coal for the engine had to be brought up on horseback – and by 1896 the funicular was in financial trouble.

Obviously regarding it as a boon for his tourists, John first tried to subsidize it. Then, in 1887, he bought it as a personal investment, his firm to act as general agents. John at once found himself opposed by local vested interests. One lot he defeated in court, but a group of local guides tried to blackmail him to the tune of some £900 a year. When John refused to pay, they burnt down the station, cut the track and threw one of his cars into the crater. A further attack, after John had rebuilt the funicular, led him to close it down altogether for six months. This forced them to come to terms, and he reopened it in June 1889. John improved the funicular and during the 1890s it showed an annual profit of about £2,000. However, it was still limited by the horse-drawn approach and so John commissioned the building of an electric railway, nearly five miles long, linking it to Pugliano and Naples.

Because of 'difficulties of obstruction as well as construction',[68] this was not completed until 1903, four years after John's death. But it will be convenient, at this point, to follow the saga through to its end. The new line climbed up from Propriano, in the southern suburbs of Naples, passing through vineyards, chestnut and acacia groves, and into the lava fields with their extraordinary brown and pink shapes. En route there were superb views of the Bay of Naples, the isles of Ischia and Capri, and the Sorrento headland. The excursion attracted many tourists, among them King Edward VII and Kaiser Wilhelm II. Thomas Cook & Son (who had acquired the line) built a hotel, the Hermitage, at the end of the railway's middle, cog-driven section. The firm understandably made much of the four braking systems on its 24-seater coaches, but it was perhaps tempting fate to advertise the railway as the only one in the world ascending an active volcano. In 1906 Vesuvius erupted, destroying the top part of the improved funicular and smothering the whole area in ash. New track was laid by 1910 and new cars, complete with electric light, were installed. They in turn had to be replaced during the 1920s to carry the increased traffic (compensating Cook for losses incurred by the funicular during the Great War.) But during the depression years losses mounted again and in 1937, partly as a response to Italian nationalism, the whole enterprise was handed over to an Italian subsidiary which Cook formed to run it. After another damaging eruption, this company sold it in 1945 to the Secondarie Meridionale Railway for 3.1 million lire. In 1949 Cook divested itself of the run-down Hermitage hotel. The funicular was replaced by a chair-lift and in 1955, when the road was improved, the railway closed.[69]

Though eager to make money, even from something as unusual as a funicular railway, John Cook was no incipient Forsyte, no mere commercial calculating machine. He had Trollopean fears about insolvency: 'It is a wonder I sleep at all when I know that at waking every morning a sum of £3000 (approximately) will have to be found for the day's payments to my employees.'[70] He worried neurotically about business and sometimes turned business away in order to reduce his worries. In 1891, when the firm celebrated its silver jubilee, the *Excursionist* noted: 'Every year our anxieties and responsibilities increase, and if we may say so without meaning to cast the slightest reflection, the travelling public becomes more and more exacting.'[71] John even showed occasional reluctance to spread Cook's empire to places painted red on the map or to countries where the white man's burden was being borne.

Although the firm was appointed agent to Cape Government Railways in 1890, for example, John did little to encourage tourism in South Africa. The following year the General Manager of Natal Railways urged him to do so. 'I can well understand your indisposition to take up new business when your hands are so full all over the world,' he wrote. But gold discoveries were rapidly bringing South Africa forward, though the railway system was not yet complete and hotels were only 'gradually improving'.[72] Perhaps for these reasons John did nothing until the Matabele war roused public interest in the whole area. In 1894, a few months after the triumph of machine-guns and civilization, Cook organized the first personally conducted party ever to visit Bulawayo. Other tourists followed. But it was not until a larger war occurred, this time against the Boers, that Thomas Cook opened a South African office, in Cape Town. As *Punch* shrewdly observed, whether trade followed the flag was open to question, but Cook's tourists certainly did. [73]

Much was made of the firm's services to the empire at the silver jubilee celebrations in July 1891. Three hundred people, including 'Princes, Peers, and Excellencies', soldiers, sailors, MPs, journalists [74] and 'all classes of society', attended a banquet in the Whitehall Room at London's Metropole Hotel. The speeches were predictable. The old Duke of Cambridge declared that the nation and the army were indebted to Cook. Sir John Gorst, who privately told John that he had been 'scurvily treated' by the government of India, said that India owed him much. [75] John replied to the tributes and toasts in characteristic fashion, by conducting an inventory of the firm's assets – 84 offices, 85 agencies, 2,692 staff (978 of them in Egypt), 45 bank accounts. But he also spoke in more idealistic vein:

> It was his belief that the world would be a pleasanter place of habitation if all the dwellers on its surface were brought closer together, and that international travel was one of the best preservatives against international wars, since it dissipated absurd notions and dangerous prejudices.

Gladstone, one of two notable absentees from the festivities, also expressed typically high-minded sentiments in his good-will message. This was not 'a mere celebration of commercial success', he said, it was the acknowledgement of a public benefactor; and Cook's competitors 'are so many additional witnesses to the real greatness of the service you have rendered'. The other absentee was Thomas Cook himself. In his speech John said that he felt the 'keenest regret' that 'extreme old age' prevented his father's attendance. [76]

Thomas was certainly blind and his 'splendid physique' had decayed, [77] but he remained impressively mobile and alert to the end. In 1888 he had visited the Middle East, a journey of 'intense interest' and almost 'complete success', despite some 'physical derangement' caused by the shaking he received on the road from Jerusalem. It was a final pilgrimage, in which happiness and sadness were alloyed.

A 'considerable company of friends and dragomans' gave Thomas a 'grand reception' at Luxor and everywhere he bade 'goodbye to friends new and old who I never expect to see again'. Thomas told John: 'I can but express my admiration of the character and provision of this great steamboat service in which you have abundant scope for the full expression of organizing and administrative power which I know will be exercised to their full.' But his further comments, expressed with affecting humility, clearly reveal the constraint that still existed between them:

> if you desire to see me to talk over any matters that have come under my notice during the trip, I shall be very glad to call at Norwood before I return to Leicester. I am almost afraid to touch any details of the unhappy disputes in Palestine . . . [and I am not] desirous to enter into any disputes which have sole reference to your management of the business . . . . I shall say nothing unless you desire it . . . . I close this letter with the most sincere love to yourself and all connected with your family.[78]

In 1890, it is true, Thomas's left leg had been afflicted by gangrene, which broke out on a scar left by a fall he had had on some glass seventy-five years earlier. However, by the time of the firm's jubilee he had recovered from this. He went to church regularly, being driven in 'a closed-in carriage something like a glorified bus'.[79] And shortly before his death the following summer he was to pay a visit to Melbourne, where he had just erected a block of almshouses, before hurrying back to Leicester to cast his vote (for Mr Gladstone). In view of all this it is difficult to quell the suspicion that John deliberately excluded his father from the anniversary celebrations. Certainly John seemed determined that no one should share his limelight, let alone steal his thunder. In his address to the staff, John said:

> it would be mock modesty on my part not to know that to a great extent they had to recognise me as being, not the founder nor the originator, but, at any rate, one who had brought about such a system as has secured the admiration of the Globe to a business which is unique at the present time.[80]

If this was immodest it was not inaccurate, as the press plaudits confirmed. Admittedly, John buttered up his neighbours in Fleet

Street. But the jubilee was no mere advertisement. It gave public recognition to a powerful purveyor of British influence throughout the world. It acknowledged the imperial, as well as the international, role of an organization embracing what Joseph Chamberlain called 'Greater Britain beyond the seas'.[81] It confirmed, too, that in the contemporary imagination Thomas Cook & Son had become totally identified with the tourist experience. As *The Times*'s report of the jubilee noted, 'They have succeeded in imposing their name and organisation so deeply upon the public mind that we cannot think of Zermatt or Oban, of the Orkneys or the Midnight Sun, without at the same time thinking of Messrs. Cook and the little books of travelling coupons that we buy at Ludgate Circus.'[82]

Reporting the death of Thomas Cook almost exactly a year later, *The Times* was moved to further encomiums, paying particular tribute to the 'indomitable courage and energy' of the Julius Caesar of modern travel.[83] This was also a theme of the Rev. W. Bishop, Cook's friend and pastor, who preached his funeral sermon to an overflowing congregation. It included Cook's three grandsons (to whom he left his entire estate, £2,497 1s. 6d., a sum which reflected his charities), but not his son John, who just failed to get back from Norway in time for the service. Bishop praised Thomas Cook as 'a Liberal in politics, a sturdy Dissenter, and an enthusiast for all legislative and social movements . . . that gave opportunities for advance in intelligence and public freedom'. Perhaps some of Cook's views 'seemed to savour of intolerance' but they expressed 'the ardour of his feelings'. Nothing was more impressive than the 'pathetic and beautiful way in which our friend bore the sorrows which thickened upon him in his last days'. He had meekly accepted blindness and bereavement while admitting: 'I cannot understand the mysterious and painful nature of these dispensations.'

Having helped to 'unite by golden links of sympathy and mutual interest our own and other people', Cook had 'engaged in acts of public duty' to the end. This came suddenly: at 8 o'clock in the evening of 18 July 1892 Cook was seized with a sudden paralysis in his side; despite the efforts of his doctor he never rallied and by 11 o'clock he was dead. 'He has gone to his grave like a shock of corn fully ripe,' said the preacher.[84] The congregation was moved to tears. Bishop's son Albert, much affected by the gloomy appurtenances of the Victorian way of death – the black drapery in which everything was swathed, the solemn silence that pervaded the chapel, the flags (including that on the Temperance Hall) flying at half-mast – later wrote:

> I was young then and impressionable but it seemed to me that I could almost hear the beat of the wings of the Dark Angel of Death and catch a glimpse of the white wings of the Angel of Light as he carried the soul of the Departed to Him who made us all leave this Earth-bound place for another life elsewhere.[85]

Autocrat of the Timetable

In the course of his jubilee address to the staff John Cook said that 'during the past few years I have taken comparatively little part in the details of the management of this business'. Having taxed himself so heavily for so long, he now wanted to hand it over to his three sons.[1] This was largely self-delusion. Wherever he went John had a secretary at his elbow and much of his time was spent dictating voluminous memoranda about the firm's transactions. His 'supervision' was so minute and so minatory that, despite his protestations, it amounted to 'general management'.[2] Moreover he clearly had no intention of imitating his father and relinquishing control to his offspring.

Nevertheless, after 1885 John did increasingly concentrate on Egypt, spending every winter there. This was partly for the sake of his health and partly because he had fallen in love with the Nile. But it was chiefly because in Egypt he was building up his greatest enterprise. At home John was just a successful entrepreneur, one who still lived, with becoming modesty, in the suburb of Upper Norwood and sometimes permitted himself the extravagance of hiring a brougham.[3] In Egypt he was soon to be 'King',[4] head of the country's largest industrial concern and commander of a fleet of Nile cruisers which, as Arthur Faulkner had prophesied, eclipsed Cleopatra's barge of burnished gold.

The first of these steamers was the *Prince Abbas*, whose maiden voyage has already been described. *Tewfik* and *Prince Mohammed Ali* followed, constructed on the same scale, and in 1887 *Rameses*, the biggest steamer ever to have sailed on the Nile, entered Cook's service after the kind of epic struggle John relished. Originally built on the Rhône for the French government, it was quite unsuited for the open sea and nearly sank in a storm when crossing the Mediterranean. Then it proved too wide to pass through the Nile Barrage, the system of locks, dams and weirs that regulated the flow of water to the delta. Undaunted, John ordered its paddle-wheels to be removed, which meant cutting through thousands of rivets. When the *Rameses* had been pulled above the barrage 150 men, working in double shifts, carried out the refit. In six days they replaced the crankshafts, paddles and paddle-boxes; they built large saloons and berths on the upper decks; they painted, decorated and furnished. John personally superintended the work, staying on board the whole time. As the *Excursionist* proudly announced, the *Rameses* not only provided a 'first-class' steamer service for tourists, 'in the event of any future troubles' it could take a regiment from Cairo to Aswan and store their kit in its hold. Yet the steamer's draught when laden was only two and a half feet.[5]

By 1888 John had three new fast mail boats, a flotilla of launches and older towing steamers, a number of specially built, steel-hulled dahabeahs, assorted sailing craft and barges, as well as the four first-class steamers. In that year he bought a valuable riverside site at Boulac, in Cairo, from a member of the Khedive's family. Here he maintained his fleet and added to it. The yard's first major task was to assemble *Rameses the Great*, which arrived from the Fairfield Works on the Clyde in nearly 4,000 crates. For eleven weeks 393 men put together this steamer, which was 221 feet long, 30 feet wide, drew $2^{1}/_{2}$ feet, carried 72 passengers and was equipped with a 22,000-candle-power searchlight which enabled it to travel at night. As John smugly remarked during a 'sumptuous luncheon' for notables at the steamer's christening, the work could never have been completed so rapidly in an England bound by trade-union regulations, whereas 'Egyptians can be turned to valuable account under European tuition and supervision.'[6] As usual John had supervised the supervisors, driving on the labour by constant nagging – about the paintwork, the insufficiency of chairs, the lack of ashtrays, the fact that separate WCs were not clearly indicated for Ladies and Gentlemen. On 8 February 1890, four days after *Rameses the Great*'s maiden voyage, he told his son Bert that he was

> so disgusted and annoyed at a number of small things that
> have been neglected in connection with this steamer that
> I feel like discharging everybody who has anything to do
> with the controlling of these matters .... I cannot bear
> the worry and annoyance of not having somebody I can
> rely upon.

Writing to his sons, John invariably signed himself 'Your affectionate Pater'. But Bert, who was helping (much against his
pleasure-loving inclinations) to manage the Egyptian side of the
business, must have been sorely tried by his father's litany of
complaints over what he himself may have considered trifles.
The dahabeahs were inadequately provisioned with biscuits and
macaroni. 'Some mean skunk' had stolen the counters from one of
the bezique boxes. There were dirty finger-marks on the woodwork
and brass fittings of steamers after voyages. It was an 'imperative
duty' to inspect them minutely and 'I want to know who is to blame
for such gross neglect.' Finally: 'I begin to wonder whether we shall
ever have business properly managed at the Cairo office.'

John became even more demanding where influential clients were
concerned. It was vital to attend 'in the most careful business manner to the smallest request of travellers', especially 'such important
people' as the Egertons. John went out of his way to 'pacify ' one
'very wealthy man' and he took a personal part in tracking down
Lord Napier's luggage when it got mixed up with Lady Brassey's.
He paid 'every possible attention' to Joseph Chamberlain, who went
up the Nile at the end of 1889.[7] The papers joked about 'Joseph in
Egypt' and Chamberlain himself found Nubia so 'bitterly cold' that
he spoke disrespectfully of the Equator. But the visit had serious
consequences. It convinced Chamberlain that Egypt should remain
under British control and it helped to turn the former radical into
'the leader of the new Imperialism'.[8]

Lord Randolph Churchill, by contrast, had a brilliant future
behind him when he cruised with Cook in 1891. Still, John was
delighted to have won him away from the rival Tewfikieh Company,
for though 'not a very profitable affair . . . they would have made a
great advertisement out of it'. As it turned out, John was not able
to do so himself. To friends at home Lord Randolph extolled life on
the Nile: he enjoyed 'good food, hock, champagne, Pilsener beer,
Marquis chocolate, ripe bananas, fresh dates, and literally hundreds of French novels' and found his 'floating home in all respects
comfortable'.[9] But Lord Randolph complained to John Cook that
his dahabeah was deficient in a number of respects, not least that it
let in water. John was frantic: it was 'about the most amazing thing
I have met with for some years in connection with our business in
Egypt'.[10] Such setbacks apart, John usually managed to gratify the
great and he was increasingly courted by them. In 1895 Sir Alfred

Milner wrote to introduce an American diplomat and his wife, Mr and Mrs White, 'popular members of the best society London can offer . . . if you can do anything to help them [on the Nile] you will add to the many obligations under which you have already placed me and other Anglo-Egyptians'.[11]

John's scrupulous attention to detail combined with a soaring vision of what he could achieve in Egypt, gave him by 1892 'practically a monopoly of the Nile'.[12] Of course, he kept a watch on Gaze and Tewfikieh, the latter now managed by the Napoleonic Rostovitz, who had previously been John's right-hand man on the Nile. But, as a friend remarked, his competitors' 'wretched' steamers were 'deservedly looked down upon by the intelligent travelling public'.[13] Certainly they were no match for Cook's floating caravanserais, their brass gleaming like gold, their decks dusted with ostrich-feather brooms, their spacious cabins and well ventilated saloons fitted with every modern comfort and convenience. There were electric bells and lights (firmly switched off at 11 p.m.), good baths (though the Nile water looked like 'a cup of chocolate'), a broad lounge with thick carpets and huge windows, a ladies' saloon, a spotless restaurant, a refrigeration room with an ice-making machine, a well furnished library and reading-room, a piano, awninged promenade decks equipped with easy chairs and windscreens. Special arrangements were made for invalids and each boat carried a doctor.

The service was immaculate. As the author Douglas Sladen recorded, 'the beautiful Arab servants, in white robes, and bright red tarbooshes, sashes and slippers, glide about, filling up tea-cups as fast as they are emptied and bringing fresh varieties of Huntley and Palmer to compel people to over-eat themselves'. The meals rivalled those served in Edwardian country houses. Breakfast, for example, consisted of porridge or cereal; bacon and eggs, fish and other hot dishes; ham, tongue, chicken and other cold ones; jam and marmalade and 'excellent' bread and butter.[14] Lunches and dinners were on the same scale and there was a wine list to grieve the heart of Thomas Cook. Picnics, too, were feasts, complete with condiments like Crosse & Blackwell sauce, mustard, pickles and chutney. As Charles Royle, John's barrister friend, told him: 'The ship ought to be called the "Crameses" instead of the "Rameses" as there has been much more cramming than ramming on board.'[15]

Most people loved this sybaritic existence, this 'materialisation of *dolce far niente*.[16] As Kipling remarked, 'For sheer comfort, not to say padded sloth, the life was unequalled.'[17] Actually passengers were just active enough to consider that there was more to the experience than mere lotus-eating. But on excursions ashore to visit bazaars or see Ozymandian monuments they were carefully chaperoned by Cook's dragomans, exotic though reassuring figures given to making such announcements as this:

> Ladies and Gentlemen – Tomorrow, at ten o'clock, we arrive at Komombo; and in about five minutes walk to the Temple of Light and Darkness. Remember the very good light in the afternoon. Monument-tickets very much wanted! No donkeys to gallop![18]

Thus passengers were almost entirely insulated from Egyptian life, which itself became little more than a picturesque backdrop to a smart social scene. The river banks were a kaleidoscope of naked brown fellahin endlessly working shadoufs, women in black robes and yashmaks carrying pitchers on their heads, youths in blue gallabeahs supervising a multi-coloured menagerie of camels, donkeys, buffaloes, goats, sheep and oxen. Behind the dirty white lateens of feluccas, tourists spied grey clusters of huts, green fields of sugar-cane, yellow patches of corn, verdant palms, emerald acacias, purple hills, golden desert. There was an occasional flash of drama, a flight of brilliantly hued birds (no shooting at wildlife was permitted from Cook's steamers) or a glorious sunset over the Nile.

Little reality was permitted to intrude into this holiday fantasy. In particular, white men in silk suits and white women in satin dresses were not to be troubled by those whose skins were brown. The real captain of Cook's steamers was not the native *reis* but the European purser. John Cook was sensitive to Egyptian susceptibilities, but on his first-class boats he imposed an informal system of apartheid. As he wrote to Bert in 1889, 'we could not allow Egyptian officers or Pachas on the upper deck in the tourist season'. Many of them, 'with due deference . . . are yet not as cleanly as they shd. be'. 'You are quite as strong upon that point as I am,' he added, but no rule should be explicitly laid down as the matter was best 'left to our discretion'.[19] Pashas and mashers did not mix.

Few Victorians were free of racial prejudice (the Queen herself was exceptional) and nearly all Cook's customers suffered from it to some degree. Jerome K. Jerome hardly ever heard English spoken abroad without also hearing 'grumbling and sneering', particularly from 'rude and assertive' female tourists.[20] Douglas Sladen, whose praise of *Rameses the Great* has been quoted, showed that males could be even deadlier. He pronounced that 'the Egyptian has no mind. Certain superficial notions and effects of civilization he assimilates – no coloured man imitates the collars of Englishmen so accurately; but in intellectual capacity and moral adaptability he is not a white man.'[21] John may have felt that business required him to concede something to ideas like this. But perhaps he was not altogether untainted by them himself, despite his fondness for frequenting native coffee-houses where he played Arabs at chequers. He may, for example, have shared the disparaging attitudes of friends who talked about watching 'our Gyppy brothers feed'[22] and nicknamed Khedive Tewfik 'the Toothpick'.

To his face, of course, John always treated Egypt's nominal overlord with elaborate respect. Apparently it was reciprocated. John once personally conducted Tewfik up the Nile, towing the Khedivah and her ladies behind in a luxurious purdah barge. Strolling through the temple at Karnak one evening, John encountered the Khedivah and, before he could draw aside, she declared: 'I have always desired to meet the great Mr Cook.' They had a brief talk, during which she said how much she was enjoying her holiday, and through her veil John could discern her transcendent beauty.[23] Courtesies of this kind, however, did not stop John collecting the Khedive's debt speedily though unobtrusively the moment the political situation became volatile again in 1895.

Obviously it was in John's interest to remain on good terms with Egypt's inhabitants, from the greatest to the least. For Cook's business remained extremely vulnerable to disruption even though it was becoming the largest British concern in Egypt. By 1891 John had twenty-four steamers (of various classes) running on the Nile and the ramifications of his enterprise were enormous. George Steevens, the *Daily Mail*'s star journalist, reported:

> You will find natives all up the Nile who practically live on him.
> Those donkeys are subsidised by Cook; that little plot of lettuce
> is being grown for Cook, and so are the fowls; those boats tied
> up on the bank were built by the sheikh of the Cataracts for the
> tourist service with the money advanced by Cook.
> Therefore, when 'the Governor' is pleased to travel up

and down the Nile, you may see the natives coming up to
him in long lines, salaaming and kissing his hand. When he
appears they assemble and chant a song with the refrain,
'Good-mees-ta-Cook'.[24]

No doubt John's habit of distributing generous baksheesh had much
to do with this devotion. He habitually travelled with great sacks full
of copper coins and scattered largesse at every village landing-stage.
But most of his charity was more discriminating. In 1891, for example, he created the first hospital for Egyptians at Luxor. It treated
over 6,000 patients in the first year and (though Cook's tourists were
encouraged to subscribe) it apparently cost John the annual sum
of £500. At the opening ceremony the Khedive paid tribute to 'the
goodness of [John Cook's] heart'.[25]
　　This was fair enough. Of course, down the ages well publicized
philanthropy has been effectively used to conceal private rapacity,
and no doubt John considered such charitable acts to be good
business. But there is ample evidence that, despite his commercial
preoccupations, John possessed at least something of his father's
altruism. As one obituarist wrote,

He could design a silver knife that would serve either for fish
or fruit, and he knew to a pigeon how many birds were used by
the cooks on his boats. Yet this was a matter of business, and
in no spirit of meanness. No man possessed of such extraordinary
capabilities for doing good was more generous-minded, more
liberal, more munificent in his charities and in his kindly
hospitality.[26]

In the firm's archives there are whole files of acknowledgements
for donations to worthy causes varying from the Railway Servants'
Orphanage (John gave it a gymnasium) to British troops in Egypt
(he sent them Christmas puddings). Many personal letters testify
to the generosity of 'the kindliest and warmest of friends'[27] – 'Surely
you are the Prince of good fellows.'[28] A lady who knew him in Egypt,
Mabel Caillard, recorded:

He never forgot old friends, and during the period of his domination of the firm of Thomas Cook and Son – and no dictator
every conveyed a stronger impression of sovereign autocracy –
many old retainers had reason to thank his long memory for past

services, or for some specific act of help or courtesy, which had
procured for their old age an honourable employment which they
were never permitted to suspect of degenerating into a sinecure.

Mabel Caillard could not decide whether John was more benevolent than despotic. But her account of him vividly conjures up his
formidable personality, the real secret of his success in Egypt. She
went on two trips up the Nile as his guest, the first in 1882 when
she was a child. On that occasion, she recalled, John ordained
that the party should rigidly adhere to an arduous programme of
sightseeing. 'Mr Cook was the veritable autocrat of the timetable. As
we owed our pleasure, so we must pay the tribute of an indefatigable
punctuality, to the King of the Nile.' Unfortunately Mabel fell off a
pylon at Karnak and broke her leg. 'This made Mr Cook terribly
angry. His plans would, or might, be disarranged by the accident;
and the plans of Mr Cook were as irrevocable as the laws of the
Medes and Persians.'[29] John never ceased in his struggle to impose
punctuality on a land where, as Kipling said, 'Time had stood still
since the Ptolemies.'[30] Sixteen years later Mabel Caillard again
went on a Nile cruise with John. On this occasion the steamer was
delayed by hitting a sandbank above Asyut and it became too late in
the day to pass through the barrage. John was in a hurry to get back
to Cairo and he asked the Scottish engineer to open the gates. The
request was refused. There was a furious altercation in which the
engineeer finally declared that he 'would not open the Barrage again
that day for God Almighty Himself. "He will open it for me," swore
Mr Cook, dispatching a sheaf of telegrams to Cairo. He did.'[31]
Applying this fierce determination to every aspect of his business,
John never allowed himself to be awed by expert opinion or by the
special claims to wisdom of the man on the spot. When his Nile
manager Dattari asserted that employing seasonal staff inevitably
led to losses, John proved him wrong. In 1894 nearly half the firm's
revenue came from the steamers and that proportion may well have
been maintained to the end of the decade, by which time net profits
had soared to £82,000 and an American journal could exclaim:
'Cook simply owns Egypt.'[32] When his captains tried to resist the
introduction of bow-steering John made his point by taking one of
the steamers out in a gale. He thus 'revolutionised Nile navigation
by the sheer force of his will'.[33]
So John Cook's growing fleet, obedient to its admiral's lightest

word, steamed serenely out of the Victorian era, a miniature British navy ruling the muddy waters of the Nile. During the last decade of the nineteenth century Egypt increasingly became 'the winter playground of a great multitude of the representatives of the fashionable world',[34] the country above all others 'à la mode'.[35] In 1889 a Cairo doctor reckoned that 6,000 visitors spent the winter in the Egyptian capital, of whom about 1,500 went up the Nile aboard Cook's cruisers (most taking the three-week voyages to Aswan which cost £50, though some preferred the cheaper trips by express steamer, fourteen days for £25 or eleven days for £20).[36] Early in 1891 the *Egyptian Gazette* reported that the French Riviera was empty while Cairo was so full that Cook's steamers were having to be used as 'floating hotels'.[37] Two years later 'nearly every berth' on every one of Cook's boats was occupied and the firm was reluctantly obliged to decline proposals to cater for special guests of the Khedive.[38] In 1896 the Egyptian season was 'one of the most brilliant on record'.[39] Despite Kitchener's Sudan expedition, the winter of 1897–8 was also an unparalleled success. As George Steevens wrote, 'Cook's facilities have resulted in a prodigious influx of every nation into Egypt for the winter time.' He estimated that there were 50,000 visitors, mainly British and American but also a 'swarm of Germans', as well as Swedes, Portuguese, Siamese, Brazilians and others.[40] In 1899 another journalist described Cairo as 'a suburb of London'.[41]

The growth of tourism prompted an improvement in amenities, and vice versa. In 1889 Egypt was said to be modernizing so fast that 'a telephone line runs almost to the ear of the Sphinx'.[42] John Cook was in the van of progress. In Luxor he had lent his former agent Pagnon £11,000 to buy the firm's hotel, which Murray's *Handbook* now described as excellent. Early in 1889, though, guests were still complaining to John himself: the food was dull and dear; there were too few amusements and not enough easy chairs; electric bells were no compensation for earth closets. In a letter to Bert he wrote that it was 'annoying for me to be having to tell people constantly that I am not the proprietor and have nothing to do with the management of the hotel'.[43] Doubtless he also remonstrated with Pagnon, for later that year the Luxor Hotel was smartened up and extended to accommodate 120 people. Soon it was making £2,000 a year and guests were describing it as a 'place of delights . . . [for] luxurious lounging'.[44] Thanks to Cook, incidentally, and to

Egypt's growing fame as a health resort, the energetic Pagnon went from strength to strength. During the 1890s he became the lessee of the Grand Hotel at Aswan, and when this proved inadequate Cook 'arranged for the erection of a large new establishment' called the Cataract Hotel, which Pagnon also leased.[45] In 1907 he opened what the *Egyptian Gazette* called the 'latest addition to M. Pagnon's palaces in Upper Egypt'. Appropriately named the Winter Palace, it had room for 200 guests and was 'the finest and most elaborately-schemed hotel within the land of Egypt'.[46]

Following Pagnon's example, Shepheard's Hotel (where Cook still had an office) was rebuilt in 1891. Later described as 'Eighteenth Dynasty Edwardian', it retained its gorgeous Oriental interior but incorporated such Western appliances as lifts and electric lights. At the behest of Cook, Cairo's facilities for sport and recreation also improved. Nor were the ancient monuments neglected, for it has always been a central paradox of the tourist industry that it seeks to preserve what it threatens to destroy. As early as 1884 John had told the Director of the Office of Antiquities, Gaston Maspero: 'I am still desirous of doing everything I can to meet your views and to carry out the proposed arrangements of protecting the antiquities, and charging the travellers a fee to cover expenses.' There had been some tourist depredations. But John said that complaints had also reached him about 'the manner in which your Guardians themselves disfigure the hieroglyphics and points of interest in the ruins', throwing stones to indicate what they were pointing at and knocking off pieces to sell to visitors.[47] John clearly saw himself as curator as well as guide to the world's largest outdoor museum. He subsidized restorations and excavations. He helped Egyptologists like Flinders Petrie and Wallis Budge. He rejoiced at such events as the 'veritable resurrection', in 1893, of the temple at Kom Ombo.[48]

Perhaps some Egyptians feared that tourism posed a threat to their cultural heritage, but most were happy to enjoy the economic benefits it conferred. As Kipling wrote, 'Granted that the tourist is a dog, he comes at least with a bone in his mouth, and a bone that many people pick.'[49] In 1889 the American edition of the *Excursionist* estimated that Cook's tourists spent two and a half million dollars a year in Egypt and this figure increased almost fourfold over the next twenty-five years.[50] No wonder *Vanity Fair* declared (as early as 1889) that: 'The chief person in Cairo is Cook.' Its roving reporter continued:

The nominal ruler [of Egypt] is Tewfik; but Tewfik takes his
orders from Baring; and Baring, I suspect, has to take his orders
from Cook. The latter Sovereign becomes more and more potent
as we get further up the Nile and here at Luxor, where a special
hotel has arisen under the light of his countenance, he figures
quite as a modern Ammon-Ra. It seems likely too that his might
and majesty will increase.[51]

About Cook's primacy Egyptians agreed. John's chief dragoman
once introduced Lord Cromer (as Baring became) to an Egyptian
provincial governor who had never heard of him but was 'very
happy to know any friend of Mr Cook'.[52] Some Egyptians actually
thought that Cook was king of England. Others regarded him as
their own sovereign, if not their saviour. At Aswan the people put up
an inscription to him in hieroglyphics which read: 'King of Upper
and Lower Egypt, John son of the sun, Cook and Son, Lords of
Egypt, Pharaoh of the boats of the north and south . . . He is a
great man, Lord of the Nile, and gives bread to the mouths of the
people of Thebes.'[53]

Another remarkable tribute came from the painter G.F. Watts,
who went up the Nile with Cook in the winter of 1886-7. As the *Pall
Mall Gazette* later reported, Watts was struck by

the distrust and grave suspicion with which the English Government and its engagements seemed to be regarded by the natives,
from pasha to fellah, and contrasted these sentiments with the
confidence and respect accorded by them to the word and deeds
of Mr John Cook, whom they have come to look upon as the
Minister of Transport in the country.

The artist felt that Cook, 'whom prejudice still sets down as a
mere tourist and ticket agent . . . [was] in reality, "an apostle of
civilization"'.[54] On a more personal level Watts was grateful for the
'intellectual and emotional enlargement of his horizon' afforded by
the Nile voyage and for the care and comfort he had enjoyed at
Cook's hands. As a token of his appreciation for all this he gave his
painting *Fata Morgana* to the Leicester Art Gallery in 1889, telling
the city corporation that it was an acknowledgement of Cook's
'admirable administration and honourable dealing' in Egypt.[55]

In Egypt, as in India, John tried to promote his firm from private
to public agency, and with similar success. In 1898 George Steevens

described Cook in Egypt as 'a kind of Government office without red tape'.[56] And thirty-five years later an internal company report said that Thomas Cook was almost 'an official British institution'. As the report made clear, this position gave the firm's managers 'access to everybody', helping it to yield 'handsome profits' and to avoid paying burdensome mooring and navigation taxes.[57] For all its patriotism and magnanimity, the firm never lost sight of the fact that it was a commercial enterprise. John Cook, in particular, did his best to exploit its unique status in Egypt during the two years (1896–8) when Britain was engaged in the process of reconquering the Sudan and defeating the Khalifa (the Mahdi's successor). On this occasion, however, he met his match in the brusque, blue-eyed, handlebar-moustached person of Horatio Herbert Kitchener.

Kitchener was both more imperious and more ruthless than the travel agent. He was also more penny-pinching, a characteristic reinforced by the fact that he had to conduct the campaign on a shoe-string. 'What a tight grip the Sirdar has,' wrote one of Cook's managers in March 1896. So far, he added, the actions of the military 'do not betoken a very friendly feeling towards us', although Kitchener 'may find himself compelled to come to terms with us'. Kitchener never did. In fact Cook's involvement in this grab for one of the last available pieces of Africa was more limited than it had been in the Gordon Relief Expedition. The army offered 'anything but a fat contract' and the firm was chiefly responsible for transporting men, animals and supplies between Balliana (the limit of the railway from Cairo) and Aswan.[58] Admittedly it made the most of this commission. As young Winston Churchill noted on his way to Omdurman, 'The versatile and ubiquitous Cook had undertaken the arrangements, as his name painted on everything clearly showed.'[59] Further south Kitchener assembled his own flotilla of stern-wheelers and gunboats. He also constructed a railway. As Churchill further observed, the River War was won on the iron road.

Nevertheless there was plenty of scope for clashes between Cook and Kitchener. Almost at once relations became 'somewhat strained' because, in the absence of a clause in the contract, the firm tried to charge the army full tariff for transporting stores and mail, whereas it allowed the Egyptian government half rates.[60] John had to accept the arbitrators' reduction. Next Kitchener wanted to requisition the *Ibis*, one of Cook's stern-wheelers. John would not agree to his terms and in any case, 'I don't believe they want Ibis for a gunboat – they want her for her carrying capacity.' Whatever the reason, Kitchener took the *Ibis*. John complained to Cromer, who acted as a benevolent arbiter between his two over-mighty subjects. He told John: 'I can only express a hope that when the present incidents are closed, you will be able to re-establish the friendly relations which formerly existed between the Egyptian authorities and yourself.'[61] The Sirdar also seized some of Cook's barges. As his tourist operations were not harmed John was delighted: 'The Sirdar is playing into our hands . . . we shall charge what we like for them . . . he puts us in the best possible position for a claim.'[62]

John was livid, though, when Kitchener forbade his steamer the *Prince Abbas* to go above the First Cataract, presumably because the general did not want tourists (particularly female ones) impeding the war effort. John sought counsel's opinion about the 'freedom of the Nile' and then instructed the *Prince Abbas* to proceed, saying: 'it is better for us to take the initiative and not to *ask* the Sirdar'.[63] Kitchener responded with characteristic vigour. He placed a guard over the steamer and a telegraph wire across the cataract, and he said that if Cook's agents disobeyed his orders they would be liable to trial under military law. John protested but capitulated. He also exacted a tiny revenge, refusing to allow his steamers to tow the barges which Kitchener had taken until the army came to terms with him over their use. All told, during the Sudan campaign Kitchener clearly defeated Cook as well as the Khalifa. As Sir George Newnes wrote, 'Egypt is now in the hands of two armies of occupation. One is composed of British soldiers, and the other of the men of Thomas Cook & Sons. The latter generals have certainly taken possession of the Nile' but elsewhere they were 'worsted with severe loss'.[64]

John Cook was doubtless chagrined, but by now he could afford the occasional reverse. Everywhere his business was flourishing as never before. Each year he was introducing tourists to new experiences and barely explored corners of the world. In 1891 the American *Excursionist* puffed the 'grandeur' of Alaska.[65] The following year the British *Excursionist* printed its first description of 'the Norwegian ski'.[66] In 1893 Cook began running steamer trips to the West Indies, much to the delight of Jamaica's *Daily Gleaner*: 'we are "discovered" in the modern sense, and if we succeed in pleasing the fastidious tastes of the class that will shortly visit us we may also in the modern sense be "made".'67 Twelve months later Morocco was puffed, as Algeria had long been, as a health resort. Simultaneously Thomas Cook & Son inaugurated new tours to Dalmatia, Bosnia and Herzegovina, 'an almost undiscovered country' whose 'exquisite scenery' could now be appreciated by their clients thanks to the development of 'comfortable railways', good roads and modern hotels. Sarajevo was 'well worth a visit', declared the British *Excursionist*,68 while the French edition recommended to its readers the 'pretty village of Berchtesgaden'.69

To satisfy the 'inexhaustible . . . desire for novelty among a large number of veteran tourists' and to cash in on the bicycling boom, Cook first organized 'Continental Conducted Cycling Tours' in 1896. The initial party of twelve (including ladies) made an 'eminently successful' trip through Normandy – the 'cobble stones, or *pavé* of French towns at first were very annoying but we soon got used to them'.70 These tours became 'extremely popular'.71 So did day trips to Boulogne, which were begun in 1897. The next year Cook arranged for the more 'adventurous traveler' to visit Khartoum, now wrenched from the Khalifa's grasp and only twelve days from London, and the Klondike, where the gold rush was in full swing and John apparently considered buying a river steamer and 400 pack mules.72 During the course of 1899 pioneer tourists travelled from St Petersburg to Vladivostok on the new trans-Siberian railway. In that year Thomas Cook & Son issued about 7 million travelling tickets (more than twice the number sold a decade earlier) and claimed to be the authorized agents of every steamship company and railroad line of repute in the world.

At the start of the 1890s John celebrated his growing prosperity by taking a 'cottage-gothic' country house at Sunbury. It was called 'Rivermead' and he filled it with mementoes of his travelling life: Japanese curios, Eastern photographs, water-colours of foreign scenery. The house contained a large library, its great bow window overlooking the lawn, and the first centrally-heated conservatory in Britain. This was the haunt of a mina bird named Jimmy. Other pets were a St Bernard called Bernard and an amorous Scotch terrier named Rob. Presiding over this 'riverside temple', John seemed, with his bald pate and his snow-white beard, a venerable figure. But as a journalist who came to interview him noticed, the managing partner of the house of Cook moved with 'business-like celerity'.73 George Steevens, too, received the impression that he was in the presence of 'a man of force': 'His white eyebrows bristle resolutely over the eyes that such a man ought to have, eyes that look out of their sockets like a gun out of a port, blue eyes that ... think as well as see.'[74] Clearly 'Rivermead' was a symbol of success, not a sign that its occupant proposed to retire into rural domesticity.

In fact, at the end of 1893, shortly before his sixtieth birthday, John set off on a round-the-world tour to inspect his empire. Unlike Thomas, he did not keep a record of his progress, but a few details survive. In Japan John met Count Ito, the Prime Minister, and overcame the opposition which had earlier prevented his opening a Japanese office – he had only had an agent in Yokohama (who rescued Kipling in 1892 when he was stranded as a result of the failure of the Oriental Banking Company). Now, with official encouragement, Cook set up a bureau at Yokohama – tragically most of the staff were to be killed when it was destroyed in the 1923 earthquake. In establishing friendly relations with the Japanese, John managed to spark off a row with British residents. He remarked publicly that they were 'in the country to make all the profits they can out of it' whereas his 'globe-trotters' spent a lot of cash on curios.[75] The English-language *Japan Gazette* reacted angrily, dubbing John 'king of the cheap trippers' and asserting that he was starving Japanese hotel keepers by his 'low rates'.

> He is the good genius of the impecunious. People who have not
> enough to live on in comfort, but travel to avoid social expenses,
> apply to COOK. They then travel like a lot of school-children.
> Rise when they are told, walk up a hill to order, and go to bed
> according to time-table.[76]

Subsequently Thomas Cook & Son did their best to encourage tourists to visit Japan, whose people, John noted, had just built their first locomotive. The American *Excursionist* recognized that the country had 'almost suddenly taken rank as one of the powers of the world' but, it declared, Japan was still 'beautiful, quaint and attractive' in its unique Oriental way.[77]

In Australia John also made a powerful impression. The Adelaide *County* was struck by his 'commanding presence' and by the favourable terms he offered prospectors to take them to the gold-fields.[78] John himself reckoned that 'the business of the firm is bound to

increase very considerably' in this region and he sent Bert assess-
ments of the different Antipodean offices. They were surprisingly
mild. He was 'very much pleased' with Sydney and 'well satisfied'
with Auckland, though the manager was 'disposed to "play off his
own bat"'. Brisbane, Dunedin, Hobart and Melbourne were also
satisfactory. The firm had an excellent agent at Invercargill, an
'Honourable'. But John's most poignant comment concerned the
Christchurch office. It was 'well conducted' but the manager, Mr
Taylor, 'has made himself objectionable . . . from the fact that . . .
he is a very prominent teetotal advocate, and is looked upon as a
leader of the prohibitionist movement in that part of New Zealand'.
Understandably John 'did not feel [he] could go into the matter'
himself but he arranged for Taylor to receive a warning.[79] Thomas
Cook must have turned in his grave.

After his global tour John devoted himself mainly to special
events, though he never lost control of the firm. Early in 1896, for
example, he peremptorily dispatched Bert to deal with problems
that had arisen in the Paris office, saying: 'we are not going to
allow our business to be injured by anyone in the service . . . and
. . . unless such complaints are put an end to at once, whoever is
concerned in them will have to go'.[80] But for the last few years of his
life John was mainly preoccupied with his most distinguished clients
– royalty. John dearly loved a monarch and he was profoundly
gratified to receive greetings from such as his 'friend' the King
of Sweden and Norway, who exclaimed: 'What a great business
yours is.'[81]

Royal commissions were even better. In 1895 the Empress
Frederick of Germany told her daughter, Crown Princess Sophia
of Greece – where the first Olympic Games since classical times
were to be held the following year – that she had heard that the
country was 'uncomfortable and ill-arranged' for tourists. 'No one
in the world could remedy this like Cook – you know what wonders
he has done in Naples and Egypt.'[82] Cook was duly summoned and
he helped to make the Olympiad a success. For developing 'the facilities of international communication' with Greece John was made
an Officer of the National and Royal Order of the Saviour.[83] Also
in 1896 one of Cook's couriers discreetly smoothed Queen Victoria's
path to Nice on the French Riviera, and so pleased was the Queen
that she made him her personal tour manager, in which capacity
he also served King Edward VII. Towards the end of this busy year

the firm organized the travel of the Tsar of Russia and his entourage from Leith to Ballater in Scotland. This was a major undertaking because there were assassination fears and the royal party brought an 'enormous amount of baggage'. John went to Scotland 'to see that everything was done in the best possible manner' and, despite various small dramas, the journey was accomplished without mishap. As tokens of thanks Queen Victoria sent two of John's senior men superb tie-pins.[84]

The following year Thomas Cook & Son helped to make Queen Victoria's Diamond Jubilee into the most successful imperial pageant ever staged. As Kipling wrote, 'London is simply packed and double packed. . . . There are 80,000 *extra* Americans in town; and Cook the tourist man has practically chartered the suburb of Richmond for their accommodation.'[85] Cook also chartered four large boats, including the *Marguerite*, the finest excursion steamer in Europe, so that clients could see every detail of the Spithead Review, an unprecedented muster of naval might consisting of 173 ships. In London the Ludgate Circus office was converted 'for the nonce' into a private club and a thousand of Cook's friends, customers, agents and staff saw the royal procession pass on its way to St Paul's. It was a glittering spectacle. The Queen, in the state landau pulled by eight cream horses, was hailed with 'unfeigned rejoicing . . . by all classes of people'. And she was supported by royalties of all sorts, including the maharajas brought from India by Cook, as well as 50,000 troops, the largest force ever assembled in the capital.

Altogether the Jubilee was enough to 'tempt Time himself to . . . lean a spectator on his scythe', and it prompted the *Excursionist* into a characteristic leap from patriotic flag-waving to commercial drum-beating. The Queen had given 'her name to an era unparalleled in the world's history for progress in the arts of civilisation'. Among the 'many marvels' of her reign 'few have had more far-reaching effects than the development of travel'. When she came to the throne not one railway ran out of London north of the Thames, no steamer had crossed the Atlantic and there was 'not a single first-class hotel in all the Metropolis'. Now London was full of luxury hotels. 'Floating palaces' reached America in five days where clippers had taken forty. A return trip by diligence to Switzerland via the Rhine which had cost £36 and taken sixty-six days could now be accomplished in two weeks for £9. Since Thomas Cook's first excursion train 'it is as if a magician's wand had been passed over the face of the globe'. It was not surprising that his firm was now 'honoured by the constant movements of almost every member of our own Royal Family' and those of nearly all European countries.[86]

John's devotion to royalty may well have been fatal to him. As one contemporary wrote, he was 'killed by the too rigid performance of a task that overtaxed his failing powers', namely organizing Emperor Wilhelm II's visit to the Holy Land in 1898. Certainly John's health had long been undermined by his 'undue devotion to business' in general,[87] and friends deprecated his embarking on a new royal venture even though it would be the 'crowning enterprise' of his career.[88] John had personally conducted the Kaiser up Vesuvius in 1896. Impressed by Cook's organization, Wilhelm then said that he would travel with him to Palestine. John promised to undertake the arrangements. Nominally the Kaiser's aim was to attend the consecration in Jerusalem of a Lutheran church, a newly converted building whose tower topped the Holy Sepulchre (and became known, because of its resemblance to a candle-snuffer, as 'Willie's Extinguisher').[89] Actually Wilhelm was indulging his inordinate love of travel – he was nicknamed the 'reise Kaiser' – and hoping to do some political fishing in Middle Eastern waters.

Having visited Sultan Abdul the Damned in Constantinople, the German Emperor landed at Jaffa in October. The imperial party consisted of 105 Germans, including the Kaiserin and her suite. They were escorted by 27 pashas, with their 80-strong entourage, and 600 Turkish troops. To transport the royal pilgrims Cook had scoured Palestine and Syria, assembling 1,500 animals, 800 muleteers and 116 landaus, carriages and carts. Under Frank Cook's guidance this colourful array set off for the Holy City, the Kaiser on horseback, his followers straggling for miles over the landscape in a haze of heat, dust and flies. As one of John Cook's friends said, 'The business was like the movement of an army in the field.'[90]

The camping was also arranged with military precision. Each evening a city of tents sprang up, furnished and carpeted with more than Oriental splendour. In the dining saloons 290 waiters and attendants served huge meals on tables groaning with solid English silver. Such was John's attention to detail that he even struck a medal which was inscribed on the obverse 'Pass to the Imperial Camp' and on the reverse 'T.C.&S.' When they all finally encamped in an olive grove outside Jerusalem the Kaiser complimented Frank Cook on the arrangements, remarking: 'You must have half a thousand tents here, Mr Cook.' (In fact, there were three hundred.) Wilhelm also shook hands with John and said: 'On Vesuvius I made you a promise. On Vesuvius you made me a promise. We have both fulfilled them, and I am gratified.' However, Wilhelm was disappointed by Jerusalem. It looked too modern. 'Yes,' John replied, 'it does from this side of the city, but they have made it more so by the whitewash they have used just now.'

The Kaiser smiled, but the citizens of Jerusalem really did make sterling efforts to welcome him. They flew flags and illuminated the streets with lanterns. They knocked a 'huge gap' in the wall next to the Jaffa gate so that the royal party could enter the city by the widened road past the Tower of David.[91] They even renovated the Holy Sepulchre. The police also took extraordinary measures, barring Moslem women from the Kaiser's route in case they had secreted stilettos in their veils. But when, on 29 October, the Kaiser entered Jerusalem in state, a romantic figure wearing a helmet surmounted by a golden eagle and a white ceremonial uniform with a voluminous cape, and sitting astride a black charger, Moslems and Christians alike greeted him with unfeigned enthusiasm. Only a few German tourists were unhappy, for at the head of the royal procession rode its English impresario, Frank Cook.

The German Emperor's 'expedition to the Orient'[92] caused fury in France and unease in Britain. Even in the United States it provoked suspicion. '*The New York Times* accused Wilhelm of trying to set himself up as 'a sort of Protestant Pope'.[93] Cook's involvement encouraged critics to express their resentment in the form of ridicule. Thus *Punch* lampooned Wilhelm as 'Cook's Crusader'.[94] Its French equivalent, *Le Rire*, which printed a cartoon of Wilhelm entering Jerusalem on an ass in emulation of Christ, suggested that he had done a lucrative deal with Cook – the Emperor would travel for nothing and take half the 'handsome profit' made from all the tourists following in his wake.[95] Actually the Kaiser paid Thomas Cook & Son £48,130 2s. 3d. for their labours.

This was not an excessive sum, for no other organization could have achieved what they did. By now John Cook was almost as much a power in the Holy Land as he was in the land of Egypt. According to an English newspaper, he was received in Jerusalem 'with the greatest demonstrations of joy and respect by the inhabitants, who regard him as scarcely inferior in importance to the Emperor himself'.[96] 'In Syria,' an American visitor recorded, 'they call him "King Cook".'[97] There, indeed, tourists mouthed the monosyllable like an incantation, an Open Sesame in a country bound by Ottoman bureaucracy and mired by medieval methods of transport. '"Cook! Cook! Cook!" we croaked,' wrote Rider Haggard, 'the only name which seems to have power in Syria; that famous name of the hydra-headed, the indispensable, the world-wide Cook.'[98] Actually, Cook did have his limitations. For all the subsequent advertisements, even a royal Cook's tour of the Middle East was not like riding on a magic carpet. Thus the Emperor curtailed his journey on account of the 'excessive heat and the discomfort of travel'.[99]

John Cook himself was badly affected by the heat and during the Kaiser's expedition he contracted dysentery. He first sought refuge in Egypt, voyaging, as a mark of special favour and in a curious reversal of roles, on board the Kaiser's dazzling yacht *Hohenzollern*. But John's condition deteriorated and he soon returned home. He died on 6 March 1899 at his new residence, Mount Felix, in Walton-on-Thames. John was buried in the family vault at Leicester, his funeral being attended by a host of dignitaries, among them Lord Cromer. In its obituary the *Excursionist* praised John's 'organising genius, his marvellous energy, and his tremendous capacity for work'. With due solemnity it concluded that his opening of Egypt to tourism was 'an event as notable as, and not altogether dissimilar to, the opening of the Egyptian ports by the progressive [Pharaoh] Psammetichus 2,500 years before'.[100]

Cook & Grandsons

John Cook's body lay a mould'ring in the grave but his soul went marching on. As one employee recorded, John's 'personality was so strong that, although he had been dead more than six years when I joined the staff, it was just as if he was still directing operations from his room overlooking Ludgate Circus'.[1] Certainly the momentum which John had given the firm, and the discipline he had instilled into its cadres, carried it successfully through the Edwardian era and beyond. This is not to say that his sons Frank Henry (1862–1931) and Ernest Edward (1866–1955) – they bought out Thomas Albert (Bert), who died in 1914 aged only forty-seven – were incompetent to run the business. Indeed, loyal members of staff like Faulkner claimed that Frank was 'a splendid combination' of his father and his grandfather. The fact was, though, that both Frank and Ernest lacked precisely their forebears' most important qualities, the creative imagination of Thomas Cook and the executive drive of John.

Part of the problem was that the brothers had for so long been overshadowed by their father, an uncompromising paternalist if ever there was one. Thus when Frank got into some serious but unspecified trouble at his public school, Mill Hill, it was John's forcefulness which saved him from expulsion. He wrote to the vice-principal, a teetotal friend named Robert Harley who had formerly been a Congregationalist minister in Leicester: 'It is true I do not know sufficient of my family but I have yet to learn that Frank has the slightest particle of vice, wickedness, untruthfulness, or dishonour in his composition.'[2] Frank and his brothers were later packed off to a college on the Rhine to learn German, and then they were set to work in the family business. Though diffident, Frank was an adventurous youth. He enjoyed the challenge of exploring new tourist areas – he had travelled by himself through the Caucasus – and he was good at acting as his father's agent in remote spots. The more effete Ernest, after some experience of the pioneering life, insisted that he would only work in the Banking Department, on the first floor of the Ludgate Circus office, which he did conscientiously and efficiently until his retirement. As if to demonstrate his family's move from clogs to spats in three generations, Bert Cook was a wild young man with extravagant tastes and a liking for liquor. Once the paternal eye was off him he set up as a country gentleman, buying Sennowe Park in Norfolk in 1902. Here he busied himself with rustic pursuits, among them nocturnal duck-shooting by searchlight (for which the coastguard fined him) and playing practical jokes on his guests (such as squirting them with water through a specially rigged-up copper branch of a huge beech tree near the house).

Unlike their father, the brothers had interests outside the business. Frank was keen on shooting and art. In 1905 he built himself a grand new house at Barnett Hill in Wonersh, Surrey, filling it with elaborate furniture, walnut panelling, decorated tiles, French tapestries and crystal chandeliers, and bringing over craftsmen from Italy to carve intricate plaster patterns on the domed ceiling over the main staircase. (During the Second World War Frank's widow gave it to the Red Cross, who now use it as their national training centre.)[3] Ernest collected paintings and was a connoisseur of architecture. He particularly admired the 'wonderful baroque domes' of Vienna and he liked to tell the story of how, as a new Cook building in Cockspur Street neared completion, 'I told them to stick a dome on top of it – *and it's all wrong.*'[4] Both brothers were conservative Conservatives. They were also excessively shy. Despite his uncanny resemblance to Kitchener – 'they might have been twin brothers'[5] – Frank was an 'extraordinarily modest, retiring man'. He later turned down the opportunity to become Lord Mayor of London. Ernest, who may well have been homosexual, subsequently became a recluse. He used his great fortune to amass an impressive collection of pictures and to preserve England's architectural heritage, restoring buildings like Montacute, Dalby Hall in Leicestershire and the Bath Assembly Rooms. James Lees-Milne, who later had dealings with him on behalf of the National Trust, found Ernest withdrawn, foxy, devious, rebarbative and strange. He remembers

> calling on Mr Cook once at his house at Sion Hill, Bath. I pressed the bell and simultaneously, without a second's lapse of time, the door opened and Mr Cook stood before me. He must have

31 Fin-de-siècle John Mason Cook

32 Frank and Bert Cook (right)
in Greek costume

33 Landed gentry: the Cook brothers after a shoot

34 Ancestor of the traveller's cheque

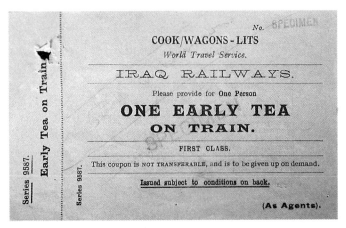

35 & 36 Vouched for by Thomas Cook

37 Le Météore en route for Versailles, 1905

38 The Edwardian excursion

been waiting with his hand on the door knob for twenty minutes
because I was (regrettably) late, having come a long distance.
Even so I was not allowed beyond the door mat. I forget the
nature of our business. It was over in a trice and I was dismissed.
He was immaculately dressed, and slightly sinister I thought . . . .
He certainly was a mystery man who shunned the limelight.[6]

Lacking their father's overweening self-confidence, Frank and
Ernest ran the business in a much more bureaucratic and less
personal fashion, though they too won the loyalty of their staff.
As one travel courier wrote, Frank was 'a model boss, firm
but fair. If any client complained about his employees he took
their part on principle . . . He placed the highest trust in people
who worked under his direction.'[7] Where they could the brothers
delegated, relying on the team that their father had assembled in
Ludgate Circus. This was a sensible policy, for as Sir Henry Lunn
discovered after his 'disastrous' failure to run tours in competition
with Cook, that firm had 'an immense organisation carried on by a
large army of experts'.[8] Lunn only succeeded in the tourist business
when he founded the specialist Public Schools Alpine Sports Club in
1903. According to his son Arnold, Lunn thus capitalized on his own
'instinctive prejudices against all foreigners', taking abroad winter
sportsmen 'who were glad to carry with them to the Alps the social
environment in which they had been born and bred'.[9] Meanwhile
the house of Cook dominated the Edwardian travel scene. Between
1900 and 1913 (inclusive) it made an average annual profit of over
£86,000.

During these years, admittedly, 'the tourist movement . . . surpassed anything of its kind ever known in the history of the human
race'.[10] The number of Britons who annually crossed the Channel
rose from around 650,000 to perhaps a million.[11] American tourism
also 'assumed enormous proportions'. In 1900 Thomas Cook's New
York manager told the *Sun* (whose great editor Charles Dana had
considered the firm 'an unmixed blessing') that he was 'fairly
stunned by indications . . . [of] a radical change in American
sentiment'. Thanks to the 'fairy tale' quality of accommodation
on board ocean liners, smart clients were now willing to cross the
Atlantic second class.[12] By 1914 some 150,000 Americans came to
Europe annually, arriving like an 'Army of Invasion'.[13]

True, before the Great War foreign tourists of all nationalities still belonged to 'a privileged class'.[14] The exiled Oscar Wilde complained ironically to his agent:

> The English are very unpopular in Paris now, as all those who
> are over here, under Cook's direction, are thoroughly respectable.
> There is much indignation on the Boulevards. I try to convince
> them that they are our worst specimens, but it is a difficult task.[15]

As always the rich tended to assume that by moving from place to place they were getting somewhere, even if it was only away from their acquaintances. But among every class a holiday of some kind was now more than a custom, it was a rite. All sorts and conditions of Edwardians aspired to enjoy a change of air, scenery, mood, pace – from those who bought Newnes' popular journal *The Traveller* (founded in 1900) to those who listened to Hilaire Belloc lecturing (in 1909) on travel as the highest form of culture.

If the climate was right for travel it was not necessarily right for travel agents. In 1900 several companies in the United States failed, leaving hundreds of Americans stranded all over Europe, some of them, according to *The New York Times*, held 'in pawn' by Venetian hotels.[16] A couple of years later Lunn nearly preceded Gaze into bankruptcy by making elaborate arrangements to bring tourists to Edward VII's coronation, which was postponed on account of the King's illness. Cook only succeeded because the firm was reckoned to be among the 'three most competent organisations in the world' – the other two being the Roman Catholic Church and the Prussian army. This reputation was not simply spread by word of mouth, it was disseminated by writers. The impoverished Wilde, for example, begged his friends not to send money by registered mail, which took eleven days, but to transfer it through Cook's office, which took three hours – 'They wire money like angels.'[17] In 1913 Kipling wrote a fulsome letter to Frank Cook acknowledging the heroic efforts of the Paris office to get him from Bourges to Athens in time to attend King George's funeral: 'I don't suppose that this sort of thing is anything new to you but it pleased me as a client and an ex-journalist more than I can say.'[18]

Even more remarkable was Mark Twain's extravagant eulogy:

All conditions of men fly to Cook in our days. In bygone times
travel in Europe was made hateful and humiliating by the wanton
difficulties, hindrances, annoyances, and vexations put upon it by
ignorant, stupid and disobliging transportation officials, and one
had to travel with a courier or risk going mad. You could not buy a
ticket for *any* train until fifteen minutes before that train was due to
leave. Though you had twenty trunks, you must manage somehow
to get them weighed and the extra weight paid for within fifteen
minutes; if the time was not sufficient, you would have to leave
behind such trunks that failed to pass the scales. If you missed your
train, your ticket was no longer good. As a rule, you could make
neither head nor tail of the railway guide, and if your intended
journey was a long one you would find that the officials could tell
you little about which way to go; consequently you often bought the
wrong ticket and got yourself lost. But Cook has remedied all these
things and made travel simple, easy, and a pleasure. He will sell you
a ticket to any place on the globe, or all the places, and give you
all the time you need, and as much more besides; and it is good for
all trains of its class, and its baggage is weighable at all hours. It
provides hotels for you everywhere, if you so desire; and you cannot
be overcharged, for the coupons show just how much you must pay.
Cook's servants at the great stations will attend to your baggage, get
you a cab, tell you how much to pay cab men and porters, procure
guides for you, or horses, donkeys, camels, bicycles, or anything
else you want, and make life a comfort and a satisfaction to you.
And if you get tired of traveling and want to stop, Cook will take
back the remains of your ticket, with 10 per cent off. Cook is your
banker everywhere, and his establishment your shelter when you get
caught out in the rain. His clerks will answer all the questions you
ask, and do it courteously. I recommend . . . Cook's tickets . . . and
I do this without embarrassment, for I get no commission. I do not
know Cook. [19]

Ironically, soon after writing this, Twain travelled from the
United States to Sweden with Cook's organization, which lost all
his luggage and failed to trace it. The author was indignant and
he penned a sinister, and in some ways a prescient, comment on
the firm:

The things is that about a year ago the German emperor travelled
to Jerusalem, also with Cook's Travel Agency. The Managing

Director for the Agency, Mr Cook himself, was so shocked by the honour that fell to him of giving service to this important person that he turned mad with pride and subsequently passed away. He took the secret of how to handle a travel agency to his grave.[20]

Apart from such exceptional lapses, though, there was little to suggest that Cook's firm was languishing under its new management. Indeed, it was taking some enterprising initiatives.

During the Boer War, for example, the Cook organization was not only employed by the government to transport 'foreign "undesirables"' from South Africa to their respective countries,[21] it also ran conducted tours of the battlefields. These attracted much attention, some of it unfavourable. Cook stressed that tourists, who paid 150 guineas for the privilege, would only visit 'accessible' sites.[22] But even this seemed in doubtful taste, for an imperial war fought against white men armed with Mauser rifles was evidently much less of a spectator sport than previous Victorian conflicts. *Punch* satirized the whole undertaking with unwonted sharpness:

In myriads behold they come,
And almost ere the guns are dumb,
The picknickers' champagne will pop
Upon the plains of Spion Kop.
O flag! O tourist! Powers twain
That all the world resists in vain,
Where 'neath the one the other picks
The wings and legs of festive chicks,
And strews the battlefield with bones,
Newspapers, orange peel, plum stones –
There is the reign of darkness done,
And Freedom's fight is fought and won.[23]

Other journalists made predictable jokes about keeping the Cook out of the Kitchener.

In the United States Cook moved to new and expanded premises, 245 Broadway, in 1900 and experienced 'the most extraordinary season' ever in transatlantic travel. This was largely due to the Passion Play at Oberammergau, Queen Victoria's visit to Dublin (where new hotels were built as England's 'Sister Isle . . . roused from her Rip Van Winkle sleep')[24] and the French Exposition in Paris. To this Cook took 1,000 people a day (some of them staying in 'specially erected hotels for visitors under our excursion arrangements') to see a huge display of the technological and other triumphs of the nineteenth century.[25] Among the exhibits was a gigantic celestial globe capable of holding 100 people and featuring a tour round the world in a series of immense panoramas, and a model of a hygienic hotel room which 'offered no refuge to the little nocturnal insects too frequently encountered' in French establishments. But more important to travellers even than this advance was the arrival of new road vehicles.

In 1900 the first electric automobile service to connect with a railway began in Washington D.C. Soon afterwards Cook was advertising excursions 'en automobile' to Switzerland and the beautiful voitures which Parisians called 'Cook's Carriages', pulled by splendid percherons,[26] were superseded by motor coaches with names like Le Météore and La Comète.[27] These were probably the first gasoline-driven conveyances ever to transport tourists on sightseeing expeditions and they ushered in a new age. The transport revolution had its snags: by 1909 Cook was advising travellers to flee from the 'petrol-reeking breath of the city'.[28] But it also promised freedom and progress on a scale never seen before. As the *Excursionist* declaimed in 1900, 'who shall say that the wildest dreams of Jules Verne may not be realised' in the twentieth century?[29]

In this optimistic spirit Frank and Ernest did much to modernize the firm during the Edwardian era. New telephone lines were installed and by 1910 there were fifty extensions in the Ludgate Circus office. New advertisments were formulated: 'There are spots on the sun but not one spot on earth you cannot visit with the aid of Cook's Tickets'; 'A Cook's Ticket like a Magic Carpet will take you anywhere you wish'.[30] In 1903 the *Excursionist* was transformed into *Cook's Traveller's Gazette*, a bland, glossy publication produced with considerable professionalism. However, what the *Traveller's Gazette* gained in dignity it lost in originality. Promoting foreign destinations, its writers used almost every cliché in the tourist lexicon. They specialized in giving spuriously romantic titles to faraway places: Ceylon was 'the Garden of the World';[31] the Rockies were 'Nature's best picture gallery'; Iceland was the 'tourist's wonderland'; New Zealand was 'the Switzerland of the Southern Hemisphere'.[32] No doubt the hyperbole was harmless, though it was also rather absurd – if Bangkok was the Venice of the East, was Venice the Bangkok of the West?

More questionable was the journal's acceptance of the grosser standards of the Edwardian era, an acceptance that would have shocked Thomas Cook and probably John too. The latter, for example, had shared his friend William Bemrose's opinion, when they visited Monte Carlo together in 1879, that the place was 'a hell upon earth'.[33] Now the *Traveller's Gazette* puffed the casino's 'magnificent play-rooms'. It also advertised horse-racing in Baden-Baden, 'one of the most delightful watering places in Europe'.[34] And it contained piquant suggestions that travel afforded exciting new opportunities for sexual dalliance. The *Gazette* quoted a contemporary author who described Boulogne as 'a gay and rather improper little town, where English and French mingle annually, without asking too many inconvenient questions'. It dwelt at length on the geisha girls of Japan. It also took to printing discreet 'pin-ups' of exotic foreign females. The caption under the photograph of a beautiful Sinhalese girl read: 'The warmth of their passions and the strength of their affections are said to be hardly inferior to the charms of their person.'[35]

Under the new dispensation Thomas Cook & Son made a calculated appeal to Edwardian men of the world. Pandering more blatantly than ever to snobbery, the firm encouraged its patrons to take their vacations in the most exclusive fashion they could afford:

> Those who find happiness in spending their holiday at Ramsgate eating shrimps, if not yearly less in number are lower down in the social scale, and all who are considered anybody by those around them look upon a continental tour as an imperative duty.[36]

For Cook's fashionable clients, the *Traveller's Gazette* suggested, holidays of various kinds were now as much part of the social round as Ascot, Henley and Cowes. November was 'the little season' when London became a staging-post for 'the Cairo crowd, the Riviera crowd, the Swiss winter sport crowd, and the more go-ahead set who are off to the States, to India or to the Colonies'.[37] Nurturing such pretensions, the firm was increasingly prone to stand on its dignity. In particular, it could no longer tolerate public attacks on vulgar and ignorant tourists. In 1903 it actually took out an injunction in New York against Clyde Fitch's play *The Girl With Green Eyes*, which introduced a group of Cook's 'gentlemen and ladies' as comic extras incapable of distinguishing the Apollo Belvedere from Diana the Huntress and indifferent to both. In court the firm asserted that its parties consisted of 'people of education and refinement'. But Cook's pompous lawsuit was punished not so much by its failure as by the comment of Clara Bloodgood, the play's leading lady, who said that 'the action is funnier than the tourists'.[38]

The American *Traveller's Gazette* hit back vigorously. It insisted that Cook's parties were 'being "taken" by a class of people that until recently would never have selected that mode of travel'. And it printed testimonials from clients who had been personally conducted through lands where '"the folks are furren and the customs queer"'.[39] Cook's tourist ventures seemed increasingly designed to attract the 'smartest of the smart'.[40] In the winter of 1902–3 the American office arranged a Mediterranean cruise on the 'exceptionally luxurious' air-conditioned, 12,000-ton SS *Moltke*, which was so successful that an additional ship had to be chartered.[41]

Cook opened up further 'winter playgrounds' for the rich – Sicily, Cuba, the Balearic Isles. Incurring what the *Bermuda Royal Gazette* called 'a heavy initial outlay on advertising . . . the world-famous firm of Thos Cook & Son'[42] also '"discovered" Bermuda as a summer resort'.[43] Throughout the Edwardian period the firm added to its steamer fleet on the Nile and continued to promote Egypt as the resort for the '*élite* of fashionable society of every nation'. In 1908 it launched the *Egypt*, 'the "Mauretania" of the Nile', joined three years later by its sister ship the *Arabia* – making a total of thirteen first-class boats. Each year the Cairo season became 'increasingly brilliant', Cook claimed. Soon, en route to the pyramids, 'the gods with very long purses' no longer had to endure 'those terrors of an *al fresco* meal' – blue-gowned donkey boys dropping hard-boiled eggs in the sand. Instead they rode in a 'perfectly appointed victoria' to enjoy a 'sumptuous luncheon' at the Mena House Hotel.[44]

Occasionally the gods with very long purses wanted something more exciting. Cook arranged balloon ascents over Mont Blanc, golfing and skiing holidays, trips to sporting events from the Cup Final and the Olympic Games (held in London in 1908) to the World Sculling Championships which in 1910 took place on the Zambezi. One of the firm's most adventurous and expensive tours began in 1903. It was a journey up the Nile to Khartoum, south to Lake Victoria, and then on to Nairobi ('the St Pancras of East Africa') and Mombasa by the new Uganda Railway.[45] This climbed through stunning, game-filled scenery to a height of 8,200 feet and was nicknamed 'the Lunatic Line'.[46] Thomas Cook & Son regarded it as a monument to 'British pluck and British brains, backed by British money', a symbol that this part of Africa was 'a white man's land' and a triumphant achievement in opening up 'the Dark Continent' to the traveller.

The *Traveller's Gazette* also declared that 'civilization has worked a striking transformation in Khartoum' since Kitchener's victory at Omdurman (Cook ran excursions to the battlefield). A new Governor-General's residence was being raised on the ruins of Gordon's palace; a two-mile promenade was laid out along the Nile and planted with palm trees; a large hotel was furnished from England. Further south, however, Cook's tourists became travellers. They had to cope with herds of marauding hippos near Gondokoro, 'a nuisance if not a source of danger'. They went on safari with native porters through 'the death-dealing miasma' of a 'foetid swamp'.[47] They camped amid primeval jungle in the heart of what Winston Churchill, who travelled through it in 1907, called a 'glittering Equatorial slum'.[48] As one pioneer wrote, 'it was just like sleeping in the Zoological Gardens, except that there were no bars to keep the animals within proper bounds, and one went to bed expecting to see an elephant's foot appearing through the side of the tent.' It also differed from the zoo in that visitors could kill the animals, which they did with abandon, enjoying 'excellent sport'.[49]

This type of adventure was particularly attractive at a time when the increasing sophistication of communications was taking the thrill out of travel. Reporting on Marconi's 'gradual perfection' of wireless, which had enabled the liner *Barbarossa* to radio news of her temporary breakdown in mid-ocean in 1903, the *Traveller's Gazette* commented on the disappearing romance of the sea. The romance of the road was also vanishing, and Cook tried to revive it with nostalgic stagecoach trips from London to Guildford and back, costing £1 for an inside seat and involving six changes of horses. Answering the call of the wild, Cook pioneered ventures into the interior of the Congo and trips to the Victoria Falls, compared with which, an American tourist remarked, Niagara was 'only a profuse perspiration'.[50] Cook also ran new tours to Petra and hitherto inaccessible regions east of the Jordan. Here, camping in the 'wilderness', far 'away from civilization', travellers could enjoy 'all the romance which made tours west of the Jordan so fascinating a quarter of a century before the days when carriage roads, hotels, railways and steamboats invaded the land'.[51]

If creating new travel confections to tickle the palates of the rich was the most glamorous part of Cook's business, the most laborious part was attending to the routine needs of the mass market. Cook issued millions of travelling tickets for events as mundane as Whit Bank Holiday excursions and as recherché as Esperanto conferences. The firm offered ten-day winter sports holidays in Switzerland (for ten guineas) and cheap day trips to the seaside. Early in the Edwardian age it initiated Popular Tours for those 'prepared to travel abroad under less luxurious conditions than those of our Select Conducted Tours' and to forgo 'wagon-lits, daily carriage drives, and palatial hotels'. Such tourists were free to arrange their own itineraries and they paid Cook a fixed sum for the 'package' of second-class travel and accommodation.[52] That led the firm to make the most important single innovation since the introduction of the hotel coupon, Independent Inclusive Travel. This system simplified the whole tourist process by offering individuals an all-inclusive tariff, as in conducted tours, and arranging the details of each itinerary in advance. Cook was able to obtain favourable terms for the independent traveller through massive buying power, guaranteeing large sales to the hotels and transport companies in return for low rates. The application of bespoke methods to individually tailored journeys not only cheapened them, it really did, as the firm claimed, take the trouble out of travel.

So, during the first thirteen years of the new century, Thomas Cook & Son flourished as never before. New departments of the business, established in the late Victorian era, proved their worth – Shipping & Forwarding, Parcel Express, Luggage Insurance. The last had sent *Punch* into an ecstasy of punning:

Bravo, Thomas Cook & Son. Not 'too many Cooks' but 'just Cooks enough'! Hitherto the traveller had only to present himself ready 'dressed' to be thoroughly 'Cook'd,' and done throughout to a turn. Now, in addition, his baggage can be book'd and Cook'd and should any 'Gravy delictum' happen to it, the value of the lost portmaneau and boxes will be handed over to the aggrieved passenger.[53]

Basking in such endorsements, the house of Cook seemed as solid
as the Edwardian furniture exported all over the world by Maples.
Like the British empire, it appeared to be enjoying a golden age.
Like the Mississippi, the firm just kept rolling along. True there
were small wars and rumours of large ones. For many years Cook
had been fearful that the business of peace might be disrupted by
some major conflict. In 1889 the *Excursionist* had written: 'With so
many millions of armed men all over Europe, a spark may cause a
conflagration.'[54] But in the glorious summer of 1914 there seemed
no hint of an impending storm.

Ireland was troublesome, of course, but elsewhere the travel scene
was bright. Germany, holding music festivals, an International
Exhibition of the book industry at Leipzig and an Industrial Exhibition at Cologne, was a particularly inviting destination. Summer
cruises to Scandinavia were also popular: special attractions were
the Baltic Exhibition at Malmö and a total eclipse of the sun, which
would be visible from Norway in August. The *Traveller's Gazette* was
heavy with advertisements: the Keptonn Treasure Garter, worn
just below the female traveller's knee (and well above the hem of
her skirt), was ideal for holding money or jewellery; Zotos cured
sea-sickness; La-rola was good for the complexion. New arteries
of communication were being opened: a motor road to Banff, the
Furka railway, a scenic railroad from Denver to San Francisco via
Salt Lake City. The Panama Canal was about to bring the East
8,000 miles nearer the West. In the Hague a huge project financed
by Andrew Carnegie was being completed, the International Palace
of Peace. In Britain the Bank Holiday weather continued and Cook
advised clients that: 'The great August Feast of St. Lubbock will
soon be upon us.'[55] Then, six weeks after the assassination of
the Austrian Archduke Franz Ferdinand at Sarajevo, when the
ultimatums, the alliances and the mobilizations had clicked into
place with the remorselessness of a railway timetable, came the
Great War.

It arrived so swiftly that some 6,000 British tourists were stranded
on the Continent. Not all of them were Cook's, but the firm made
valiant efforts to bring them back and some were actually rescued
from enemy territory. This was largely due to the work of Edward
Huskisson, a descendant of the politician who had joined the firm in
1898. He raced to Geneva with £500 in gold, mustered refugees from
European holiday resorts (including Carlsbad) and sent them home

by roundabout routes in special trains. Similar evacuations, though on a smaller scale, took place elsewhere. For example, Cook's man in Constantinople, W.K. Jeffery, helped British people to get out of Turkey. But if the firm reacted promptly to the first wartime emergency it was slow to appreciate the implications of Armageddon.

So were other institutions, of course, at a time when the national watchword was 'business as usual'. But initially Cook seemed unwilling to acknowledge the very existence of the war. The *Traveller's Gazette* continued to advertise tours to many places in Europe, North America, Egypt, South Africa, Australia and the Far East, assuring its readers: 'There is no reason why the holiday should be abandoned.'[56] During October 1914 there was an 'exodus abroad' and Cook's 'conductors escorted some sixty travellers to resorts in the south of France, Italy, and Switzerland'. The 'usual Christmas programmes' were available at England's seaside hotels and elsewhere.[57] And in the New Year even *The Times* recommended holidays in France. Despite travel problems (the journey from London took twenty-one hours, five more than in peacetime) and new passport regulations, tourists would have no difficulty in reaching the Riviera with 'the expert help of Messrs. Thomas Cook & Son'. There they would have the dual satisfaction of relieving the hardships of 'anti-Teutonic' hoteliers and of finding everything 'considerably cheaper than heretofore'.[58] Not being 'fashionably thronged', the Côte d'Azur would be 'invested with new charms' and although it could offer no carnival fêtes there would be a variety of entertainments.[59] A.E. Housman paid his first visit to the Riviera in the spring of 1915 'when the worst classes who infest it are away'.[60]

By then it was becoming clear that tourism and total war did not mix. In March Cook announced that despite 'stray' enquiries from 'would-be visitors . . . we have not the slightest intention of organising . . . sight-seeing expeditions' to the battlefields of the Western Front. 'When the war is over it will be different.' But while fighting continued the French were 'strongly opposed' to such trips,[61] though some Americans and privileged Britons were given conducted tours of selected trenches.[62] At Easter and Whitsun the usual excursion trains were suspended in Britain and people were encouraged to spend their holidays at home, 'a blank and depressing prospect' according to *The Times*.[63] Instead of tourist information Cook printed the names of 580 of its staff who had volunteered to serve in the forces. Some tourists did continue to visit France, though by September the only organized parties were restricted to Paris. There were also other Continental and domestic tours, popular and select. But Cook was increasingly defensive about them.

Holidays, the *Traveller's Gazette* argued, were necessary to promote health and efficiency. To abolish them would be a 'false economy'.[64] This theme was repeated in 1916. People would not 'seek the same gaiety and pleasure' in vacations while 'so many are facing danger and death in the various fields of the world-war'. But to recruit themselves before and after labour was an act of patriotism. So Cook offered to prepare itineraries and supply couriers for individuals and families visiting the Continent. By then 'touring on the other side of the channel' was 'practically out of the question' for organized parties.[65] But British tours still went to Canada and the United States, and the firm puffed places like Atlantic City, 'The Seashore Pleasure Ground of America'. It also advertised other remote destinations. Literally and figuratively, it promoted castles in Spain. Motoring in the Philippines was recommended. South America 'has taken the place for the present of the Old World as a field of travel'.[66]

Early in 1917 travel was 'virtually tabooed' for British citizens except for the strictest 'business and health purposes'. Anticipating the later slogan, 'Is your journey really necessary?' the government appealed to the public to ease pressure on the railways for the sake of the war effort. To encourage compliance, the railway companies raised fares, diminished services and restricted baggage allowances. Tourism became distinctly unpatriotic and Cook was limited to offering 'The Friendly Hand' to those '*compelled*' to travel. Although some newspapers continued to advertise Monte Carlo as a resort even in the grim winter of 1917–18, the British tourist business now virtually collapsed. Cook suffered badly. The *Traveller's Gazette* shrank to twenty-eight pages. Staff took severe pay cuts. The Vesuvius railway made considerable losses. Cook in Egypt was almost defunct: the Nile steamers had stopped running in 1914 and were taken over by the government for war purposes; the Winter Palace at Luxor had become a hospital; Aswan was 'like a city of the dead'.[67] In Palestine, anyway out of bounds because of the war, the Turkish army had seized all Cook's camping equipment. About the only new venture the firm could undertake in the last year of the war was to organize drives round 'the chief "wonder places" of London' for colonial troops. This it did at the request of King George and Queen Mary.[68]

There were a few bright spots on Cook's commercial horizon. The Shipping & Forwarding Department grew enormously, becoming one of the most efficient freight services in the world. Despite redundancies, the firm managed to keep a nucleus of experts together. This was largely due to the government, which gave them the work of handling enemy mail. Through Cook's Amsterdam office in neutral Holland, Britons were thus able to keep in contact with relations and friends domiciled in enemy territory. Most of Cook's foreign offices remained open for business, running a huge variety of tours to regions of the world 'where peace prevails and beauty reigns'. In February 1917, the American bureau, which took 'elite' parties anywhere from Alaska to the South Sea Islands, went so far as to say that 'the closing of many once-popular regions by war may well be forgotten. It is now a negligible factor in the situation.' Even more crassly, a few months after the United States had entered the war, the American edition of the *Traveller's Gazette* informed readers that it was better to join the army of tourists as a volunteer 'than to wait until your doctor conscripts you'.[69] Other Cook's offices tried to ignore the war altogether. The Far Eastern edition of the *Traveller's Gazette* filled its pages with lyrical articles extolling places like Japan as tourist resorts. Snow-capped Fujiyama, cherry blossom in springtime, autumn chrysanthemums in Kyoto, the pearl fisheries of Yamada, the golf course near Nagasaki, white sails skimming over the sea at Ise Bay, automobiling from Yokohama to mountain resorts with geysers, hot springs and comfortable hotels – Japan was an escapist's dream.

There was no escaping the fact, though, that the house of Cook was seriously damaged by the war. At the most fundamental level, 153 of more than 1,000 members of staff who served in the armed forces were killed. Wounds rendered many others unfit to return to their (guaranteed) jobs. Altogether between 1914 and 1918 the firm made a financial loss of about a quarter of a million pounds. Cook's global organization was severely disrupted. As the *Traveller's Gazette* wrote shortly after the armistice in 1918, 'Peace and Travel are inseparable sisters . . . . The flight of the one is the extinction of the other.'[70] Yet the Great War was only the first of several shattering blows which Thomas Cook & Son were to be dealt by the twentieth century.

Cook & Wagons-Lits

After the sacrifices of the world war an exhausted people looked forward to the rewards of peace, few of which were more alluring than holidays. In the summer of 1919 the British made for the shores of their island like lemmings. Although thousands of military vehicles were re-bodied as charabancs to take passengers by road, the railway system was almost overwhelmed. The seaside resorts were engulfed. Yarmouth and Clacton had never seen such crowds. More than 300,000 people invaded Blackpool, where many had to sleep on the beach. Others walked the streets all night or returned home because they could find no lodgings. Some women and children were accommodated in police cells.[1] None of this worried a nation released from the thrall of war. As the *Daily Telegraph* said, 'After having been "pent up" for years the public would have been taken with a passion for "getting away" somewhere if travelling had been three times as bad and five times as expensive.'[2]

When overseas travel restrictions were eased, in the spring of 1919, there was also a considerable exodus to Europe. Many of those who crossed the Channel did so to visit the scenes of the conflict. Cook ran six-day tours of the battlefields by motor coach, a vehicle which was to change the face of European tourism during the 1920s. The firm justified these excursions somewhat anxiously. Tourists came 'not because of a morbid desire to view the wilderness of devastation, but in token of their heartfelt gratitude for the blessings of peace'. They were paying 'homage to the memory of the Glorious Dead'.[3] Thus the war contributed to the postwar boom and the travel industry benefited immediately. Thomas Cook & Son netted a profit of £139,268 in 1919, just over the 1913 figure and well under those for the next decade, when average profits amounted to more than £200,000 a year.

A small item in the accounts for 1919 was earned by a momentous new means of transport, aviation. At Easter Cook became the first travel agency to offer pleasure trips by air. They were made in converted Handley-Page bombers which cruised at about 70 miles an hour. Cook assured clients that this biplane was not 'a "stunt" machine'; it could not 'loop' or do 'trick flying'; it could stay aloft using half its power; and anyway neither the two-engined nor the four-engined version would be loaded to full capacity, twenty and fifty passengers respectively. The half-hour joy-rides cost two guineas, including light refreshments served by an attendant en route. A thousand people made their way to Cricklewood in order to experience this thrilling new dimension in travel.

Cook was not always quick off the mark between the wars. But evidently someone in the organization, perhaps the adventurous Frank, appreciated the further possibilities of these wood-and-canvas contraptions which braved the skies. In 1919 the firm became passenger agents to the principal aerial companies. It issued an illustrated booklet entitled *The New Highway in the Air* and forecast that 'Space will be annihilated, the cities of the world will be brought within the reach of all.' A couple of years later Cook was booking clients on flights from London to Paris and Brussels, with links to more remote destinations. As the *Traveller's Gazette* somewhat optimistically pronounced, a 'trip to the Continent by air' had become a 'recognised part of the modern tourist's programme'.[4] The firm was also organizing the transport of goods by aeroplane and arranging airborne excursions over the battlefields. Cook's aerial business, which included the first escorted tour by plane (from New York to Chicago in 1927 to see the Dempsey–Tunney heavyweight boxing contest) and Zeppelin flights across the Atlantic in 1928, grew steadily but slowly. Fears about safety persisted, though airlines gave a generous allotment of free tickets to travel agents, on the theory that they would afterwards recommend flying to their clients. But passengers' confidence could hardly have been increased when, before taking off, they, as well as their suitcases, were weighed. Despite subsidized progress, made after the formation of Imperial Airways in 1924, fewer than 50,000 passengers a year were flying from Britain to foreign parts by the end of the decade.

On the ground another revolution was taking place during the early 1920s. As travel facilities were restored, as excursion trains began to run once more, as the regular Dover–Calais service was resumed and tourism revived generally, many people enlisted in a great new 'army of sun-hunters'.[5] In the past fashionable people had avoided the sun, wearing hats, veils and kid gloves (as advised by Baedeker) and cultivating the peaches and cream complexion associated with gentility. But after the drab days of the war there was a sudden 'fetish [for] sunburn'[6] and within a remarkably short time a Mediterranean tan was *de rigueur*. Mad dogs and Englishmen went out in the midday sun.

Doubtless cultural forces, such as Impressionism and naturism, were at work. But the change was also encouraged by medical opinion, which had previously regarded the sun's rays as dangerous – a view reviving today. In 1922 Dr Eve told the British Association that 'sunshine is the source of practically all the energy on the earth'.[7] The following year Auguste Rollier, 'the high priest of modern sun-worshippers', published an influential book entitled *Heliotherapy*. The effects of the 'solar revolution' were profound.[8] The French Riviera, until then an exclusive winter resort, now became a popular summer one. It became, in fact, the forerunner of today's Spanish 'costas', with their formula of sun, sea and sex (not to mention double gins for sixpence), which Britain could never duplicate because of her climate. By the mid-1920s the streets of Nice and Menton were packed with 'bronzed armies of *flâneurs*'.[9] Noting that Cook had risen to fame 'on the upper middle-class tourist', *The Observer* said that the firm's 'newest customers are of a more democratic kind still', haunters of the Côte d'Azur 'to whom it would never have occurred before the war to go further than Margate'. In 1926 one French newspaper suggested that Cannes was full of British unemployed who had spent their dole money on a trip to the Riviera.[10]

Preposterous though this was, the *Traveller's Gazette* acknowledged that 'every report of thronged stations and tripled boat trains has its tale of the exodus of Mr and Mrs Everyman and their families'.[11] What Cook's journal did not acknowledge was that new or improved travel agencies were rising to cater for this class of tourists. The Workers' Travel Association (founded in 1922) was growing rapidly. The Polytechnic Touring Association, having anticipated Cook's use of display advertisements, made progress. Dean & Dawson was expanding. So was American Express, which had firmly established itself as a European travel organization by 1909 despite its President James C. Fargo's objection to having 'gangs of trippers starting off in charabancs from in front of our offices the way they do from Cooks'.[12] Sir Henry Lunn's brother

George, 'full of brilliant ideas in connection with developing and operating new tours',[13] was widely regarded as 'the biggest man in the travel business' during the 1920s, 'a giant among travel agents'.[14] Even so, Cook remained supreme. Aspiring travellers of any pretensions were quick to imitate Owen Rutter's hero Tiadatha (Tired Arthur):

> Then along Pall Mall he hastened . . .
> Round to Thomas Cook in Pall Mall,
> Thomas Cook, the ever-helpful,
> Thomas Cook, the trouble-saver . . .[15]

Tourism was encouraged by a strong pound and by foreign inflation. It benefited from, and fostered, further female emancipation. It was promoted by new bodies – for the first time governments began to appreciate that tourism was, as Lord Derby said, an 'invisible export of great value'.[16] In 1924 the International Union of Official Organizations for Tourist Propaganda was founded (later changing its name to omit the last word). Five years later the precursor of the British Tourist Authority came into existence. Economists now saw tourism as an industry, one that certain nations were particularly well placed to develop. One remarkable forecast was made as early as 1923:

> it is even possible that the part ultimately reserved for the British
> Isles in the scheme of the international division of labour will be
> that of a playground and park and museum to exercise the youth
> and soothe the declining years of the strenuous industrial leaders
> congregated on either side of the Pacific ocean.[17]

Other novelties stimulated the growth of tourism during the 1920s and were duly exploited by Thomas Cook & Son. The Prince of Wales was an 'indefatigable traveller'. He set a good example, in Cook's view, as a peripatetic peacemonger, and he added glamour to faraway places from Udaipur to Uganda.[18] The Bolshevik Revolution had aroused much interest in the Communist experiment and by 1929 Cook's 'Russian business was well established'. This was due largely to the efforts of John Harmshaw, who believed passionately that the Soviet Union would be 'the country of the 20th century, just as the United States was of the 19th'.[19] Italy was more attractive now that Mussolini had supposedly made the trains run on time. As the *Traveller's Gazette* asserted in 1923, with 'typical Fascista thoroughness' the dictator had made 'discipline among the staff' and the 'regular working' of railway services 'two highly important accomplished facts'.[20] And in New York publicity manager Malcolm La Prade exploited the new medium of radio with a popular programme called 'The Man from Cook's'.

In Switzerland skiing overtook skating as the most popular winter sport, a fact Cook recognized by presenting a Ski Challenge Cup. In France the discovery of prehistoric cave paintings near Toulouse drew Cook's tourists. There was a vogue for the 'radio-active waters' of Disentis and Bad Gastein, which were good for 'nervous troubles, anaemia and overwork'. In Florida 'splendid new cities . . . [had] arisen as if by magic' and what had recently been an 'almost uncharted wilderness' was by the Jazz Age 'the Riviera of America'. In England Cook acted as chief passenger agents and guides to the British Empire Exhibition at Wembley, 'a world's shop window of stupendous proportions' which attracted 17 million visitors in 1924 and was reopened the following year. The firm promoted new destinations such as Mesopotamia, 'a land fit for tourists'. It recommended new types of holiday: trail-riding in the Canadian Rockies, a thousand-mile trip up the Amazon to the port of Manaus, Citroën safaris to Timbuktu. It also made skilful use of anniversaries, such as the tercentenary of the voyage of the *Mayflower* and the eighty years of Cook's round-the-world tours. 'By indomitable persistence,' the *Traveller's Gazette* intoned, 'country after country was won, until the world became our playground'.[21]

One of the most fortunate events of the 1920s, from Cook's point of view, was Howard Carter's famous archaeological discovery in the Valley of the Kings. Prone to hyperbole though it was, the *Traveller's Gazette* scarcely exaggerated when it said that 'the whole world is agog with excitement over the tomb of Tutankhamen'.[22] Until then tourism in Egypt had been held back by sporadic outbreaks of violence following the nationalist rebellion of 1919, though some of Cook's Nile steamers did resume service in 1920. During the disturbances of 1921 five or six of Cook's stern-wheelers were actually used as patrol boats by the navy, though their only engagement seems to have been a spectacular New Year's Eve revel fuelled by the Political Officer's luggage – a case of whisky.[23] The opening of Tutankahmun's tomb in 1923, and the revelation of its astonishing treasures, persuaded tourists to ignore the political troubles. They returned to Egypt in droves. Although the price of a three-week cruise from Cairo to Aswan and back had gone up to £80, Cook was by 1926 filling seven steamers which 'embody every known improvement, are lavishly furnished throughout and for comfort, convenience and cuisine are unsurpassed on the river'.[24] This first-class fleet was augmented by seven private steamers and about half a dozen dahabeahs. Thomas Cook & Son could rightly boast about the 'extent and permanence of our organisation'. They remained, as the famous French traveller who wrote under the name of Pierre Loti called them, 'the veritable sovereigns of Egypt'.

Actually, caring as he did about the conservation of antiquities, Loti was anything but an admirer of Cook or his tourists. He protested, for example, about their sacrilegious picnics in the temple of Abydos: 'They wear cork helmets, and the classic green spectacles, drink whisky and soda, and eat voraciously sandwiches and other viands out of greasy paper, which now litters the floor.' The litter was cleared up but the 'ugliness associated with the name of Cook' remained. To account for it Loti repeated a story he had heard:

> 'The United Kingdom, justifiably jealous of the beauty of its daughters, submits them to a jury when they reach the age of puberty; and those who are classed as too ugly to reproduce their kind are accorded an unlimited account at Thomas Cook & Sons, and thus vowed to a course of perpetual travel, which leaves them no time to think of certain trifles incidental to life.'[25]

Many such old-fashioned prejudices against tourists were expressed during the interwar years. Edith Sitwell denounced visitors to Italy as 'the most awful people with legs like flies who come into lunch in bathing costumes – flies, centipedes'.[26] Beverley Nichols was equally hysterical about Britons he encountered on the Riviera: 'Ye Gods, the people! Drunken, debauched, heartless, of an incredible vulgarity – swooping, screaming, racketing.' American writers were just as bad. Scott Fitzgerald inveighed against the 'fantastic neanderthals' who crossed the Atlantic in the late 1920s. They came in droves and in luxury, he said, and they 'had the humane values of Pekinese, bivalves, cretins, goats'.[27] Yet in addition to the familiar cries of social and intellectual snobbery there were valid concerns, given new urgency by the sheer volume of traffic, about preventing tourists from destroying the very things they had come to see.

During the years of the 'holiday boom' Cook's most spectacular achievement was to conduct several round-the-world cruises abroad the *Franconia*. These were smarter than the ones begun by American Express or than Cook's other impressive ventures afloat in the early 1920s. The 20,000-ton Cunard liner, specially built after the war for the task, was 'the most magnificent and luxurious of all cruising vessels'.[28] On these cruises she carried nearly 400 passengers, mostly American, mainly elderly, all rich. Everyone travelled first-class, wore evening dress for dinner and expected to be entertained and cosseted the whole time. Cook's representative on board was Ross Skinner, so experienced that he was said to have begun his career as cruise director to Noah. Skinner was assisted by a staff of fourteen, plus two lecturers, two chaplains, two hairdressers, a bookseller, a photographer, a cinematograph operator and a dentist. All went well on the first cruise, a circumnavigation of the northern hemisphere in 1926, until the visit to Peking had to be cancelled because of the Chinese civil war. A 'mutinous situation' then developed among the passengers. One old lady shrilled: 'I *demand* to be taken to Peking.' Others practically accused Thomas Cook of starting the civil war. In due course the tactful Skinner calmed everyone down and the 4¹/₂-month voyage was eventually pronounced a triumph. Over £7,000 was spent in the bar and Americans described their experience as a 'world booze'.

Eighty of the same passengers booked to go on the *Franconia*'s southern-hemisphere cruise the following year. Despite the appearance of a gang of cardsharps, discovered and dealt with by Skinner, and a somewhat frosty welcome in Australia, where the Melbourne *Morning Post* criticized the 'blasé outlook' and 'self-importance' of the well-upholstered tourists, this voyage was also a success.[29] Further evidence of Cook's expertise in this sphere, incidentally, was the appointment of one of the firm's couriers to make all the sightseeing arrangements during George V's Mediterranean cruise in 1925. Unhappily Queen Mary was a bad sailor and the convalescent king was difficult to please: 'Abroad is awful. I know. I have been.'[30] But the courier, who lived with the upper servants and was known as the 'curry man', displayed great efficiency. Only one slip-up occurred, when a car failed to appear at Naples. Queen Mary promptly took a tram; the occupants ignored her; and Lieutenant-Commander Agar of the royal yacht *Victoria and Albert* 'had the honour of paying for her fare'.[31]

Cook's unprecedented prosperity in the decade after the Great War renewed the firm's self-confidence. As Frank casually remarked to one of his couriers in 1920, 'If Homer's Odysseus had had some kind of Cook's guide there wouldn't have been so many mistakes on the journey; in fact there wouldn't have been any mistakes at all.'[32] To safeguard their gains Frank and Ernest transformed Thomas Cook & Son into a limited company in 1923, crediting themselves with £1.6 million and each holding half the nominal share capital of £1 million. In 1924 they incorporated Thomas Cook (Bankers) Ltd. Two years later they moved their head office from Ludgate Circus to Berkeley Street, in the heart of London's West End (a similar move in 1921 had established the chief Paris bureau at a large new white-stone corner house in the Place de la Madeleine). In what had once been the garden of Devonshire House, 1,500 Cook's employees now ran the biggest office in London.

In fact, it was too big. For some time the fifth floor remained almost empty, spare space being rented to the Pullman Car Company which also ran the management dining-room. Nor was the office entirely modern. Some of the Dickensian stools and desks were brought over from Ludgate Circus, and counter clerks were not given their own telephones. They had to leave their posts and go to a central kiosk, an 'incredible system [which] lasted until the war years'. At first, too, there were practically no customers, for Cook was the first commercial enterprise in the newly widened Berkeley Street and 'the public didn't know where we were'.[33] They were soon told. In display advertisements the firm's address was given as 'The Temple of Travel, Berkeley Street, W.1.' The porters of luxury hotels, whose construction may well have attracted Cook to the West End in the first place, were given commissions for obtaining new business. Journalists also helped. Under a typical headline, 'Bagdad Wonder Outshone in Berkeley Street', the *Daily Chronicle* enthused: 'A trip to Timbuctoo, a jolly camel cruise in Arabia, a flight across the Indian Ocean, a six months tour of the world; you begin them all in Berkeley Street.'[34] By 1980 over 50 million people had called at Cook's Mayfair headquarters.

The new building contained generous amenities for the staff, including a restaurant, lounge and two recreation rooms, one for each sex. Nor were they forgotten financially. The firm paid out some £40,000 a year to make good losses suffered through the reduction of salaries during the war. And in 1926 it introduced a new pension scheme. By the beginning of 1928 the company's prospects had never looked rosier. The *Traveller's Gazette* (of which there were now ten foreign editions, including Dutch, Danish, Spanish and Italian) commented on the 'amazing development of travel within the last few years'. Compared with 1914 and 1920

> our Programme of Summer Holiday Arrangements for the present year has an air of robustness and prosperity that points to our being more than ever a nation of inveterate globe-trotters. From being originally a somewhat uninspiring catalogue of fares and places it has assumed the proportions of a readable manual of travel at home and abroad, brightened by a little gallery of travel pictures.[35]

Then came a bolt from the blue. On 8 February 1828 Frank and Ernest Cook sold the firm lock, stock and barrel to the Compagnie Internationale des Wagons-Lits of Belgium for the sum of £3^1/$_2$ million.

It is not known whether the sale was prompted by shrewd intimations of the coming slump or whether the brothers simply wanted to retire from the business. Undoubtedly, though, Cook's employees, from pin-stripe-suited managers to brilliantined office boys, regarded the disposal of the family firm as a tragic abdication of trust and a fatal snuffing-out of tradition. G. H. Hargreaves later remembered how Frank Cook broke the news at the Paris office:

> [He] made a few – very few – remarks on the necessity of the fusion [with Wagons-Lits] and then passed round in complete silence, to shake hands with each of us. Very sad though the occasion was, I could not repress the thought that the undertaker would soon come to the scene to say 'members of the family may go upstairs if they so desire'.[36]

'Fusion of interests' was the approved euphemism to disguise the radical nature of the change. For the same reason Frank briefly remained chairman of the board. But it was now dominated by representatives of Wagons-Lits and its British backer, the International Sleeping Car Share Trust Ltd, namely Lord Dalziel of Wooler (for a short time before his death) and then his former private secretary Stanley Adams. The latter was a 'skilful and dynamic' businessman who became the chief force in the firm for the next three decades.[37]

If the circumstances of the purchase are obscure, those of the sale are positively murky. It was apparently arranged by that great commercial *éminence grise*, Dudley Docker.[38] He preferred to work behind the scenes but there are intriguing signs of his involvement. For example, he soon acquired an office on the fifth floor of Berkeley Street. His former valet, John Barker, was given a job as Cook's front liftman – it was his practice to shoo lesser members out of the lift if senior managers appeared. Cook's branch offices received a directive that Docker's Paints must be used in any redecoration. *The Times* also let slip the fact that 'Mr F. Dudley Docker's group' was interested.[39] Evidently Docker's role was not just to bring the parties together but to raise, through City associates, the additional capital needed to buy Thomas Cook, from which they would all profit at the subsequent share issue. After Dalziel's death in April 1928, Docker's nominees, men like Follett Holt and Sir Edmund Wyldbore-Smith, took an important part in directing Cook/Wagons-Lits. Interestingly enough, Stanley Baldwin, then Prime Minister, was canvassed as its future head, but he refused to 'go guinea-pigging'.[40] Docker believed that British enterprises had to be international in scope and, profit apart, he was obviously convinced by the logic of combining 'the two most important travel agencies in existence'. By amalgamating the companies, preserving the best features of each and taking advantage of increased negotiating power with principals like hotels and railways, a new organization would be created which was 'universal, economical and practical'.[41]

This sounded plausible. Wagons-Lits, which had been founded in the 1870s by George Nagelmackers, son of the banker to King Leopold of the Belgians, was a large and powerful concern. Nagelmackers started with the idea of providing travelling carriages more luxurious than anything Pullman had built, palaces on wheels. Assisted by royal patronage, he spread his coaches, sleeping cars and restaurant cars throughout Europe.[42] By 1928 Wagons-Lits was carrying over two million passengers a year (as well as boarding some of them in its splendid hotels) and the introduction of second-class Pullman cars promised a further increase in trade.

Wagons-Lits would be able to sell even more tickets if its large network of offices was supplemented by that of Cook.

Although Cook also complemented Wagons-Lits, being strong in areas where the Belgian concern was weak, the fusion was far from satisfactory. The Wagons-Lits company was not unreasonable: it appreciated the 'general usefulness for travel business of the organisation of Cook's as it exists, and the necessity to utilise it and extend it rather than to attempt to introduce W.L. systems'. So, in the major reorganization that followed the merger, only 'obvious duplications' were eliminated. However, this did involve the closure of forty Cook offices. Consequently there was much intrigue and bad feeling as the men from Cook's dragged their feet. Edward Huskisson, for example, engaged in a struggle that lasted for years to protect what he saw as the interests of the British firm and its staff. Partly this was chauvinism: despite Cook's international operation, the company was 'the most British of British institutions'[43] and resented the intrusion of foreigners. Partly it was conservatism: Cook's Civil-Service-style hierarchy was reluctant to change. Partly it was high-mindedness.

A Berkeley Street memorandum insisted that 'the "tips" evil', which was prevalent among Wagons-Lits staff, should not contaminate Cook's employees, who were told that anyone accepting gratuities would be liable to instant dismissal.[44] Cook's managers successfully protected their Egyptian operation from encroachments by Wagons-Lits with the help of the High Commissioner, Sir Percy Loraine. He wrote: 'The Anglo-Saxon tourists who formed about 80% of the whole body of tourists felt they got a square deal from Cooks but would not feel the same confidence on the point if they had to deal with an actual Wagons-Lits under a Cook's façade.'[45] Cook's managers were also keen to guard against the corruption of their 'specialist', multilingual, omnicompetent couriers, who were 'always in plain clothes and will be found socially acceptable'.[46] Here they did not entirely succeed. As the Vice-President of the LMS Railway later wrote, Cook's

close association with CIWL [i.e. Wagons-Lits] has, I think, been detrimental to the business done in the name of Cooks. CIWL methods with their accompanying graft have made the combined CIWL/Cooks offices on the Continent most unpopular with the travelling public, and it is a pleasure to come across one of the old Cook's staff in one of these offices and usually I find when I do so that they very much feel the way CIWL are damaging the name of Cooks.[47]

If morale was low among Cook's employees, tourism itself seemed buoyant in the spring of 1929. Europe promised many fairs, festivals and exhibitions. Almost every resort offered some fresh attraction, from motor-boat racing in Venice to new illuminations at Blackpool. Promoting its transatlantic business, the American *Traveller's Gazette* noted portentously that the 'regular migration of many hundreds of thousands of people from one continent to another and back is a unique phonemenon of world-significance'.[48] In the autumn everything changed. While Cook still struggled to come to terms with Wagons-Lits the entire travel scene was overwhelmed by what Ramsay MacDonald called 'the economic blizzard'.[49] After the Wall Street crash (to quote the pardonable exaggeration of one tourist agent) 'the American traveller disappeared'.[50] In Europe the Depression took longer to bite, but Cook's profit of nearly £100,000 in 1929 turned into a loss of almost twice that sum by 1931. During those years 45 per cent of Cook's business vanished.

The 'annus terribilis' was 1931 itself,[51] when Britain went off the gold standard. The *Illustrated London News* compared the crisis to that of 1914:

> thousands of English people [were] scattered all over Europe . . . need[ing] immediate help in order to save them from an awkward and often ignominious situation. It is in emergencies like these that the national as well as the individual value of such a world-wide travel and banking organisation as that of Thomas Cook and Son becomes apparent.[52]

After this expensive rescue operation Cook had to pay its outstanding Continental bills in depreciated pounds. Docker and Wyldbore-Smith had to negotiate a five-month loan of £250,000 from the Midland Bank. Holidays abroad were now 'practically 50% dearer for English people'. Many of Cook's clients could still have afforded them, but as a measure of national economy the government imposed a 'moral ban of foreign holidays'. In the face of official discouragement Cook's winter sports traffic shrank alarmingly: 5,066 clients went in 1930/1 compared to 661 in 1931/2.[53]

Interestingly, during this period Russia was the only foreign country with which Cook's business actually expanded (though some of this was trans-Siberian traffic to the Far East). The apparent collapse of the capitalist past doubtless inspired bourgeois tourists to see the Communist future at work.

Stanley Adams, who became Managing Director of Thomas Cook & Son in 1930, realized as well as anybody that 'vulnerability is the outstanding feature of [the firm's] business'. Its profit margins were 'small', its costs were 'inelastic', its income exceptionally sensitive to 'world conditions'.[54] Adams could do little about the profit margins; he even failed to prevent the airlines from reducing Cook's commission on ticket sales below 10 per cent. However he did institute drastic economies. He reduced salaries. He cut staff – by the end of 1932 only 2,544 remained, just enough to sustain 'the goodwill of the business'.[55] In 1932 Adams suspended the company's contributions to its employees' pension fund and stressed the need for their 'unremitting work and . . . unswerving loyalty'.[56] He shut some offices and disposed of most of the Nile fleet. In 1935 he sold the freehold of the firm's Berkeley Street headquarters to the Prudential Assurance Company, though Cook continued to lease the premises.

To increase revenue, Adams encouraged business wherever he could. In spite of the slump air traffic continued to grow. There was a 'remarkable vogue for pleasure cruising'. This was caused, the *Daily Telegraph* explained, by 'a patriotic determination to divert our spending for health and pleasure from foreign to home industries'. Advertisements extolled 'Cook's for Cruises' and the firm benefited from 'our good relations with the Steamship Companies'. 'Thrift Tours to Egypt' (inclusive for £32) were also promoted. But during the Devil's Decade Cook made more from its engineering works at Boulac (which did valuable work for the Royal Air Force) than from the few steamers that kept running. Of course, many of them were getting old, and Wagons-Lits were anxious to fill their new Pullman and sleeper trains (the Birmingham-built *Star of Egypt* and *Sunshine Express*) to Luxor and Asyut. However, the depression seems to have ruined Nile navigation generally: according to one report, Cook's steamers spent 157 hours on sandbanks during 1931/2 and the narrow channels were often 'blocked with gyasses waiting for Allah (or Cook) to move them over'.

Despite famine and purge the USSR continued to attract Westerners, and in 1935 Cook published a new programme of tours which was billed as 'a landmark in world travel history'. Under the tsars it had been 'almost a matter of policy for the authorities to obstruct and inconvenience visitors' and the Soviet Union had previously 'been the most backward of all civilised lands in encouraging and facilitating foreign travellers'. But now, thanks to the Intourist organization (founded five years before), 'a highly developed and competitive travel-world' had been established in Russia.[57] The USSR had another, less well-known connection with Thomas Cook: in at least one major city, Shanghai, secret agents of the Communist International used its office as a dead-letter-box.[58]

Cook continued to promote new tourist attractions of all sorts, from the International Congress of Sex Research in London to the newly discovered site of Sodom. Clients were taken to the Schneider Trophy Race and to the inauguration of New Delhi. They were conducted to Boy Scout jamborees and to 'the unique opera house, known as Glyndebourne'. They visited a theatre festival in Moscow and the Berlin Olympics. They attended Vancouver's golden jubilee and Adelaide's centenary. They witnessed the maiden voyage of the *Queen Mary* and the first flight of the airship *Hindenburg*. Above all they found royal events compelling. Few, admittedly, were willing to pay £325 to go to the coronation of the Emperor of Ethiopia in 1930, though the *Traveller's Gazette* promised big-game hunting and 'splendid pageantry', including a chance to see the imperial coach which had once belonged to Wilhelm I of Germany and a royal bodyguard whose busbies had been made in England from the manes of African lions.[59] By contrast George V's Silver Jubilee and George VI's coronation significantly assisted Cook's recovery after the slump. So did the Canadian Legion Pilgrimage in 1936. Cook made the travel arrangements for 6,300 ex-servicemen, led by Brigadier-General Alexander Ross, who crossed the Atlantic to attend the inauguration of the Canadian National War Memorial on Vimy Ridge. Pilgrims of the traditional kind were also important, sometimes making up 15 per cent of Cook's customers. For many years the Pope appointed the firm official pilgrimage agent to Lourdes and Rome, and its brochures bore the Papal emblem.

Such was the need to raise revenue after 1929 that Cook also embarked on a bewildering variety of new enterprises, anything from a laundry service at Port Said to a kiosk at Berkeley Street selling flowers and fruit. In 1930 the firm offered to find houses for people making long stays in foreign countries. It opened a Scholastic

Department to help parents (usually those abroad) choose schools for their children and to make the termly travel arrangements. The following year Cook set up a translation and typewriting bureau. The French office provided a Shopping Service, whereby a Cook's representative accompanied clients on buying expeditions, advised on costs and attended to shipping, customs and so on. The firm also formed a Travel Lecture Agency, offering independent speakers on a professional basis. It acquired theatre tickets for clients. And it advertised 'Books through Cooks', obtaining travel literature for its customers. Cook's own guide-books (which sold 10,000 five-shilling copies a year) were re-written and improved. As a senior member of staff said, they had been started as

> a useful sideline, paying their way and providing a permanent
> means of propaganda. They were used for the latter purpose
> rather blatantly at first, and their reputation as guidebooks
> suffered accordingly . . . booksellers refused to regard as a
> trade proposition a series which they considered as merely an
> advertisement for Cook's.

As a result the guide-books had '"run to seed" a little' and the intention, never quite realized, was to build them into a 'really reputable' series.[60]

At the top end of the social scale Cook 'dabbled in yachting', renting, for example, the 500-ton *Argosy* to David Lloyd George for a Mediterranean health cruise. The firm retained a certain Captain G., who was supposed to interest fellow members of White's and Boodle's in Cook's services, among which was arranging private East African safaris.[61] It made special arrangements to transport celebrities as exotic as Harry Houdini and Coco the Clown. From established organizations it accepted unusual commissions. One of the trickiest was bringing two king cobras from Burma to London Zoo – they travelled 'not as tourists but as freight'. Cook ferried boxes of programmes over to Radio Luxemburg. The company also introduced its Shopping Service to England: fashion trips were organized by Barbara Budden and much attention was paid to 'Sightseeing à la Mode'.[62] With his staff of nine, Donald White, the quintessential 'Man from Cook's' (he was proud of featuring on a cigarette card), graciously welcomed distinguished visitors at Victoria Station. White acted as a kind of major-domo to the metropolis. Hitler's ambassador Ribbentrop once asked him, with reference to the lanky Foreign Secretary Lord Halifax: 'Hullo, where's old Daddy-long-legs got to?'[63]

For some of the better-off among the eight million additional wage-earners who became entitled to holidays with pay after the 1938 legislation, Cook provided a holiday camp at Prestatyn in North Wales. Like Thomas Cook's initial excursions, holiday camps stemmed from a strong Victorian desire to improve the common lot. Their pioneers were teetotallers like John Cunningham and 'the non-conformist philanthropists, evangelizing socialists, trade unionists and cooperative societies who simply aspired to comrade-ship in the fresh air and togetherness in tents'. Chalets eventually superseded tents and huts, some made from old tramcar bodies, at the Caister Socialist Holiday Camp (begun in 1906) and the first major commercial camp was opened by Billy Butlin at Skegness in 1936.[64] His offer of three meals a day plus free entertainment for between 35s. and £3 a week proved so popular that by 1939 over 100 other holiday camps had been set up, with accommodation for half a million people each season.[65]

'The Chalet Village by the Sea' at Prestatyn was a product of a partnership between Cook and the LMS Railway, which together put up the capital of £250,000. It was designed as a showpiece by the LMS architect and built (in six months) on 'the most up-to-date lines'. It had striking 'marine' features, a kind of deck overlooking the swimming-pool and a curious oblong conning-tower. The cha-lets were arranged in courts with communal washrooms at the centre. Prestatyn offered a complete 'holiday package', though it lacked a 'pleasure park'.[66] Still, nearly 2,000 campers could bask in 'an atmosphere of cheerful warmth, so reminiscent of the French Riviera'. They could enjoy the games room, the sun lounge and the bars, the beauty contests, the string orchestra and the popular stage and floor shows.[67] Apparently there was less regimentation than at Butlin's, and one postwar visitor to Prestatyn was pleasantly sur-prised not to find himself in 'a cross between a concentration camp and an Ensa music hall'.[68] Probably Thomas Cook & Son attracted a smarter type of visitor than Butlin's. Certainly they aspired to do so: an advertisement showed the ballroom at Prestatyn packed with campers in full evening dress. Unfortunately the inauguration was marred by a staff crisis in which Stanley Adams and other dignitaries ended up washing the dishes. And Prestatyn opened just in time to become an army camp, though in the twelve weeks before the outbreak of war it did make a net profit of £6,000.

All these new expedients helped Cook, as Stanley Adams said, 'to avoid an outcome which might have been disastrous'.[69] Nevertheless, the firm needed the assistance of bankers 'to tide through' 1931.[70] So did Wagons-Lits, which had ordered more coaches during 'the "boom" years' and was left during the slump with 'rolling stock much in excess of requirements'.[71] However, such was the strength of the combined company, which had 350 offices throughout the world, that it had no trouble raising money and throughout the 1930s the press commented on Cook's 'exceptionally strong liquid position'.[72] Smaller travel agencies were not so well placed and many collapsed. George Lunn was the most spectacular casualty. Unlike Sir Henry Lunn, George was not able to insinuate his travel literature into the pews of Nonconformist chapels; when he spent money in an effort to advertise his way out of the Depression he went bankrupt to the tune of £130,000.

Agencies that survived became more competitive. When the economy began to improve and it was no longer deemed unpatriotic to spend vacations abroad, a price-cutting war broke out, forerunner of epic struggles in more recent times. Dean & Dawson did particularly well by chartering trains for cheap Continental holidays. But in 1934, fearing further bankruptcies, nine of the rivals formed the Creative Tourist Agents' Conference and agreed on a fixed price structure. By cooperating they drove down hotel and transport charges, lowered still further by the devaulation of the franc. In 1936 it was possible to have a fortnight's all-inclusive holiday in Switzerland for under £10. So the travel business recovered, reaching its apogee in 1937 when Cook's profit rose to the unprecedented figure of almost £270,000. At this stage Thomas Cook & Son still dominated the travel market. Cook collected more fares than the Railway Clearing House and attracted more than twice as many clients as all the other agencies put together, a global total of about 5 million a year.[73]

The firm also maintained its tradition of being a kind of travel Civil Service, with well trained representatives scattered all round the globe. Jack Hyde, one of a handful who have recorded their reminiscences, was a typical member of this cadre. He started at Ludgate Circus in 1920, earning 25s. a week. Nine years later he was sent to Bombay, where he served with a staff of 120 in the Hornby

Road office. Much hard work was relieved by occasional diversions, such as drying out thousands of pounds' worth of currency notes soaked by monsoon rains or cheering on the office race-horse (which always seemed to come last). Hyde married on his first home leave, in 1934. And his wife May (after surviving initial shocks like finding the cook straining their soup through his apron) soon became acclimatized to India. Together they made a dozen moves round the subcontinent during the next twenty years, often travelling in trains where the only cooling devices were an electric fan and a tin bath which was filled with ice at stops. Hyde's duties were routine, though he sometimes had to make travel arrangements for exotic figures like the Maharajas of Travancore and Mysore, and for the Theosophist Annie Besant. Prosaic activities like supervising the transfer of air-freight in Karachi also involved unexpected excitements: before his office was fitted with a safe Hyde secreted consignments of gold bars under his bed.[74]

Despite such enterprising and experienced employees, there were distinct signs by the mid-1930s that the firm was running out of steam. Stanley Adams was energetic in a slightly inhuman way – staff later nicknamed him 'the desiccated calculating machine'.[75] But he knew more about the stock market than about the travel business. Perhaps for this reason he commissioned an assessment of the company by a management consultant, Harold Whitehead, an imaginative move in 1935. Whitehead reported that there was a 'general appreciation of the reliability and thoroughness of the service'. Cook's 'extensive organisation and connections' also deserved the 'highest admiration'. However, the firm was 'more expensive' than competitors. It was not as effective at selling, particularly its subsidiary services. And its staff, though of 'excellent quality', were somewhat bureaucratic. Furthermore, the company was 'old-fashioned', with 'a suggestion of mid-Victorianism' about it. Cook was less 'a commercial organisation' than 'an "institution", something like the Crystal Palace'.[76] This was a particularly unfortunate analogy as, within a few months, the Crystal Palace was burnt to the ground.

Still, the report was essentially correct. The firm was living off a capital of dynamism that had been slowly diminishing since John Cook's death. It was becoming ossified by tradition. For example, the accounts of the banking and tourist companies were kept separate simply because this had always been the practice;

but in the 1930s the former was sometimes in profit while the latter showed a loss, and the business as a whole thus incurred very large and quite unnecessary tax bills. Some of Cook's managers, particularly those who had been with the firm all their working lives, rejoiced in its conservatism. One of them acknowledged that Polan Banks's proposed historical novel, *The Man from Cook's* (1938), might be 'an excellent means of propaganda'. However, 'we have a good many old-fashioned principles and . . . we cannot permit our name to be linked with any sloppy fiction'. The book was rather sloppy but, hoping for a Hollywood film which never materialized, the firm did eventually give Banks some help. It also persuaded him to delete the undignified fact that Thomas Cook's first excursion had been accompanied by a brass band.[77]

Taking such care of its public image, riding out the economic crisis, preserving its identity and a good measure of its independence despite the amalgamation with Wagons-Lits, the house of Cook seemed a reassuring edifice at a time when a global regression to barbarism appeared imminent. It was even a symbol of civilization. 'The whole world is civilised now, isn't it,' a character in one of Evelyn Waugh's novels remarked sardonically, 'charabancs and Cook's offices everywhere.'[78] Certainly those who travelled with Cook experienced a comforting sense of security. One English visitor to Europe in 1938 found that several hotels devoted 'special attention to us as "Cook's clients"' and she paid tribute to the power of 'Cook's mighty hand . . . which had enabled two defenceless women, ignorant of the language, to survive the Balkans without a serious scratch'. She also returned home, it must be said, 'singing Hitler's praises'. Germany and Italy were 'quite the pleasantest places on the Continent; and quite the most exciting Brave New Worlds in the making, and well worth emulating'.[79] Such political views may not have been as untypical as future generations would like to think, for tourists, like tourist agencies, looked firmly on the bright side.

Cook did not go quite as far as the Poly, which advertised Germany with a romantic picture of the Rhine, a Swastika flag and a slogan, 'The Land of Dreams Come True'.[80] But Cook's brochures did recommend the Nazi state for 'art, life and music', adding that its hotels were 'exceedingly comfortable'.[81] Having a vested interest in peace, the firm did its best to banish the thought of war. Early in 1939 it issued a 434-page handbook of tours containing everything

39 The original Vesuvius funicular bought by John Cook in 1887

40 Cook's Vesuvius Railway in 1934

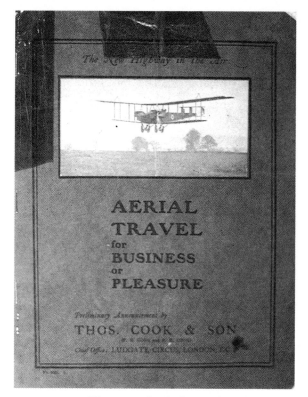

The New Highway in the Air

AERIAL
TRAVEL
for
BUSINESS
or
PLEASURE

Preliminary Announcement by

THOS. COOK & SON
(T. H. COOK and J. M. COOK)
Chief Office, LUDGATE CIRCUS, LONDON, E.C.

41 The age of aviation arrives
42 The first conducted charter flight –
to the Dempsey–Tunney fight in Chicago, 1927

43 Cook's tourists depart for Italy from Victoria Station, Easter 1937.
Donald White, the quintessential 'Man from Cook's', is in the background

44 A Cook's party waiting for the bus at Nice Station, 1930s

45 Thomas Cook's Ludgate Circus office
– decorated for Queen Victoria's Diamond Jubilee, 1897

46 Famous faces as seen by *Punch* in the booking hall,
including Oscar Wilde, Lord Salisbury, Ellen Terry and Bernard Shaw

47 Thomas Cook in the Place de la Madeleine, Paris

48 Thomas Cook on Broadway

THE NEW HEAD OFFICE OF THOS. COOK & SON, LTD., BERKELEY STREET, PICCADILLY, LONDON, W.1.
TO BE OPENED EARLY IN 1926.

49 'The Temple of Travel', Mayfair

50 The booking hall at Cook's head office
in Berkeley Street soon after it opened in 1926

51 Thomas Cook's Peterborough headquarters

52 Thomas Cook in the high street

from Blackpool excursions to journeys by regular air service 'Round
the World in 30 Days'. In September the *Traveller's Gazette* noted that
a Thomas Cook Day had been celebrated at the World's Fair in
New York. At this event the president of the American company,
Harold White (who had started as a clerk at Ludgate Circus in
1911, earning £75 a year), praised its founder as 'a great believer
in internationalism'. He said that 'expositions, bringing together
the arts, industries and sciences of the various nations, could
accomplish much in the cause of world peace'. Readers were also
told that Germany was 'preparing energetically for the Fifth Winter
Olympiad', that Japan was not many miles from 'Fairyland' and
that 'You will like Poland.' (This was almost as poignant as the
notice which appeared in the window of a Warsaw travel agent in
1980, when Russian forces were poised to crush Solidarity: 'Visit
the Soviet Union Before the Soviet Union Visits You.')[82]

When war did break out, in September 1939, the *Traveller's Gazette*
was extinguished immediately and permanently. This unique record of the rise of tourism had lasted eighty-eight years, about
a thousand days longer than the Crystal Palace which it was
established to promote. Whereas the lamps had gone out slowly
in 1914, the blinds came down at once in 1939. And for tourism
the blackout was complete. Cook made hectic preparations to face
the war. Within a few weeks the staff at Berkeley Street shrank from
2,000 to 200. Those who remained had all the experience to start the
business again once hostilities ceased. But as Charles Holt, one of
Adams's ablest lieutenants, wrote, the head office of Thomas Cook
& Son which had 'hummed like a dynamo from year's end to year's
end' was now 'a ghost of its former self'.[83]

The Sleeping Giant

Cook's fortunes reached their lowest ebb during the Second World War. After what had by now become almost a routine operation – the rescue of British tourists from the Continent and the repatriation of foreigners stranded in Britain – the firm helped to take hundreds of British children to North America, an affluent version of the large-scale evacuations from town to countryside. Early in 1940 the Berkeley Street office was actually requisitioned by the Children's Overseas Reception Board. But it soon became clear that keeping children in England was safer than sending them across the Atlantic as, in a grimly literal sense, the Board's activities were torpedoed. Cook's employees remained busy running the Expeditionary Force Supplies Service, which packed and dispatched three-quarters of a million parcels to troops abroad. Shipping & Forwarding also continued to grow. But after Dunkirk Cook's main task was once again to operate the Enemy Mail Service, its skills recently honed by the experience of transmitting mail between opposing sides (through Gibraltar) during the Spanish Civil War. Although the duties were onerous, so much correspondence having to be returned because it contravened the regulations in some way, they were not enough to keep employees fully occupied. Edward Huskisson wrote: 'There is a period in midwinter when we could comfortably drop 50% of the staff.' Despite the 'unfortunate prunings' and the fact that salaries had been 'cut ruthlessly at the outbreak of the war', the situation grew worse. In 1941, Cook's centenary year, the firm sustained a bigger loss than ever before, nearly £150,000.[1]

Cook put a brave face on it, feeding the press with optimistic titbits on its hundredth birthday. These were mainly concerned with the company's past. *The Times*, for example, recollected the Kaiser's personally conducted visit to the Holy Land and wondered whimsically: 'What would be an appropriate Cook's Tour for the present rulers of Germany?' But the paper also peered into the future: 'When peace comes, [Cook's] will have a great work to do for civilisation in helping to reopen the channels of intercourse between the nations.'[2] Meanwhile the war was engulfing the whole world. It banished pursuits like tourism and cut off Cook's offices abroad, some of which were closed temporarily, others permanently.

The Germans had already interned the British caretaker of the Place de la Madeleine, though they did not requisition the building, apparently because he told them that it was British property.[3] In Shanghai Cook's chief employees were also interned, and their families were only allowed to see them for ten minutes a year. In Malta Cook's manager found work as Bread Distribution Officer and Controller of Firewood for Ovens. In Egypt the remaining steamers were used for war purposes. Some, like the *Sudan* (built in 1921 and surviving until 1989, a relic as evocative in its way as the ruined monuments of the Pharaohs), became officers' clubs. Although Boulac, with a workforce of over 3,000, was operating at ten times its normal capacity, mainly constructing light coastal craft, much of the Nile equipment – tugs, barges, the floating dock – was sold to the British army.[4] At home the Berkeley Street office was hit by a land-mine. Luckily there was only one casualty, a fire-watcher in Curzon Street, but the restaurant and kitchen were badly damaged and the booking hall was littered with lumps of brick and concrete.

Cook's centenary year might well have culminated in a financial collapse. This was partly because the firm's parent company Wagons-Lits had fallen into German hands after the invasion of France in 1940. The British Custodian of Enemy Property then took control of Cook, which severely limited the firm's freedom of action, particularly in money matters. The Custodian had no funds to keep the company going and by 1941 it faced bankruptcy. According to Stanley Adams, he persuaded his 'old friend Winston Churchill', a once and future client of Cook's, to save the firm.[5] According to Sir John Elliot, later Chairman of Cook, Adams consulted Montagu Norman, Governor of the Bank of England, who said: 'Let Cook's be bought by the mainline Railway Companies for the duration of the war. The French [who now had a prime interest in Wagons-Lits] may not like it but they will have to lump it.'[6] Actually the process, which involved delicate negotiations and elaborate provisions, was more complicated than that. For instance, Wagons-Lits was to retain a 25 per cent stake in Cook's overseas assets after the war. And

Cook's banking business, though not foreign exchange or traveller's cheques, was to go to Grindlay and Co. But essentially Norman's formula was adopted. In 1942, through a transaction ratified by act of parliament,[7] Cook's share capital was vested in Hay's Wharf Cartage Co. Ltd, a subsidiary of the four mainline railway companies. They made good the travel agency's losses (nearly £500,000 by 1945) and it was through their intervention that Cook survived the war.

The price of survival was high. Once again the firm was involved in a struggle to preserve its independence. As Edward Huskisson stoutly maintained in 1942, 'We are not Railway servants any more than we were Wagons-Lits servants.' But the railway companies proved harder taskmasters than Wagons-Lits, and in that year further cuts were made, reducing Cook's global staff to 1,082, of whom 427 worked in the United Kingdom. Other 'key men' were lost to the forces – many of these were engaged in movement control.[8] The Railway Clerks' Association also persuaded many junior employees to join their trade union. Hitherto the staff had been 'almost completely unorganised from a trade union point of view'[9] and this move, which led to the introduction of proper salary scales and conditions of service, was a vote of no confidence in the firm's traditional methods of paternalism. Cook's leading men – Adams and Huskisson, Charles Holt, known as the 'uncrowned king of the tourist world', and Cecil Garstang, a 'loyal "Cookite"'[10] nicknamed 'Mr Travel' in the press – had good cause to be apprehensive about the changes peace would bring.[11] Meanwhile the business of peace continued to make its contribution to the war, a particularly direct one in the United States. As Harold White wrote, 'The Armed Services of America made many landings on enemy-held territory [in the Pacific] after being briefed with information and photographs furnished by the successors of Thomas Cook and his son John.' They were thanked for their 'complete cooperation' by the US government.[12]

After the Axis defeat and the Labour victory in the British general election there was a 'protracted wrangle' about the fate of Thomas Cook & Son. According to Elliot the Prime Minister, Clement Attlee, personally prevented the firm from being handed back to Wagons-Lits, despite vociferous protests from General de Gaulle.[13] A new overseas company was formed, in which Wagons-Lits had a quarter share, but at home the firm remained a fief of the railway companies. It had no time to worry about such matters, however, being much occupied with repatriating refugees, to whom the United Nations Relief and Rehabilitation Agency gave travel vouchers which could only be exchanged for tickets at Cook offices. More important still, the postwar holiday boom showed every sign of exceeding that of the 1920s. As Stanley Adams told *The Times* in April 1946, 'the urge to travel is sweeping the people of this and other war-weary lands like an epidemic'. Long queues formed at Berkeley Street, which received a larger mail than ever before, and employees complained of being 'inundated' and 'overwhelmed'.[14] The management took on more staff, opened new offices, refurbished Prestatyn, published a fresh programme including battlefield tours, and 'by some miracle restored their travellers' cheques system to full use'.[15] Despite these efforts the season was disappointing. Foreign currency allowances were restricted (and remained so, at various levels, until 1959). There were transport bottlenecks and accommodation shortages. Indeed, the whole period was one of austerity, punctuated by occasional economic crises.

For that reason, no doubt, even more Britons – about a quarter of a million – tried to escape abroad after the grim winter of 1947. Once again Cook was deluged and the firm was driven to advise customers to book for the following year. According to one observer, the head office, now nearly back to its full complement of 2,000 staff, resembled 'a great cosmopolitan railway terminus – you expect to see engines puffing out at the other end'. But much of this activity ceased in August when, faced by an acute shortage of exchange, Attlee's government imposed a ban on foreign holidays. The firm was reduced to promoting tourism within the sterling area – 'Cook's Sterling Holidays'. It assisted emigrants, managed official visits and developed subsidiary services, shipping, air freight, schools and so on. At Christmas it organized a convalescent holiday in Marrakesh for Winston Churchill, 'an exacting but not a difficult client'. When the Hotel Mamounia refused to book a mere VIP, Churchill was persuaded to let Cook use his name. Berkeley Street thus received two cables: 'Very important party regret impossible'; 'Churchill d'accord.'[16] Cook also set up a Business Travel Service, which began with a staff of three and is today the largest such agency in the world, making travel arrangements for over 12,000 companies.

The travel ban was lifted early in 1948 and Sir Stafford Cripps,

Chancellor of the Exchequer, remarked benevolently that the 'name, Thomas Cook, will always be pleasantly associated with the long tradition of annual mass exodus'.[17] This was not a gratuitous compliment so much as a proprietorial pat on the back, for on 1 January 1948 the railways had been nationalized and Thomas Cook was now a state enterprise. In the short term this change of ownership hardly affected the company, which had preserved its identity and its *esprit de corps* through all vicissitudes. Indeed, Cook benefited in various ways, not least by an accretion of official dignity and by an incidental expansion. Dean & Dawson, possessing thirty-one branches and previously owned by the London & North Eastern Railway, was also nationalized and its services became largely amalgamated with those of Cook. In any case, the Berkeley Street office was still preoccupied with the postwar travel boom. This continued, fostered by such events as London's 'austerity Olympics' in 1948, and not seriously hampered by interruptions. The most important of these was the massive devaluation of the pound in September 1949, when Cook's overseas offices were besieged by angry clients whose traveller's cheques had lost almost a third of their value overnight. The firm itself benefited from a windfall profit of £88,000 on its foreign-currency holdings.

By 1950 the demand for foreign holidays, promoted and exploited by Cook, had become immense. About a million Britons went abroad that year. And some 200,000 North Americans visited the United Kingdom, 10 per cent of them booked through Cook's chain of 24 offices and 1,000 sub-agents, which extended throughout the United States and Canada. The firm's sales there were worth nearly £4 million and tourism received increasing official encouragement in Britain as the country's 'biggest dollar-earning industry'.[18] All told, Cook and Wagons-Lits now had 350 branches in 64 countries. Cook's staff numbered 10,000. The Berkeley Street office alone handled 5,000 telephone calls and 500 visitors a day; during the year it received 40 tons of mail and sent out twice as much again. Cook had arrangements with 200 airlines, 500 railway companies and 6,600 hotels; issued 250,000 brochures and dealt with 7 million clients; sold £10 million and nearly $6 million worth of traveller's cheques. The firm's net profit in 1950, £389,184, broke all previous records. Cook was the largest travel agency on earth and, as Charles Holt said, the world's 'chief mechanic of tourism'.[19] The company was determined, as its General Manager James Maxwell said, to stay in 'the vanguard of the present vast international movement and merchandise by air, land and sea'.[20]

However, there were already indications that Cook would not be able to maintain its preeminence and that state ownership would harm the company in the long term. Nationalization reinforced its customary conservatism at a time when able new competitors were coming into the industry. They took advantage of the spare aviation capacity left over from the Berlin airlift – 32-seat Dakotas could be hired for half a crown a mile – and began to organize cheap package holidays to the Continent. The most radical tour operator was a Reuter's journalist called Vladimir Raitz, founder of Horizon Holidays. In 1950, using '£2,000 left him by his Russian grandmother',[21] he chartered a plane and organized a two-week 'package' tour to Corsica (where his passengers lived in tents) for £35 10s. Actually Thomas Cook had already run inclusive air holidays, to the Riviera, just before the war. But now, as living standards rose and aircraft grew more sophisticated – the Comet, the first jet passenger plane, entered service in 1952 – skyborne package holidays were to develop apace. Raitz merely applied to aeroplanes 'Cook's principle that full bookings could command low prices'.[22] Later he scathingly criticized Cook's top management for not doing the same, attributing their failure to 'sheer inertia'.[23]

In fact there was much to be said for caution in such a volatile business – Horizon itself collapsed in 1974 – and Stanley Adams certainly was the embodiment of old-fashioned commercial caution. Having nursed Cook through the Depression, he was determined that the firm should not stray far from the safe and respectable business of taking commissions from the transport companies. He disapproved of advance commitments and risky speculations. He set his face against 'fly-by-night adventures' and would not even charter a motor coach. Adams got his way, for he ruled the company with a rod of iron and Cook's managers regarded him as 'God with a capital G'.[24] State ownership also discouraged the firm from taking bold initiatives. Its nominal overlords simply did not want that kind of bother. The British Transport Commission barely mentioned Cook in its annual reports and its successor, the tight-fisted Transport Holding Company, was known in Berkeley Street as 'the Transport Holding-Back Company'.[25] As a journalist later wrote,

Of an accidentally nationalised industry, what more could be asked than that it should make no trouble, call for no capital, and lose no money? All this Cook did. It grew set in its ways: it cut out troublesome business; it missed the chance American Express seized, and it missed, for a decade, the boom in package travel. But it was an institution.[26]

Nowhere was Cook more of an institution than in Egypt. After the war the remainder of the fleet had been sold because nationalist troubles continued and Cook's managers believed that travellers 'no longer had the time or the inclination to proceed to Upper Egypt by steamer'.[27] But in 1950 the firm made one last effort to turn the clock back to the great days of its ascendancy. The private dahabeah *Memnon* set off on Cook's first postwar cruise. One of the passengers was the writer Roderick Cameron. He thought it significant that 'Cook's landing stage' at Cairo 'is next to that of the King' and he said that their gleaming paddle-steamer resembled 'an Edwardian country house . . . transplanted by chance to the Nile'. Everything was organized in the most elaborate fashion, from the eight-course meals to the engraved paper, sealing wax and pens with clean nibs on the desks. The *Memnon*'s crew was equally smart, each man wearing a dark blue sweater embroidered in red with the legend, 'Cook's Nile Service'. The British were unpopular in Egypt, Cameron noted.

> However, the political situation does not seem to have affected Thomas Cook and Sons' position in the country. They are still all-powerful, a kind of East India Company of our time, nabobs of the Middle East. Thos. Cook at home one regards as any other travel agency, but here it is quite a different matter. They have ramifications as extensive as big companies such as Shell Oil . . . . You travel with Cook in Egypt and you are quite somebody, the big effendi.[28]

This privileged status could not last. The violence worsened and during the riots of January 1952 various traditional British institutions were set on fire – the Turf Club, Shepheard's Hotel and Cook's office. The firm tried to continue from Boulac. But political hostilities, culminating in the Suez invasion of 1956, finally destroyed Thomas Cook's traditional position as 'uncrowned king of Egypt'.[29]

Back in Britain the firm attracted hostility in some quarters simply because it was a nationalized industry. In 1950, for example, Cook was attacked for sending out printed cards saying that clients' letters could not be answered by return because of 'the extraordinary demands made . . . on our staff dealing with Continental travel in connection with Holy Year in Rome and other special events, together with an abnormal influx of visitors from overseas'. In fact, as James Maxwell said, this practice was caused by the acute shortage of typists, and the card at least gave clients 'the opportunity of making alternative arrangements'.[30] The energetic, red-faced Maxwell, who travelled 100,000 miles a year, was infuriated by suggestions that state control had incapacitated Cook. 'We're nationalized, not sterilized,' he declared.[31]

He could point to all sorts of initiatives and innovations. Cook took a prominent part in organizing travel to the Festival of Britain and to Queen Elizabeth's coronation. At Berkeley Street a mechanized accountancy system was installed in 1952, telex a few years later. New tours were launched. In 1955 Cook conducted the first world cruise party ever to enter Nepal. The firm also helped to thaw out travel relations with the Soviet Union which, during the Cold War, was only willing to deal with ideologically sound organizations like the nationalized Cook. (The Intourist delegation to London was convinced that 'Potemkin' shops had been specially stocked with goods for their benefit while elsewhere Britons queued for bread, until Cook's negotiations manager, Sidney King, took them on a tour of suburban bakeries.) In 1956 there were three Cape to Cairo safaris, offering tourists the opportunity to meet both pygmies and the giant warriors of the Watusi tribe, all for £980. And Cook arranged specialist visits like the one to Les Eyzies with the archaeologist Glyn Daniel, chairman of the popular television quiz game 'Animal, Vegetable or Mineral'. After much argument Charles Holt was persuaded to reverse his ill-judged and ineffective policy of trying to keep Cook's *Continental Timetable* out of the hands of rival travel agents. Sales boomed and today the timetable unit's annual turnover exceeds £1 million, achieving 'the highest contribution per head of any Thomas Cook trading department'.[32]

The firm also tackled the problem of dwindling demand for its Shipping & Forwarding service. Thanks to the popularity of flying – in 1952, for the first time, more people crossed the Atlantic by air than by sea – 'suitcases and even handbags replaced trunks, portmanteaux and crates' (thus encouraging the trend towards

greater informality of dress).[33] Cook filled the gap with an astonishing miscellany of cargoes. The firm transported a complete
factory from Britain to Australia, a motor cruiser to New Zealand,
seventeen road rollers to Egypt, rats, mice and frogs for medical
research, polo ponies to India, kangaroos to Osaka, a state coach to
Iraq, a fortune in banknotes to Persia and an entire sewage system
to Tristan da Cunha. And the Film Location Department took all
the actors, baggage and equipment to Ceylon for the shooting of
David Lean's film *The Bridge on the River Kwai*. Cook also used
two other freight-forwarding firms which it had acquired and ran
under their original names, Perrotts & Hernu, Peron & Stockwell,
to provide spurious competition – they generated more business by
offering lower rates to prospective customers.

Cook's record profits, which were running at well over half a
million pounds a year during the late 1950s, seemed to be a
guarantee of the firm's continuing success. In fact its share of
the market, still 40 per cent in 1954, shrank rapidly. The other
old travel firms suffered the same fate as the growth of tourism
produced a proliferation of agencies almost inconceivable before
the war. When the Association of British Travel Agents (ABTA)
was formed in 1950 it consisted of 106 companies with 250 offices; by
1960 it contained 450 companies with 1,400 offices. ABTA was run
from the fifth floor of Thomas Cook's Berkeley Street headquarters,
a fact barely disguised by its using the address of 40 Stratton Street.
But its members and other new agencies undercut Cook savagely. In
1955 Whitehall Travel offered air 'packages' to the Costa Brava for
£10 less than Cook's equivalent holidays by rail. Similarly, in 1959
British European Airways scheduled return flights to Barcelona
cost £33 12s. while travel agencies were offering a complete package
holiday by chartered aircraft for £33 15s.

As the *Financial Times* wrote, in an article entitled 'Foreign Travel
off the Peg',

It has been on the crest of the package holiday wave that most
of the newer travel agents have broken into the business. Pick on
a suitable underdeveloped resort [like the village of Benidorm],
make a deal with a hotelier, charter a plane or a train, advertise –
the tour operator need only net £1 per head to make a handsome
profit if he can send a thousand or so off to his resort during the
two and a half months summer season.[34]

Meanwhile, acknowledging that they were old-fashioned, Cook continued to promote conducted tours catering for 'a select clientele whose special requirements differ from those of the more popular holiday tour clients, who do not ask for the same detailed personal attention'.[35] James Maxwell was well aware that 'the small man is seeping away from us much valuable traffic'. But, addressing Cook's staff, he would 'not agree with those among us who say we are only scratching the surface because I believe and know that our slice of the cake is a considerable one'.[36]

This view was supported by Sir John Elliot, who succeeded Stanley Adams as Cook's chairman in 1959 (though in a non-executive capacity). Elliot had done long service for the railways and was no innovator. Nor was the suave, efficient Charles Holt, who was made Managing Director and really ran the company, though he was bitterly disappointed not to be stepping into Adams's shoes. Holt was a 'dyed-in-the-wool' conservative[37] who (like nearly all Cook's top men at this time) had risen from the clerking ranks. And he was delighted that there had not been 'a scrap of change in our organisation' since he had joined it in 1920.[38] Elliot was told by loyal employees that the firm was 'a bit stick-in-the-mud at times'.[39] Moreover the trade press was increasingly prone to suggest that 'the cautious giant' was complacent, 'top-heavy' and 'old-fashioned'.[40] Yet Elliot declared in 1960: 'If the organisation is efficient, there's no point in interfering . . . . I have seen no need for any changes of policy, and at present I don't foresee any changes in the future.' He would leave novelties such as travel credit cards and 'go-now-pay-later' schemes to other agencies. He was not even particularly enthusiastic about the growth of traveller's cheques, despite the marvellous flow of cash they created. One weekend when British Railways ran short of money Thomas Cook enabled them to pay their staff. And, as Charles Holt had recently pointed out, 'the results of about one quarter of our business subsidise the other three-quarters and still have a small margin of profit'.[41] Elliot insisted: 'We are interested principally in travel rather than the banking business. I am a transport man.'[42]

Cook was certainly well managed under Charles Holt, who 'ran an exceedingly tight ship'. He also pinched pennies. Finding that there was now little or no profit in the 5 per cent commission made from selling railway tickets, he encouraged booking staff to impose a further handling charge on customers who looked likely to pay it.

This unofficial and unstandardized charge, known in the business as 'agency', was 'the cream of the commission'. But taking such cream was a dubious practice and it could only be fostered *sub rosa*. Otherwise Holt was, in the spirit of Stanley Adams, 'cautious and unimaginative'.[43] Behind the scenes Elliot supposedly applied 'the gentle spur'.[44] But he was a weak man and, as befitted one who claimed to have introduced the American term 'public relations' to Britain (in 1925), his effort was mainly cosmetic. More was spent on advertising and publicity. Five 'travel roadshows' went round Britain and 300,000 people a year saw films promoting Cook's tours. *Punch* printed a cartoon in which a middle-aged man on a French beach tells his wife: 'I can't relax. I keep wondering whether we're here because *we* want to be here or because Thomas Cook & Son Ltd. want us to be here.'[45]

Elliot also encouraged dignified stunts like Miss Jemima Morrell's Swiss Tour in 1963, brainchild of the enterprising Publicity Manager, Bill Cormack. This was a centenary repetition of Thomas Cook's first Alpine tour (of which Jemima's diary record was now published), led by his great-great-grandson and namesake dressed in a deerstalker and knickerbockers. The other members of the party also wore Victorian dress, the ladies sporting crinolines and the gentlemen carrying Gladstone bags. Their trip was widely reported and at Interlaken some 20,000 people turned out to greet them. Cook organized other 'prestige events'. There were luxury adventure holidays on the Golden Road to Samarkand, to the Mountains of the Moon, to Ayers Rock in central Australia, round Cape Horn in a square-rigger. There was ballooning in the Alps. There were 'Welcome Tours', once-in-a-lifetime journeys to India, the Far East, South America, and round the world. Cook ran winter cruises on the *Queen Mary* and the *Mauretania*, helping the shipping lines in their 'struggle for survival'.[46] Having earlier complained that 'the unsavoury aspect of London-by-night' was keeping away tourists,[47] the firm ran expensive tours of 'Paris-by-Night', visiting four clubs and seeing, as one newspaper remarked, large numbers of girls catching cold.[48] It also gave a costly face-lift to Prestatyn, now a 'pigmy by holiday camp standards' and hoping to attract the 'professional class'.[49]

Cook did make some efforts to appeal to the cheaper end of the market. In 1960 the firm began 'Thrift Coach Tours' and in 1964 it initiated 'Topstar' budget holidays by charter aircraft. In the same year, having previously spurned the credit schemes of its rivals, Cook offered 'travel on tick'.[50] Charles Holt ingenuously explained: 'We believe this will result in increased business.'[51] But he did not attempt to emulate the 'direct selling' techniques adopted so successfully by Max Wilson's Travel Savings Association. More seriously, Cook 'stayed aloof from the commercial credit card orbit'.[52] Indeed, Elliot and Holt turned down the chance to produce a joint credit card with American Express, who launched their own card in Britain in 1963 and established a dominant position in this exceedingly lucrative market.

At the time this did not seem such a mistake. Traveller's cheques were making fat profits and moving into the credit card market involved heavy expenditure for hypothetical rewards. Anyway, travel itself, as Holt said, was 'the new industrial giant', the most dynamic enterprise in the world.[53] Most of Cook's operations reflected its spectacular growth. The firm's chain of shops was expanding. The Business Travel Service now had 400 accounts. The Autotravel Department, begun to cater for motorists in 1954, was increasing its turnover by some 15 per cent a year. Despite challengers, Cook was still the largest British travel agency and had the 'lion's share' of the individual trade.[54] No one knew better how to take three lady ornithologists to watch flamingos in the Camargue or a posse of British bookmakers to the race tracks of North America, a Texas oilman to the Kremlin or south-eastern football league clubs to fixtures in England, a gaggle of train enthusiasts to Agra (only one of whom bothered to see the Taj Mahal) or a Chinese circus (including 77 performers, 40 security agents, tons of baggage and 250 live fish) to the West. Cook was equal to making travel arrangements for Princess Margaret and for the Pope, for 8,000 Boy Scouts, 48 Russian Intourist agents and 12 Egyptian belly dancers. For royalty, incidentally, staff booked space in their own names, just as they avoided references to Israel which might be seen in Arab countries by christening it 'Williams Territory'. In 1965 the company's net profit exceeded £1 million for the first time.

That year 114 million people throughout the world travelled abroad, among them 14 million Americans and 5 million Britons, and it seemed as though nothing could stop the boom. Indeed tourism had become such a prominent feature of life, especially in the West, that it attracted renewed attention from a number of social critics. Daniel Boorstin described the modern tourist experience as 'diluted, contrived, prefabricated' and full of 'pseudo-events'.[55] Hans Magnus Enzensberger argued that tourists were engaged in a hopeless quest for freedom from bourgeois industrial society, hopeless because they found only what they sought to escape – 'history as a museum', 'nature as a botanical garden', experience as a commercial product and a status symbol.[56] Summing up all this and more, Malcolm Muggeridge coined the paradox that 'Travel narrows the mind', though he also said that 'tourism today is a more dynamic force than revolution, swaying as it does crowns and thrones; Thomas Cook and the American Express, not the *Internationale*, unite the human race'.[57]

At a popular level Hollywood mocked the know-nothing tourist in the feature film, *If It's Tuesday, This Must Be Belgium* (actually a variation on an ancient *Punch* joke at the expense of a 'philosophical excursionist' in one of Cook's parties).[58] In more serious vein, L. Turner and J. Ash later denounced tourists as 'the barbarians of our age of leisure'. Foreign holidays, they said, were a 'form of officially sanctioned deviancy', a licensed Saturnalia which would make the tourist more amenable to 'social control' once he returned home. They admitted that Thomas Cook had been 'tourism's noblest apologist'. But now his firm and others were engaged in a 'new form of colonialism': they assisted people from rich countries to invade the privacy of those in poorer ones, whom they exploited like animals in a game reserve.[59]

The last criticism was a reference to Cook's Adventure Holiday programme, particularly to the 'tribal tour' of Papua New Guinea. On this expedition twenty people paid £800 each to walk a hundred miles through the jungle during the rainy season, encountering crocodiles, pythons and reformed Biami cannibals. Understandably one newspaper called it a 'package *ordeal*'.[60] Although carefully contrived by Cook, it hardly presented the intrepid visitors with nature as a botanical garden. But most Cook's tourists went to Europe and North America, continents which were scarcely obvious victims of neo-colonialism let alone willing hosts to deviants, licensed or not. Of course, some holiday-makers did behave badly and few tourists assimilated more than a smattering of the culture of countries they visited. Yet this had always been the case, as was made plain by hostile comments on Cook's early parties and on Grand Tourists before them.

The revolutionary change of the 1960s, and still more of the '70s and '80s, was the advent of mass tourism. For the first time millions of working-class people took their holidays abroad. There they at least had the chance to widen their horizons as well as briefly to shed the yoke of routine toil. Yet social critics could not resist the temptation to brand them as a noxious breed of louts and philistines. Boorstin was particularly insulting about the intelligence of the new tourists, who were under no illusions about the factitious elements in their recreations. They were happy to enjoy fantasies like Madame Tussaud's or Disneyland as well as cheap, standardized foreign holidays. It was a measure of Cook's detachment from the mass tourist market that the firm's employees were themselves inclined to make fun of the new class of holiday-makers. Cook's hostesses told the press that they were asked questions like, 'What's à la carte in French?' and 'Who was General Charlemagne, who fought in the last war?'[61] Cook's staff magazine reported that one tourist had disembarked the rest of his party at Aachen Hauptbahnhof, assuring them: 'That's German for Cologne.'[62]

Naturally the firm defended tourism in general. This was easy, for despite the strictures and the growing worries of conservationists almost everyone now appreciated its value, especially as an invisible export – tourism provided Spain, for example, with 40 per cent of her foreign earnings. The United Nations designated 1967 International Tourist Year and passed a unanimous resolution recognizing tourism as 'a basic and most desirable human activity, deserving the praise and encouragement of all peoples and all Governments'.[63] But Cook was reluctant to embrace popular tourism unreservedly. The firm seemed 'content with its middle-class clientele'.[64] It appeared glad, as Eric Kitchen, President of Cook's 1841 Club, said, not to have a 'Majorca with chips' image.[65] Above all, it was unwilling to take risks, especially at a time when turnover was mounting annually. 'We might be bold,' the staff were informed, 'we might also lose our money. If we are cautious we are also willing to learn. We may be a little traditional but that is part of our value.'[66]

There was much truth in this, but Cook's traditional methods proved sadly inadequate to deal with the crises of the late 1960s and early '70s. This was an era of competition more cut-throat than had ever been seen in the travel business. The relaxation of restrictions on charter flights and a new generation of short-distance jets, notably the Boeing 727, resulted in even cheaper package holidays. But tour operators were 'hypersensitive about prices. Their future is balanced on razor-thin profit margins netting only one or two per cent on turnover.'[67] In July 1966 Harold Wilson's new Labour government re-imposed the £50 travel allowance as part of a series of measures to hold down inflation. This allowance remained in force until 1970 and it hurt Cook more than other travel agencies because a third of the firm's tours fell beyond the limit. A new programme had to be printed and the scramble for business in the charter market became even fiercer.

Cook fell behind while agencies like Horizon, Cosmos, Clarkson's and Thomson's forged ahead. The arrival of the Thomson conglomerate, which took over Universal Sky Tours and Riviera Holidays in 1965, marked a new trend for 'big financial empires to "move in" on the travel industry'.[68] It was an international trend: in 1968 the Furgazy Travel Bureau, third largest agency in the United States after American Express and Cook, was bought by Diner's Club. And as one English journal said, the arrival of these business leviathans promised a 'slow but far-reaching reorganisation' in the travel industry, from which would emerge 'a few large groups, well armed for a massive onslaught in the 1970s, on some of the 45 million stay-at-home Britons'.[69] Such giants could well afford to invest in 'vertical integration', the increasingly common practice whereby travel companies acquired airlines and hotels in order to gain control over the entire holiday package. There were, indeed, great risks attached to this policy: in 1968 British Eagle Airways, owned by Harold Bamberg, who had purchased Lunn-Poly, went into liquidation. But for a successful entrepreneur the rewards could be colossal and Thomas Cook, despite a long history of owning or controlling tourist accommodation and means of transport, notably in Egypt, did not really grasp this opportunity.

Admittedly Cook's position was difficult. The firm was inhibited from acquiring an airline because this would have brought it into direct competition with the large operators for whom much of its gigantic agency work was done. And it was unwilling to invest state money in 'time charters', the new system of hiring aircraft at cheap rates for several thousand hours at a time. For although potentially lucrative, time charters were hazardous because they could not be cancelled if passengers failed to materialize. So, in 1968, with profits slipping and the company in danger of being

squeezed out of the popular market altogether, Cook teamed up
with British European Airways (also facing losses because of stiff
competition from charter flights) to promote 'Silver Wing' package
holidays. Here was 'a determined attempt to capture a bigger share
of the mass market'[70] while simultaneously 'trying to maintain an
image of old-world reliability'. It was accompanied by a costly
advertising campaign, organized by J. Walter Thompson. Plans
were even made in Berkeley Street 'to build a chain of holiday
hotels in the Mediterranean'.[71] There was also a 'major shake-up',[72]
mainly because, having such a large staff, Cook was badly hurt by
Selective Employment Tax, which cost the company £1,000 a day.
At first it looked as though all this effort would pay dividends. In
1969 Cook seriously contended with Clarkson's and Thomson's
for dominance in the popular market-place, taking some 150,000
people on Silver Wing holidays. But the following year, unable
to compete on price, the men from Cook's 'severely curbed their
package ambitions'.[73] In 1970, too, travel allowances were lifted
and jumbo jets first landed at Heathrow. So Cook gratefully looked
to the more expensive, long-distance market, running, for example,
the first package tour to Mount Everest.

For all the ballyhoo that surrounded expeditions like this, there
was no disguising the fact that the firm had suffered a major setback. For some time critics had been calling Cook 'the sleeping
giant'[74] and saying that the company 'followed a policy of living
on a good name rather than on developing more enterprise'.[75]
One journalist had described the 'strangely monastic atmosphere'
at Berkeley Street, where 'the polished panels and white-coated
stewards of the managerial fifth floor bring to mind an expensive
nursing home'.[76] After the Silver Wing failure there were more
such comments, especially when the government announced (in
January 1971) that Cook was to be sold.

Then the *Financial Times* held forth on the firm's 'lack of
managerial-entrepreneurial spirit', its rigid, Civil-Service-style 'system of rank and promotion' and the 'enormous cavern' of a
booking-hall at Berkeley Street, which gave little indication of
'"modern techniques". The décor is 1930s brown; acres of space
are unused; the bustling supermarket atmosphere that pervades
most of Cook's rival outlets (regrettable perhaps, but profitable)
is missing.'[77] Cook had once been 'the Harrods of travel', said the
Daily Telegraph, but was now 'rather more Gamages'.[78] *The Times*

opined that Cook had 'grown into something of a juggernaut'.[79] Vladimir Raitz, who wanted to buy Cook, declared: 'There are brilliant people right inside the Thomas Cook organisation who are chafing at the bit and raring to go but they have been held back by a moribund top management and possibly the heavy hand of state ownership.'[80]

Here was the nub. Much of the criticism was inspired by a wish to knock down this 'state monolith' so that it could be rebuilt as a monument to private enterprise.[81] Earlier Barbara Castle, Labour Minister of Transport, had described Cook as 'a valuable national asset which must continue to be maintained and vigorously developed'.[82] (She might have been less enthusiastic had she known that Thomas Cook continued to function in Rhodesia after its unilateral declaration of independence, disguising the fact by omitting its branches from the printed list of offices). The Conservatives, anticipating the policy of privatization which came to fruition under Margaret Thatcher, considered that the travel agency should not be in state hands, where it had stagnated, and could only be revived by exposure to market forces. There was much in this view, just as there was substance to press and other strictures on Cook. As Sir John Elliot said,

> It should never have been state-owned; the business was – and still is – international, and state ownership did nothing to help it. Indeed, our masters inhibited Cook's from going into the charter business, and gave no encouragement to any development of its travellers' cheque network.[83]

Yet this special pleading hid the firm's real postwar successes. For, despite everything, there is much to commend in Thomas Cook's achievement as a nationalized industry.

Above all, in the tradition of its philanthropic founder, the firm was a public service. Its new rivals were tour operators. They packaged trips on which tourists often had to fend for themselves and sometimes arrived in resorts to find their hotels 'either still in the concrete mixer or grossly overbooked'. Cook was a travel agency. As *The Times* acknowledged, the firm had 'a history of public service that has made the name Thomas Cook a by-word for reliability, whatever the return on capital employed'.[84] Indeed, some members of staff with strong trade union principles believed that Thomas Cook should not make a profit at all but should cater for public needs in the same spirit as the National Health Service.

Cook also maintained the highest standards: as the travel writer Arthur Eperon said, 'I have seen the same hotel called "comfortable second class" by Thomas Cook, "top second" by another agent and "first class" by a third.'[85] Cook provided unique adjuncts to tourism such as the *Continental Timetable*, edited by the remarkable John Price and described by Paul Jennings as 'a master-text of the restless modern world from which material could be drawn for a dozen sociological and political theses'.[86] Cook's staff worked together as a team, with little back-biting and less back-stabbing. The firm had 'a continuity that defies analysis' and its employees were loyal to each other and to the job.[87] They were thoroughly professional. It took two years' training to become a booking clerk in Berkeley Street and on the fifth floor the School of Travel (founded in 1947) ran specialized courses for seniors as well as juniors. Thus 'most of the "chefs" in the travel business are to be found in Cook's'.[88] Other companies, which mostly made do with cheap, unskilled labour, would pay a premium to inveigle an experienced man from Cook's into their employment.

By 1971 Cook had 110 shops (which now began the profitable business of selling their rivals' holidays) and traveller's cheques continued to give the firm a 'cash flow' which was the envy of competitors.[89] In other words, Cook had achieved its own kind of 'vertical integration'. This stood the firm in good stead, as did its perennial caution, during the price-cutting war of the early 1970s. Then companies like Thomson's, Clarkson's and Horizon made huge losses while Thomas Cook remained in profit. As the *Guardian* wrote, 'This makes Cook's decision not to get too deeply involved in the cut throat end of the market a lot more justifiable.'[90]

No wonder there were six serious bidders for Cook in the spring of 1972. They included the Thomson Organization, Trafalgar House, Great Universal Stores, a group led by Barclays Bank, and a consortium headed by Midland Bank which included Trust House Forte and the Automobile Association. Midland, 'a pioneer of diversification outside the confines of traditional banking operations',[91] had for some time been stalking Thomas Cook, with which it had long had dealings. In 1963, for example, Midland had considered taking over the firm 'to exploit the potential of Cook's travellers cheques . . . the only effective competition to . . .

American Express'. The bank's representatives went so far as to discuss matters with Charles Holt. After further deliberation they concluded that Thomas Cook must be acquired, if at all, as a homogeneous whole: 'To take the banking side of the travellers cheques without the travel agency might, in time, leave us with an empty shell . . . the one is in many respects dependent on the other for its name and reputation.'[92]

In October 1970, after Edward Heath's surprise victory in the general election, Sir Archibald Forbes, chairman of Midland, had got together his consortium, including the AA because it 'would still further increase the "respectability", in the eyes of the Government, of our bid'.[93] They joined in pressing the new Minister of Transport, John Peyton, to privatize the company. He was nervous, believing that he would have difficulty in defending such a novel policy in the House of Commons. Thomas Cook could certainly not be disposed of abroad, or broken up, or sold to one of the 'crook organisations in the tourist industry which are not too squeamish about the safety of their customers'.[94]

Not content with the sale particulars issued by Henry Schroder Wagg and the accounts audited by Peat, Marwick, Mitchell (which valued Cook's tangible assets at £13^1/2 million), Midland carried out its own investigation. It heard that the old firm was slow-moving, introspective, inflexible, traditionalist, run by committees, hampered by a policy of promotion from within and tied by trade-union wage scales. But Cook's traveller's cheques, with their favourable cash flow, the firm's international chain of offices, and other departments such as Shipping & Forwarding, were considerable assets.[95] So were the incomparable experience of its staff and 'the wide international acceptance of its name as synonymous with reliability and security'.[96]

Just how much this made Cook worth Midland found it difficult to gauge: estimates ranged from what bank experts admitted was the ridiculous sum of around £3 million to £15 million. Sir Reginald Wilson, Elliot's successor as Cook's chairman and himself a distinguished accountant, was simultaneously wrestling with the same problem and finding it equally intractable. Favouring a bank as purchaser, he concluded that 'the acceptance of any figure less than £20 million, or at least £17^1/2 million, will require a lot of public justification'.[97] In the event, Midland and its junior partners, who were bought out five years later, offered £22.5 million. This was substantially more than rival bids, and they emerged victorious. In the light of modern economic developments, becoming part of a great financial and service industry was probably the most logical outcome for Thomas Cook. Sir John Elliot told Forbes: 'The Midland Bank-Cook combination is a "natural" and will be a great success.'[98] Needless to say, there were those at Thomas Cook who resented the sale, whatever the price. As the President of the 1841 Club said, reflecting on the value of 'our inheritance from the past' and expounding the faith of all loyal employees, 'Cook's is worth more than money.'[99]

• 16 •

The Global Future

So dawned a bright new era for Thomas Cook, though there were also dark moments to come. Midland Bank had bought Cook for its international services and for its name. This, it has been estimated, is the seventh most recognizable trademark in the world, and there was some suggestion that the Bank might even change its own name to Thomas Cook. Nothing came of that, but Midland did cease to sell its own traveller's cheques in favour of Cook's. However, some senior figures in the Bank disapproved of the diversification and they hankered to get rid of the new acquisition. Not until 1987, fifteen years after the purchase, did Midland Bank unequivocally commit itself to keeping and expanding its venerable subsidiary. Part of the trouble, initially, was that, despite its earlier enquiries, Midland did not entirely know what it had bought. Once in control, the Bank conducted a rigorous examination of the affairs of Cook and was perturbed by further revelations. The accounting system, in particular, was 'unbelievably archaic' and in some cases there was not even double-entry book-keeping.[1] For the rest the investigators, a professional body called the Stanford Research Institute, concluded that Thomas Cook was badly managed, ill-organized and not sufficiently profit-minded. It could and should make money, like its competitors, by creating and selling package tours.

The dangers of this procedure were cogently pointed out by Sir Reginald Wilson, who defended the company against its critics. But Wilson also recognized that 'adjustment and rejuvenation'[2] were long overdue and Midland Bank appointed a new chief executive to carry out the necessary reforms. He was Simon Kimmins, who was well connected socially and formerly head of a finance corporation. Kimmins 'came in like a tornado',[3] in a 'rash, fierce blaze of riot'. He was clever, dynamic, enthusiastic, impatient, charming, volatile, arrogant and ambitious. He had a flair for publicity and he 'worked incredibly hard'.[4] He had no experience of the travel industry but he predicted a 'progressive future' for the company after the 'trial and strain [of] the last few years'.[5] Kimmins claimed that he was not proposing to bring about an 'instant revolution' at Cook. But the firm's employees, who regarded him as 'a whiz kid', feared that he meant to make all things new – and in his own image.[6] They were less worried about the introduction of new measures than new men. Midland Bank's appointee as Deputy Chairman, for example, was Malcolm Wilcox, who had 'a mind like a razor'[7] and (it was thought) inclinations to match. At Berkeley Street he was nicknamed 'Papa Doc', and employees watched anxiously as his 'Tonton Macoutes' went to work. Some ancient blood was spilt and much new blood was recruited. There was also a growing polarization between the Old Guard, on whom Wilson kept a benevolent eye, and the young radicals, with Kimmins in the van.

He moved at a frenetic pace, pushing through a reorganization of the corporate structure, realizing some assets and maximizing profits. For some time the firm had been planning to move its headquarters out of London, where costs were high and conditions cramped, and it had actually bought a site in Swindon for the purpose. But Kimmins decided that Peterborough had more to offer and he initiated the construction of a large new office block beautifully situated in green fields beside the River Nene.[8] Employees were encouraged to participate more critically in the decision-making process, and for the first time women (who had been allowed on Cook training courses since 1947) took a more outspoken role in the company's affairs. They proceeded to complain, quite rightly, about the male chauvinist tone of the Staff Magazine.

Discovering that 'the Cook signal to the public was weak and confused', Kimmins employed the advertising agency McCann Erickson to improve matters. This resulted in a new emphasis on 'the most illustrious name in travel', one preeminently suggestive of personal service, and the emergence of a standardized 'logo'.[9] The T in Thomas and the k in Cook were slightly lowered to give unity to the whole and to separate the magic words from anything coming after them (the '& Son Ltd' disappeared altogether), and the letters were henceforth printed in 'flame' red, a 'young, active' colour.[10] In the United States Cook launched a multi-million-dollar advertising campaign to increase sales and in Australia the firm used television commercials for the first time. Kimmins could point to 'increased awareness of Thomas Cook in the media'.[11] But not all his enterprises were successful, particularly in the

United States, where losses mounted remorselessly. The plans to
build two Nile cruisers were not realized. And some of Kimmins's
initiatives seemed little more than gimmicks. In 1974, for example,
the *Guardian* reported cattily that Cook was 'about to galvanise itself
into commercial life with the help of that portly predictor from the
Hudson Institute, Dr Herman Kahn', whose expensive advice the
firm had solicited. It turned out to be a spectacular demonstration
of the fatuity of futurology: Kahn forecast that Latin America would
be the world's next Mediterranean. He added helpfully that he had
run a survey on British girls taking holidays in Italy and found that
two-thirds of them had affairs there, and that you could get 700
people into a Boeing 747 if they were packed horizontally – a case
of literal lateral thinking.[12]

All the same, Kimmins had impressed many observers and in
June 1974 *Travel News* announced that the shake-up at Cook was
complete and that the company 'now seems poised for take-off'.[13] In
fact, Kimmins was still grappling with intractable problems. For
he had had the ill luck to arrive at a time when the whole travel
industry was in a crisis caused by the recession, the devaluation
of sterling, the rise in oil prices and a disastrous price-cutting war.
Altogether the top forty-nine travel companies lost £8 million in
1971 and £6 million in 1972, and this at a time when nearly 10
million Britons a year were going abroad and tourism had become
the 'largest single item of world trade'.[14] Some firms went to the
wall; others amalgamated; all the major ones changed their top
managements. In 1974 Court Line, the massive company which
had absorbed Clarkson's and Horizon, collapsed leaving 40,000
tourists stranded and many more out of pocket. Cook's response was
prompt and masterly. The firm launched a Money-Back Guarantee
scheme which ensured that people who booked with Cook should
never again suffer from the failure of a tour operator. Nor did they:
for example, when Laker Airways collapsed in 1982 Cook's clients
received full compensation within twenty-four hours. The travel
press was jubilant about this revolutionary initiative:

> The sleeping giant has awoken with a roar that has taken
> everyone by surprise. Just when the travel trade is in its most
> vulnerable position for years – under attack from all sides –
> Britain's biggest travel agency chain has begun dictating terms
> with a vengeance.[15]

But although Cook 'came through the bad times better than most, its good name being a great asset', the firm was by no means unscathed. Kimmins's methods had been, to say the least, controversial and, not having found 'much in the way of management talent or system to support him', he had failed to create the necessary infrastructure to sustain the drive for growth.[16] To quote the *Investor's Chronicle*, when he tried to speed up the machine 'the wheels had flown off'.[17] In 1975 the firm declared the worst loss in its history, over £3.4 million. That summer Midland Bank brought in its experienced and successful 'troubleshooter' Tom Fisher to find out what had gone wrong. A plain, blunt Midlander, Fisher soon returned to Malcom Wilcox's office and slapped down a thick report on his desk saying: 'I can give it to you in a sentence: it would take ten Tom Fishers five years to put this thing right.' Wilcox looked up sharply and replied: 'You start on Monday.'[18] Fisher was appointed chief executive of the Thomas Cook Group. And Kimmins, who admitted that he had found tourism 'an extremely difficult trade',[19] departed in dudgeon.

Fisher's instructions were to stop the rot, to 'be as hard as iron to cut losses' and if possible to turn them into profits.[20] He did just that. In the words of Sir John Cuckney, who was chairman of Cook between 1978 and 1987, Fisher was 'largely responsible for the Group's strong and effective recovery'. Remaining in post until 1980, he initiated a phase of the firm's activity 'comparable to the great years of its development between 1865, when Thomas Cook moved to London, and 1873 when he made his first world tour'.[21]

From the start Fisher made no bones about the company's inadequacies. In private and in public he was gloriously outspoken. He told the men from Cook's that Midland had bought 'a pig in a poke' and that he had found 'a can of worms'.[22] He was not sure whether he had been 'called in to act as undertaker or midwife'.[23] At one early staff meeting Fisher declared that Cook's homegrown management was 'lamentable', 'genteel', 'relaxed', 'juvenile' and 'top-heavy'. The firm's £3.4 million loss would have been doubled if it had included the pension-fund deficiency and 'Maybe you'd have been better off if you'd remained nationalised.' European losses were also frightening – the Paris office had not made a profit since before the war. In the United States twenty-four out of forty-five branches were 'grossly unprofitable' and 'we are comprehensively broke'. The indictment was remorseless. Cook's freight charges had not been raised for fifteen years. 'Last year we spent £4,000 on rubber bands. We have 80 years' stock!'

Finally Fisher waxed furious about the fact that Thomas Cook was the only major company in Britain not to have accrual accounting.[24] This meant that there was no up-to-date financial information available to the firm's managers. The equipment was equally antiquated. In Berkeley Street Fisher found '1926 Mercedes accounting machines' slung from the ceiling on metal ropes so that the rickety tables on which they rested should not collapse. They 'had been written off long ago' and the systems used by their operators 'related to the last century in many respects'.

> To establish what Cook owed a principal supplier, there was no recourse but to ring that supplier up. The key document warranting payment to suppliers could take more than 80 different forms.[25]

By contrast Wagons-Lits used seventeen vouchers and American Express used one, and unlike Thomas Cook they did not issue them in quintuplicate. Cook's business, Fisher concluded, was living off 'the fat of former years'.[26]

In an effort to modernize the company Fisher bullied, hectored and fulminated like some latter-day John Mason Cook. He had an explosive temper and 'could go from flat calm to volcanic lava in two seconds'.[27] The model of an 'authoritarian chief executive', he could 'make counter staff weep at fifty paces'.[28] Fisher himself denies this, but there is no doubt that he was sometimes exceedingly abrasive. At a sales conference, when a garrulous Australian manager asked if he could have two more words, Fisher replied: 'Yes, if they're good-bye.'[29] Fisher also had a penchant for direct action which caused 'shaking, shivering and weeping' at Berkeley Street.[30] Having quickly concluded that the Cook bureaucracy spent far too much time administering itself, he determined to stop the endless meetings which were interfering with business. Consulting no one, he arrived at the office early one morning, locked all the doors of the conference rooms and pocketed the keys. By 9.15, as he later recorded, the corridors were jammed with a 'milling mass of the creme de la creme of our management raring to get round their allotted tables'. Fisher brusquely informed them that the committee rooms were closed until further notice and that their function was not to debate but to direct.[31] Needless to say, such tactics did not make him popular. But in the interest of galvanizing the company he was prepared to 'live with the blood-red results and all the tooth and claw'.[32] Moreover, as some employees discovered, under Fisher's formidable exterior beat the proverbial heart of gold. In the words of one senior figure, 'When members of staff became ill he was the kindest man imaginable – even if he had made them ill in the first place.'[33]

Like John Cook, Fisher believed that 'the devil is in the detail' of the travel industry[34] and he told Cook's staff ominously: 'If I am running the business properly I tidy everything up.'[35] But, unlike other new brooms, he did not altogether want to sweep away the past. For instance, he readily agreed to John Price's imaginative suggestion that the fiftieth anniversary of the Cook/Wagons-Lits merger should be marked by the purchase of a Wagons-Lits dining car, to be leased for £1 a year to Peterborough's Nene Valley Railway – where it is still in service. Fisher also prized the firm's Victorian legacy, which had left Cook with 'unrivalled benefits . . . a world network of branches, each with its long-derived expertise and awareness of local needs, customs and prejudices, and . . . a reputation for solidity and integrity, highly valued in the Middle and Far East'.[36] Of course he was determined to shake off 'our Kipling image of pith helmets and paddles up the river'. But he was equally determined to exploit 'the prestige of the Thomas Cook name'.[37]

This did not mean head-on competition with Thomson's in the popular market-place, for Fisher believed that Cook was a different sort of animal. The company's strength lay in financial services, retailing, business travel and the arrangement of first-rate tours. Fisher made a virtue of Cook's prestige, the very quality which had inhibited the firm from producing successful cheap package holidays for the million. However, Fisher did not propose to get 'stranded at the wrong end of the market'[38] and he tried to increase holiday sales in the middle range. He offered incentives to families, attracted more people from the North of England, increased the variety of tours and gave fixed-price guarantees. The company's share of the British holiday market was now between 3 and 4 per cent and Cook's shops sold five rival holidays for every one of its own. Fisher improved this position by adopting a clever slogan which advertised the firm as much as the product: 'Thomas Cook – go for the experience.'

Fisher also made a huge effort with other areas of the business. He pressed ahead with the issuing of Thomas Cook traveller's cheques in foreign currencies and opening exchange bureaux in good locations such as cross-Channel ferries. He thus expanded still further sales which grew by 700 per cent between 1972 and 1978. He made Thomas Cook more of a presence in British high streets; by 1978 there were 150 shops and Cook had 'reached the point of dominating the retail travel industry'.[39] Fisher also did his best to ensure that the shops gave efficient service. 'My objective,' he declared, 'is to be the Marks & Spencer of travel.'[40] Actually it had long been a company joke that, during the winter, ticket-issuing staff divided themselves into the chess section and the embroidery section because there was nothing else to do. Fisher kept them busy by making them omnicompetent, training those on the travel side to help those on the financial side and vice versa. He also wrote and issued a pamphlet on 'The Art of Being a Good Manager'. He rewarded bad management in the Rome office (where it was compounded by corruption) by literally shutting up shop and personally directing frustrated customers to the nearest branch of Wagons-Lits.

Fisher was equally forceful in the United States, where a similar situation prevailed. He blamed top management for the continuing losses – 'The fish smells from the head down'[41] – and within a few days of arriving he dismissed the director of American operations. He then sent one of Kimmins's ablest recruits, Ralph Kanter, across the Atlantic on a 'kill or cure mission'.[42] 'Tough, professional and direct to the point of bloody rudeness', Kanter cut costs and staff viciously, sometimes, it was said, 'lowering his voice to a scream'.[43] He created a new accounting system and taught branch managers how to use it, converting them in the process from being 'old-fashioned readers of timetables'. Above all he 'went very aggressively after corporate accounts',[44] those of large companies whose travel needs Cook could meet on advantageous terms.

Until then Thomas Cook, which remained too small in the United States to obtain attractive discounts for leisure travellers, had only made tentative ventures in this direction. With the help of Midland Bank the firm expanded fast, purchasing Executive Travel Inc. of Detroit and becoming the largest business-travel organization in the

United States. By 1978 nearly half of Cook's $200 million turnover came from its corporate customers, nearly 1,500 of them, including Atlantic Richfield, International Harvester and Standard Oil. In Detroit Cook had the largest and most sophisticated business-travel centre in North America, catering for such companies as Ford, Chrysler and Bendix. Cook also arranged travel for official bodies such as the United Nations in New York, the Organization of American States in Washington, the World Health Organization in Geneva and (a long-standing and little-known office) for the House of Commons in London. Elsewhere Fisher opened more branches, in the Middle East, the Far East, South Africa and Australia, where eight new offices began work in 1978 alone. But he was also ruthless in closing down unprofitable enterprises. The holiday camp at Prestatyn, the Boulac land and the freight business were all sold. Autotravel, superfluous now that motorists could easily book their own holidays, was disbanded. Two years after his arrival Fisher could declare: 'We have stopped bleeding, and although we are still sick in bed we have enough strength to chase the nurses.'[45]

This vitality stemmed partly from an investment of capital by Midland Bank, some £10.5 million. As a further reflection of its confidence in Cook, Midland not only bought out the minority shareholders in England, it also purchased the quarter stake in Cook's foreign interests still held by Wagons-Lits, though the two companies continued to work closely together, having between them by 1978 a network of over 900 offices in about 140 countries. Without Midland Bank Fisher would not have been able to undertake nearly such an ambitious programme of modernization.

He renewed everything – plant, machinery, structure, procedures. He introduced a new accounting system which enabled the 'state of each outlet to be examined every month'.[46] He ensured that the new Peterborough headquarters would be 'a showpiece for the Company'.[47] This new temple of tourism, a gleaming white building set on a thirty-acre freehold site, cost nearly £11 million and was equipped with the most advanced travel technology. For example, its computers speeded up the automated holiday reservation system which had been in operation since 1966. Fisher was particularly keen on going to Peterborough because it would stanch the perpetual haemorrhage of staff who, having been trained by Cook, had acquired a 'highly negotiable "certificate"'.[48] Actually, the move was not without its traumas. Many employees preferred to resign rather than leave London and the rest were 'so bloody miserable', according to one senior man, that the company had been obliged to offer them the incentive of generous 'relocation allowances'.[49] Fisher thought that they were far too generous and tore up the agreement, which scarcely added to his popularity. However, as a further item of what he took to be good housekeeping Fisher did introduce a pay and productivity scheme in 1977. Nor did he neglect the Berkeley Street office. By 1980 it had been turned into the largest and most advanced travel centre in the world, offering a range of services from passports to car hire, from traveller's cheques to vaccinations. Fisher was especially proud of the vaccination centre, which he persuaded a reluctant Midland Bank to support by offering to accept its franchise in lieu of his pension. He himself retired in 1980, chagrined not to be made a member of Midland''s board but conscious that he had done a 'fabulous job' at Thomas Cook.[50] In that year the pre-tax profits of the Cook group were nearly £11 million on a turnover of £2.5 billion. Not since the time of John Mason Cook had the firm been so 'revitalised and strengthened'.[51]

But Cook's troubles were not over, as the 'highly intelligent'[52] new chief executive Alan Kennedy soon discovered. Kennedy was a former submarine commander – in 1971 he had become the first Briton to take his craft, HMS *Dreadnought*, under the polar ice-cap. He had solid experience of the travel industry, some of it acquired in the United States where he had improved on Kanter's reforms, and he was much liked by Cook's staff. This was not only because he was 'very able'[53] but because he had done something to shield them from his predecessor's 'withering blast'.[54] Once in control, Kennedy employed his superb management skills to encourage teamwork and to exploit 'the enormous fund of good will from the staff to the company which still remained'.[55] But he was faced with two major sets of difficulties, global and local.

In some ways the early 1980s, a time of massive inflation and fierce competition in the travel industry, resembled the early 1970s. Cook suffered accordingly, as did other leading tour operators, who lost nearly £10 million in 1982. Cook also suffered as a result of the serious problems with plagued Midland Bank during the early 1980s. At the beginning of the decade Midland bought the Crocker Bank in the United States. This turned out to be a disastrous investment and it also meant that Thomas Cook was forced by the Securities and Exchange Commission to part with its American subsidiary. Midland's further difficulties, largely caused by its heavy loans to Third World countries, restricted capital outlay and inhibited Cook's ability to expand. Midland Bank itself endured 'a certain amount of pain' from being associated with a travel business which it found hard to understand and, not for the first time, it contemplated selling Thomas Cook.[56] Instead it decided, somewhat hesitantly, to complete the work of Tom Fisher. There were further redundancies. Payrolls and overheads were slashed. Bureaucracy was diminished and efficiency increased. A rolling reorganization occurred, outlasting Kennedy and continuing into the time of his successors, Bernard Norman (1986–8) and Peter Middleton (1988–), and taking various forms. This reorganization was given added impetus by Midland's recovery: in 1986 it sold Crocker and the following year it received a 'cash injection' of £310 million from the Hong Kong & Shanghai Bank. The result was massive further investment in Thomas Cook – £18 million in 1990 alone. There was also a determined and successful effort to achieve a 'leaner, less costly structure, with fewer layers of management' and to 'shake off our old-fashioned and expensive image'[57] – poignant echoes of the 1930s as well as the 1960s.

Of course, there were difficulties and reverses, especially abroad. In India the government forced Thomas Cook to 'go public' – such was the power of the ancient name that the issue was over-subscribed fifteen times. Other mergers, in New Zealand and South Africa, expanded the company's network but reduced its coherence. The traveller's cheque business was particularly tricky. For example, after the return of the Ayatollah Khomeini in 1979 many Iranians invested in Cook's convertible currency, locally known as 'mattress money' because of its supposed hiding place. This was fine, but meanwhile revolutionary guards threatened to expropriate the firm's remaining stock, some $6 million. Their move was only just thwarted by Cook's man on the spot, Jim Kane, who persuaded them to give him access to the bank vault and cut up the entire amount with an industrial guillotine. The company was less fortunate over £3.4 million worth of traveller's cheques which it lost when a Saudi Arabian money-changer named Al Rahji went bankrupt in 1982.

Yet despite the setbacks, and perhaps because of the internal convulsions of the 1980s, this was a period of astonishing advance

for the company. At the beginning of the decade Cook's traveller's cheques were already benefiting enormously from having an
effective monopoly in Libya, where most expatriate workers were
paid in this form. Reciprocal agreements were then made with
European banks and with Mastercard and new Cook's Euro traveller's cheques were launched These were an immediate success.
Thomas Cook's traveller's cheques quickly doubled their share
of the world market and today, issued in twelve currencies, they
hold about 18 per cent. A comprehensive refund service was
introduced and now operates through 105,000 outlets all over
the world (including banks, Hertz and Wagons-Lits offices). It
handles 30,000 claims a year. The most remarkable, it is often said,
was made by a woman whose traveller's cheques had been eaten by
baboons in an East African safari park. But after the Argentinian
invasion of the Falkland Islands an even more extraordinary claim
was made. One of the Royal Marine guards lost his cheques during
the initial skirmish at the Governor's mansion and telephoned the
New York refund centre from Uruguay, where he was taken as a
prisoner. Having explained the circumstances, he was surprised to
be asked routine questions such as why he had made no police
report. But he got his refund. Today most cheques are cashed about
a month after their date of purchase. But occasionally very ancient
traveller's cheques turn up and, having enjoyed the interest for so
long, Thomas Cook is happy to honour them. However, there were
some glum faces in Berkeley Street when the safes of the *Titanic* were
raised to the surface.

It had been a standing joke since the 1890s that whenever bank
clerks were asked for foreign currency they popped out of the back
door and fetched it from the nearest Cook's office; by the 1980s
Cook had become one of the world's largest wholesale dealers in
banknotes, enabling many financial institutions to supply their
customers. Cook's business travel agency, catering for 12,000 companies, established a major position in the global market during the
1980s. It not only met the travel needs of international organizations
and stage-managed complete sales conferences in all parts of the
world, it also served entire government departments. In 1985 Cook
set up Compass Travel to organize more specialized projects along
the same lines. As for individual 'senior executives', they could
take advantage of new services such as the Carte d'Or, which
gave them immediate credit of £2,000 as well as other benefits.

In 1985 Cook sold the unprofitable Madeleine office in Paris for
£5.5 million and bought Blue Sky Travel, British Caledonian's
chain of thirty shops, and Frame's forty-six shops. This gave an
important fillip to Cook's already large retail chain, which continues
to expand rapidly at home (where it has more than 340 shops) and
abroad – approaching 1,000 outlets in over 100 countries.

Further enormous investment was made in travel technology. A
Travel Information Bank was established in 1980 which now gives
all branches access to 40,000 'pages' of up-to-the-minute data, such
as the air fare between Sydney and Singapore; passport, visa and
health requirements in Thailand; the temperature in Dallas; bank
opening hours in Germany and car hire rates in Vancouver. Cook's
Air Fare Warehouse was set up to offer customers the most competitive rates and the firm's private data communications system,
christened FAST, was linked to the information networks of major
airlines, tour operators and other travel suppliers, as well as to
Midland Bank. A computerized hotel-reservation system known
as HOTELTECH was developed. In 1988 a national toll-free
telephone booking system COOK DIRECT was inaugurated, soon
followed by a similar operation for small companies, BUSINESS
DIRECT. Today Thomas Cook's computer centres handle over half
a million traveller's cheques a day. To cope with the administration
the company installed a sophisticated electronic distribution and
settlement system in major centres. In addition an automatic sales
system called CHEQUEMATE, which immediately brings stock
records up to date and has proved particularly attractive to the
Japanese, is available for larger agents. Cook so relies on computerized technology that the Group created a contingency computer
centre, called FASTBAK, where vital systems could be operated
if some disaster occurred at the Peterborough headquarters. This
commercial service proved its worth in 1988 when a fire in the
basement damaged some of the firm's main electronic equipment.

Despite the emphasis on finance and technology, Cook continues
to provide a personal service. This naturally appeals to the rich and
famous though, just as naturally, the company claims that it treats
all its customers like VIPs. Certainly it manages to attract celebrities, not least Middle Eastern oil potentates who make demands
unequalled since the extravagant days of the maharajas. Recently
one such figure (and his entourage) tested the travel agency almost
to breaking point. It could cope with chartering yachts at short

notice, with hiring white Rolls-Royces and with getting large amounts of luggage (including firearms) through the customs. It had no difficulty in booking £2,000-a-night suites in Italian hotels and arranging that they should be stocked with freshly cut flowers and special brands of champagne and cigarettes. It could conjure up £70,000 in petty cash on a Friday evening, visas on demand and instant shark-fishing expeditions. But what really threw them out at Berkeley Street was their distinguished client's habit of changing all his plans at the last moment and arriving late everywhere into the bargain. On one occasion an enterprising man from Cook's delayed the *Queen Elizabeth II* for an hour so that his client could sail with her.

Cook appealed to a much larger section of the market by continuing to run imaginative tours to glamorous places. After the difficulties and defeats in the short-distance package market (and with hindsight Alan Kennedy reckons that he continued the costly struggle too long) one of the brightest spots in the company's career during the 1980s has been the expansion of its long-distance tours programme. It is true that the acquisition of the specialist firm Rankin Kuhn in 1982 barely helped this process. But specialized tours, pioneered by the holidays' director Erich Reich, have been outstandingly successful. Indeed, when the painful decision was finally taken, in 1988, to quit the short-distance package-tour market altogether there were no redundancies, staff being redeployed in the long-distance sector and in other expanding areas of the business.

Today separate brochures set out a host of exotic itineraries to India, China and Thailand. 'Faraway Holidays' offer independent travellers favourable rates for transport to, and hotels at, the best international resorts. 'Discovery Flights' perform much the same service for Canada, Australia and New Zealand. 'Escorted Journeys' provide an increasingly wide range of personally conducted tours all over the world. Those to North America have been particularly successful over the past few years. Interestingly enough, Cook first presented the Escorted Journey as 'an exciting new concept . . . . It's not a trip for the tourist but a voyage of discovery for the traveller, not just an enjoyable holiday but also an enriching experience.'[58] Today, however, the company has returned to that runic formula, 'Cook's Tours'. During the 1980s Thomas Cook also set out to re-establish its position in Egypt and it is now the most popular high-quality travel service operating there. In 1989, thanks to Reich's successor Simon Laxton, it even returned to the boat business. It took a major part in planning, fitting out and supervising a spacious new cruiser, the MS *Nile Rhapsody*, which exclusively serves Cook's clients in the British market. At the time of writing another cruiser is under construction, the *Royal Orchid*, and a third, the *Nile Empress*, is at the planning stage. In its brochures the company pertinently recalls that Victorians nicknamed the Nile 'Cook's Canal'.

Furthermore Cook continues to exploit its distinctive history, organizing a number of commemorative luxury tours. In 1984 the Gordon Centenary Nile Cruise celebrated the firm's part in the attempt to relieve Khartoum. Gordon's grand-nephew, John Phillips, was one of the lecturers and, to everyone's amazement, another member of the party turned out to have even closer links with the eminent Victorian. He was an Australian lawyer named Beresford Love, whose great-uncle was Lord Charles Beresford (the eloquent denigrator of Cook's steamer the *Fersaat*) and whose *father* had not only taken part in the relief expedition but had been in Khartoum with Gordon as early as 1879. Building on this success, Cook ran an ambitious tour all round India in 1987 to commemorate the firm's role in Queen Victoria's Golden Jubilee a century before. It included many special events, encompassed fascinating relics of the British Raj and culminated with a grand ball in Delhi attended by British and Indian dignitaries. Cook also gained much publicity by helping to promote the performance of operas in spectacular settings – *Aida* at the temple of Luxor in 1987, and *La Traviata* and *André Chénier* at Versailles in 1989, part of the celebrations marking the bicentenary of the French Revolution. At the time of writing plans are being made to commemorate the 150th anniversary of Thomas Cook's first excursion.

All these initiatives take place at a time when tourism is once again getting a bad press. And once again the reason is its unprecedented expansion. Tourism is now the largest and fastest-growing industry in the world. In 1988 20 million Britons and 40 million Americans went abroad, out of a global total of 355 million tourists. The sheer weight of numbers has actually prompted the authorities in resorts such as Venice and the Algarve to consider imposing restrictions on tourism. It has inspired fresh worries about pollution by tourism and about the creation of 'a new slave trade'[59] – not an altogether absurd concept when one considers that every year

1.5 million Japanese go to South-East Asia on organized 'sex tours'.[60] It has also alienated sympathetic commentators like the distinguished travel-writer Jan Morris. Having for years defended tourism as a valuable asset to poor regions and 'a necessary outlet for the urban millions', she recently denounced it as a colossus whose shadow darkens the world.

> I went to the coast of Maine, and found its old seaports swamped one and all by Collectible Shoppes, Sea'n'Surf restaurants and Davy Jones Boutiques. I went to the Caribbean island of St Maarten, and found its old Dutch waterfront garishly dominated by duty-free shops for cruise passengers, I went to the Côte d'Azur, and ran away again. I went to Oaxaca, in southern Mexico, and found the high mysterious stronghold of the Zapotecs criss-crossed by sheep-like convoys of sightseers, and littered with the detritus of the morning's coach-tours.

Like earlier social critics, Jan Morris now wishes that 'opportunities for travel could be limited to the congenial few'; for it is 'the volume of tourism, not tourism itself, that is making it a curse rather than a benefit to mankind'.

That the present scale of tourism causes serious problems cannot be denied. It can be a blight as well as a blessing. It endangers the environment, undermines indigenous cultures and threatens to kill the thing the tourist loves, the uniqueness of foreign lands. Yet this is no reason for wanting to stifle '*every* manifestation of organised tourism . . . however cultivated, however benevolent'.[61] As one of her critics pointed out,

> Morris's elitist impulse to limit tourism to 'a congenial few' is worse than no solution. It is a step backwards to the day when only upper-class imperialists could afford to 'do the continent', and locals starved in idyllic beauty. Despite the devastation, we are *all* better off for the invention of mass tourism.[62]

Obviously governments agree, for they do their utmost to promote, and to share in the colossal rewards of, this industry. In 1988 two trillion dollars were spent on tourism. This is twice was much as the international arms budget, it is larger than the gross national product of any country apart from the United States and it represents some 12 per cent of the global economy. Tourism has been described as 'the fourth dimension of economic growth' because it is an unimaginably powerful catalyst, stimulating all-round development and creating a vital infrastructure.[63] How much of the wealth generated by tourism actually filters down to those who need it most is debatable, but many poor countries regard it as their salvation. Tourists, too, find their holidays a form of emancipation as well as recreation – and this is to say nothing of tourism as a source of cultural enrichment and international understanding. Whatever its advantages or disadvantages, though, nothing is going to reduce tourism to Victorian dimensions. So the real question for the twenty-first century is how the world can best come to terms with this mass movement. How can we prevent tourists from destroying the objects and qualities which attract them while continuing to foster tourism as a liberating experience for more and more people?

The question casts a shadow over Thomas Cook's future, though this is more promising and perhaps more exciting than at any time in the firm's history. Of course, snags and difficulties remain, some of them serious. In such a volatile business the organization needs constant reorganization, with all the attendant strains which that entails. New challenges produce new conflicts. Growth involves dislocation and big is not always beautiful. Another review of Cook's internal workings, carried out by American efficiency experts in 1988, may have been administratively helpful but it had an unhappy effect on staff morale. Both the emergence of long-distance package tours and the obsolescence of traveller's cheques pose a threat to the company. Thomas Cook remains peculiarly vulnerable to world conditions. Government repression in China, communal violence in Sri Lanka, street crime in South America, trouble almost anywhere in the world can have a disastrous effect on tourism. And while the firm has been able to maintain its integrity and its *esprit de corps* through many vicissitudes, good leadership can turn into bad leadership overnight – with appalling consequences.

On the other hand there is evidence that Thomas Cook is experiencing what the *Financial Times* calls 'a genuine renaissance'.[64] Profits, which reached £22.5 million in 1989, continue to break records and annual turnover, now around £10 billion, has never been so buoyant. For all sorts of reasons, not least the Thomas Cook Travel Book awards, the 'public image' projected by the company remains exceptionally attractive. There is a new partnership between management and staff, known as GEMINI, which offers incentives to individual enterprise as well as joint cooperation. Peter Middleton has given the remarkable assurance that he will only stay as chief executive while he retains the confidence of his own juniors, Cook's senior managers. Bureaucracy is being cut to a minimum: where there were once nineteen grades of status there are now four. New training programmes and leisure facilities for staff are being developed. A potentially effective system of global management is evolving which is designed, paradoxically, to foster both cohesion and devolution: control is maintained from the centre by means of uniform technology (standardized computer equipment employing satellite communication) but regional managers are given every encouragement to use their initiative. The current maxim is, 'Think global, act local.'[65] Already enormous strides have been made.

In Egypt Thomas Cook once again rules the tourist roost. In Canada, thanks to a joint venture with the leading retailer Eaton's, Cook's outlets have just increased from about a dozen to almost a hundred, giving the firm a nationwide scope which is soon to be widened still further. Expansion is taking place in Australia (where the company is market leader, with a turnover of a billion dollars) and New Zealand (where John Reid has brilliantly developed his business). Recently Middleton has been able to regain control of Cook's operation in the United States, a tricky exercise involving negotiations with its owner, Robert Maxwell. The merger with Crimson Travel and Heritage Travel makes Cook the third largest travel agency in the United States, with 325 branches and sales exceeding 1.3 billion dollars a year. With the help of the Hong Kong & Shanghai Bank, ambitious plans are being made to expand in the Far East, where travel is growing faster than anywhere else in the world. A similar programme is being implemented to increase Thomas Cook's presence in Europe, the world's largest area of international travel expenditure. In 1987 Cook finally broke its link with Wagons-Lits in order to be free to develop its services here and elsewhere. This has resulted in a number of recent agreements with travel companies like Via Voyages of France and Viajes Internacional Expreso of Spain. In short, a world-wide travel and servicing network is being established which will give Thomas Cook a presence in 140 countries and in every major city on earth.

Plans are in train, too, for a Thomas Cook credit card. The company is experimenting with 'smart' cards (containing a mass of data encoded on a magnetic strip) which may one day supersede traveller's cheques. Thanks to modern technology and a three-year £35 million investment plan, the shops are also changing their faces. They are providing 'stores within stores' (i.e. separate centres for separate needs) and soon buying a holiday will become an electronic, as much as a personal, consultation. Retail staff will greet customers and then introduce them to a computer terminal at which they can indicate their requirements, see videos of possible destinations together with details of transport, accommodation and price, make their choice and have their booking processed automatically. Automation will also help to give Cook's corporate clients, such as British Telecom, the best deals and greater personal attention. As multinational corporations look for a consistent approach, the company's share of the world's business travel market, itself worth $300 billion a year, is set to increase. Tourists will also benefit from automation as the chain of 500 retail bureaux de change is updated and expanded – with the aim of making Cook 'the preferred global money changer'.[66]

In fact, 150 years after Thomas Cook's excursion from Leicester to Loughborough, his business bids fair to become one of only two truly global travel conglomerates (the other being American Express). But while extending its international scope with an entrepreneurial zeal which John Mason Cook would have admired, the firm strives to maintain the tradition of public service which was the hallmark of its founder.

Manuscript Sources

A: Thomas Cook Archive (TCA)
By far the most important source for this book is the firm's archive at Berkeley Street, which contains a mass of holograph correspondence, unpublished diaries, business reports, company documents, travel guides, brochures, staff magazines, press-cuttings, pictures, posters and ephemera. It is at present being re-catalogued so I have omitted the bin numbers, hitherto used, and referred only to TCA, giving further identification such as names and dates of correspondence where possible. The archive also contains a full run of the *Excursionist* (and *Traveller's Gazette*) from 1851 to 1939 in its various editions (though not the post-1939 Latin-American continuation).

B: John Price Papers
A remarkable collection of manuscripts, cuttings, articles and memorabilia collected by John Price during his years with Thomas Cook.

C: Bill Cormack Papers
An interesting collection of articles and memoranda including a valuable 'History of Holidays in Great Britain from 1812'.

D: Richard Webster Papers
The diaries of Lucilla, Elizabeth and Marian Lincolne, who went on Cook's first Continental tour in 1855.

E: Public Record Office (PRO)
The most important sources from the point of view of this book were the papers of Colonel Ardagh, H. H. Kitchener and Lord Cromer.

F: India Office Library (IOL)
Various letters and reports concerning Thomas Cook's work in India, especially to do with the pilgrim traffic.

G: Midland Bank Archives (MBA)
Papers mainly relating to the Bank's relations with its subsidiary.

H: Sir Reginald Wilson Papers
Letters, reports and memoranda kept by Sir Reginald Wilson, Chairman of the Board of Thomas Cook between 1968 and 1976.

I: John Mason Papers
Papers collected by former Cook archivist, especially concerning the firm's work in India.

Notes

Chapter 1: *The Birth of Tourism* (pages 5–17)

1 J. Pudney, *The Thomas Cook Story* (1953), 53.
2 *Cook's Excursionist*, 13 Sept. 1856. This publication went through various metamorphoses and changes of name between its birth in 1851 and its demise in 1939. In these notes the English edition will be abbreviated as *Exc* until 1903, other editions being indicated by reference to their country or area of origin. After that date it will be referred to as *TG*, short for *Cook's Traveller's Gazette*.
3 C. Hamilton Ellis, *The Midland Railway* (1953), 3.
4 J. Simmons, 'Railways, Hotels, and Tourism in Great Britain 1839–1914' in *Journal of Contemporary History* XIX (1984), 209.
5 *Temperance Messenger* II (1841), 101.
6 *Leicestershire Mercury*, 10 July 1841.
7 *L[eicester] C[hronicle]*, 10 July 1841.
8 P. Ziegler, *Melbourne* (1976), 338.
9 *LC*, 10 July 1841.
10 *Temperance Messenger* II, 126.
11 J. Simmons, 'Thomas Cook of Leicester' in *The Leicestershire Archaeological and Historical Society Transactions* XLIX (1973–4), 18.
12 L. Turner and J. Ash, *The Golden Hordes* (1975), 52.
13 *LC*, 23 July 1892.
14 *Railway Gazette*, 30 Jan. 1959.
15 J. Wraight, *The Swiss and the British* (1987), 218.
16 W. Löschburg, *A History of Travel* (1979), 143–4.
17 M. Feifer, *Going Places: The Ways of the Tourist from Imperial Rome to the Present Day* (1985), 29.
18 T[homas] C[ook] A[rchives], cutting from *The English Illuminated Magazine* (1885).
19 L. Casson, *Travel in the Ancient World* (1974), 32, 266 and 310.
20 Löschburg, *History of Travel*, 35.
21 C. Hibbert, *The Grand Tour* (1969), 228.
22 Feifer, *Going Places*, 119.
23 C. Hibbert, *The Grand Tour* (1987), 170.
24 J.E. Norton (ed.), *The Letters of Edward Gibbon* (1956) I, 180–1.

25 J. Boswell, *The Life of Samuel Johnson* (1941, Everyman edn.) II, 25.
26 G. Hindley, *Tourists, Travellers and Pilgrims* (1983), 11.
27 J. Black, *The British and the Grand Tour* (1985), 2.
28 *Observer* Colour Magazine, 24 Dec. 1967.
29 H. K. Cook, *Over the Hills and Far Away* (1947), 82 and 173.
30 *Daily Universal Register*, 29 Aug. 1786.
31 T. Morgan, 'Travelling Troubles' in *New Monthly Magazine* V (Oct. 1829), 337–8.
32 Feifer, *Going Places*, 164.
33 Hibbert, *Grand Tour* (1987), 87.
34 Hindley, *Tourists*, 214.
35 A.B. Granville, *Spas of England* (1841), II, 6, and I, 33.
36 Granville, *Spas*, II, 121.
37 A. Adburgham, *A Punch History of Manners and Modes 1841–1940* (1961), 49.
38 Simmons, *Journal of Contemporary History* (1984), 205.
39 T. Cook, 'Travelling Experiences' in *Leisure Hour* (June 1878), 374.
40 P. Laslett, *The World We Have Lost* (1965 edn.), 147.
41 R. S. Hawker, *Footprints of Former Men in Far Cornwall* (1870), 163.
42 A. P. Stanley, *The Life and Correspondence of Thomas Arnold* (1846 edn.), 204.
43 French *Exc*, Aug. 1900.
44 W. G. Hoskins, *Devon* (Newton Abbot, 1972 edn.), 152.
45 [H. B. Wheatley], 'Stage-Coaches' in *Temple Bar* (Jan, 1873), 263.
46 C. P. Moritz, *Travels in England in 1782* (1924), 212 and 217.
47 L. A. G. Strong, *The Rolling Road* (1956), 58.
48 J. A. R. Pimlott, *The Englishman's Holiday* (1976 edn.), 76.
49 *Exc*, 18 Mar. 1878.
50 J. Murray, *A Handbook for Travellers on the Continent* (1836), 182.
51 A. I. Shaw, *Old-Time Travel* (1903), 49.
52 *New Monthly Magazine* (Dec. 1829), 545.
53 Hibbert, *Grand Tour* (1987), 49.
54 Cook, *Over the Hills*, 88.
55 A. and P. Burton, *The Green Bag Travellers: Britain's First Tourists* (1978), 17.
56 W. T. Jackman, *The Development of Transportation in Modern England* (1962 edn.), 345 and 605.
57 F. C. Mather, 'The Railways, the Electric Telegraph and Public Order during the Chartist Period, 1837–48' in *History* (Feb. 1953), 40 ff.
58 J. R. Kellett, *The Impact of Railways on Victorian Cities* (1969), 91.
59 B. Disraeli, *Sybil* (1954 edn.), 105–6.
60 *TG*, Feb. 1917.

61 [Wheatley], *Temple Bar* (Jan. 1873), 267.
62 H. Perkin, *The Age of the Railway* (1970), 119.
63 J. Ruskin, *Fors Clavigera* (1896 edn.) I, 92.
64 C. Hibbert, *Venice* (1988), 221.
65 Stanley, *Arnold*, 678.
66 *Exc*, July 1854.
67 H. Pearson, *The Smith of Smiths* (1948 edn.), 331.
68 Perkin, *Age of Railway*, 87.
69 G. Sigaux, *History of Tourism* (Geneva, 1966), 73.
70 J. Francis, *History of the English Railway* (1831) I, 290.
71 *Times*, 2 July 1891; Pudney, *Cook Story*, 16; and *London Echo*, 25 Jan. 1873.

Chapter 2: *A Mission in Life* (pages 18–37)

1 *Exc*, 13 Sept. 1856.
2 *Exc*, Christmas Supplement 1873.
3 TCA.
4 *Times*, 2 July 1891.
5 J. T. Budge, *Melbourne Baptists* (1951), 16.
6 J. R. Godfrey, *Historic Memorials of Barton and Melbourne General Baptist Churches* (Leicester, 1891), 129 and 140.
7 Budge, *Melbourne Baptists*, 21.
8 T. Cook, . . . *Memoir of . . . Samuel Deacon* (Leicester, 1888), 190–2.
9 Budge, *Melbourne Baptists*, 41
10 P. W. Clayden, 'Off for the Holidays: the rationale of recreation' in *Cornhill Magazine* XVI (Sept. 1867), 316.
11 J. J. Briggs, *The History of Melbourne* (n.d.), 29.
12 *Exc*, July 1854.
13 *D[ictionary of] N[ational] B[iography]*.
14 J. L. and B. Hammond, *The Village Labourer* (1948 edn.), 163–4.
15 Briggs, *History of Melbourne*, 29.
16 *Exc*, 26 May 1859.
17 Briggs, *History of Melbourne*, 73.
18 E. Cleveland-Stevens, *English Railways* (1915), 3.
19 G. Hindley, *A History of Roads* (1971), 63.
20 Briggs, *History of Melbourne*, 24.
21 *Exc*, 21 June 1851.
22 Godfrey, *Historic Memorials*, 171.
23 Quoted (from 1874) by the *Buxton Chronicle and Observer*, 8 June 1972.
24 *Exc*, 1 Oct. 1867.

25 *Exc*, June 1854.
26 *Barton Church Magazine* (Oct. 1892).
27 Godfrey, *Historic Memorials*, 170.
28 Pudney, *Cook's Story*, 24.
29 *General Baptist Magazine* (1876), 185.
30 Cook, *Deacon*, 201.
31 Godfrey, *Historic Memorials*, 171.
32 Cook, *Deacon*, 201.
33 Godfrey, *Historic Memorials*, 171.
34 S. W. A. Moisey, 'Joseph Foulks Winks' in *Baptist Times*, 30 Nov. 1950.
35 *The Anti-Smoker and Progressive Temperance Reformer* II (1842), 12.
36 Budge, *Melbourne Baptists*, 31.
37 W. Fraser Rae, *The Business of Travel* (1891), 19.
38 Budge, *Melbourne Baptists*, 42.
39 *Cook's Scottish Tourist Official Directory* (Leicester, 1861), 36.
40 Cormack Papers.
41 TCA, Albert H. Bishop's Reminiscences.
42 *General Baptist Magazine* (1876), 235.
43 *Exc*, 1 June 1868.
44 TCA, Bishop Reminiscences.
45 J. Bland, *Bygone Days in Market Harborough* (Market Harborough, 1924), 89.
46 TCA, T. Cook, *Brief Notes on the Life, Labour, Sufferings, and Death of Mrs Marianne Cook* (1884).
47 *Exc*, 1 Feb. 1867 and 2 Mar. 1868.
48 *Anti-Smoker* II, i.
49 M. Girouard, *Victorian Pubs* (1975), 25.
50 A. Prentice, *Historical Sketches and Personal Recollections of Manchester, 1792–1832* (Manchester, 1851), 216–7.
51 G. B. Wilson, *Alcohol and the Nation* (1940), 229.
52 *Temperance Messenger* II, 86.
53 B. Harrison, *Drink and the Victorians* (1971), 41, 100 and 86.
54 A. Bell, *Sydney Smith* (Oxford, 1980), 149–50.
55 TCA, T. Cook, *Temperance Jubilee Celebrations at Leicester and Market Harborough* (Leicester, 1886).
56 B. Harrison, *Dictionary of British Temperance Biography* (1973), 112.
57 [A. Griffiths], 'John Cook' in *Blackwood's Magazine* CLXVI (Aug. 1899), 211.
58 *Temperance Messenger* II, 43 and 132.
59 *Temperance Messenger* I (1840), 172.
60 *Anti-Smoker* II, 1.
61 *Temperance Messenger* I, 45 and 119.

62 *[National] Temperance Magazine* II, 95.
63 *Temperance Messenger* I, 11.
64 *Temperance Messenger* II, 125.
65 *Temperance Messenger* I, 11, and II, 43 and 1.
66 *Anti-Smoker* II, 17.
67 *Temperance Magazine* II, 130.
68 *Temperance Messenger* II, 50.
69 *Temperance Messenger* I, 28.
70 *Anti-Smoker* II, 3.
71 P. Bailey, *Leisure and Class in Victorian England* (1978), 47, 167 and 29.
72 *Exc*, 13 Sept. 1856.
73 *Exc*, June 1854.
74 *Temperance Messenger* II, 148.
75 A. Temple Patterson, *Radical Leicester* (Leicester, 1954), 247.
76 M. Elliott, *Victorian Leicester* (1979), 39.
77 *Temperance Messenger* I, 27.
78 T. Cook, *Guide to Leicester* (Leicester, 1843).
79 Cook, *Leicestershire Almanack* (Leicester, 1843).
80 Cook, *Guide to Leicester*.
81 *Anti-Smoker* II, 17 and 1.
82 Patterson, *Radical Leicester*, 367.
83 *Temperance Magazine* II, 28.
84 Cook, *Temperance Jubilee Celebrations, 28–9.*
85 *Temperance Magazine* II, 91.
86 *Anti-Smoker* III (1843), 21.
87 E. Swinglehurst, *The Romantic Journey* (1974), 34.
88 *Temperance Magazine* III, 132.
89 T. Cooper, *The Life of Thomas Cooper* (1873), 142.
90 *LC*, 6 Jan. 1844.
91 *Temperance Magazine* II, 504
92 *LC*, 11 July 1846.
93 *Temperance Magazine* III (1845), 190.
94 *Temperance Messenger* II, 132, 127 and 138.
95 T. Cook, *Handbook of the Trip to Liverpool* (Leicester, 1845), iii.
96 *LC*, 5 Oct. 1844.
97 *Railway Chronicle* I (1844), 166.
98 C. C. Eldridge, *England's Mission* (1974), 246.
99 *Liverpool Albion*, 16 Oct. 1843, quoted in Cook's *Trip to Liverpool*.
100 T. Cook, *Handbook of Belvoir Castle* (Leicester, 1848), 3.
101 Cook, *Trip to Liverpool*, iii.
102 *LC*, 2 Aug. 1845.
103 TCA.

104 *Exc*, 4 June 1856.
105 Pudney, *Cook Story*, 78.

Chapter 3: *Tartan Tours* (pages 38–56)

1 T. Carlyle, *Scottish and Other Miscellanies* (Everyman edn., n.d.), 87. Earlier, of course, Ossian had stimulated a romantic interest in Scotland.
2 *Exc*, 1 July 1868.
3 *Exc*, 3 May 1851.
4 *Exc*, 16 Aug. 1836
5 *Exc*, 9 July 1872.
6 *Exc*, 11 July 1863.
7 *LC*, 4 July 1846.
8 Cook, *Temperance Jubilee Celebrations*, 58.
9 R. E. Turner, *James Silk Buckingham 1786–1855* (1934), 395.
10 *Chambers's Edinburgh Journal* (29 Oct. 1853), 281.
11 *LC*, 4 July 1846.
12 S. Nowell-Smith, *The House of Cassell* (1958), 6.
13 *Temperance Magazine* III (July 1846), 279.
14 *Temperance Magazine* III (Aug. 1846), no page reference in the British Library copy and wrongly bound between pages 291 and 292.
15 *Leicester Journal*, 7 Aug. 1846.
16 *LC*, 1 Aug. 1846.
17 *Temperance Magazine* III (Aug. 1846), between 291 and 292.
18 *Cambridge Chronicle*, 9 Nov. 1850, and TCA.
19 *Barton Church Magazine*, Oct. 1892.
20 TCA.
21 Cook, *Belvoir Castle*, 24.
22 J. Mason, 'Thomas Cook and horse-drawn transport' in *Horse-Rider* (Nov.–Dec. 1983).
23 Cook, *Belvoir Castle*, 24 and 4.
24 Rae, *Business of Travel*, 38.
25 *All the Year Round* (7 May 1864), 303.
26 H. Cunningham, *Leisure in the Industrial Revolution* (1980), 86.
27 Cook, *Belvoir Castle*, 22.
28 *Temperance Messenger* II (1841), 1.
29 Patterson, *Radical Leicester*, 360
30 *LC*, 10 June 1848.
31 *LC*, 17 June 1848.

32 M. Hovell, *The Chartist Movement* (1943 edn.), 118.
33 Patterson, *Radical Leicester*, 376–7.
34 T. Cook, *A Retrospect of 40 Years* (1881).
35 Cook, *Temperance Jubilee Celebrations*, 55.
36 *Exc*, 26 Apr. 1862.
37 *Exc*, 23 Aug. 1858.
38 *Exc*, 2 Sept. 1853.
39 *Exc*, 3 June 1858.
40 Pudney, *Cook Story*, 85–8.
41 *Exc*, 13 Sept. 1856.
42 *Exc*, 19 Sept. 1859.
43 *Exc*, 25 June 1859.
44 *Cambridge Chronicle*, 2 Sept. 1854.
45 *Exc*, 15 Aug. 1856.
46 *Chambers's Edinburgh Journal* (29 Oct. 1853), 281.
47 *Exc*, 12 Aug. 1861.
48 Cook, *Scottish Directory*, 31.
49 *Exc*, June 1854.
50 TCA.
51 *Exc*, 25 June 1858.
52 TCA.
53 *Exc*, 15 May 1860.
54 *Exc*, 4 June 1856.
55 *Exc*, June 1854.
56 *Exc*, 3 June 1858.
57 *Exc*, 13 Sept. 1856.
58 *Exc*, 15 Aug. 1856.
59 *Exc*, 3 June 1858.
60 *Exc*, 13 Sept. 1856.
61 *Exc*, 4 June 1856.
62 *Exc*, 26 May 1859.
63 For the photograph of Balmoral see T. Whittle, *Victoria and Albert at Home* (1980), 77, plate 14. *Illustrated London News*, 2 Oct. 1858.
64 *Exc*, 19 Sept. 1859.
65 T. Cook, *Letters to His Royal Highness . . .* (1870), 21.
66 *Exc*, 18 July 1860.
67 Cook, *Scottish Tourist Directory*, 22.
68 Cook, *Scottish Tourist Directory*, 36.
69 *Exc*, 27 Apr. 1861.
70 *Exc*, 25 June 1859.
71 E. Swinglehurst, *Cook's Tours: The Story of Popular Travel* (1982), 35.
72 *All the Year Round* (7 May 1864), 302.
73 *All the Year Round* (7 May 1864), 303.

74 Cook, *Scottish Tourist Directory*, 22.
75 *Exc*, 18 July 1860.
76 *Exc*, 6 June 1864.
77 *Exc*, 3 June 1858.
78 Simmons, *Leicestershire Transactions* XLIX, 26.
79 C. Harvie, *Scotland and Nationalism* (1977), 88.
80 *Exc*, 26 May 1859.
81 R. W. Butler, 'Evolution of Tourism in the Scottish Highlands' in *Annals of Tourism Research* XII (1985), 377.
82 *Exc*, 25 June 1858.
83 *All the Year Round* (7 May 1864), 302.
84 *Exc*, 25 June 1858.
85 *Exc*, Sept. 1860
86 *Exc*, 5 May 1860.
87 G. P. Neele, *Railway Reminiscences* (1974 edn.), 140.
88 *Exc*, 19 Oct. 1861.
89 *Exc*, 24 May 1862.
90 *Exc*, 6 June 1863.
91 To quote the title of Leslie Stephen's book (1871).
92 *Exc*, 6 June 1863.

Chapter 4: *The Napoleon of Excursions* (pages 57–80)

1 E. Green, *Debtors and their Profession. A History of the Institute of Bankers, 1879–1979* (1979), 12, and *Exc*, 3 May 1851.
2 *Times*, 12 Jan. 1850.
3 *Exc*, 20 July 1872.
4 J. Murray, *A Handbook for Travellers in Syria and Palestine* I (1858), xlix.
5 *The Tourist and Traveller*, 15 July 1884.
6 *LC*, 24 Sept. 1853.
7 E. G. Barnes, *The Rise of the Midland Railway* (1966), 137.
8 V. Markham, *Paxton and the Bachelor Duke* (1935), 126.
9 S. Weintraub, *Victoria* (1987), 214.
10 A. Briggs, *Victorian People* (1972), 58.
11 *Exc*, 3 May 1851.
12 Quoted from the *Working Man's Friend* (1850) in Nowell-Smith, *Cassell*, 30.
13 A. Briggs, *1851* (1951), 24.
14 Swinglehurst, *Romantic Journey*, 35.
15 Pudney, *Cook Story*, 101.
16 Neele, *Railway Reminiscences*, 30.

17 *Exc*, 3 May 1851.
18 *Exc*, 21 June 1851. By 1864 the *Excursionist* was appearing roughly once a month and circulation was just over 2,000. In 1867 he sold a total of 58,000 copies, i.e. nearly 5,000 a month.
19 *Saturday Review*, 26 Aug. 1871.
20 A. Ogilvy, 'Tickets and Tourists Wholesale' in *Once a Week* (29 Sept. 1866), 362.
21 *Exc*, 18 Sept. 1865.
22 *Exc*, 21 June 1851.
23 *Exc*, 3 May 1851.
24 *Exc, passim.*
25 John Cook claimed that he was chiefly responsible for the *Excursionist* after 1865 (*Exc*, 1 Feb. 1899), but Thomas's influence is visible at least until the mid-1870s.
26 US *Exc*, 1 Mar. 1873.
27 Y. ffrench, *The Great Exhibition* (1950), 219.
28 *Times*, 2 May 1851.
29 *Exc*, 3 May 1851.
30 *Times*, 17, 2 and 3 May 1851.
31 G. O. Trevelyan, *The Life and Letters of Lord Macaulay* (1895 edn.), 551.
32 *Times*, 29 May 1851.
33 *Exc*, 1 May 1865.
34 *LC*, 23 July 1892.
35 *Exc*, 15 Aug. 1868.
36 *Exc*, 15 June 1860.
37 *Exc*, 23 Aug. 1858.
38 Cook, *Handbook to Liverpool* (1852), 5.
39 *Exc*, June 1854.
40 *Exc*, June 1854.
41 *Exc*, 2 Sept. 1861.
42 F. D. Bridges, *A Lady's Travels Round the World* (1883), 1.
43 *Exc*, July 1854.
44 *Exc*, 4 June 1856.
45 *Exc*, 7 Apr. 1860.
46 TCA, 'History of the Negotiations between Thomas Cook and the Midland and South Eastern Railway Companies'.
47 Cook said it numbered forty, but this was perhaps the total number who travelled with him throughout the various stages of the tour.
48 Diaries of Lucilla, Elizabeth and Marian Lincolne (1855), in possession of Mr Richard Webster.
49 *Exc*, 6 Aug. 1855.
50 *Exc*, 12 Sept. 1855.

51 *Exc*, 6 Aug. 1855.

52 *Exc*, 21 June 1851.

53 *Exc*, 6 Aug. 1855.

54 *Exc*, 4 June 1856.

55 Viator Verax, *Cautions for the First Tour* . . . (1863), 10, 47–50.

56 A. Sketchley, *Out for a Holiday with Cook's Excursion through Switzerland and Italy* (1870), 27 and 35.

57 Gaze referred to two pamphlets of 1858 advertising, respectively, 'Messrs. Holmes and Co., Late Christy and Co.'s Cheap Excursions to the Contintent' and 'Henderson's Series of Cheap Continental Tours' in his *Outline Sketch of the Rise and Progressive Development of the Tourist System of Henry Gaze & Son* (1881), TCA.

58 *Exc*, 23 Aug. 1858.

59 *Exc*, 25 June 1858.

60 *Exc*, 4 June 1856.

61 *LC*, 24 Sept. and 19 Nov. 1853, 23 Dec. 1892.

62 Elliott, *Victorian Leicester*, 30.

63 Simmons, *Leicestershire Transactions* (1973–4), 27.

64 *Exc*, 18 Aug. 1857.

65 *Uttoxeter New Era*, 6 Aug. 1856.

66 *Exc*, 10 Dec. 1900.

67 *Exc*, 15 May 1860.

68 *Exc*, 13 June 1860.

69 *Exc*, 19 July 1861.

70 *Exc*, 16 July 1860.

71 TCA.

72 *Exc*, 27 Apr. 1861.

73 *Exc*, 5 June 1861.

74 *Illustrated London News*, 8 June 1861. See also *Manchester Guardian*, 24 May 1961.

75 *Exc*, 5 June 1861.

76 *Times*, 8 Oct. 1861.

77 *Exc*, 5 Oct. 1861 – presumably the journal was actually issued after that date.

78 *Times*, 8 Oct. 1861.

79 *Exc*, 19 Oct. 1861.

80 *Exc*, 6 Sept. 1862.

81 *Illustrated London News*, 10 May 1862.

82 *Exc*, 6 Sept. 1862.

83 T. Cook, 'Twenty Years on the Rails', 16. This pamphlet is bound into *Cook's Scottish Tourist Official Directory* (1861).

84 *Exc*, 7 May 1863.

85 *Exc*, 15 May 1863.

86 TCA. This figure seems excessive but it was given by John Cook.
87 *Guide to Cook's Tours on the English and French Coasts and Channel Islands* (1865), 3.
88 *Exc*, 7 May 1863.
89 *Exc*, 15 May 1863.
90 *Exc*, 6 June 1863.
91 J. Morrell, *Miss Jemima's Swiss Journal: The First Conducted Tour of Switzerland* (1963), 40.
92 *Exc*, 11 July 1863.
93 *Exc*, 28 Aug. 1863.
94 Verax, *First Tour*, 33.
95 Morrell, *Swiss Journal*, 15–16.
96 *Exc*, 2 Aug. 1865. According to Mark Twain, in *The Innocents Abroad*, the time allotted to dinner at Dijon was half an hour, so perhaps Cook exaggerated.
97 *Exc*, 30 Sept. 1863.
98 *Exc*, 4 Aug. 1864.
99 H. Pearce Sales (ed.), *Travel and Tourism Encyclopaedia* (1959), 86.
100 *Exc*, 11 July 1863.
101 *Civil Service Gazette*, 14 May 1864.

Chapter 5: *John Bull Abroad* (pages 81–100)

1 E. S. de Beer (ed.), *The Diary of John Evelyn* (1959), 256.
2 Cook, *Over the Hills*, 185.
3 Hibbert, *Grand Tour* (1969), 90.
4 J. Ruskin, *Modern Painters* (1897 edn.) I, 307.
5 J. Ruskin, *Praeterita* (1949 edn.), 103.
6 R. Fitzsimons, *The Baron of Piccadilly* (1967), 149–150.
7 *Exc*, 4 Aug. 1864.
8 Morrell, *Swiss Journal*, 37, 50 and 66.
9 TCA, Edward Miell's Diary of a Swiss Tour, August 1865.
10 T. G. Bonney, *The Building of the Alps* (1972), 350.
11 L. Stephen, *The Playground of Europe* (1946 edn.) 134.
12 F. Harrison, *Memories and Thoughts* (1906), 240.
13 *Exc*, 6 June 1864.
14 *Exc*, 28 Aug. 1863.
15 [J. C. Parkinson], 'Tripping it Lightly' in *Temple Bar* (12 Aug. 1864), 588–9 and 586.
16 A. Lunn, *Come What May* (1940), 108.
17 R. Storrs, *Orientations* (1945), 19.
18 *Temple Bar* (12 Aug. 1864), 586.

19 E. Downey, *Charles Lever: His Life and Letters* (1906) II, 98.

20 G. de Beer, *Travellers in Switzerland* (Oxford, 1949), 306.

21 *Daily News*, 5 Aug. 1869.

22 *Exc*, 4 Aug. 1864.

23 *T[homas] C[ook] S[taff] M[agazine]*, Nov–Dec. 1949.

24 *Exc*, 2 Aug. 1865.

25 'Cornelius O'Dowd' in *Eclectic Review* (May 1865), 462.

26 Morrell, *Swiss Journal*, 33.

27 *Exc*, 1 July 1856.

28 *Exc*, 6 June 1864.

29 Pimlott, *Englishman's Holiday*, 203.

30 TCA, William Chater, Diary of a Tour of Switzerland in 1865.

31 R. Lewis and A. Maude, *The English Middle Class* (1973 edn.), 49.

32 Pudney, *Cook Story*, 166.

33 *Exc*, 1 Feb. 1884.

34 *Observer*, 31 Jan. 1926.

35 TCA, William Chater's Tour.

36 Cook, *Letters to HRH*, 31.

37 T. Cook, *Guide to Cook's Excursions to Paris . . . Switzerland and Italy* (1865), 18.

38 *Exc*, 7 May 1863.

39 *Exc*, 4 Aug. 1864.

40 *Exc*, 15 May 1863.

41 [J. A. Lomax], 'John Bull Abroad' in *Temple Bar* (Sept. 1890), 60 and 56–7.

42 A. Trollope, *Travelling Sketches* (1866), 43–4.

43 E. Yates, 'My Excursion Agent' in *All the Year Round* (7 May 1864), 303.

44 TCA, W. L. White, Journal of a Trip to Switzerland and Italy (Sept–Oct. 1864).

45 *Leicestershire Mercury*, 27 Aug. 1864.

46 TCA, Miss Riggs's Diary: Egypt, Nile and Palestine, 1869.

47 *Exc*, 6 June 1864.

48 TCA, E. J. Webb, 'A Trip to Rome and Venice' (1905), 112.

49 H. James, *Italian Hours* (1909), 94–5.

50 TCA, quoted in an unidentified article by James Laver on 'Foreign Travel'.

51 Quoted from Newman's *Idea of a University* by J. L. Hammond, in *The Growth of Common Enjoyment* (1933), 22.

52 W. H. Mallock, *In an Enchanted Island* (1889), 3.

53 J. Pemble, *The Mediterranean Passion* (Oxford, 1988), 76.

54 *Exc*, 1 May 1865.

55 US *Exc*, Feb. 1877.

56 *Exc*, 1 May 1865.
57 de Beer, *Travellers in Switzerland*, 354.
58 Stephen, *Playground of Europe*, 128.
59 W. Plomer (ed.), *Kilvert's Diary* (1973) I, 79.
60 'The World in Wideawakes' in *P[all] M[all] G[azette]* (19 Sept. 1871), 10.
61 Cornelius O'Dowd [i.e. Charles Lever], 'Continental Excursionists' in *Blackwood's Magazine* (Feb. 1865), 231.
62 Downey, *Lever*, II, 255.
63 *Blackwood's* (Feb. 1865). 230–1.
64 *Leisure Hour* (June 1878), 396.
65 *Exc*, 6 June 1864.
66 *PMG*, 11 Feb. 1865.
67 [A. I. Shand], 'Rambles Round Travel' in *Blackwood's Magazine* (May 1877), 621.
68 [W. Barry], 'A Popular Swiss Tour' in *Temple Bar* (Aug. 1868), 73.
69 *Temple Bar* (12 Aug. 1864), 584–5 and 598.
70 *All the Year Round* (7 May 1864), 303.
71 *PMG* (19 Sept. 1871), 10.
72 A. Hare, *The Years with Mother* (1952), 33.
73 TCA, G. C. Heard, 'Three Weeks in Switzerland and North Italy' (1865), 128–9.
74 J. Pope Hennessy, *Robert Louis Stevenson* (1974), 123.
75 J. R. Green, *Stray Studies from England and Italy* (1876), 31.
76 *Blackwood's* (May 1877), 620.
77 Cook, *Letters to HRH*, 50.
78 *Exc*, 3 Apr. 1865.
79 *Exc*, 1 May 1865.
80 S. Koss, *The Rise and Fall of the Political Press in Britain* (1981) I, 123.
81 *Morning Star*, 11 Sept. 1865.
82 *Exc*, 6 June 1864.
83 *Exc*, 1 May 1865.
84 *Exc*, 18 Sept. 1865.
85 *Exc*, 6 June 1864, 22 May and 18 Sept. 1865.
86 *Exc*, 9 June 1871.
87 *Exc*, 1 May 1865.
88 E. Hodder, *On Holy Ground* (1874), 4.
89 *Exc*, 3 Feb. and 13 and 25 Aug. 1877.
90 *Exc*, 10 Oct. 1867.
91 *Exc*, 15 Aug. 1868.
92 *Exc*, 1 Nov. 1871.
93 *Saturday Review*, 6 Sept. 1873.
94 US *Exc*, Aug. 1905.

95 F. Kemble, *Further Records* (1860) II, 132.
96 *Illustrated London News*, 7 Sept. 1878.
97 *The Citizen*, 11 Apr. 1885.
98 Adburgham, *Punch History*, 250.
99 *Exc*, 8 Aug. 1891.
100 Cook, *Letters to HRH*, 50.
101 *Exc*, 4 July 1864.
102 *Exc*, 25 Apr. 1864.
103 *General Baptist Magazine* (1876), 235.
104 *Exc*, 4 Aug. 1864.
105 *Exc*, 25 Apr. 1864.
106 *Times*, 4 Aug. 1891.
107 *Exc*, 4 Aug. 1864.
108 Cook, *Excursions to Paris . . . Switzerland and Italy*, 80–1.
109 *Exc*, 6 June 1864.
110 *Exc*, 24 June 1865.
111 Rae, *Business of Travel*, 60.
112 TCA, J[ohn] M[ason] C[ook] to T[homas] C[ook], letter written between 29 Nov. 1877 and 19 Jan. 1878.
113 TCA, Miell, Swiss Tour.
114 *Exc*, 4 Aug. 1864.
115 *Exc*, 17 Apr. 1867.
116 TCA, JMC to TC, 29 Nov. 1877–19 Jan. 1878.

Chapter 6: *Cook & Son* (pages 101–19)

1 TCA.
2 *Blackwood's* (Aug. 1899), 211.
3 *Exc*, 1 Feb. 1899.
4 *Blackwood's* (Aug. 1899), 211.
5 US *Exc*, Mar. 1896.
6 *Exc*, 11 Aug. 1890.
7 *Blackwood's* (Aug. 1899), 222.
8 *Exc*, 1 Nov, 1871.
9 *Blackwood's* (Aug. 1899), 212.
10 TCA, JMC to TC, 29 Nov. 1877–19 Jan. 1878.
11 *Blackwood's* (Aug. 1899), 214 and 221.
12 *Exc*, 1 Oct. 1867.
13 *Exc*, 1 Nov. 1871.
14 *Blackwood's* (Aug. 1899), 212.
15 Cook, *Guide to Paris, Switzerland and Italy*, 37.
16 *Citizen*, 11 Apr. 1885.

17 *Exc*, 26 Feb. 1866.
18 *Exc*, 26 Feb. 1866.
19 Pudney, *Cook's Story*, 142–4.
20 *Exc*, 26 Feb. 1866.
21 W. S. Caine, *A Trip Round the World in 1887–8* (1888), 31.
22 *Exc*, 26 Feb. 1866.
23 C. Van Doren, 'Opening up American Travel' in *Time Traveller* iii, 4.
24 *Exc*, 28 July 1866. See also TCA, P. Newby, 'Thomas Cook in America, 1866'.
25 US *Exc*, June 1874.
26 *Exc*, 25 Nov. 1867.
27 *Exc*, 28 May 1867.
28 Hibbert, *Grand Tour* (1969), 135.
29 D. Ganzel, *Mark Twain Abroad* (Chicago, 1968), 130.
30 *Exc*, 24 Sept. 1874.
31 *Exc*, 1 May 1866.
32 H. Jones, *The Regular Swiss Round* (1865), 45.
33 de Beer, *Travellers in Switzerland*, 205.
34 *Exc*, 3 Apr. 1865.
35 *Exc*, 1 May 1866.
36 *Globe*, 12 Feb. 1886.
37 P. Howarth, *When the Riviera Was Ours* (1977), 67.
38 *Exc*, 1 May 1866.
39 *Exc*, 15 Mar. 1867.
40 *Exc*, 9 Apr. 1867.
41 *The [Liverpool] Albion*, 8 July 1867.
42 *Exc*, 14 Aug. 1867.
43 Quoted in *Exc*, 7 May 1867.
44 *Morning Star*, 28 Feb. 1867.
45 TCA, JMC to TC, 29 Nov. 1877–19 Jan. 1878.
46 *Exc*, 7 Sept. 1867.
47 *Exc*, 25 Nov. 1867.
48 *Exc*, 15 Aug. 1868.
49 *Exc*, 1 June 1868.
50 *Exc*, 2 July 1866.
51 *Exc*, 3 May 1869.
52 *Exc*, 15 May 1869.
53 *Exc*, 21 Oct. 1872.
54 *Exc*, 20 June 1868.
55 P. P. Bernard, *Rush to the Alps: The Evolution of Vacationism in Switzerland* (New York, 1978), 200.
56 *Exc*, 3 May 1869.
57 *Graphic*, 23 Sept. 1871.

58 *Saturday Review*, 26 Aug. 1871.
59 *Exc*, 1 June 1869.
60 *Graphic*, 23 Sept. 1871.
61 TCA, *Tourist System of Henry Gaze*.
62 *Blackwood's* (Aug. 1899), 212.
63 US *Exc*, 1873 Supplement.
64 TCA, JMC to TC, 12 Feb. 1873.
65 *Blackwood's* (Aug. 1899), 218.
66 *Exc*, 20 Apr. 1872.
67 J. Bentley, *Oberammergau and the Passion Play* (1984), 34.
68 *Exc*, 1 Aug. and 18 July 1870.
69 *Times*, 8 Aug. 1870.
70 *Times*, 18 Aug. 1870.
71 *Exc*, 15 May 1871.
72 *Observer*, 4 Sept. 1870.
73 *Times*, 13 Sept. 1870.
74 L. Wake (ed.), *The Reminiscences of Charlotte, Lady Wake* (1909), 301–2.
75 *The Globetrotter*, Apr. 1923.
76 Pudney, *Cook Story*, 176.
77 *Times*, 8 Feb. 1871.
78 *Exc*, 19 July 1891.
79 *Exc*, 6 Aug. 1869, quoting the *Standard*.
80 *Morning Star*, 2 June 1869.
81 *Daily Telegraph*, 30 Mar. 1872.
82 *Exc*, 20 June 1871.
83 *Exc*, 1 Nov. 1871.
84 TCA, JMC to TC, 29 Nov. 1877–19 Jan. 1878.

Chapter 7: *Egypt and Beyond* (pages 120–40)

1 *Exc*, 3 May 1869.
2 D.Cumming, *The Gentleman Savage: The Life of Mansfield Parkyns* (1987), ix.
3 *Stamford Mercury*, 26 Apr, 1872.
4 TCA.
5 Murray, *Syria and Palestine* (1858), 12.
6 A.W. Kinglake, *Eothen* (Lincoln, Neb., 1970), 152–3.
7 Murray, *Syria and Palestine* (1858), xlix.
8 M. Twain, *The Innocents Abroad* (1881 edn.), 573–4.
9 V. Noakes (ed.), *Edward Lear: Selected Letters* (1988), 209.
10 J. Murray, *Handbook for Travellers in Egypt* (1847), 126.

11 Murray, *Egypt* (1880), 7.
12 Murray, *Syria and Palestine* (1858), lvi.
13 G. W. Steevens, *Egypt in 1898* (1898), 217.
14 *Exc*, 3 May 1869.
15 Murray, *Egypt* (1847), 128.
16 Murray, *Syria and Palestine* (1858), lvi–lvii.
17 *Times*, 9 June 1874.
18 *Times*, 12 June 1874.
19 *Exc*, 1 Nov. 1876.
20 TCA, Riggs Diary. Miss Riggs's party used the temporary 'Fell' railway over the Mont Cenis Pass, opened in 1868 and replaced by the new tunnel in 1871.
21 *Stamford Mercury*, 26 Apr. 1872.
22 M. A. P. Ripley, *Teetotaler and Traveller: The Life of John Ripley* (1893), 203.
23 *Exc*, 3 May 1869.
24 TCA, Riggs Diary.
25 *Exc*, 15 and 3 May 1869.
26 TCA, Riggs Diary.
27 *Exc*, 3 May 1869.
28 *Stamford Mercury*, 26 April 1872.
29 *Exc*, 3 May 1869.
30 P. Magnus, *King Edward the Seventh* (1967 edn.), 136.
31 W. H. Russell, *A Diary in the East* (1869), 145–6.
32 P. Brendon, *Our Own Dear Queen* (1986), 80.
33 Cook, *Letters to HRH*, 44.
34 A. Sattin, *Lifting the Veil: British Society in Egypt 1768–1956* (1988), 139–40 and *Exc*, 3 May 1869.
35 Russell, *Diary*, 321.
36 Cook, *Letters to HRH*, 3, 19 and 8.
37 Russell, *Diary*, 321–2.
38 *Exc*, 21 Oct. 1873.
39 *Exc*, 1 and 15 June 1869.
40 TCA, Riggs Diary.
41 *Exc*, 3 May 1869.
42 TCA, Riggs Diary.
43 *Exc*, 1 Aug. 1870.
44 TCA, Riggs Diary.
45 *Stamford Mercury*, 26 Apr. 1872.
46 TCA, Riggs Diary.
47 *Exc*, 15 May 1869.
48 *Exc*, 3 May 1869.
49 *Exc*, 4 May 1872.

50 *Exc*, 30 Mar. 1872.

51 R. Hill, 'Tourists on the Nile: A Story of Navigation and Travel, 1837–1914', 8/1. I am grateful to John Price for letting me study this unfinished manuscript.

52 *Exc*, 21 Apr. 1873.

53 J. Burns, *Helpbook for Travellers to the East . . . with tourist arrangemnts by Thomas Cook* (1870), 162–3, 181–2, 169.

54 *Nile Season 1893–94: Thos Cook & Son's Arrangements* (1893), 4.

55 *Times*, 9 and 12 July 1874.

56 *Exc*, 20 July 1872.

57 Burns, *Helpbook*, 10.

58 A. Moorehead, *The While Nile* (1976 edn.), 147.

59 Burns, Helpbook, 11–12.

60 Burns, *Helpbook*, 8.

61 *Punch*, 18 May 1861.

62 Burns, *Helpbook*, 13, 12 and 209.

63 *Exc*, 20 July 1872.

64 US *Exc*, Mar. 1877. Gaze developed a similar system.

65 *Exc*, 6 Nov. 1875.

66 I. Burton, *The Inner Life of Syria, Palestine and the Holy Land* (1875) II, 18–19.

67 *Exc*, 15 May 1871.

68 Burton, *Inner Life* II, 20.

69 TCA, George Jager Jnr, Diary of a Visit to the Holy Land and Egypt.

70 Murray, *Syria and Palestine* (1858), lvi.

71 Burton, *Inner Life* I, 2.

72 W. H. Leighton, *A Cook's Tour to the Holy Land in 1874* (1947), 49.

73 *Exc*, 12 Nov. 1889, and N. Shepherd, *The Zealous Intruders: The Western Rediscovery of Palestine* (1987), 179.

74 W. J. Loftie, *A Ride in Egypt* (1879), 365.

75 TCA, TC to *New York Observer*, 11 June 1873.

76 *Exc*, 1 June 1869.

77 Noakes (ed.), *Lear Letters*, 209.

78 C. D. Bell, *A Winter on the Nile* (1888), 255.

79 P[ublic] R[ecord] O[ffice], Ardagh Papers, 30/40, §2, 75, Sankey to Ardagh, 1 Dec. 1884.

80 W. N. Willis, *Anti-Christ in Egypt* (1915), 30.

81 S. Low, *Egypt in Transition* (1914), 147.

82 TCA, Jager Diary.

83 PRO 30/40, §9, f3.

84 In 1877–8, for example, another Italian who went down the Nile on board a Cook's steamer observed that the manager 'treated me with

every kindness. The food was excellent.' P. Santi and R. Hill, *The Europeans in the Sudan 1874–1878* (Oxford, 1980), 209.

85 TCA.
86 Low, *Egypt in Transition*, 142 and 145.
87 *Exc*, 1 Nov. 1877.
88 *Blackwood's* (Aug. 1899), 214.
89 Murray, *Egypt* (1880), 450, and (1888), 451.
90 TCA, JMC to Pagnon, 25 Mar. 1880.
91 Murray, *Egypt* (1880), 386.
92 J. Lehmann, *All Sir Garnet* (1964), 338.
93 TCA, JMC to Edgar Vincent, 15 Feb. 1884.
94 M. Caillard, *A Lifetime in Egypt 1876–1935* (1935), 55.
95 *Exc*, 1 July 1882.
96 *Andover Townsman* (USA), 21 Oct. 1887.
97 TCA, JMC to Plagge and to Cates, both 3 Mar. 1884.
98 Pudney, *Cook Story*, 189.
99 *TCSM*, Christmas 1970.
100 Murray, *Syria and Palestine* (1858), 3.
101 H. P. Parsons, *Letters from Palestine: 1868–1912* (1981), 29–134, *passim*.
102 *Edinburgh Daily Review*, 24 Dec. 1869.
103 Turner and Ash, *Golden Hordes*, 59.

Chapter 8: *Around the World* (pages 141–59)

1 *Daily News*, 5 Aug. 1869.
2 *Exc*, 21 Sept. 1872.
3 TCA, JMC to TC, 18 July 1872.
4 *Exc*, 21 Sept. 1872
5 *Exc*, 8 June 1872.
6 *Exc*, 31 Aug. 1872.
7 *Saturday Review*, 28 Sept. 1872.
8 *Exc*, 20 July 1872.
9 *Exc*, 21 Sept. 1872.
10 TCA, JMC to TC, 29 Nov. 1877–19 Jan. 1878.
11 TCA, TC to M[arianne] C[ook], 16 Feb. 1873.
12 TCA, TC to MC, 6 Oct. 1872.
13 Cook, *[Letters from the sea and from foreign lands, descriptive of a tour round the] World* (1873), 13 and 18.
14 TCA, TC to MC, 20 Oct. 1872.
15 Cook, *World*, 21 and 14.

16 Cook, *World*, 55.
17 TCA, TC to MC, 28 Nov. 1872.
18 Cook, *World*, 23.
19 TCA, TC to MC, 28 Nov. 1872.
20 Cook, *World*, 28.
21 TCA, TC to MC, 28 Nov. 1872.
22 Cook, *World*, 30.
23 Verax, *First Tour*, 36 and 39.
24 TCA, TC to MC, 8 Dec. 1872.
25 Cook, *World*, 31.
26 TCA, TC to MC, 25 Dec. 1872.
27 Cook, *World*, 33, 75, 63 and 36.
28 TCA, TC to MC, 9 Jan. 1873.
29 Cook, *World*, 76–7.
30 Cook, *World*, 35, 77, 37, 79 and 37.
31 Cook, *World*, 38, 42, 43 and 40.
32 TCA, TC to MC, 7 Feb. 1873.
33 TCA, TC to MC, 24 Mar. 1873.
34 *Exc*, 21 May 1873.
35 Cook, *World*, 67.
36 TCA, TC to ?, 29 Oct. 1873.
37 See R. Escaich, *Voyage au Monde de Jules Verne* (1955), 233.
38 M. Allotte de la Fuÿe, *Jules Verne, His Works and His Life* (1954), 137.
39 *Exc*, 20 Oct. 1879.
40 *Exc*, 1 Feb. 1879.
41 *Exc*, 29 July 1873.
42 M. M. Ballou, *Due West* (Boston, 1884), 2.
43 US *Exc*, July 1883.
44 G. A. Sala, *The Life and Adventures of George Augustus Sala* (1895) II, 236 and 239.
45 [V. Paget], 'On Modern Travelling' in *Macmillan's Magazine* 69, (Feb. 1894), 307.
46 *Exc*, 29 July 1873.
47 *London Echo*, 25 Jan. 1873.
48 TCA, JMC to W. Gregory, 2 Mar. 1875.
49 TCA, JMC to TC, 29 Nov. 1877–19 Jan. 1878.
50 J. London, *The People of the Abyss* (1903), 2. As late as 1930 Cook took 2,000 people annually on evening tours of the East End. *Times*, 16 Sept. 1931.
51 TCA, JMC to A. McDougall, 25 Mar. 1880.
52 *City Press*, 2. Apr. 1884.
53 TCA, Faulkner to Cates, 31 Oct. 1883.
54 *City Press*, 2 Apr. 1884.

55 US *Exc*, Oct. 1894.
56 *Punch*, 10 Aug. 1889.
57 *Scope*, June 1946.
58 *TCSM*, May–June, 1971.
59 TCA.
60 TCA, JMC to Cates, 24 Mar. 1884.
61 TCA, JMC to Bredall, 18 Feb. 1884.
62 TCA, Faulkner to Cates, 3 Dec. 1883.
63 TCA, Faulkner to Cates, 20 Nov. 1883.
64 TCA, JMC to Faulkner, 19 Feb. 1884.
65 TCA, Faulkner to Spiller, 8 June 1883.
66 *Exc*, 25 Sept. 1875.
67 *Exc*, 1 Dec. 1874.
68 TCA, JMC to Cates, 18 Feb. 1884. Caygill seems to have set up on his own in about 1879.
69 TCA, JMC to Plagge, 18 Feb. 1884.
70 TCA, JMC to Cates, 3 Mar. 1884.
71 TCA, JMC to Lany, 25 Feb. 1884.
72 TCA, JMC's Jubilee Address, 22 June 1892.
73 TCA.
74 *Art Journal*, Oct. 1873.
75 *Exc*, 9 Aug. 1873.
76 *Exc*, Christmas Supplement 1873.
77 *Exc*, 21 May 1872.

Chapter 9: *Cook, Son & Jenkins* (pages 160–81)

1 *Exc*, June 1874.
2 *Exc*, 5 Aug. 1872.
3 *N[ew] Y[ork] T[imes]*, 1 July 1872.
4 *Exc*, 21 May 1872.
5 *NYT*, 24 June 1872.
6 *NYT*, 1 July 1872.
7 *Exc*, Christmas Supplement 1873.
8 US *Exc*, 1 Mar. 1873
9 US *Exc*, Mar. 1892.
10 US *Exc*, June 1874.
11 *Minneapolis Tribune*, 26 Mar. 1873.
12 *Springfield Rupublican*, 7 Apr. 1873.
13 *NYT*, 31 May 1873.
14 Quoted by *John O'London's Weekly*, 10 July 1920.

15 TCA.
16 Pudney, *Cook Story*, 171.
17 *Times*, 23 July 1891.
18 J. V. Fifer, *American Progress* (Chester, Conn., 1988), 207.
19 US *Exc*, Feb. 1877 and 1873 Supplement.
20 *Exc*, 3 Aug. 1876.
21 *Exc*, 19 Dec. 1876.
22 Quoted by P. Banks, *The Man from Cook's* (1938), 184.
23 Swinglehurst, *Romantic Journey*, 110.
24 *Daily News*, 15 Sept. 1873.
25 *Exc*, 22 Sept. 1873.
26 *Exc*, 19 Apr. 1879.
27 *Annual Register* (1874), II, 86.
28 TCA. Relations with the LC & D Railway afterwards deteriorated.
29 *Exc*, 29 June 1875.
30 *Exc*, 12 July 1877.
31 *Exc*, 9 Dec. 1875.
32 *Exc*, 25 Sept. 1875.
33 TCA, JMC to TC, 16 Nov. 1877.
34 *Exc*, 1 Feb. 1878.
35 *Times*, 6 Aug. 1878.
36 TCA, 25 Jan. 1875.
37 TCA, 26 Apr. 1877, and JMC to Jenkins, 6 Apr. 1875.
38 Fifer, *American Progress*, 207.
39 TCA.
40 US *Exc*, Apr. 1876.
41 TCA, JMC to Jenkins, 28 July 1876.
42 TCA, JMC to TC, 19 Nov. 1877.
43 TCA, JMC to TC, 22 Dec. 1877.
44 TCA, JMC to TC, 29 Nov. 1877–19 Jan. 1878.
45 TCA, JMC to TC, 16 Nov. 1877.
46 TCA, JMC to TC, 4 Jan. 1878.
47 TCA, JMC to TC, 19 Nov. 1877.
48 TCA, JMC to TC, 27 Nov. 1877.
49 TCA, JMC to TC, 22 Dec. 1877.
50 TCA, JMC to TC, 15 Jan. 1878.
51 TCA, JMC to TC, 29 Nov. 1877–19 Jan. 1878.
52 TCA, JMC to TC, 27 Dec. 1877.
53 TCA, JMC to TC, 22 Feb. 1878.
54 TCA, JMC to TC, 8 Aug. 1878.
55 TCA, JMC to J. Allport, 15 Nov. 1878.
56 *Exc*, 1 Apr. 1879.
57 *Exc*, 1 Feb. 1888.

58 TCA, JMC to Annie Cook, 13 Dec. 1878.
59 Swinglehurst, *Romantic Journey*, 121.
60 *Leicester Daily Post*, 9 Nov. 1880.
61 TCA, Bishop Reminiscences.
62 Cook, *Marianne Cook*.
63 M[idland] B[ank] A[rchives], K9 and K34. I owe these references to Edwin Green.
64 TCA, TC to JMC, 1 Feb. 1888.
65 US *Exc*, 1 Feb. 1879.
66 TCA.
67 *New York Tribune*, 3 June 1883.
68 TCA, Faulkner to JMC, 5 Nov. 1883 and 1 Dec. 1883.
69 TCA, Faulkner to Cates, 31 Oct. 1883.
70 TCA, Faulkner to JMC, 10 Dec. 1883.
71 US *Exc*, 15 Oct. 1879.
72 TCA, Faulkner to Cates, 3 Dec. 1883.
73 US *Exc*, 27 Dec. 1880.
74 US *Exc*, Oct. 1883.
75 US *Exc*, Nov. 1888.
76 French *Exc*, Mar. 1888.
77 US *Exc*, Nov. 1888.
78 *Exc*, 16 Dec. 1880.
79 US *Exc*, Nov. 1888.
80 US *Exc*, Feb. 1883.
81 F. R. Dulles, *Americans Abroad* (Ann Arbor, Michigan, 1964), 106.
82 US *Exc*, Sept. 1891.
83 *Standard*, 23 Oct. 1883.
84 *Exc*, 10 Aug. 1885.
85 *Tourist and Traveller*, 1 Jan. 1885.
86 Rae, *Business of Travel*, 159.
87 *Cincinnati Commercial*, 5 Apr. 1880.
88 Dulles, *Americans Abroad*, 106.
89 *Exc*, Aug. 1891.
90 Hindley, *Tourists*, 216.
91 C. Robertson, *The International Herald Tribune* (New York, 1987), 55.

Chapter 10: *King of Egypt* (pages 182–200)

1 Bailey, *Leisure and Class in Victorian England*, 82.
2 *Exc*, 10 Aug. 1883.
3 J. Walvin, *Beside the Seaside* (1978), 75.

4 C. Thubron, *Behind the Wall* (1987), 66.
5 Kellett, *Impact of Railways*, 98.
6 US *Exc*, May 1873.
7 *Exc*, 22 July 1879.
8 US *Exc*, 1 Apr. 1879.
9 TCA, *Excursions to Europe* (1882), 4, and US *Exc*, Jan. 1884.
10 French *Exc*, Jan. 1883.
11 *Exc*, 8 Aug. 1908.
12 TCA.
13 A. Gould Lee, *The Empress Writes to Sophie* (1955), 203.
14 *Exc*, 2 Feb. 1880.
15 *Exc*, 1 Feb. 1888.
16 TCA.
17 TCA.
18 TCA, JMC to Higgins, 19 and 24 Mar. 1884.
19 TCA.
20 TCA, JMC to Spiller, 6 Mar. 1882.
21 TCA, Faulkner to Spiller, 8 June 1883.
22 TCA, JMC to Faulkner, 18 Feb 1884, and to Spiller, 7 Mar. 1884.
23 Australian *TG*, 1 Jan. 1904.
24 TCA.
25 A. Kershaw, *A History of the Guillotine* (1958), 74.
26 *Exc*, 19 Apr. 1884.
27 *Exc*, 12 Dec. 1883.
28 *Tourist and Traveller*, 15 July 1884 and Aug.–Sept. 1887.
29 Trollope, *Travelling Sketches*, 106.
30 Ward Muir, *The Amazing Mutes* (1910), 29–30.
31 Murray, *Egypt* (1880), 9.
32 Banks, *Man from Cook's*, 172.
33 US *Exc*, Oct. 1882.
34 *Exc*, 10 Mar. 1883.
35 *Exc*, 7 Sept. 1883.
36 US *Exc*, Aug. 1883.
37 TCA, 15 Feb. 1884.
38 TCA, JMC to Cates, 3 Mar. 1884.
39 TCA, JMC to Cates, 7 Mar. 1884.
40 *Exc*, 2 Feb. 1885.
41 *Exc*, 1 Mar. 1884.
42 TCA, JMC to Cates, 18 Feb. 1884.
43 TCA, JMC to Cates, 24 Mar. 1884.
44 Lehmann, *Garnet*, 351.
45 TCA, JMC to Pagnon, 25 Mar. 1880.
46 J. Symons, *England's Pride* (1965), 129.

47 Rae, *Business of Travel*, 192.
48 PRO 30/40, §2, f48, Buller to Ardagh, 8 Nov. 1884.
49 A. Preston (ed.), *In Relief of Gordon: Lord Wolseley's Campaign Journal of the Khartoum Relief Expedition 1884–5* (1967), 67.
50 Lord Charles Beresford, *Memoirs* (1914), I, 225.
51 TCA, Diary of Colonel G. A. Furse.
52 W. F. Butler, *The Campaign of the Cataracts* (1887), 119.
53 Beresford, *Memoirs*, I, 226.
54 *Proceedings of the Royal Geographical Society* VII (1885), 124.
55 TCA, J. M. Cook, *Mr John M. Cook's Visit to the Sudan in Connection with the Expedition of 1884–85* (1885), *passim*.
56 Preston (ed.), *Relief of Gordon*, 48.
57 TCA, Cook, *Visit to the Sudan*, 24, and H. J. Coke, *Travels of a Rolling Stone* (1905), 345.
58 *Proceedings of Geog. Soc.* (1885), 125.
59 *Exc*, 2 Feb. 1885.
60 P. Magnus, *Gladstone* (1970 edn.), 322–4.
61 *Exc*, 2 Feb. 1885.
62 Calcutta *Englishman*, 2 Aug. 1884.
63 PRO 30/40, §9, f4.
64 Rae, *Business of Travel*, 194–5.
65 *Daily Telegraph*, 4 Mar. 1899, and C. Royle, *The Egyptian Campaigns* (1900), 554. Admittedly Royle and John Cook were friends.
66 PRO 30/40, §9, f4.
67 TCA, JMC to Ardagh, 1 Apr. 1885.
68 PRO 30/40, §9, f3, Ardagh's Official Report (27 Feb. 1887).
69 TCA, 11 July 1887, and JMC to the Surveyor General of the Army, 18 July 1887.
70 TCA, G. Royle to JMC, n.d. (?1889).
71 Hill, 'Tourists on the Nile', 4/3.
72 TCA, Furse Diary.
73 PRO 30/40, §2, f111, Buller to Ardagh, 7 June 1885.
74 *Exc*, 11 Oct. 1886.
75 TCA, Faulkner to Dattari, 6 Aug. 1886.
76 E. A. W. Budge, *By Nile and Tigris* (1920), 86–8.

Chapter 11: *Booking Clerk to the Empire* (pages 201–22)

1 TCA, JMC to Lord Granville, 5 Nov. 1881, and to E. Fleck, 2 Nov. 1881.
2 *Daily Telegraph*, 4 Mar. 1899.
3 *Exc*, 16 Dec. 1880.

4 W. E. Gladstone, '"Locksley Hall" and the Jubilee' in *The Nineteenth Century* CXIX (Jan. 1887), 9.
5 *Exc*, 15 June 1897.
6 TCA, J. H. N. Mason, 'History of Thomas Cook in India 1873–1982', 4.
7 *Exc*, 4 June 1898.
8 E. Longford, *Queen Victoria* (1964), 464.
9 Pudney, *Cook Story*, 222.
10 TCA.
11 TCA.
12 *Cook's Indian Tours* (1881), 9.
13 *Exc*, 21 Apr. 1881.
14 *Exc*, 12 Dec. 1881.
15 W. S. Caine, *Picturesque India* (1890), ix.
16 TCA.
17 TCA.
18 TCA, G. E. Howse to JMC, 13 May 1884.
19 A. Rutherford (ed.), *Early Verse by Rudyard Kipling 1879–1889* (Oxford, 1986), 238.
20 J. Murray, *Handbook for Travellers in India and Ceylon* (1891), xvii–xviii.
21 TCA, Howse to JMC, 13 May 1884.
22 TCA, Frank Buckley's Diary.
23 *Times of India*, 9 Nov. 1885.
24 *Madras Mail*, 19 Jan. 1895.
25 TCA, F[rank] C[ook] to JMC, Oct. 1886.
26 J. M. Cook, *The Mecca Pilgrimage* (1886), *passim*. The only extant copy of this pamphlet seems to be in the I[ndia] O[ffice] L[ibrary].
27 *Bombay Gazette*, 16 Jan. 1895.
28 Cook, *Over the Hills*, 144.
29 IOL, 1441, Comment on JMC's letter to H. Hill, 29 Sept. 1886.
30 TCA, JMC to FC, 4 Oct. 1886.
31 R. Kipling, *Something of Myself* (1951), 40 and 94.
32 *Exc*, 26 Mar. 1887, quoting an unsigned article from the *Civil and Military Gazette*, obviously written by Kipling.
33 Mason, 'Cook in India', 10–11.
34 TCA, JMC to FC, 4 Oct. 1886.
35 *Times*, 12 Feb. 1895.
36 TCA, JMC to FC, 4 Oct. 1886.
37 *Times of India*, 19 Jan. 1895.
38 IOL, Report of the Haj Committee (1931), 131.
39 *Times*, 2 Feb. 1895.
40 *TCSM*, May–June 1977.

41 Mason, 'Cook in India', 14.
42 *Richmond Herald*, 29 Oct. 1954.
43 Pudney, *Cook Story*, 227.
44 *John Bull*, 6 Feb. 1954.
45 Murray, *Handbook for . . . India* (1891), xx.
46 W. S. Caine, *A Trip Round the World in 1887–8* (1888), 307 and 311.
47 *Exc*, 2 Feb. 1891.
48 US *Exc*, Jan. 1905.
49 *Daily Telegraph*, 14 July 1971.
50 *Exc*, 1 Mar. 1898 and 11 Aug. 1906.
51 TCA, JMC to FC, 4 Aug. 1887.
52 TCA, JMC to Chairman of Victoria Railways, 22 Dec. 1887.
53 TCA, JMC to FC, 22 May 1888.
54 Rae, *Business of Travel*, 291–2.
55 *New Zealand Herald*, 21 Nov. 1888.
56 TCA, Bilborough to FC, 13 Dec. 1889.
57 TCA, JMC to FC, 26 Feb. 1888.
58 *Times*, 14 Sept. 1888.
59 US *Exc*, Apr. 1890.
60 *Exc*, 11 Aug, 1888.
61 J. Verschoyle, 'Where to Spend a Holiday' in *Fortnightly Review* 56 (Aug. 1894), 305.
62 *Times*, 11 Sept. 1888.
63 *Exc*, 1 July 1890.
64 US *Exc*, July 1889.
65 *Exc*, 25 May 1889.
66 *Exc*, 20 July 1889.
67 TCA, William Bemrose's Diary (1882).
68 *Exc*, 10 Dec. 1903.
69 For many of these details I am indebted to John Price's article in *TCSM*, Jan.–Feb. 1984.
70 *Blackwood's* (Aug. 1899), 222.
71 *Exc*, 18 July 1891.
72 TCA, Hunter to JMC, 9 Oct. 1891.
73 *Punch*, 18 Apr. 1900.
74 *Times*, 23 July 1891.
75 TCA, Sir John Gorst to JMC, 15 Nov. 1894.
76 *Exc*, 8 Aug. 1891.
77 *LC*, 23 July 1892.
78 TCA, TC to JMC, 15 Mar. and 28 Apr. 1888.
79 TCA, Bishop Reminiscences.
80 TCA, JMC's Jubilee Address.
81 D. Judd, *Radical Joe* (1977), 180.

82 *Times*, 23 July 1891.
83 *Times*, 20 July 1892.
84 *LC*, 23 July 1892.
85 TCA, Bishop Reminiscences.

Chapter 12: *Autocrat of the Timetable* (pages 223–42)

1   TCA, JMC's Jubilee Address.
2   *Exc*, 15 June 1897.
3   TCA, JMC to Barattoni, 20 Apr. 1880.
4   Royle, *Egyptian Campaigns*, 554.
5   *Exc*, 1 Mar. and 10 Oct. 1887.
6   *Exc*, 1 Mar. 1890.
7   TCA, JMC to B[ert] C[ook], *passim*.
8   J. L. Garvin (and L. Amery), *The Life of Joseph Chamberlain* (1932–)
    II, 401 and 455.
9   W. S. Churchill, *Lord Randolph Churchill* (1906) II, 440.
10 TCA, JMC to BC, 29 Nov. 1890 and 15 Jan. 1891.
11 TCA, Milner to JMC, 25 Aug. 1895.
12 *Exc*, 2 May 1892.
13 TCA, C. Royle to JMC, 17 Mar. 1895.
14 D. Sladen, *Egypt and the English* (1908), 414, 419 and 415.
15 TCA, C. Royle to JMC, 17 Mar. 1895.
16 D. Sladen, *Queer Things about Egypt* (1910), 389.
17 R. Kipling, *Letters of Travel* (1920), 241.
18 Sladen, *Egypt and English*, 442.
19 TCA, JMC to BC, 15 Nov. 1889.
20 J. K. Jerome, *Diary of a Pilgrimage* (1891), 141.
21 Sladen, *Egypt and English*, 73.
22 TCA, A. Harrington to JMC, 8 Feb. 1889.
23 Caillard, *Lifetime in Egypt*, 55.
24 Steevens, *Egypt in 1898*, 271.
25 *Exc*, 14 Mar. 1891.
26 *Blackwood's* (Aug. 1899), 223.
27 *Blackwood's* (Aug. 1899), 212.
28 TCA, G. Royle to JMC, 16 Jan. 1889.
29 Caillard, *Lifetime in Egypt*, 54, 58 and 61.
30 Kipling, *Letters of Travel*, 254.
31 Caillard, *Lifetime in Egypt*, 62.
32 US *Exc*, Aug. 1897.
33 *Blackwood's* (Aug. 1899), 212.
34 *Letters from an Egyptian . . . Upon the Affairs of Egypt* (1908), 57.

35 French *Exc*, Jan. 1890.
36 F. M. Sandwith, *Egypt as a Winter Resort* (1889), 2 and 107.
37 Egyptian Gazette, 11 Feb. 1891.
38 Egyptian Gazette, 11 Feb. 1893.
39 US *Exc*, 14 Dec. 1896.
40 Steevens, *Egypt in 1898*, 269–70. This figure was probably too high, though F. C. Penfield's estimate of 8,000 was certainly too low in *Present-Day Egypt* (1899), 1.
41 *Standard*, 4 Mar. 1899.
42 US *Exc*, July 1897.
43 TCA, JMC to BC, 10 Jan. 1889.
44 C. A. Cooper, *Seeking the Sun* (Edinburgh, 1892), 85.
45 Hallil J. Kemeid, *Cairo and Egypt and Life in the Land of the Pharaohs* (1900), 152.
46 *Egyptian Gazette*, 19 Jan. 1907.
47 A. Cooper, *Cairo in the War 1939–1945* (1989), 37, and TCA, JMC to Maspero, 31 Mar. 1884.
48 French *Exc*, July 1893.
49 Kipling, *Letters of Travel*, 231.
50 Low, *Egypt in Transition*, 146.
51 *Vanity Fair*, 23 Feb. and 9 Mar. 1889.
52 Royle, *Egyptian Campaigns*, 554.
53 Swinglehurst, *Cook's Tours*, 106.
54 *PMG*, 28 Aug. 1889.
55 TCA, Watts to Leicester corporation, 15 Dec. 1889.
56 Steevens, *Egypt in 1898*, 175.
57 TCA, R. Margot's Report on Cook in Egypt, May 1933.
58 TCA, ? to JMC, 26 Mar. 1896.
59 F. Woods, *Young Winston's Wars* (1972), 70.
60 TCA, JMC to FC, 25 Aug. 1896.
61 PRO FO 633/8, Cromer to JMC, 24 Oct. 1896.
62 TCA, JMC to ?, 7 Aug. 1896.
63 TCA, JMC to ?, 1 Sept. 1896.
64 Kemeid, *Cairo and Egypt*, 161.
65 US *Exc*, Apr. 1891.
66 *Exc*, June 1892.
67 US *Exc*, Feb. 1893.
68 *Exc*, Feb. 1896.
69 French *Exc*, Mar. 1894.
70 *Exc*, 1 July and 2 Nov. 1896.
71 *Exc*, 18 Mar. 1899.
72 TCA.
73 *London World*, 21 Oct. 1891.

74 Swinglehurst, *Romantic Journey*, 127.
75 *Times*, 4 Jan. 1894.
76 *Japan Gazette*, 21 Feb. 1894.
77 US *Exc*, Feb. 1896.
78 TCA.
79 TCA, JMC to BC, 12 Jan. 1894.
80 TCA, JMC to BC, 3 Feb. 1896.
81 TCA, Cook's Norwegian agent to JMC, 18 July 1896.
82 Lee, *Empress Frederick Writes*, 203.
83 *Exc*, 14 Dec. 1896.
84 US *Exc*, Dec. 1896.
85 C. Carrington, *Rudyard Kipling* (1978 edn.), 309.
86 *Exc*, 15 June 1897.
87 *Times*, 6 Mar. 1899.
88 *Blackwood's* (Aug. 1899), 220.
89 TCA.
90 *Blackwood's* (Aug. 1899), 220.
91 TCA.
92 A. Palmer, *The Kaiser* (1978), 91.
93 TCA.
94 *Punch*, 15 Oct. 1898.
95 TCA.
96 *City Press*, 2 Nov. 1898.
97 US *Exc*, Sept. 1895.
98 H. R. Haggard, *A Winter Pilgrimage* (1901), 2.
99 TCA.
100 *Exc*, 18 Mar. 1899.

Chapter 13: *Cook & Grandsons* (pages 243–57)

1 *TCSM*, Nov.–Dec. 1960.
2 TCA, and TCA, JMC to R. Harley, ?1878.
3 I owe the details about Bert to his grandson, Thomas Cook, and those about Frank to Colonel Cary-Elwes and Veronica Marchbanks, Archives Assistant at Barnett Hill.
4 *The Ernest Cook Collection*, introduced by F. David, (n.d.), 3.
5 Paris *Herald-Tribune*, 9 May 1958.
6 *Surrey Advertiser*, 2 Jan. 1932. John Pudney was apparently shocked by what he took to be evidence of Ernest's homosexuality. Private information – James Lees-Milne.
7 F. N. Wagner, *Grosse Welt und Kleine Menschen* (Zürich, 1942), 32. I am grateful to Dr Richard Overy for translating this for me.

Unfortunately Wagner's account of Thomas Cook's origins is so inaccurate that it can only be regarded as fiction.

8 H. Lunn, *Nearing Harbour* (1934), 59.

9 Lunn, *Come What May*, 110.

10 L. J. Lickorish and A. G. Kershaw, *The Travel Trade* (1958), 38.

11 Walvin, *Seaside*, 142.

12 US *Exc*, May 1893 and June 1900.

13 Paris *Herald-Tribune*, 23 June 1914.

14 A. J. Norval, *The Tourist Industry* (1936), 45.

15 R. Hart-Davis (ed.), *The Letters of Oscar Wilde* (1962), 758.

16 *NYT*, 6 Sept. 1900.

17 Private information – John Mason. Hart-Davis (ed.), *Letters of Wilde*, 655.

18 TCA, Kipling to FC, 1 Apr. 1913.

19 M. Twain, *Europe and Elsewhere* (1923), 214–6.

20 *TCSM*, Jan.–Feb. 1964.

21 TCA.

22 US *Exc*, 2 Apr. 1900.

23 *Punch*, 18 Apr. 1900. Similar but more bitter reflections about battlefield tourists are to be found in Philip Johnstone's fine poem 'High Wood' in *The Nation*, 16 Feb. 1918.

24 *Exc*, 21 Apr. 1900.

25 *Exc*, Aug. 1900.

26 French *Exc*, Aug. and July 1900, Oct. 1902 and Aug. 1897.

27 TCA.

28 *TG*, 7 Aug. 1909.

29 *Exc*, 10 Dec. 1900.

30 *TG*, 22 July 1905 and 15 June 1908.

31 US *TG*, Jan. 1905.

32 *TG*, 17 June, 25 May and Sept. 1905.

33 TCA, W. Bemrose, 'Our Trip to Italy' (1879).

34 *TG*, Feb. 1905 and Aug. 1903.

35 *TG*, Aug. 1903 and Oct. 1912.

36 *Exc*, 27 May 1899. This was an unacknowledged plagiarism from Trollope's *Travelling Sketches* (101), written over thirty years before.

37 *TG*, Nov. 1909.

38 *TG*, May 1903.

39 US *TG*, 1 June 1904.

40 Oriental and Australasian *TG*, Feb. 1904.

41 US *TG*, Dec. 1902.

42 *Bermuda Royal Gazette*, 10 Apr. 1900.

43 US *TG*, May 1904.

44 *TG*, Nov. 1905 and Oct. 1908.

45 *TG*, 10 Dec. 1903.
46 J. Morris, *The Spectacle of Empire* (1982), 119.
47 *TG*, Nov. 1903.
48 P. Brendon, *Winston Churchill* (1984), 46.
49 *TG*, Nov. 1903.
50 TCA, E. M. Thomson, 'Diary of a Trip to Victoria Falls' (1918).
51 *TG*, 11 Dec. 1907.
52 *TG*, 23 June 1908.
53 Banks, *Man from Cook's*, 184–5.
54 *Exc*, 1 Feb. 1889.
55 *TG*, 18 July 1914.
56 *TG*, Sept. 1914.
57 *TG*, Dec. 1914.
58 *Times*, 9 Jan. 1915.
59 *TG*, Feb. and Jan. 1915.
60 E. S. Turner, *Dear Old Blighty* (1980), 48.
61 *Times*, 31 Mar. 1915.
62 *Tatler*, 17 Mar. 1915.
63 *Times*, 27 Mar. 1915.
64 *TG*, June 1915.
65 *TG*, 15 June 1916.
66 *TG*, 22 July and Dec. 1916.
67 *TG*, Mar., Jan. and Oct. 1917.
68 *TG*, Apr. 1918.
69 US *TG*, Jan., Feb. and Aug. 1917.
70 *TG*, Dec. 1918.

Chapter 14: *Cook & Wagons-Lits* (pages 258–77)

1 R. Graves and A. Hodge, *The Long Weekend* (1950 edn.), 30.
2 *TG*, Sept. 1919.
3 *TG*, Mar. and Apr. 1920.
4 *TG*, May 1919 and June 1921.
5 *TG*, Feb. 1923.
6 R. G. Studd, *The Holiday Story* (1950), 94.
7 *TG*, Oct. 1922.
8 J. Weightman, 'The Solar Revolution' in *Encounter* (Dec. 1970), 9.
9 *TG*, Oct. 1926.
10 *Observer*, 31 Jan. 1926.
11 *TG*, Jan. 1926.
12 A. Hatch, *American Express* (New York, 1950), 106 and 102.
13 TCA.

14 Studd, *Holiday Story*, 98.
15 O. Rutter, *The Travels of Tiadatha* (1922).
16 *TG*, Nov. 1931.
17 D. Robertson and S. Dennison, *The Control of Industry* (Cambridge, 1960 edn.), 25.
18 *TG*, Feb. 1930.
19 TCA, J. W. Harmshaw's Report, 18 Feb. 1931.
20 *TG*, Dec. 1923.
21 *TG*, July and May 1930, Jan. 1926, Oct. and Dec. 1923, Dec. 1921.
22 *TG*, Dec. 1923.
23 *The Coastguard*, Dec. 1959.
24 *TG*, Aug. 1926.
25 P. Loti [i.e. J. Viaud], *Egypt* (1928), 141, 135 and 137. This book was originally published in the Edwardian age but it was evidently considered accurate enough to merit printing in translation as late as 1928.
26 P. Fussell, *Abroad: British Literary Travelling Between the Wars*, Oxford, 1980), 40.
27 Feifer, *Going Places*, 220.
28 *TG*, Aug. 1921 and May 1927.
29 J. Bisset, *Commodore* (1961), 180, 171 and 196–7.
30 Brendon, *Queen*, 110.
31 A. Agar, *Showing the Flag* (1962), 151.
32 Wagner, *Grosse Welt*, 33.
33 R. Smyrk in J. H. Price Papers.
34 *Daily Chronicle*, 13 Dec. 1926.
35 *TG*, Apr. 1928.
36 *TCSM*, Nov.–Dec. 1955.
37 TCA.
38 R. P. T. Davenport-Hines, *Dudley Docker* (Cambridge, 1984), 212.
39 *Times*, 29 Feb. 1928.
40 T. Jones, *Whitehall Diary* II (1969), edited by K. Middlemas, 138.
41 *TG*, Mar. 1928. I owe nearly all this paragraph to John Price, who has written two valuable papers on the subject: 'Wagons-Lits/Cook: New Light on the 1928 Merger' and 'Lord Ashfield and Wagons-Lits'.
42 G. Behrend, *Grand European Expresses* (1962), 48 ff.
43 *Observer*, 31 Jan. 1926.
44 TCA, 1929.
45 PRO FO 141/546.
46 *TG*, June 1929.
47 TCA, quoted by John King to J. H. N. Mason, 17 Jan. 1988.
48 US *TG*, Feb. 1929.

49 D. Marquand, *Ramsay MacDonald* (1977), 519.

50 Studd, *Holiday Story*, 140.

51 R. Skidelsky, *Politicians and the Slump* (1967), 280.

52 *Illustrated London News*, 14 Nov. 1931.

53 TCA.

54 TCA, Thomson McLintock Report, 30 Aug. 1940.

55 TCA.

56 TCA, Stanley Adams's Report to the Staff, Apr. 1933.

57 TCA.

58 F. W. Deakin and G. R. Storry, *The Case of Richard Sorge* (1966), 188.

59 *TG*, June 1935 and Sept. 1930.

60 TCA.

61 *TCSM*, Nov. 1974

62 *TG*, Aug. 1938 and May 1939.

63 *Leader*, Aug. 1946.

64 C. Ward and D. Hardy, *Goodnight Campers! The Story of the British Holiday Camp* (1986), 1 and passim.

65 C. L. Mowat, *Britain Between the Wars* (1978 edn.), 501.

66 *TG*, Sept. 1938.

67 TCA. Prestatyn was run by a subsidiary company called British Holiday Estates Ltd, which also owned the Farringford Hotel on the Isle of Wight.

68 *TCSM*, July–Aug. 1956.

69 TCA.

70 TCA.

71 TCA.

72 *Times*, 10 Jan. 1936.

73 In 1931 Britain provided 47% of Cook's business, US and Canada 17%, Germany 13.5%, India 6%, South Africa 5%, Australia and New Zealand 3.5%, Far East 3%, others 5%. In Egypt, though, 43% of Cook's clients were English and 28% American.

74 Private Information – John Mason.

75 Private Information – J. H. Price.

76 TCA.

77 TCA.

78 E. Waugh, *A Handful of Dust* (Penguin, 1981), 172.

79 TCA, letter from Louise Hayward, June 1938.

80 Studd, *Holiday Story*, 155.

81 *TG*, July 1934.

82 M. Craig, *The Crystal Spirit* (1986), 194.

83 *TCSM*, July–Aug. 1947.

Chapter 15: *The Sleeping Giant* (pages 278–97)

1 TCA, Huskisson's 'Very Confidential File', 10 July 1942.
2 *Times*, 5 July 1941.
3 Paris *Herald-Tribune*, 9 May 1958.
4 TCA.
5 Private Information – Bill Cormack.
6 J. Elliot, *On and Off the Rails* (1982), 102–3.
7 Railways Companies (Thos. Cook & Son Limited Guarantee) Act, 1942: 5 & 6 Geo. 6.
8 TCA, Huskisson's 'Very Confidential File', 10 July 1942.
9 *Transport Salaried Staff Journal* (June 1951), 249.
10 Elliot, *Rails*, 103–4.
11 *TCSM*, Jan.–Feb. 1972.
12 H. White, *Thomas Cook & Son John* (pamphlet, n.d.) in TCA.
13 Elliot, *Rails*, 103.
14 *Times*, 27 Apr. 1946.
15 *Evening News*, 28 Mar. 1946.
16 *TCSM*, July–Aug. 1947 and Jan.–Feb. 1965.
17 *Times*, 17 Mar. 1948.
18 *Radio Times*, 6 Nov. 1949.
19 TCA, 'Report on Cook, 1 Nov. 1948–31 Oct. 1949'.
20 *Travel Trade*, June 1949.
21 W. D. C. Cormack, 'Going Away', 127–8. I am grateful to Bill Cormack for giving me a copy of his unpublished 'History of Holidays in Great Britain'.
22 *Statist*, 28 Jan. 1966.
23 *Travel News*, 24 June 1971.
24 Private Information – Bill Cormack.
25 Private Information – John Price. Actually the Transport Holding Company's meanness was something of a myth. Later it did encourage Cook to expand its retail chain and, in 1970, to market the tours of other operators.
26 *Investor's Chronicle*, 8 July 1977.
27 Hill, 'Tourists on the Nile', 4/1.
28 R. Cameron, *My Travel's History* (1950), 42–4.
29 *New Statesman*, 6 Feb. 1954.
30 *Time & Tide*, 12 Aug. and 9 Sept. 1950.
31 *Go*, Oct.–Nov. 1954.
32 J. H. Price, 'Timetables as a Business' (1987), 55.
33 TCA, Memo from Jack and Mary Hyde.
34 *Financial Times*, 16 June 1959.

35 *International Hotel Review*, June–July 1950.
36 *TCSM*, June 1957.
37 Private Information – Sir Reginald Wilson.
38 Paris *Herald-Tribune*, 9 May 1958.
39 Elliot, *Rails*, 104.
40 *Travel Topics*, July 1960.
41 TCA, Holt's Report, 3 Feb. 1958.
42 *Woman & Home*, Oct. 1960.
43 Private Information – Bill Cormack.
44 Elliot, *Rails*, 104.
45 *TCSM*, Sept.–Oct. 1963.
46 *Financial Times*, 20 Mar. 1963.
47 *Daily Sketch*, 25 Nov. 1954.
48 *Sunday Telegraph*, 28 June 1964.
49 *T[ravel] T[rade] G[azette]*, 20 Nov. 1964.
50 *Daily Telegraph*, 15 Feb. 1964.
51 *TTG*, 31 Jan. 1964.
52 *Financial Times*, 9 Nov. 1963 and 10 Sept. 1965.
53 *Travel World*, Feb. 1961.
54 *Financial Times*, 18 June 1964.
55 D. Boorstin, *The Image* (1961), 79.
56 *Observer* Colour Magazine, 24 Dec. 1967.
57 *New Statesman*, 6 May 1966.
58 Pudney, *Cook Story*, 155.
59 Turner and Ash, *Golden Hordes*, 11, 91, 53, 249 and 171.
60 *Sunday Times*, 25 Mar. 1973.
61 *Evening Advertiser*, 27 May 1961.
62 *TCSM*, Jan.–Feb. 1963.
63 A. J. Burkart and S. Medlik, *Tourism* (1974), 57.
64 *Time*, 2 Aug. 1968.
65 *TCSM*, July–Aug. 1971.
66 *TCSM*, Sept.–Oct. 1965.
67 *Statist*, 28 Jan. 1966.
68 *TTG*, 17 Feb. 1967.
69 *Director*, Sept. 1968.
70 *Guardian*, 6 July 1968.
71 *Financial Times*, 20 Nov. 1969.
72 *Economist*, 12 Apr. 1969.
73 *Financial Times*, 28 July 1970.
74 *Travel Agency*, Dec. 1967.
75 *TTG*, 14 June 1968.
76 *Modern Woman*, Mar. 1964.
77 *Financial Times*, 28 and 29 Jan. 1971.

78 *Daily Telegraph*, 14 July 1971.
79 *Times*, 29 Nov. 1971.
80 *Travel News*, 24 June 1971.
81 *TCSM*, July–Aug. 1972.
82 *TTG*, 2 Feb. 1968.
83 Elliot, *Rails*, 108.
84 *Times*, 31 Dec. and 29 Nov. 1971.
85 *Sun*, 24 Dec. 1965.
86 *Observer*, 2 Jan. 1966.
87 Private Information – Bill Cormack.
88 C. Squarey, *The Patient Talks* (1955), 58. Training courses were initiated at Thomas Cook in 1937.
89 *Financial Times*, 22 Dec. 1970.
90 *Guardian*, 27 May 1972.
91 E. Green, *The Making of a Modern Banking Group* (1979), 103–4.
92 MBA, 200/246, 8 Aug. 1963 and 6 Jan. 1966.
93 MBA, Thomas Cook & Son Ltd, Correspondence File, 1967–72, Lord Crowther (of Trust House Forte) to Forbes, 12 Dec. 1970.
94 MBA, 200/366.
95 MBA, 200/368, 'Thomas Cook & Son Ltd: A Paper for Mr Adam Thomson' by Duncan Haws, December 1971.
96 MBA, 'Thomas Cook and Son Ltd: Preliminary Work and Background Papers 1969–1972'.
97 Sir Reginald Wilson Papers, 'Cooks and the THC', 16.
98 MBA, Thomas Cook & Son Ltd, Correspondence File, 1967–72, 28 May 1972.
99 *TCSM*, July–Aug. 1971.

Chapter 16: *The Global Future* (pages 298–316)

1 Private Information – Sir John Cuckney.
2 *TTG*, 1 Aug. 1969.
3 Private Information – Sir John Cuckney.
4 Private Information – Sir John Cuckney.
5 *TCSM*, May–June 1973.
6 Private Information.
7 Private Information – Sir Reginald Wilson.
8 T. Bendixson, *The Peterborough Effect* (1988), 173.
9 *Thomas Cook International News*, June 1974.
10 *TCSM*, Nov. 1974.
11 *TCSM*, Jan. 1975.
12 *Guardian*, 25 May 1974.

13 *Travel News*, 20 June 1974.
14 L. J. Lickorish, 'Tourism' in *Reviews of United Kingdom Statistical Sources*, ed. W. F. Maunder (1975), 25.
15 *TCSM*, Oct. 1974, quoting *TTG*.
16 *Evening News*, 29 July 1975.
17 *Investor's Chronicle*, 8 July 1977.
18 *Spectator*, 30 Aug. 1986, 19.
19 *TCSM*, June 1975.
20 *TTG*, 19 Oct. 1977.
21 *TCSM*, Apr. 1980.
22 Private Information – John Price.
23 *Business Week*, 3 Oct. 1977.
24 Private Information – John Price.
25 *Investor's Chronicle*, 8 July 1977.
26 *Daily Telegraph*, 27 Oct. 1977.
27 Private Information.
28 *TTG*, 18 May 1984.
29 Private Information – Alan Kennedy.
30 Private Information.
31 Fisher to the author, 18 Jan. 1989.
32 Private Information – Tom Fisher.
33 Private Information.
34 Private Information – Tom Fisher.
35 Private Information – John Price.
36 *Eastern Times*, 2 Feb. 1978.
37 *Daily Telegraph*, 27 Oct. 1977.
38 *TCSM*, Mar.–Apr. 1977.
39 *TCSM*, Jan.–Feb. 1978.
40 *Management Today*, Oct. 1978.
41 *Times*, 9 Aug. 1977.
42 *Business Week*, 3 Oct. 1977.
43 *TTG*, 18 May 1984.
44 *Business Week*, 3 Oct. 1977.
45 *TTG*, 19 Oct. 1977.
46 *TTG*, 19 Oct. 1977.
47 *TTG*, 1 Apr. 1977.
48 *TTG*, 19 Oct. 1977.
49 Private Information.
50 Private Information – Sir John Cuckney.
51 *TCSM*, Apr. 1980.
52 Private Information – Sir John Cuckney.
53 Private Information – Tom Fisher.
54 Private Information.

55 Private Information – Alan Kennedy.
56 *Travel News*, 31 Mar. 1983.
57 *TCSM*, Nov.–Dec. 1982 and Aug. 1986.
58 *Escorted Journeys* brochure, 1987.
59 J. B. Allcock, 'Yugoslavia's Tourist Trade: Pot of Gold or Pig in a Poke?' in *Annals of Tourism Research* 13 (1986), 132.
60 J. Jafari, 'Tourism for Whom? Old Questions Still Echoing' in *Annals of Tourism Research* 13 (1986), 566.
61 *Independent*, 9 Dec. 1987.
62 *Independent*, 11 Dec. 1987.
63 S. R. Waters, *The Big Picture* (New York, 1988), 17.
64 *Financial Times*, 23 Feb. 1990.
65 *Globe: The Thomas Cook Newspaper*, I, 1.
66 Private Information – Peter Middleton.

Bibliography

In view of the fullness of the notes it seems otiose to compile anything more than a list of the most useful books relating to Thomas Cook and the history of popular tourism. The following works are published in London unless otherwise stated.

Banks, P. *The Man from Cook's* (1938)

Behrend, G. *Grand European Expresses* (1962)

Bernard, P. P. *Rush to the Alps: The Evolution of Vacationism in Switzerland* (New York, 1978)

Burkart, A. J., and Medlik, S. *Tourism* (1974).

Burton, A. and P. *The Green Bag Travellers: Britain's First Tourists* (1978)

Cook, T. *Letters Descriptive of a Tour round the World* (1873).

Dulles, F. R. *Americans Abroad* (Ann Arbor, Michigan, 1964)

Elliot, J. *On and Off the Rails* (1982)

Feifer, M. *Going Places: The Ways of the Tourist from Imperial Rome to the Present Day* (1985)

Fifer, J. V. *American Progress* (Chester, Connecticut, 1988)

Fussell, P. *Abroad: British Literary Travelling Between the Wars* (Oxford, 1980)

Green, E. *The Making of a Modern Banking Group* (1977)

Hibbert, C. *The Grand Tour* (1969 and 1987)

Hindley, G. *Tourists, Travellers and Pilgrims* (1983)

Leighton, W. H. *A Cook's Tour of the Holy Land in 1874* (1947)

Lickorish, L. J., and Kershaw, A. G. *The Travel Trade* (1958)

Löschburg, W. *A History of Travel* (1979)

Morrell, J. *Miss Jemima's Swiss Tour: The First Conducted Tour of Switzerland* (1963)

Norval, A. J. *The Tourist Industry* (1936)

Pemble, J. *The Mediterranean Passion* (1988)

Pimlott, J. A. R. *The Englishman's Holiday* (1976 edn.)

Pudney, J. *The Thomas Cook Story* (1953)

Rae, W. F. *The Business of Travel* (1891)

Robinson, J. *Wayward Women: A guide to Women Travellers* (Oxford, 1990)

Sattin, A. *Lifting the Veil: British Society in Egypt 1768–1956* (1988)

Shepherd, N. *The Zealous Intruders: The Western Rediscovery of Palestine* (1987)

Sigaux, G. *History of Tourism* (Geneva, 1966)

Sketchley, A. *Out for a Holiday with Cook's Excursion through Switzerland and Italy* (1870)

Steevens, G. W. *Egypt in 1898* (1898)

Studd, R. G. *The Holiday Story* (1950)

Swinglehurst, E. *The Romantic Journey* (1974)

Swinglehurst, E. *Cook's Tours: The Story of Popular Travel* (1982)

Turner, L., and Ash, J. *The Golden Hordes* (1975)

Wagner, F. N. *Grosse Welt und Kleine Menschen* (Zürich, 1942)

Walvin, J. *Beside the Seaside* (1978)

Waters, S. R. *The Big Picture* (New York, 1988)

Ward, C., and Hard, D. *Goodnight Campers! The Story of the British Holiday Camp* (1986)

· *Index* ·

TC stands for Thomas Cook, JMC for John Mason Cook

WESTERN HEMISPHERE